17774

STUDIES IN THE FOURTH GOSPEL

OTHER BOOKS

STUDIES IN
THE FOURTH GOSPEL

by

LEON MORRIS

Principal of Ridley College
Melbourne

WILLIAM B. EERDMANS PUBLISHING COMPANY
GRAND RAPIDS, MICHIGAN

PRINTED IN THE UNITED STATES OF AMERICA

/09

Acknowledgments

IN THIS BOOK I HAVE MADE USE OF MATERIAL FIRST PUB-
lished elsewhere in the form of articles and lectures. I am
grateful to the editors and publishers who so freely gave
permission to republish. The articles in question and the
volumes in which they were published are as follows:
"History and Theology in the Fourth Gospel" (*Faith and
Thought*, Vol. 92, No. 3, Summer 1962); "History and
the Fourth Gospel" (*TSF Bulletin*, Vol. 46, Autumn
1966); "Synoptic Themes Illuminated by the Fourth
Gospel" (*Studia Evangelica*, Vol. II, ed. F. L. Cross,
Berlin, Akademie-Verlag, 1964); "The Fourth Gospel and
History" (from *Jesus of Nazareth: Saviour and Lord*,
ed. C. F. H. Henry, Grand Rapids, Eerdmans, 1966);
"The Dead Sea Scrolls and St. John's Gospel" (Campbell
Morgan Memorial Lecture, 1960); "The Problem of His-
tory and the Gospel" (I.V.F. Annual Lecture in Queens-
land, 1966; subsequently reprinted in *Interchange*, Vol. 1,
No. 1, April 1967).

Acknowledgment is also made to the Viking Press, Inc.
for permission to make quotations from *The Dead Sea
Scrolls* © 1955 by Millar Burrows and *More Light on the
Dead Sea Scrolls* © 1958 by Millar Burrows.

Contents

Preface

THE CONSERVATIVE EVANGELICAL WHO WRITES SERIOUSLY on biblical topics is apt to find himself the target of a certain amount of criticism. If he decides simply to state the facts as he sees them, and to be silent about the works of more radical critics, he finds himself accused of obscurantism. If, on the other hand, he decides to take notice of what others have been writing, and to quote them, he may find himself accused of citing authors who do not really agree with his essential position (an English bishop took me to task for this offense *inter alia*, in a review of a recent book of mine).

In facing this issue I fear that I am unrepentant. I unhesitatingly adopt the second-mentioned course. I read books by men of all sorts of opinions and profit not least from those with whom I disagree most fundamentally. So I have repeated my crime in this book, and have cited all sorts of opinions from a variety of scholars. I have never hitherto thought it necessary to defend this practice, but in view of the strictures of the good bishop perhaps I should make it clear that when I cite any author, whatever his theological position, I cite him for the words quoted and no others. I do not mean to imply that he is in agreement with my essential position. I mean to imply no more than that the words quoted have interest and value in connection with the topic under discussion.

A further disadvantage under which the conservative evangelical labors is that it is often held that his conclusions are given in his premises (the bishop to whom

I have referred maintained that I imposed my pattern on the evidence; it is so incredible that I should have *found* it there that he does not even discuss the possibility). Your conservative, it is held, is the slave of his presuppositions. He is bound to reach certain conclusions. Therefore his arguments need not be taken seriously. I hope that conservative evangelicals may be pardoned for wondering whether there is not perhaps a kind of radical obscurantism (if I may be permitted to use the word against those who are so free with it themselves), whereby objections that evangelicals at any rate regard as really serious are simply dismissed with no attempt at a reasoned answer. Just as it seems to the radical that the conservative is simply refusing to face real objections to his position, so it seems to the conservative that the radical will not face some part of the evidence, notably that which shows that the Bible is an inspired book.

Let me put the objection in the words of one who will not be suspected of a too tender approach toward conservative evangelicals (for he vigorously repudiates what he calls "fundamentalism"), nor of lacking a critical approach to the Bible, namely J. V. Langmead Casserley. He says: "From within the biblical tradition we must insist and confidently expect that the more profoundly and validly we understand and interpret the Bible, the greater the religious depth with which it will challenge and speak to us. It is precisely here that modern biblical scholarship has proved itself so insipid and unstimulating. We are confronted with the paradox of a way of studying the word of God out of which no word of God ever seems to come, with an imposing modern knowledge of the Bible which seems quite incapable of saying anything biblical or thinking biblically. Kant and Hegel and other German philosophers always seem to be standing in the background, but the immanent spirit of the Bible itself has long since departed from the scene."[1] Elsewhere he says, "We need both the categories of modern history and of inspiration in order to do justice to the phenomena with which we are confronted."[2] The point I am trying to make

---

[1] *Toward a Theology of History*, London, 1965, p. 116.
[2] *Ibid.*, p. 96.

is that, while it seems painfully obvious to the normal run of critical scholars that the conservative evangelicals are trying to work out everything on the basis of evangelical presuppositions, it is just as clear to the conservatives that their more critical brethren are leaving out or at any rate minimizing precisely that category which is most significant.

In writing in this way I am not claiming that I have some way of resolving the conflict. Nor do I claim to have done what so many others have failed to do, namely achieve the perfect balance between recognizing the consequences of inspiration and the use of the critical method. It is rather that I, as a conservative evangelical, want to assure the reader that I have made a serious attempt to deal with the great questions raised in this book. I have not tried to defend any preconceived position or to follow a party line. As far as I am able, I have let the facts lead me where they will. I have little hope that the typical modern scholar will have much patience with this book, for I have had the temerity to argue that the Fourth Gospel was probably written by John the apostle, and that it contains good historical material. But I ask him to see this as a work meant as seriously as is his own. And I ask him to deal with the argument on its merits, and not simply to assume that I am engaging in special pleading. He is, of course, free to disagree with me fundamentally. But I want to assure him that at the least this is a sincere effort to grapple with the problems on the basis of the evidence.

For some years now I have been at work on a commentary on the Fourth Gospel. My primary interest has been to inquire into the meaning of the text, and I have not been so closely concerned with questions like those of authorship, relationship to the Synoptics, and the like. But it has not been possible to overlook them, and I have gathered some of my notes together to make up this book. It is not a complete introduction to John, but an examination of some of the problems associated with that Gospel. I can claim no other principle of selection than that these problems interest me. And since up-to-date discussions on this Gospel from the standpoint of the conservative

evangelical are not exactly plentiful I venture to send
this one forth in the hope that it will prove of some
interest and value.

These are ecumenical days, and it is interesting to see a
readiness in many quarters to read and profit from the
writings of men who stand in a variety of traditions. Thus
critical Protestant scholars and Roman Catholics are
reading one another's works and discussing one another's
writings with charity and mutual profit. Perhaps it is not
too much to hope that both will include the conservative
evangelicals within the scope of their reading and their
charity. In the hope that it will make some small contribution to the continuing dialogue this book goes forth.

— LEON MORRIS

Abbreviations

ALQ	Frank M. Cross: *The Ancient Library of Qumran*, New York, 1958
BJRL	*Bulletin of the John Rylands Library*
CGT	*The Cambridge Greek Testament*
CQR	*The Church Quarterly Review*
DSS	Millar Burrows: *The Dead Sea Scrolls*, New York, 1955
EGT	*The Expositor's Greek Testament*
ET	*The Expository Times*
FGRCI	W. F. Howard: *The Fourth Gospel in Recent Criticism and Interpretation* (rev. C. K. Barrett), London, 1955
Guide	A. R. C. Leaney, R. P. C. Hanson and J. Posen: *A Guide to the Scrolls*, London, 1958
HDB	James Hastings (ed.): *A Dictionary of the Bible*, Edinburgh, 1898 (5 vols.)
HTFG	C. H. Dodd: *Historical Tradition in the Fourth Gospel*, Cambridge, 1963
IB	*The Interpreter's Bible*
ICC	*The International Critical Commentary*
IFG	C. H. Dodd: *The Interpretation of the Fourth Gospel*, Cambridge, 1953
JBL	*The Journal of Biblical Literature*
JQR	*Jewish Quarterly Review*
JTS	*The Journal of Theological Studies*
ML	Millar Burrows: *More Light on the Dead Sea Scrolls*, New York, 1958
MNTC	*The Moffatt New Testament Commentary*

NTS   *New Testament Studies*

S Bk   H. L. Strack and P. Billerbeck: *Kommentar zum Neuen Testament aus Talmud und Midrasch*, Munich, 1922-1928 (5 vols.)

SE, I   K. Aland, F. L. Cross, J. Danielou, H. Riesenfeld and W. C. van Unnik (edd.): *Studia Evangelica*, Berlin, 1959

SE, II   F. L. Cross (ed.): *Studia Evangelica*, Vol. II, Berlin, 1964

SE, III   F. L. Cross (ed.): *Studia Evangelica*, Vol. III, Berlin, 1964

SNT   Krister Stendahl (ed.): *The Scrolls and the New Testament*, New York, 1957

TBC   *Torch Bible Commentary*

TNTC   *Tyndale New Testament Commentary*

Quotations from the Bible are normally taken from the American Revised Version (unless otherwise noted). The Mishnah is cited from the translation by H. Danby, the Talmud from the Soncino translation, and Philo and Josephus from the translation in the Loeb edition.

Chapter One

The Relationship of the Fourth Gospel to the Synoptics

UP TILL QUITE RECENTLY IT WOULD HAVE BEEN TRUE TO say that the great majority of scholars held that John had one or more of the Synoptists before him as he wrote his Gospel. Most agreed that he had Mark, and a good number held that he also used Luke. All agreed that the case for his employment of Matthew is less cogent, if not highly unlikely; but dependence on the former two was held to be reasonably certain.[1] And this was a question on which conservative and radical critics were in general agreement. The former said that he wrote to supplement the Synoptists and the latter that he aimed at correcting them. But both agreed that he knew of their work and wrote with it in mind.

This is the case with the most recent substantial commentary on this Gospel, that by C. K. Barrett. That writer thinks it probable that John was familiar with Mark, probable also, "though in a smaller degree, that he knew

---

[1] E. F. Scott maintained that John used all three Synoptics (*The Fourth Gospel*, Edinburgh, 1906, pp. 32f.). More recently R. H. Lightfoot has come to the same conclusion (*St. John's Gospel*, Oxford, 1956, p. 29).

Luke."[2] This does not mean that he had these Gospels actually before him as he wrote and that he used them as Matthew, for example, used Mark. Barrett is asserting that John "had read Mark, and was influenced both positively and negatively by its contents — that is, that he reproduced in his own way some Marcan substance and language, and also emended some of the Marcan material — and that a few of John's statements may be most satisfactorily explained if he was familiar with matter peculiar to Luke."[3]

The evidence on which Barrett chiefly relies is the fact that a number of passages "occur *in the same order* in both Mark and John,"[4] and that there are some verbal resemblances. Here is his list:[5]

			Mark	John
(a)	The work and witness of the Baptist		1:4-8	1:19-36
(b)	Departure to Galilee		1:14f.	4:3
(c)	Feeding the Multitude		6:34-44	6:1-13
(d)	Walking on the Lake		6:45-52	6:16-21
(e)	Peter's Confession		8:29	6:68f.
(f)	Departure to Jerusalem		9:30f. 10:1, 32, 46	7:10-14
(g)	The Entry	⎰ trans- ⎱ posed in ⎰ John	11:1-10	12:12-15
	The Anointing		14:3-9	12:1-8
(h)	The Last Supper with predictions of betrayal and denial		14:17-26	13:1 – 17:26
(i)	The Arrest		14:43-52	18:1-11
(j)	The Passion and Resurrection		14:53 – 16:8	18:12 – 20:29

With all respect, this is not a very impressive list. For example, (a) obviously has to come first. Where else are we to locate the work of the Baptist? And (b) must come somewhere later than (a), unless Galilee is to be omitted.

---

[2] C. K. Barrett, *The Gospel according to St John*, London, 1955, p. 14.

[3] *Ibid.*, p. 34.

[4] *Ibid.* (Barrett's italics). He italicizes the same words again a little later (p. 36). Clearly he regards the point as important.

[5] *Ibid.*, pp. 34f.

But that we should not put too much emphasis on the point is shown by the fact that the departure to Galilee comes 6 verses later in Mark and 79 verses later in John. Since the feeding of the multitude took place in Galilee, (c) had to follow (b), and in this case Mark puts it 211 verses later and John 99 verses later. The conjunction of (c) and (d) is more impressive, and is in fact the kind of sequence out of which a case might be built up were there enough examples. The next incident might also be included under the same heading were it not for the fact that there is grave doubt as to whether Mark and John are describing the same event. If they are not (and in my opinion they are not: their incidents are quite distinct), then this item should not be included. The departure to Jerusalem could not come before the end of the Galilean ministry, so that (f) could scarcely be elsewhere in the list, while (g) had to follow (f). It could not possibly precede it. It is not without its interest that Barrett brackets two items under (g), but that they are in the reverse order in the two Gospels. It is difficult to see how the triumphal entry, the Last Supper, the arrest, and the passion and resurrection could go in any other order.

The list can hardly be called decisive. It boils down to a single sequence of two events as alone worth notice, and considering the length of the two Gospels this is not remarkable.

The case for verbal dependence is little more convincing. Barrett lists twelve passages with verbal coincidences, mostly single verses and rarely agreeing very closely. As there are about 12,000 words in Mark this is not really very convincing. Indeed the impression left is that if this is the best case that can be made out for dependence on the part of the Fourth Evangelist then the case is not strong. Presumably Barrett has not neglected any relevant piece of evidence.

The case for dependence on Luke is even less convincing. Barrett cites two lines of evidence, the fact that certain persons are named in these two Gospels alone of the four, and certain details common to these two but not found elsewhere. Of the persons the complete list is as follows: Mary and Martha (John mentions their brother Lazarus and Luke uses this name in a parable), a disciple named Judas other than Judas Iscariot, and Annas. This is not a large number. Of the details that link the two Gospels Barrett notes the following: the betrayal is due to the possession of Judas by Satan; Peter's denial is made at the Supper and not after it, "and the language of John 13.38 is closer to Luke 22.34 than to Mark 14.30"; the high priest's servant had his *right* ear cut off; at the tomb on Easter morning there were two angels, not one; finally, "The details of the Johannine anointing story recall the Lucan as well as the Marcan narrative."[6] This is not a lengthy list, and there are some discounts even here. Thus Luke tells us that Satan entered Judas before he first sought out the high priests (Luke 22:3); John links Satan with Judas at the Supper (John 13:2, 27). The language of the denial in John does indeed more closely resemble that in Luke than in Mark, but it does not resemble either very much. Certainly it is difficult to see direct dependence. Again one is inclined to say that if there is no better case than this for dependence the two Gospels may well be regarded as independent.[7] One wonders what would have been the result of Barrett's investigation if in this

---

[6] *Ibid.*, p. 37. J. A. Bailey puts a good deal of emphasis on the anointing. He treats it first, out of chronological order, apparently because he thinks that of itself it proves that John has Luke before him. He maintains that John drew from Luke the anointing of the feet and the wiping with the hair (*The Traditions Common to the Gospels of Luke and John*, Leiden, 1963, pp. 1-8). That Luke and John both mention these incidents is interesting, but scarcely sufficient to demonstrate dependence in view of the great dissimilarities in the remainder of the narratives. Yet Bailey bases much of his case on this. He can go so far as to say at a later point, "but, as the anointing pericopes once and for all show, this view of the chronology of the gospels (i.e. that John is earlier than Luke) is not justified by the evidence of their contents" (p. 92, n. 3). This is a somewhat optimistic inference when the basis is so flimsy.

[7] G. B. Caird notices in connection with Luke's special material "its remarkable affinities with the fourth Gospel." He points to both similarities and dissimilarities (both are important) and concludes, "The unavoidable inference is that Luke and John were relying on two allied streams of oral tradition" (*The Pelican Gospel Commentaries, Saint Luke*, Harmondsworth, 1963, pp. 20f.). But this is not the same thing as saying that John knew Luke.

section he had applied the same rigid tests for determining dependence as those by which he excludes Ignatius and Justin from a knowledge of John.[8]

RESEMBLANCES BETWEEN JOHN AND THE SYNOPTISTS

IT SEEMS TO ME THAT THE EVIDENCE FOR LITERARY dependence, even on Mark, comes far short of demonstration. There are, to be sure, some resemblances. But then some resemblance is involved in the very idea of writing a gospel. A gospel is not a universal literary form. It arose only with the early Christians, and there are not very many examples even among them. They did not produce a variety of gospel types. The potential gospel author thus was not offered a variety of approaches. Of the gospels that survive all show common traits. As far as we know if a man wished to write a gospel he would have to produce a document with some resemblances to other examples of this genre.

It must further be borne in mind that none of the four Gospels was written in a vacuum. We cannot suppose that the writer of the first of them (whoever that was) sat down and composed a completely original narrative out of his own head. It is agreed by all responsible critics that there was a period when the essentials of the gospel message were carried on by oral tradition, and that the four Evangelists drew heavily on that tradition,[9] whatever use they may also have made of matter peculiar to themselves. Naturally, oral tradition often varies from place to place. Slight modifications creep in locally, despite the general trend toward stereotyping. And, as someone has remarked, the Oriental memory, though retentive, was not a tape recorder. Striking sayings or incidents might

---

[8] *Op. cit.*, pp. 93f.

[9] Cf. P. Gardner-Smith: "Whoever he was, the author of the Fourth Gospel must have been a member of some local congregation, and as such he must have been instructed in the traditions of the Church. It is a fallacy, obvious yet strangely common, to think that he can only have learnt about the life of Christ and the incidents of the ministry from the perusal of some written document" (*Saint John and the Synoptic Gospels*, Cambridge, 1938, p. xi). The same thing could be said of the writers of the other Gospels.

well be preserved without modification, but the lesser elements in stories transmitted orally might suffer alteration. It is thus to be expected that when two writers are drawing on oral tradition they will have certain agreements, but also, if their oral tradition has come to them by different channels, they are likely to differ in other places. Much, moreover, will depend on the writers' attitude to the tradition. One man may follow it fairly closely, not feeling himself free to modify it other than in insignificant detail.[10] Another may treat it with greater freedom, especially if he or someone known to him was involved in some of the events, or if he has some other independent knowledge of those events. Thus if two men in the second half of the first century of our era set themselves to compose gospels without knowledge of one another, and without either's seeing the work of the other, we would be justified in conjecturing that, while there would certainly be major differences in the finished products, there would also be certain resemblances. We should also expect that these resemblances would occur not only in the general thrust of the narratives, but would now and then concern detail. Striking expressions have a way of being preserved in oral tradition, and the climax of any story may well be identical in several lines of tradition.

Nor should we overlook the fact that certain written documents existed embodying some of the tradition in circulation in the church. New Testament critics discern such documents as Q, M, and L, and Luke himself tells us that many had set forth narratives (Luke 1:1). Accordingly it is not at all impossible that, say, Mark and John had access to a common source or sources now lost to us.[11] I would not myself be inclined to set much store by this suggestion. But the possibility is undoubtedly

---

[10] This will be especially the case if it is true, as Cullmann maintains, "that the New Testament regards the Lord exalted to the right hand of God as the direct author of the tradition of the apostles, because he himself is at work in the apostolic transmission of his words and deeds" (*The Early Church*, London, 1956, p. 59).

[11] Thus E. R. Goodenough thinks that there may have been a document which John shares with Mark, and which underlies John 6 (JBL, 64, 1945, pp. 157f.).

there, and it should not be overlooked. In other words a certain amount of resemblance between John and one or other of the Synoptists may be due to mutual access to some early written source, rather than to direct literary dependence.

Such reasoning, of course, settles nothing. It concerns no more than possibilities. But I am concerned to insist that they are possibilities, so that when we examine the evidence we shall look for more in the way of proof of literary dependence than the occasional likenesses which appear to have satisfied some. We must bear in mind differences as well as resemblances and make up our minds with a due regard to both. In the case of the Synoptists such a procedure leaves us with no doubt but that there is literary dependence. The Synoptic problem is not an easy one, but few today would hold that it can be solved along the lines of oral tradition. There are differences between, say, Matthew and Mark, but the resemblances are such that the most natural explanation is that one of these writers had before him a copy of the other. So with Luke. There is surely an interrelationship among these three that cannot be explained short of direct literary dependence. The question in the case of the Fourth Gospel is whether the resemblances are such as to demand a similar explanation, or whether the differences are weighty enough to demand a different explanation. It will be contended here that the latter is the case. In taking up this position I am not unmindful of the very real resemblances, nor that these have been sufficient to convince most critics up till recent times. The resemblances are real and they are important. But I do not think that sufficient attention has been paid to the small amount of the total bulk that they occupy, nor to the equally striking differences.

It is important to realize that the situation with regard to the Fourth Gospel is not the same as in the case of the other three. A solution that is perfectly satisfactory in the Synoptic problem will not necessarily fit the facts when we turn to the relation of the Fourth Gospel to the others.[12] The two problems are not the same.

---

[12] R. P. Casey does not seem to give sufficient attention to this.

DIFFERENCES

THERE ARE IMPORTANT DIFFERENCES OF A BROAD GENERAL character between John and the Synoptics. John's account of the ministry of Jesus is largely concerned with Jerusalem, theirs with Galilee.[13] They have a good deal to say about the parables of Jesus; John says nothing.[14] He records long disputes between Jesus and His opponents in what I. Abrahams has recognized as the typical rabbinic style, and they have nothing like this. Such a passage as the Sermon on the Mount differs markedly in both structure and content from anything in John. The Synoptics make quite a feature of the exorcisms performed by Jesus. John mentions none. The broad general plan of John's Gospel provides for a ministry of longer duration and different character from that which we see in the Synoptics. It is, of course, possible that John had before him one or more of the other Gospels, and writes

---

He objects to Goodenough's contention that John is a primitive Gospel, and he says *inter alia*, "To substitute the independent impact of oral traditions on our Gospels for the documentary hypothesis as an explanation of the close similarities between them, and to ignore the evidence of editorial procedure and evolution transforming Mk into Mt and Lk, and all three into Jn is the substitution of complexity for simplicity as the mark of truth" (JBL, 64, 1945, p. 537). This insistence on dealing with all four Gospels together seems to me unwarranted. Casey appears to be saying that if oral tradition be accepted as the explanation of the Synoptic problem it must also be accepted as the explanation of the resemblances between John and the Synoptics.

[13] G. H. Tremenheere suggests that, except on His last visit, Jesus was not accompanied to Jerusalem by the Twelve, but only by John and perhaps James. He points out that the Twelve are not mentioned as being with Him in Jerusalem on these earlier occasions (*Theology*, 16, 1928, p. 260). This cannot be proven beyond doubt, but it is quite reasonable. Why should Jesus have taken all the Twelve with Him each time he went on the not inconsiderable walk to Jerusalem? And since the Twelve are not mentioned as having been with Jesus in Jerusalem at the earlier visits they may well not have accompanied Him. If they did not, then it would not be surprising that the Synoptists do not mention these visits.

[14] See below, pp. 268f., for the view that there are traces of the parables in John. But whatever view is taken of this question there is no denying that John does not have parables in the typical Synoptic form. Thus the statement in the text is scarcely affected.

to supplement or correct them, as many critics affirm.[15] But as far as the evidence goes it indicates a lack of dependence. And it remains to be seen whether the evidence does or does not point to a deliberate attempt to supplement or correct.

COMPARISON OF JOHN WITH THE SYNOPTICS

IF WE COMPARE THE FOURTH GOSPEL WITH THE OTHERS we certainly get an impression of independence.[16] Thus in the first five chapters John appears to have only two things that appear in the Synoptics, the ministry of John the Baptist and the cleansing of the temple. This in itself raises the question of whether if John did have any of the others before him as he wrote he would have made such a radically different beginning. There is nothing like his Prologue in the others, and, after John's ministry, there is not much in the opening that resembles the Synoptic story.

The work of the Baptist is summed up very simply in the Fourth Gospel, "There came a man, sent from God, whose name was John. The same came for witness, that he might bear witness of the light, that all might believe through him" (John 1:6f.). This Evangelist knows the Baptist simply as a witness to Jesus, and he brings out this thought several times (see John 1:15,

---

[15] A. H. N. Green-Armytage thinks that the way John and Mark supplement one another is significant. "Where Mark is fullest, John is briefest; what Mark passes over slightly, John emphasizes. The two Gospels are almost like a mask and a face or a casting and its mould. Where one sticks out the other is recessed. And so they can be harmonized together almost like chorus and semichorus in a tragedy, each capping the other's verses" (*John Who Saw*, London, 1952, p. 115). "No one who had not read the second Gospel could possibly have been so accurate in avoiding just those parts of the story which had been already told" (p. 116). This is an interesting point of view, but the situation has not seemed quite so clear to other students. And I am not at all sure that the analogies of mask and face and of casting and mould are applicable.

[16] J. A. Bailey, in a work avowedly given over to an examination of the traditions common to Luke and John, deals only with John 1:19, 27 and 12:1-8 before he comes to the passion narrative (*op. cit.*). This of itself is sufficient to show that these two Gospels are basically independent.

19, 32, 34; 3:26 [cf. 3:28]; 5:33). He records a dialogue between the Baptist and certain "priests and Levites" who came from Jerusalem to question him about his position. This is an occasion for denying that he was the Messiah or a messianic figure, and for him to bear his witness (John 1:23, 26f.). John tells us that this man baptized, though interestingly he does not record anyone as actually being baptized. That was not his interest. His interest was witness. He does not even record the baptism of Jesus, which is such an important event in the Synoptics. But he does tell us (as they do not) that the Baptist hailed Jesus as "the Lamb of God" (John 1:29, 36), and that he persuaded some of his disciples to leave him and follow Jesus. Again, Mark does not record any of Jesus' ministry until after the Baptist was cast into prison (Mark 1:14). John, however, speaks of Jesus as having been active before that time and he pictures the Baptist as continuing to bear witness to Jesus after our Lord's ministry had been in progress for a time (John 3:23ff.). To sum up, for the Synoptists the really important things about the Baptist are his practice of baptism for repentance, his baptizing of Jesus, his preaching that the Messiah was coming, and (in Luke) his ethical teaching. In John there is none of this except the looking forward to the Messiah, and this is made central. In short, the scope of the Baptist's work is as different in the Fourth Gospel as it could possibly be and yet describe the same ministry.

Perhaps the points of closest connection in the ministry of John are those which concern the application to him of Isaiah 40:3, and the words about loosing the sandal thong. Concerning the former it must be noted that the prophecy is applied to John in all four Gospels. Clearly it was strongly marked in the tradition. But, whereas in the first three Gospels it is the Evangelists who explain that these words apply to John, in the Fourth Gospel it is the Baptist himself who makes the application. This does not look like dependence.

Nor is the case much improved if we go on to notice the reference to Christ as coming after the Baptist, who is not worthy to loose His sandals. The relevant words in the four narratives are as follows (words shared by John and one or more of the other Gospels are underlined).

...tthew 3:11	Mark 1:7	Luke 3:16	John 1:26
΄σω μου	Ἔρχεται ὁ ἰσχυρότερός	ἔρχεται δὲ ὁ	μέσος ὑμῶν στήκει ὃν
...ος ἰσχυρότερός	μου ὀπίσω μου οὗ	ἰσχυρότερός μου, οὗ οὐκ	ὑμεῖς οὐκ οἴδατε, ὁ ὀπίσω
...ιν, οὗ οὐκ	οὐκ εἰμὶ ἱκανὸς	εἰμὶ ἱκανὸς λῦσαι τὸν	μου ἐρχόμενος, οὗ οὐκ
...ὼς τὰ	κύψας λῦσαι τὸν	ἱμάντα τῶν	εἰμὶ ἐγὼ ἄξιος ἵνα λύσω
...ιτα βαστάσαι	ἱμάντα τῶν	ὑποδημάτων αὐτοῦ	αὐτοῦ τὸν ἱμάντα τοῦ
	ὑποδημάτων αὐτοῦ		ὑποδήματος

There are certainly resemblances. John shares with Mark ὁ ὀπίσω μου, with all three οὗ οὐκ εἰμί, with Mark and Luke τὸν ἱμάντα and with Matthew ὁ ὀπίσω μου ἐρχόμενος. But for the rest the interesting thing is the number of differences the Fourth Evangelist has managed to pack into such a small compass. His use of ἄξιος where all three Synoptists have ἱκανὸς is noteworthy, as is his choice of the singular ὑποδήματος against their plurals. He uses a ἵνα clause over against their infinitive. Again he has a section μέσος . . . οἴδατε which they do not parallel. He uses the emphatic ἐγώ (according to the probable text), and he places αὐτοῦ differently. The three all refer to Christ as ἰσχυρότερός μου, for which John has no equivalent. In view of these significant differences it scarcely seems likely that dependence on one or more of the Synoptists is the explanation of the resemblances.

There remains the Baptist's witness to Jesus. Here the striking thing is that, while the Synoptists have as their central feature the baptism of Jesus, the Fourth Gospel says nothing about this. All four record the Baptist's words about baptizing with water, but, though the saying cries aloud to be completed with a reference to baptism in the Holy Spirit, and though all three Synoptists do just this, John does not. Later, however, he does tell us that Jesus would baptize with the Holy Spirit (John 1:33).

Summing it all up, then, there are undoubted resemblances between John's account of the Baptist and the

Synoptic accounts. But the total impression is different, and the few coincidences in detail are not weighty enough to counterbalance the differences. It seems that oral tradition is a better explanation of the resemblances, all the more so since the features most likely to be retained in oral tradition are the ones that John shares with the Synoptists. Literary dependence is far from being proven, and, on the contrary, seems unlikely.

In the rest of John 1 there is nothing resembling the Synoptics. I think we must distinguish between the call to discipleship in this Gospel and that to the apostolate in the Synoptics. But even if it be held that the incidents that John records in connection with the impact of Jesus on the followers of the Baptist are to be identified with those that Mark records by the sea of Galilee, it is obvious that they are not taken from the same source. Whatever else may be said about them they are independent narratives.

In chapter 2 the marriage in Cana has no Synoptic affiliations. The cleansing of the temple is, however, a notorious crux. It is usually held by scholars that the account in John is a variant account of the same incident as is recorded in the Synoptics. This may or may not be the case. For our present purpose the point is irrelevant. What is quite clear is that John's account is not derived from the Synoptic version. The following points are to be noted:

1. There is the important time difference. John puts the incident at the beginning of Jesus' ministry, the Synoptists at the end.

2. The words common to the two narratives are few (ἐξέβαλεν, κολλυβιστῶν, τραπέζας, πωλοῦντας, περιστεράς); and it would be practically impossible to tell a story of temple cleansing without them. We need more than this to demonstrate dependence.

3. Several features of the narrative are peculiar to John, such as the references to the sheep and the oxen, and to the scourge of cords. He alone uses the word κερματιστής for the changers of money (John 2:14); he alone refers to the "pouring out" of the money and to the command, "Take these things hence."

4. Peculiar to the Synoptic account is the prohibition of carrying anything through the temple, i.e. making a short cut of a way through the temple precincts.

5. For "overthrew" John uses ἀνέτρεψεν and the others κατέστρεψεν.

6. The Synoptists tell us that Jesus quoted from Isaiah, "my house shall be called a house of prayer for all peoples" (Isa. 56:7), and then from Jeremiah, "Is this house, which is called by my name, become a den of robbers in your eyes?" (Jer. 7:11) in explanation of His action. John does not speak of Jesus as citing any passage from the Bible, but he tells us that the disciples remembered the words, "For the zeal of thy house hath eaten me up" (Ps. 69:9).

7. In the Synoptics objection is made to the dishonesty being practiced ("a den of robbers"). In John there is no reference to dishonesty and objection is made to the practice in itself ("make not my Father's house a house of merchandise").

There may be some doubt as to whether the two accounts tell of the same incident. Some will remain firmly convinced that this is so and that either the Synoptists or John have placed it in the wrong setting for purposes of their own. Others will be sure that there were two cleansings. But it can scarcely be maintained that John is dependent on Mark for his information. These accounts are independent of one another.

John 3 – 5 is purely Johannine. There is nothing in the Synoptics to parallel the story of Nicodemus or the subsequent meditation and the reference to John the Baptist and his followers. And there is no Synoptic parallel to John's story of the woman at the well. While there are some who think that the healing of the nobleman's son in John 4:46-54 tells of the same incident as that described as the healing of the centurion's servant in Matthew 8:4-13 (=Luke 7:2-10), this is not at all obvious to others. In any case the manifest differences, so great as to make many scholars think (in my judgment rightly) that these are two separate incidents, are clear evidence that the Johannine story is not de-

pendent on the other. Then neither the healing of the
lame man by the pool of Bethesda, nor the discourse that
follows, is to be found in the Synoptics. It is plain enough
that so far John has little connection with the Synoptic
narratives.

In John 6, however, for the first time we come across
more significant points of contact. Here we have the
story of the feeding of the five thousand, the only miracle story (apart from the resurrection) in all four Gospels. There is no doubt but that John is describing the
same incident as the others. But does he derive it from
them? This seems most unlikely. In the first place the
setting is different. The Synoptists put it at the end
of a day of teaching, whereas John does not mention
this. They tell us that the disciples had been on a mission, and that on their return Jesus took them off to a
deserted place, but that there they were sought out by
the crowds. John says nothing of all this. When we come
to the miracle itself there are several significant divergences. Gardner-Smith puts it this way:

> John's account of the miracle differs in almost every
> possible way from that of Mark. In Mark the disciples
> intervene with the suggestion that Jesus should send
> the multitudes away while there is yet time for them to
> buy food, and it is only when Jesus replies 'Give ye
> them to eat' that they answer 'Shall we go and buy two
> hundred pennyworth of bread and give them to eat?'
> Jesus ignores the implied rebuke, and asks how many
> loaves they have. After enquiry, they reply 'Five, and
> two fishes (δύο ἰχθύας)'. In John, Jesus assumes the
> need of feeding the great crowd and initiates the con-
> versation with Philip, 'Whence shall we buy bread that
> these may eat?' Philip replies, 'Two hundred penny-
> worth of bread are not sufficient for them that each
> may take a little'. Then Andrew breaks in with the
> remark, 'There is a lad here who hath five barley loaves
> and two small fishes (ὀψάρια), but what are they among
> so many?'
> It may be claimed with some confidence that this is a
> completely independent account. The words used are
> different, the speakers are different, the only point of
> contact is in the single phrase διακοσίων δηναρίων ἄρτοι and

even that is accusative in Mark and nominative in John.[17]

It is difficult to see how Gardner-Smith's conclusion can be resisted. The differences between John and the Synoptics admittedly are in more or less minor points, and the accounts can be reconciled without much difficulty. But our point is that John can scarcely have derived his account from Mark or the others.[18] His is a quite independent account of the same incident.

A different approach is to set this story in its context. Linguistically it undoubtedly differs from the Synoptic accounts, but some have pointed out that there is a suggestive repetition of similar themes in John 6 and in Mark 8. In this latter chapter E. R. Goodenough discerns, in addition to a miraculous feeding (which incidentally is that of the four thousand; Mark's account of the feeding of the five thousand is in 6:35-44), "a crossing in a boat (but not of miraculous stilling of the waves, vv. 10 and 13), the demand for a sign (vv. 11, 12), and, after a healing of a blind man which may well have suggested the ninth chapter of Jn, the confession of Peter (vv. 27-33). The demand for a sign is echoed in Jn 6:30, where, however, a sign is given, the true bread of the eucharist in contrast to the manna of the wilderness: in Mk all signs are categorically refused."[19] But though he sees these parallels Goodenough just as firmly as Gardner-Smith rejects the idea that John depended on Mark.

---

[17] *Op. cit.*, pp. 29f. H. E. Edwards similarly says, "There is no sign of literary dependence whatever. If he is quoting S. Mark, it must be from memory, in which case his memory must have been one that retained all the facts and forgot all the phrases" (*The Disciple Who Wrote These Things*, London, 1953, p. 104).

[18] This is not faced by many commentators who assume dependence. Thus G. H. C. MacGregor simply states that "In characteristic fashion he [i.e. John] selects from the mass of Synoptic material dealing with the Galilean ministry an outstanding miracle which will serve to introduce the symbolical exposition of the meaning of the Lord's Supper which follows" (*The Gospel of John*, MNTC, London, 1928, p. 128). But no evidence is cited. All is assumption. There is no attempt to deal with the kind of evidence we have noted above. R. H. Strachan, by contrast, sees no dependence (*The Fourth Gospel*, London, 1955, p. 181). He appeals to Gardner-Smith's examination as conclusive.

[19] *Op. cit.*, p. 157.

For if the author of Jn took these from the completed
Gospel of Mk it is astonishing that he should have
reproduced with great care just this one cluster of
stories from a special part of Mk, or this one and the
Passion group, and done so with these two groups alone.
In these sections, far from reproducing his source,
whatever it was, with utter disregard for tradition, the
author of Jn has reproduced it in his own words to be
sure, but still has done so very faithfully indeed. The
conclusion is unavoidable that he may have reproduced
so few Marken stories in this way precisely because
he had so few to reproduce.[20]

Thus this approach no more than that of those who
compare words and phrases yields evidence for dependence. Goodenough may or may not be right in his contention that there is a common source underlying these
sections of John and Mark, but it is plain that neither of
these Evangelists drew his story from the other.

It is the same through the rest of chapter 6. The discourse on the living bread certainly did not come from
the Synoptics,[21] nor did the story of Peter's confession.
The situation with regard to this confession is rather
similar to that in respect to the cleansing of the temple:
scholars may differ as to whether the confession at
Caesarea Philippi (Mark 8:27ff. and parallels) refers to
the same incident as that in John 6:66ff., but there is no
question of literary dependence. These are not from the
same source.[22]

---

[20] *Ibid.*

[21] Though it may agree with Synoptic teaching. C. J. Wright,
speaking of John 6:45, says, "Nothing is truer to the mind of
Jesus as portrayed by the Synoptists than this 45th verse" (*Jesus
the Revelation of God*, London, 1950, p. 177).

[22] Pierson Parker compares John 6 with the Synoptics and concludes in this way: "Finally, where John vi does accord with the
Synoptics, it is not always with the same one. Sometimes John
sides with Luke against the first two, sometimes with both of these
against Luke, sometimes with the Second Gospel alone, or with
the First alone — and this is true both in its subject-matter and
in the few expressions it has in common with the other gospels.
For there to have been literary dependence, the Fourth Evangelist
would have had to keep all three of the Synoptic books open before
him, culling one phrase from one, another from another, but mostly
disregarding them all and going his own separate way" (NTS, 9,

John is manifestly independent in chapters 7 – 10. We cannot find the incident at the Feast of Tabernacles in the Synoptics, nor the discourse on the Light of the world, nor the healing of the blind man at the pool of Siloam, nor the Good Shepherd passage. Those who see connections, by asserting for example that the healing of the blind man in John 9 is derived ultimately from a blending of the stories of blind Bartimaeus and that of the blind man in Mark 8:22ff., do but demonstrate the impossibility of literary dependence. If that were the way of it (which I would strongly deny) then John certainly did not have Mark before him. The differences are too great.

THE ANOINTING AT BETHANY

NOR IS THE CASE ANY BETTER AS WE MOVE ON. THE STORY of the raising of Lazarus in John 11 gives rise to problems of its own, but it certainly does not come from any Synoptic narrative. John 12 gives more scope for Synoptic parallels. The chapter opens with an anointing of Jesus by Mary of Bethany. There are accounts of an anointing of Jesus by a woman in all four Gospels, Matthew 26:6-13; Mark 14:3-9; and Luke 7:36-50, as well as here. Luke places the anointing in Galilee earlier in Jesus' ministry, and locates it in the house of a Pharisee called Simon. Some connect this with the fact that Mark's anointing also took place in the house of a man called Simon, this one being distinguished as "the leper." But Simon was a very common name, so probably not too much weight should be placed on this. Luke describes the woman as "a sinner" and does not give her name. She first wet Jesus' feet with her tears, then wiped them with her hair, then kissed them, and finally anointed them. Simon deduced from all this that Jesus could not be a prophet and thus opened the way for the Master to speak about the woman's love. This story seems quite distinct from the other three. Matthew, Mark, and John, however, all speak of an anointing in Bethany toward the end of Jesus' ministry,

---

1962-63, p. 332). This well brings out the improbability of it all. There are resemblances; the traditions behind the four Gospels are not disparate and unrelated. But any hypothesis of dependence runs up against insuperable difficulties.

and almost all critics agree that they tell the story of the same event. We might list the similarities between John and Mark in this fashion:

1. Both locate the incident at Bethany.

2. Both use the unusual expression νάρδου πιστικῆς for the perfume (though Mark's adjective for "costly" is πολυτελοῦς and John's πολυτίμου).

3. Both record the suggestion that the unguent should have been sold and the proceeds given to the poor.

4. The sum of three hundred denarii is mentioned in both (though Mark says the perfume might have been sold for more than this; a small point is that the order of the two words δηναρίων and τριακοσίων is reversed in the two accounts).

5. Jesus' answer includes "Let her alone" (though with a slight difference; Mark has Ἄφετε αὐτήν and John Ἄφες αὐτήν) and a reference to His burial (Mark εἰς τὸν ἐνταφιασμόν, John εἰς τὴν ἡμέραν, τοῦ ἐνταφιασμοῦ μου).

6. Jesus further says, "The poor ye have always with you; but me ye have not always" (though Mark inserts after "you" the words "and whensoever ye will ye can do them good"; there is also a slight textual doubt, for the words are missing from the Johannine account in D Syrsin).

These similarities have been sufficient to convince many that John had Mark before him.[23] But against them we should set some divergences which are very curious if John did in fact have Mark.

1. There is a difficulty in the time. Mark appears to place the incident after the triumphal entry, whereas John puts it before.[24]

2. Mark speaks of an anointing of the head and John of an anointing of the feet.

---

[23] E.g. G. H. C. MacGregor, who says, "The close verbal agreements with Mark and Matthew are clear proof of John's dependence" (op. cit., p. 258). But his case is weakened by the fact that he does not consider the difficulties.

[24] Actually neither Matthew nor Mark dates the incident with any precision. They simply place it immediately before Judas' act of betrayal. They may be more concerned with dramatic contrast than with chronological precision.

3. John names the woman as Mary and plainly indicates that she was the sister of Martha. Neither Matthew nor Mark gives either piece of information.

4. John does not say where the supper was held, whereas the other two inform us that it was in the house of Simon the leper. John does not mention this name anywhere in his story.

5. The amount of the unguent in John's account is very large, namely a pound. It has been pointed out that an alabaster box strong enough to hold this quantity would be difficult for a woman to break as Mark tells us she did.

6. Mark tells us that the protest was made by "some," Matthew by "the disciples," and John by Judas.

7. In Mark the whole leads up to the resounding saying, "Wheresoever the gospel shall be preached throughout the whole world, that also which this woman hath done shall be spoken of for a memorial of her." This is completely absent from John.

8. There is a difficulty about Jesus' words in John, "Suffer her to keep it against the day of my burying" since she had just done the reverse of keeping it. There seems no good reason why John should alter Mark's straightforward saying into these difficult words.

It will be seen that we have an interesting combination of resemblances and differences. The most important coincidences are in the name of the unguent, in the mention of three hundred denarii, and in Jesus' words about not having Him always present in contrast with the poor. But it may fairly be said that each of these is the kind of thing that would persist in oral tradition.[25] It is such striking details that linger in the memory. But the

---

[25] Cf. F. C. Grant, "For any raconteur knows that he hears identical stories in a great many forms, and that two things survive most often the wear and tear of insensitive repetition. The first of these is the catch-words. So the 'valuable pistic nard ointment' and the three hundred denarii would long survive a total loss of the original place or circumstances of the incident, or even of the characters involved" (*The Gospel of John*, New York and London, 1956, p. 153). It is true that some of the story is omitted by Matthew, who certainly had Mark before him. But it is Matthew's habit to do away with Mark's picturesque details as he abbreviates the narrative.

differences are difficult to explain if John had Mark before him. Why should he speak of Mary as anointing Jesus' feet and not the head? Why should he place the incident at a different time? Such alterations are inexplicable. Altogether the differences are such as to make it hazardous to hold that John had Mark before him. The probability is that the resemblances come from oral tradition.

THE ENTRY INTO JERUSALEM

NOR IS IT OTHERWISE WITH THE TRIUMPHAL ENTRY, THE next incident to be recorded in the Fourth Gospel. Here there is one striking coincidence with Mark, namely the use of the words, "Hosanna: Blessed is he that cometh in the name of the Lord." The expression occurs in exactly the same form in the two Gospels. But note the following points of difference:

1. John dates the incident on the Sunday preceding the Passover, whereas Mark leaves the time indefinite. But he and the other Synoptists have it just after Jesus' visit to Jericho. This would make it take place just as Jesus was arriving at Jerusalem for this visit. John records it after the anointing at Bethany.

2. Mark puts the sending for the ass at the beginning of the story. Jesus sent for the ass and rode in. Then, as the multitude saw Him riding in, they greeted Him and spread clothing and branches in the way. John speaks rather of Jesus as sitting on the ass after the enthusiasm had started.

3. John tells us that the branches were palm branches. None of the others mentions this, and palms were not so very common in the vicinity of Jerusalem.

4. John links the incident with the raising of Lazarus ("The multitude therefore that was with him when he called Lazarus out of the tomb, and raised him from the dead, bare witness"). Nothing of this is found in the other accounts.

5. John records, as the others do not, the fact that the disciples did not understand the significance of what was being done at the time.

6. It is to John that we owe the record of the pessimistic verdict of the Pharisees, "Behold how ye prevail nothing; lo, the world is gone after him."

7. The multitude in the Synoptics appears to be the Galilean pilgrims going up to Jerusalem for the feast. In John the crowd "went forth to meet him," i.e. evidently *from* Jerusalem (the crowd in John is described as "a great multitude that had come to the feast," but the direction is different).

The differences are not serious. But they do appear to indicate that the accounts are independent. The one striking similarity is an impressive but short saying, the kind of thing that might well remain identical in more than one line of oral tradition.

The rest of John 12 scarcely gives rise to serious questions of parallels. And, though some of the events referred to in chapter 13 are mentioned in the earlier Gospels, there is no good reason here for seeing dependence. The same goes for the long section, John 14 — 16, for this discourse is without parallel in the Synoptic Gospels. Not only are there no striking parallels in this whole section, but there are some serious problems. Thus the Synoptists mention, as John does not, the institution of the Eucharist. By contrast John has the feet-washing, which they all omit, and also the great high-priestly prayer (John 17). There is also the well-known crux of whether the Last Supper was the Passover (as the Synoptics seem to indicate) or a meal the day before (as John appears to place it). Difficulties of this kind make it difficult to think that John was writing with the others before him.

It would be possible similarly to go through the passion and resurrection stories. I refrain from doing this for two main reasons. One is that this examination is already quite long enough and there is scarcely point in prolonging it. If John had before him the Synoptics or one of them there is not the slightest reason for thinking that he would wait until this point before beginning to rely on them. The other is that the comparison has often been made, and the conclusion of practically all students is that in this part of his Gospel John is certainly independent of the others. A typical verdict is that of C. H. Dodd:

"... The variation in detail is considerable, and the amount of verbal resemblance to the Synoptics is almost the minimum possible if the same story is to be told at all. Certainly there is not nearly so much as is ordinarily required to prove literary dependence."[26]

NO DEPENDENCE

THE DIFFICULTIES IN THE WAY OF SEEING DEPENDENCE ON any of the Synoptics are thus considerable. John characteristically makes use of incidents that they do not employ. Even when he is recording the same thing his account always has distinctive traits, such distinctive traits indeed that it is impossible to think that he is dependent on the others. It is not simply that he uses matter that they do not have. Had this been the case it would have been quite possible to postulate a process wherein John had before him, say, Mark and some other source. One could say that he often preferred the other source, but that he sometimes made use of Mark. But there is more to it than the fact that he does not use Synoptic language when relating Synoptic incidents. His form of expression is often such that it is difficult to think that he knew the Synoptic narrative. Take, for example, his handling of the relationship between John the Baptist and the prophet Elijah. In the Synoptics it is clear that Jesus taught that the Baptist fulfilled the

---

[26] IFG, p. 450. Similarly B. F. Westcott, "It is a superficial and inadequate treatment of his narrative to regard it as a historical supplement of the other narratives, or of the current oral narrative on which they were based. It does (it is true) become in part such a supplement, because it is a portrayal of the main spiritual aspects of the facts illustrated from the fulness of immediate knowledge, but the record is independent and complete in itself" (*The Gospel According to St. John*, Grand Rapids, 1954, II, p. 261). An interesting treatment of the subject is that of Ivor Buse. Accepting Vincent Taylor's division of the Marcan narrative into two strata, the basic narrative A, and Petrine and other Semitic material B, he shows that John has no parallels to material in A but that he has to a number of passages in B. He concludes, "It is impossible to imagine the evangelist, if he had the whole of Mark in front of him or in mind, carefully choosing out the very passages which Vincent Taylor recognizes as B and ignoring with such exactness all that is classified as A" (NTS, 4, 1957-58, p. 219).

prophecy of Malachi 4:5 (Matt. 11:13f.; 17:10-13; Mark 9:11-13). But John tells us that when the Baptist was asked whether he were Elijah he answered "I am not" (John 1:21). A reconciliation between these two statements is not at all difficult. The Baptist was Elijah in the sense foretold by the prophet. That is to say, he went before the Messiah in the spirit and power of Elijah. But he was not Elijah *redivivus*, which was what the Jews meant. In one sense he was Elijah, in another sense he was not. But the point is that, had John had Matthew or Mark before him (in either case with all the authority that comes from acceptance by the church), he would scarcely have left the Baptist's comment as it was, without a word of explanation. It would not have needed more than a sentence or two to make the position quite clear.

A similar comment might be made at various other points. A sentence would have distinguished between John's narrative of the call of the first disciples and the Synoptic call to the apostolate. Minor alterations to his account of the feeding of the multitude would both have brought in extra information and have made it quite clear that he was not contradicting a Gospel accepted as authoritative in the church. It would not have taken much to relate his statement that Bethsaida was "the city of Andrew and Peter" (John 1:44) with Mark's that these two apostles had a house in Capernaum (Mark 1:29), nor his statement that Jesus carried the cross (John 19:17) with Mark's that Simon of Cyrene, coming from the country, was pressed into doing this service (Mark 15:21). There are other examples. In the face of them all it is very difficult to maintain that John was familiar with the Synoptics or even with any one of them. The most satisfactory conclusion is that John wrote his Gospel quite independently of the others.[27] He had access to oral tradition and to what other sources we have no means of

---

[27] Cf. F. C. Grant: "The generally-held view among present-day scholars appears to favor the complete independence of John" (*op. cit.*, p. 10) ; or again, "the distinctive, characteristic features of Mark, Luke or Matthew, the peculiar and unique impress given the tradition, or its specific interpretation, by the earlier evangelists — none of this is traceable in John, either positively or negatively" (*ibid.*).

knowing. But he seems to have written his account without seeing the other canonical Gospels.

ORAL TRADITION

THE PLACE OF ORAL TRADITION HAS RECEIVED A GOOD DEAL of attention in recent years. It is surely obvious that at first all the information now in our Gospels circulated in the form of oral tradition. No one would, I think, venture to affirm that it was written down during our Lord's lifetime. For some time the stories and the sayings were passed on by word of mouth. Then when written records did appear we have no reason for thinking that oral tradition simply disappeared. There is a well-known passage in which Papias tells us that he preferred the living voice to information taken from books,[28] and we have no reason for thinking that this was an unusual position to take. The continuance of oral tradition is important, for it gives us an explanation of the fact that John sometimes reproduces striking expressions identical with those in the Synoptics, as we have seen. But the tradition he selects is not the same in all points as that which they select. It is important to be clear that John does have access to the tradition of the church.[29] The occasional close verbal agreements are very significant here, as are also the general structure of the Gospel and the form of some of the incidents narrated therein. This Gospel did not descend out of the clear blue sky upon an astonished church somewhere around the end of the first century,

---

[28] He says, "And if anyone chanced to come who had actually been a follower of the elders, I would inquire as to the discourses of the elders, what Andrew or what Peter said, or what Philip, or what Thomas or James, or what John or Matthew or any other of the Lord's disciples; and the things which Aristion and John the elder, disciples of the Lord, say. For I supposed that things out of books did not profit me so much as the utterances of a voice *which liveth and abideth*" (cited from *A New Eusebius*, ed. J. Stevenson, London, 1963, p. 50; the passage is from H. E. III, 39; the italicized words are regarded as a quotation from I Pet. 1:23).

[29] Eusebius tells us that John "used all the time a message which was not written down" (H. E. III, 24.7; Loeb translation), which appears to point to a preference for oral proclamation. Eusebius also speaks of John as having written last of all. This I doubt, but the emphasis on oral proclamation may be significant.

the work of a theologian who wanted a suitable vehicle for some radical ideas he was seeking to put forward. It is rooted in the tradition of the church.

No one has done more in recent years to make this clear than C. H. Dodd. Some time ago he wrote:

> . . .Leaving the Gospels aside, we can recover from the New Testament a clearly articulated picture of the place which the historical tradition of Jesus occupied in the early Church, and of the general character of its contents. From the very beginning of things, the life of the Church grew up about this central tradition, which remained normative of its thought, its worship, and its practice through all the rapid and far-reaching development which it underwent in the apostolic and sub-apostolic periods.
>
> The Gospels are to be regarded primarily as the deposit, or crystallization, of this tradition in narrative form. They result from the gathering together of material of various kinds about a central strand of testimony embodied from the first in the preaching (*kerygma*) and teaching (*didaché*) of the Church. Both elements, preaching and teaching, reappear in our Gospels.[30]

In a later work he has pointed out how important it is to realize all this if we are rightly to understand the Fourth Gospel. Many have gone astray by taking it for granted that written sources were the really significant things, and that we can safely neglect oral tradition. He reminds us that most critics have assumed that John used the Synoptics. They have "held the opinion, almost as a dogma," that John used the Synoptics or Mark at the least, "altering them in accordance with special motives of his own. Since the 'alterations' are so drastic at times, the dogma tended to throw a cloud of discredit upon the Johannine narrative." This is very important. It was not anything in the Johannine narrative as such that brought about this discredit. It was the "dogma" assumed all too readily by many critics. Dodd goes on, "That opinion however rested upon an assumption, which was not usually avowed, and of which the critic perhaps was hardly aware, that the writings of early Christianity must have

---

[30] *History and the Gospel*, London, 1938, pp. 73f.

formed a documentary series, in literary dependence on one another. It is now widely recognized that the main factor in perpetuating and propagating the Christian faith and the Gospel story was oral tradition in its various forms. There is therefore no strong *a priori* presumption that resemblances in early Christian documents are due to literary dependence. The presumption is rather the other way."[31]

More recently still this great scholar has turned his attention to the problem of the nature of the tradition behind the Fourth Gospel. He has subjected this Gospel to a rigorous examination and sums up the result in these words: "The above argument has led to the conclusion that behind the Fourth Gospel lies an ancient tradition independent of the other gospels, and meriting serious consideration as a contribution to our knowledge of the historical facts concerning Jesus Christ. For this conclusion I should claim a high degree of probability."[32] I do not see how this conclusion can be resisted. Dodd's work is a patient exhaustive examination of the material and he demonstrates, in my judgment conclusively, that again and again our best explanation of the facts is that John is quite independent of the Synoptics, but that he has access to an early tradition.[33]

AN INTERLOCKING TRADITION

I HAVE BEEN CONCERNED TO INSIST THAT THERE IS LITTLE evidence for direct dependence and that John must be held to be independent of the three Synoptics. But this does not mean that there is no connection between the tradition that John enshrines and the tradition that the Synoptists use each in his own way.

---

[31] IFG, p. 449.

[32] HTFG, p. 423. He immediately adds that "certainty in such matters is seldom to be attained."

[33] J. A. T. Robinson shares this view and in some respects goes further: "Whatever the circumstances and the environment in which this Gospel was eventually put out, there is little doubt in my mind that it rests upon oral tradition with a southern Palestinian milieu prior to A.D. 70, parallel to, and independent of, the Synoptic tradition" (NTS, 4, 1957-58, p. 264, n. 2).

A careful examination of the evidence, such as Pierson Parker undertakes in his article, "Luke and the Fourth Evangelist,"[34] shows that the relationships are very complex. Mostly John does not agree with any of the Synoptists. But when there is shared material all sorts of things happen. Sometimes John agrees with Matthew and Mark against Luke,[35] sometimes with Luke against Matthew and Mark,[36] sometimes with Matthew alone,[37] and sometimes with Mark alone.[38] While there appear to be more agreements with Mark than with either of the others there is no real pattern. All this shows that the tradition behind the Fourth Gospel has its connections with the Synoptic traditions.[39] There is an interlocking.

There is a great deal of evidence that shows that each needs the other for its complete understanding. We are so used to reading any one of the Gospels with what the others say tucked away somewhere in the inner recesses of our mind that we do not always notice that quite a number of passages in the first three Gospels present very real difficulties taken by themselves, but seem capable of solution when considered in the light of what the Fourth

---

[34] *Op. cit.*, pp. 317-336.

[35] Parker cites such things as the place of the anointing at Bethany, and Jesus' reply to the objection (Matt. 26:6-13; Mark 14:3-9; Luke 7:36-50; John 12:1-8); the releasing of a prisoner at the feast (Matt. 27:15f.; Mark 15:6f.; John 18:39); and the scourging of Jesus (Matt. 27:15f.; Mark 15:6f.; John 18:39).

[36] Notably in the resurrection appearances, though Parker lists a considerable number of smaller points.

[37] Jesus orders Peter to resheathe his sword (Matt. 26:52; John 18:11: contrast Mark 14:47f.; Luke 22:61); Caiaphas is mentioned at the beginning of the trial (Matt. 26:57; John 18:12-14: contrast Mark 14:53; Luke 22:54); Joseph of Arimathea is called a "disciple" of Jesus (Matt. 27:57; John 19:38: but not Mark 15:43; Luke 22:50).

[38] Parker mentions the disciples' rowing when Jesus walked on the water and the omission of Peter's attempt to imitate his Master (Matt. 14:22-36; Mark 6:45-52; John 6:15-21); the use of the word κράβατον (John 5:8f.; Mark 2:11f.), etc.

[39] Parker thinks that "John shows no literary dependence on the other gospels. Indeed, he probably had not read any of them" (*op. cit.*, p. 335). He sees a sharing of oral tradition, and conjectures that John "must somewhere, some time, have been associated with Luke in the Christian missionary enterprise" (p. 336).

Gospel says.[40] Indeed, C. H. Dodd regards this as true of
the general picture quite apart from details. He says, "I
believe that the course which was taken by Leben-Jesu-
Forschung (*'The Quest of the Historical Jesus'*, according
to the English title of the most important record of that
'Quest') during the nineteenth century proves that a
severe concentration on the Synoptic record, to the
exclusion of the Johannine contribution, leads to an
impoverished, a one-sided, and finally an incredible view
of the facts — I mean, of the *facts*, as part of history."[41]
And what is true of the general picture is true also of a
number of specific incidents. This is important for an
understanding of the relationship between the Gospels.
It tells us nothing about the question as to whether John
had read the Synoptics (or at least one of them). But it
does show that the traditions on which John was drawing
cohere with those on which the Synoptists drew. There
is a kind of intermeshing which indicates that, though
the portraits are different, it is the same Subject that is
before all the Evangelists.

1. *The Judean Ministry*. The most obvious of these points

---

[40] Cf. R. H. Lightfoot: "Let the reader attempt the almost impossible task of forgetting, for the moment, the existence of St.
John's gospel and all that he has learned from it and by means of
it in reference to the Lord's incarnate life, and then let him consider whether he would not find considerable difficulty in answering
certain questions which might be put to him. How, for example, is
he to answer the question, 'What think ye of Christ?' In what sense
is he to regard the Lord Jesus as the Jewish Messiah? What is
the relation between His coming as Jesus of Nazareth and the
future coming of the Son of man? What is the meaning of the
mysterious title, the Son of man? Above all, how does the Lord
remain a living force in mankind, the fountain head of vital religion? Did His disciples only transmit a message about His life and
death and work and teaching, or had they, and have they, a
further, greater, and more vital task? It is to St. John that we
owe the definitive answers to those questions" (*St. John's Gospel*,
Oxford, 1956, p. 32). He thinks it "nearer the truth" to say that
"without St. John's gospel the earlier gospels are largely a puzzle"
(p. 34). Similarly W. F. Lofthouse cites certain sayings of Christ
from the Synoptic Gospels and says, "The riddle of such words
from such a man would be insoluble if we had not the key furnished
by the fourth gospel" (*Ethics and Atonement*, London, 1906, p.
284).
[41] IFG, p. 446.

is the fact which has often been pointed out that the Synoptic accounts require the Judean ministry that John alone records. The Three describe a ministry that is practically confined to Galilee until the last few days, when Jesus went up to Jerusalem and died there. It seems, moreover, to be a fairly short ministry, lasting perhaps a year. And when Jesus did go to Jerusalem He was killed in very short order.

Now if we were not so familiar with it this would surely strike us as nothing short of astonishing. It is somewhat difficult to see how Jesus could have attained such influence in Galilee as the Synoptists attest during a ministry as short as the one the Synoptists record. But the really astonishing thing is that the Jerusalem authorities acted in such haste to put the Galilean to death. Admittedly the triumphal entry would not have endeared Him to the chief priests, nor would the cleansing of the temple. But these two things, even taken together, scarcely seem sufficient reason for the extremes to which the chief priests went. They are a good reason for opposition, but not a good reason for an execution, not unless there is something more behind it all. And it is asking a lot to believe that the superior Jerusalemites would be sufficiently disturbed by reports emanating from Galilee of a short ministry there to take strong action. Notice further that it cannot, on Synoptic premises, be anything other than a quick decision, for Mark speaks of the authorities as beginning to plan Jesus' death only after His arrival in Jerusalem, and within two days of the feast (Mark 14:1).

Moreover there are indications in the Synoptic narratives that something has been omitted. Thus Mark records a saying of Jesus, "Day after day I was within your reach as I taught in the temple, and you did not lay hands on me" (Mark 14:49, NEB). This is passing curious if there is nothing more than Mark records, for up till this point he has spoken of but two days when Jesus taught in Jerusalem. With it we must consider the fact that according to this same Evangelist Jesus knew where to find an ass in a village in the immediate vicinity of Jerusalem, though Mark has not yet recorded that He was ever in the

vicinity (Mark 11:1ff.), and the further fact that He
knew of and could secure for His use a furnished upper
room in the city itself (Mark 14:12-16).[42] How would a
stranger have such contacts?

All this falls into place if we accept the Johannine
evidence that the ministry was longer than a year, and
that there was a not inconsiderable part of it spent in and
around Jerusalem. Given the clue we can find hints of this
in the Synoptics. Thus Matthew tells us that Jesus said to
the Jerusalemites, "How often would I have gathered thy
children together" (Matt. 23:37; cf. Luke 13:34). This
certainly implies more than one visit, and the impression
is strengthened by the following "Behold, your house is
left unto you desolate." This is explicable after repeated
failure to heed the claims of Jesus, but not after a single
visit. There is textual difficulty, but Luke appears to tell
us that at one time Jesus was preaching in the synagogues
of Judea (Luke 4:44).[43] He speaks of a crowd including
people from Judea and Jerusalem as following Jesus in
Galilee (Luke 6:17). He also records Jesus as having wept
over the city, "because thou knewest not the time of thy
visitation" (Luke 19:44).[44] Luke knows of Martha and
her sister Mary, and even relates an incident that took
place in their home (Luke 10:38-42). But they lived in
Bethany (John 11:1). Unless they had two homes, which
is improbable and for which there is no evidence, Luke is
speaking of something that happened in Judea. It may
also be relevant that he relates the story immediately
after the parable of the Good Samaritan, where the
setting is the road from Jerusalem to Jericho. But though

---

[42] Mark also tells us that Jesus was present at a banquet in the
home of Simon the leper in Bethany (Mark 14:3). This seems to
indicate another Judean friendship.

[43] της Ιουδαιας is read by P[75], ℵ B C L f1 157 al syr[sin];των Ιουδαιων
by W; της Γαλιλαιας by A D K Θ Ψ f13 28 33 565 latt bo[pc]. Nearly all agree that the former reading is to be preferred.

[44] Cf. V. H. Stanton, "It is inconceivable that Jesus should not
have regarded His own coming, His own preaching and working
amongst them, as not included in their 'day of visitation,' their day
of opportunity (as we should more commonly say), and should
regard that day as already over though He had never exercised any
ministry there" (*The Gospels as Historical Documents*, Part III,
The Fourth Gospel, Cambridge, 1920, p. 232).

the Synoptists give us these hints it is John alone who lets us see that Jesus came into conflict with the authorities in Jerusalem at an early date, and that this conflict was carried on at intervals through a ministry lasting at least three years.

2. *The Last Journey to Jerusalem.* The Synoptists tell us that Jesus went up to Jerusalem, knowing that He would be killed. Why then did He go up? In a deeper sense we can say that He must fulfil His destiny in this way. But the question concerns the immediate occasion of the journey. The Synoptists give us no reason. Mark, for example, simply says, "They were on the way, going up to Jerusalem; and Jesus was going before them: and they were amazed; and they that followed were afraid" (Mark 10:32). Clearly the journey was one to be regarded with trepidation. Why then was it to be undertaken? Mark supplies no answer. Neither does Matthew (Matt. 20:17), nor Luke (Luke 18:31). All three Synoptists present us with a picture of Jesus leading His disciples up to Jerusalem into danger, and even into certain death for Himself. But they do not tell us why He did it.

John, however, does give a reason. He tells us that a friend of Jesus, Lazarus by name, was ill, and that the sisters of the sick man sent for Jesus (John 11:1ff.). Both Jesus and the disciples knew the danger, but the Lord insisted upon going up to help His friends (John 11:7ff.).

3. *The Denial.* The Synoptists place Peter within the high priest's courtyard at the time of the denials (Matt. 26:58, 69ff.; Mark 14:54, 66ff.; Luke 22:54ff.). But none of them explains how this Galilean secured admittance to the place where another Galilean was being held. On the surface it seems unlikely enough. But John has an explanation. He tells us that there was one disciple who was known[45] to the high priest and that this man spoke to the

---

[45] On the word for "known" in John 18:15 Dodd remarks, "It is now generally recognized that γνωστός implies something more than mere acquaintance. It means that the person so described was a member of the High Priest's circle, possibly a kinsman and himself of priestly birth, or at any rate one who stood in intimate relations with the governing high priestly family" (HTFG, pp. 86f.).

doorkeeper on Peter's behalf, thus securing his admission (John 18:15f.). The point is a small one, but none the less illuminating.

4. *"Destroy this Temple."* The charge made by certain false witnesses at Jesus' trial was "We heard him say, I will destroy this temple that is made with hands, and in three days I will build another made without hands" (Mark 14:58; cf. Matt. 26:60f.). Nor did the charge die there. Mockers revived it on Calvary (Matt. 27:40; Mark 15:29). And later still, Stephen's opponents said, "We have heard him say, that this Jesus of Nazareth shall destroy this place" (Acts 6:14). The repeated emphasis on this saying shows clearly that Jesus said something which His enemies remembered, and which they held against Him. At least they remembered it in a garbled form, for their witness did not agree (Mark 14:59).

What was this saying? Once again the Synoptists lead us to a situation for which their story has not prepared us. We cannot find a suitable saying among those recorded in any of the Synoptics. But John tells us that Jesus once said, "Destroy this temple, and in three days I will raise it up" (John 2:19). There has been a good deal of discussion as to exactly what this saying means. John says that the temple in question was "his body." Many discussions are concerned with the correctness or otherwise of this interpretation. I do not wish to go into this. Whatever the precise meaning, the saying is enigmatic. It might thus be interpreted (or misinterpreted!) in more ways than one. But it does not sound complimentary to the temple and all that it stood for. Thus it is not surprising that Jesus' enemies held it against Him, and regarded it as a suitable accusation to be used at the critical moment. Notice further that John places the saying early. If about three years elapsed between the utterance of the words and their use against Jesus at His trial we can understand why the witnesses did not agree on exactly what was said. Once again John enables us to make good sense of some Synoptic passages.[46]

----

[46] J. E. Davey regards this saying as one of his "foundation pillars of *John's* historicity ... fragments which are obviously independent and historical" (*The Jesus of St. John*, London, 1958,

5. *The Roman Trial.* There are many difficulties about the trial of Jesus, one of which bears on our present subject. Mark does not account for the trial before Pilate which he records. He speaks of a trial before the high priest, and then records what looks like a verdict and sentence, "And they all condemned him to be worthy of death" (Mark 14:64). But then, inexplicably, they take Jesus off to the Roman governor and the chief priests appear as accusers (Mark 15:1-3). John does not record anything in the nature of a trial before the high priest, but seems to indicate that what took place there was in the nature of a preliminary examination. The real trial took place before Pilate. The point of this appears when Pilate offered to let the chief priests try the case in their own jurisdiction. They replied that they had no power to put a man to death (John 18:31). The question whether they did or did not have power to put men to death under any circumstances is an intricate one. But what is beyond doubt is that the Romans had supreme power and that only they could procure a crucifixion. John gives a reasonable account of the way Jesus and His accusers came to be before the Roman governor. And, in fact, John makes quite a feature of the Roman trial. Here, however, it is sufficient to notice that the Synoptic accounts give no real reason for bringing Jesus before Pilate, whereas John does.[47]

Temple makes the further point that we need the Fourth Gospel to make clear the meaning of the Synoptic

---

p. 34). He says of it, "Here, as in quite a number of cases, we see *John* elucidating, supporting and even enlarging the Synoptic tradition itself, in ways which are historically probable" (*op. cit.,* pp. 38f.). But it seems to me that he makes difficulties by putting the saying late (he accepts the common view that there was one cleansing of the temple and that the Marcan date is to be preferred), and by rejecting John's explanation in favor of the view that the temple building was meant. He does not face the difficulty of the inability of the false witnesses to recall the words of what, on his showing, was a straightforward saying uttered within a very few days of Jesus' trial.

[47] C. H. Dodd stresses the point that behind the Fourth Gospel in the trial narrative there is an old and reliable tradition, and he concludes that John "clarifies" the Synoptic accounts (HTFG, p. 120).

Gospels at the Jewish stage of the trial. Thus Mark records a trial before the high priest on the night that Jesus was arrested (Mark 14:53-65). The next morning there is a solemn assembly of chief priests, elders, scribes, and the whole sanhedrin. These "held a consultation," as a result of which they bound Jesus and took Him to Pilate (Mark 15:1). But if they had gone over the whole affair during the night, why the "consultation" in the morning? Mark does not say. But John tells us that when He was arrested Jesus was taken first to Annas (John 18:12-14) Subsequently Annas sent Him off to Caiaphas (John 18:24). John enables us to see that Mark's nighttime assembly is an informal inquiry before Annas, while what took place in the morning was the official meeting of the sanhedrin, necessary before further action could be taken.[48]

6. *Jesus' Enemies.* This point I will give in the words of A. H. N. Green-Armytage:

> ... It is an argumentative Gospel. There is much debate between Jesus and his opponents, many angry and provocative speeches by Jesus, many tart rejoinders. There is no sign of that 'gentle Jesus meek and mild' who has distorted the vision of many and induced in them a mental picture of an inoffensive curate with a seraphic smile who went about doing good (and whose crucifixion is therefore totally inexplicable). In St. John it is abundantly clear why, and how, Jesus made so many enemies — and any man worthy of the name is bound to make enemies.[49]

I would not go so far as to say that the Synoptics give us no reason for Jesus' having made enemies. They do. But the point Green-Armytage is making is that John

---

[48] William Temple, commenting on the words, they "led him to Annas first" (John 18:13), says "Only St. John tells this; it is one of the facts recorded by him alone which make intelligible the Synoptic narrative where it otherwise would be, at best, obscure. ... St. John tells us that the earlier trial was an informal enquiry at the house of Annas, at which the decision was reached, though sentence could not there be pronounced. Then, very early in the morning, the Sanhedrin met in full session and rapidly confirmed in legal verdict and sentence what had been informally decided during the night" (*Readings in St. John's Gospel*, London, 1947, *ad loc.*).

[49] Green-Armytage, *op. cit.*, p. 43.

brings the picture more sharply into focus. The Jesus of St. John could not but make some very bitter enemies, and this makes more intelligible the cross of which the Synoptists write.

7. *The Sabbath.* It is plain enough from all four Gospels that Jesus' attitude toward the sabbath aroused some very bitter opposition. This is somewhat curious in the Synoptic Gospels, since there the ministry is set in Galilee where the evidence indicates that there was not the same ceremonial strictness as in the capital.[50] There were so many Gentiles there that Galilee could be spoken of as "Galilee of the Gentiles" (Matt. 4:15). The Law was not studied with as great strictness as in Jerusalem, and all in all the general attitude of the largely rural Galilee was very different from that in the capital.[51]

This makes it quite surprising that Jesus very early came into conflict with Jewish leaders on the matter of sabbath observance. It is true that His opposition came from Jerusalem (Mark 3:22; cf. 7:1; Matt. 15:1), but this is itself even more surprising. Why should the religious leaders think it worthwhile to send emissaries to oppose the Galilean Carpenter? Nothing in the Synoptic Gospels explains this opposition from such a long range.

---

[50] For a comparatively minor example cf. a saying of R. Judah concerning *Terumah* ("Heave-offering") : "If the vow was of undefined *Terumah*, in Judea the vow is binding; but in Galilee it is not binding, since the men of Galilee know naught of the *Terumah* of the Temple-chamber. (And if the vow was of) undefined devoted things, in Judea it is not binding, but in Galilee it is binding, since the people of Galilee know naught of things devoted to (the use of) the priests" (*Mishnah, Ned.* 2.4; Danby's translation). In each case the reason for the different rule in Galilee is the local neglect of a ritual point observed in Judea.

[51] Cf. A. Edersheim: "... They were looked down upon as neglecting traditionalism, unable to rise to its speculative heights, and preferring the attractions of the Haggadah to the logical subtleties of the Halakhah. There was a general contempt in Rabbinic circles for all that was Galilean" (*The Life and Times of Jesus the Messiah*, I, London, 1890, p. 225) ; "The very neighbourhood of the Gentile world, the contact with the great commercial centres close by, and the constant intercourse with foreigners, who passed through Galilee along one of the world's great highways, would render the narrow exclusiveness of the Southerners impossible" (*op. cit.*, p. 223). See the *Mishnah, Ned.* 2.4 (quoted in the previous note) ; *Yad.* 4.8, for examples of contempt for the Galileans.

The explanation may well be found in John 5. Here we read that Jesus on a sabbath day cured a lame man in Jerusalem and that He came into violent conflict with the Jewish leaders as a result. Jesus' defense was, "My Father worketh even until now, and I work" (John 5:17).[52] The Jews were enraged "because he not only brake the sabbath, but also called God his own Father, making himself equal with God" (v. 18). "Brake" is the translation of ἔλυεν, where the imperfect tense denotes not a single, isolated happening, but a continuing practice. Moreover this practice was not aimless, nor due to religious carelessness or the like. It proceeded from Jesus' idea of His relationship to the heavenly Father. It was because He was the Son that He acted as He did on the sabbath. Therefore the Jews saw in His attitude to the sabbath not merely the breaking of one of the commandments, but blasphemy, and that of the most serious kind: "making himself equal with God." Small wonder that they persecuted Him into Galilee.

The Synoptic narrative by itself is difficult. It presents us with a picture of determined opposition on a point of ceremonial observance in Galilee, which is against all the probabilities as we know them. But with the Johannine evidence before us this is not only understandable, but inevitable.

8. *The Healing Miracles.* The Synoptic Gospels deal with a number of miraculous cures wrought by Jesus. Commonly such a narrative ends with words like "Thy faith hath saved thee; go in peace." Faith is presupposed and the miracle is the response to it. It would be too much to say that the Synoptics give us no reason for the miracles. The compassion of Jesus for the sufferers is mentioned many times (e.g. Matt. 9:36; 14:14; Mark 1:41; Luke 7:13). Again, His answer to the question from the imprisoned John the Baptist shows that the miracles were a means of accrediting Him (Matt. 11:4ff.), and

---

[52] This is accepted by J. E. Davey as the first of his "foundation pillars of *John's* historicity" (*op. cit.*, pp. 34f.). He thinks that in view of Gen. 2 and the attitude of both Jews and Christians to the Old Testament it would not have been invented.

several passsages show that they revealed God (e.g. Luke 7:16; 9:43).

But John speaks of the miracles as inducing faith. Thus he concludes his story of the healing of the nobleman's son with the words, "himself believed, and his whole house" (John 4:53). He quotes Jesus as saying, "The works which the Father hath given me to accomplish, the very works that I do, bear witness of me, that the Father hath sent me" (John 5:36). He also records that Jesus once blamed people for following Him because they were fed and not on account of the miracles (John 6:26). John's characteristic word for these great acts is not "miracles" or "mighty works," but "signs."[53] For him the miracles point men to spiritual truth. They are not ends in themselves. They have Christological significance.[54]

The point of this is that John gives meaning to the miracles in a way that the Synoptists do not. As Bishop Cassian puts it (with specific reference to the accounts of the healing of the centurion's servant in the Synoptics and the nobleman's son in John), "In both cases the healing is due to faith, but John completes: faith is not only the condition of the miracle but its aim, or, with different words, the object of the faith is not the possibility of healing but the person of the Healer."[55] It is impossible to think that the end of the faith we see so splendidly set forth in the miracle stories was simply the cures. There is more to it than that. The end of the faith was surely increased knowledge of and love for and faith in the Person. But it is only John who makes this clear.[56]

There is another point in connection with the miracles.

---

[53] Actually John makes a great deal of use of the term "works" for Jesus' miracles. What to us is a miracle is to Him no more than a "work." But we are concerned here not with John's treatment of the miracles in all its details, but rather with the fact that he saw them as signs rather than as works of power.

[54] Cf. H. Latimer Jackson: ". . . His 'signs' are proof of his divine omnipotence and manifest his glory" (*The Problem of the Fourth Gospel*, Cambridge, 1918, p. 65).

[55] SE, I, p. 146.

[56] R. H. Strachan notes a typical Jewish story narrated by Josephus and proceeds, "There the technique of the healer is

In the Synoptics there is often the question of whether Jesus is willing to heal (e.g. Mark 1:40; 9:22), but nothing is said about the patient's will to be healed. This is often implied, as in the faith that is shown or the determined way in which, say, the friends of the paralytic battled on till they were able to bring him before Jesus. But in John it is explicit. Thus in the story of the man at the pool of Bethesda Jesus asks, "Wouldest thou be made whole?" (John 5:6). This makes it quite plain. The patient must *will* to be healed.[57]

9. *The Call of the Disciples*. Matthew and Mark first refer to Peter and Andrew when they narrate their call to be apostles: "And walking by the sea of Galilee, he saw two brethren, Simon who is called Peter, and Andrew his brother, casting a net into the sea; for they were fishers. And he saith unto them, Come ye after me, and I will make you fishers of men. And they straightway left the nets, and followed him" (Matt. 4:18ff.). It is exactly the same with James and John (Matt. 4:21f.). There are no preliminaries. Jesus sees these men, apparently for the first time. He calls them and they leave everything to follow Him. This leaving of everything, as the sequel shows, was something far-reaching. They joined Jesus in His peripatetic ministry and had no opportunity of practicing their craft. They left their jobs. They left their homes. They left the familiar routine of their lives and abandoned all the security they had hitherto enjoyed. Why did they do all this? What made them enter into such a far-reaching commitment to a

---

magical, and the purpose of the story is to magnify the power of the spells at his disposal. No personal bond is forged between healed and healer" (*op. cit.*, p. 4, n. 1). John makes it clear that in the case of the miracles of Jesus the personal bond was real and important.

[57] Cf. C. H. Dodd: "The 'faith' of the woman with the haemorrhage (Mark v. 34), of Bartimaeus (Mark x. 52), of the friends of the paralytic in the Marcan story (Mark ii. 5), and of the Canaanite mother in Matthew (xv. 28), is exhibited in the sheer determination with which they press for a cure, whether for themselves or for those they represent. The question, therefore, 'Have you the will to be healed?' is implicit in such stories. John makes it explicit" (HTFG, p. 177).

total stranger, and that on the spur of the moment? The Synoptists do not tell us.

But John's first chapter is given over, after the Prologue, to a recounting of certain incidents in connection with John the Baptist. From this it transpires that the Baptist had spoken of One to come, and that he directed certain of His followers to Jesus as that One. Andrew and Peter are specifically named as having been introduced to Jesus in this way (John 1:40-42), and most scholars hold that John was the man who first went with Andrew to see Jesus (John 1:35ff.). The events of Matthew 4 are more intelligible if they follow after those of John 1 than if they represent the first contact that the men there spoken of had had with Jesus. Once more John helps us to understand a Synoptic narrative.

10. *Making Jesus King.* At the conclusion of the story of the feeding of the five thousand both Matthew and Mark record that Jesus sent the disciples away by ship while He Himself remained behind to dismiss the people (Matt. 14:22; Mark 6:45). The word they use for sending the disciples away is a strong term, ἠνάγκασεν, i.e. He "compelled" or "constrained" them. And when He had taken His leave, He went up into the mountain to pray. While all this is perhaps not totally inexplicable it at least leaves us wondering why the disciples were not permitted to be with Jesus at the end of the day, and why, having got rid of His close followers, He speedily withdrew from the multitude. John tells us that the miracle had such an effect on the people that they wished to proclaim Jesus King (John 6:15). Clearly high hopes had been aroused, and not unnaturally they turned to high political hopes. John's little addition to our knowledge helps us to see the naturalness of the action recorded in the earlier Gospels. Jesus packed the disciples off before they got caught up in the king-making fever. Then He separated Himself from the crowds in order to discourage them from proceeding further with their revolutionary nonsense.

11. *Prayer.* The Synoptic teaching on prayer is nothing less than astonishing. Perhaps equally astonishing is the calmness with which we take it. Take, for example,

the well-known words of Matthew 7:7f., "Ask, and it
shall be given you; seek, and ye shall find; knock, and
it shall be opened unto you: for every one that asketh
receiveth; and he that seeketh findeth; and to him that
knocketh it shall be opened." These promises are absolutely without qualification. Nothing is mentioned in the
way of faith, agreement with the will of God, or anything
of the sort. Nothing other than asking, seeking, knock-
ing. If we stopped to reflect on this it would strike us
as very strange teaching indeed.

Or take Jesus' words about the mountain: "Have
faith in God. Verily I say unto you, Whosoever shall
say unto this mountain, Be thou taken up and cast into
the sea; and shall not doubt in his heart, but shall believe that what he saith cometh to pass; he shall have
it. Therefore I say unto you, All things whatsoever ye
pray and ask for, believe that ye receive them, and ye
shall have them" (Mark 11:22-24). Similarly Matthew
records the words, "If ye have faith as a grain of mus-
tard seed, ye shall say unto this mountain, Remove hence
to yonder place; and it shall remove; and nothing shall
be impossible unto you" (Matt. 17:20). In the same
strain Jesus tells the father of the epileptic boy, "All
things are possible to him that believeth" (Mark 9:23).
In these examples faith is necessary. Once Matthew
speaks of the necessity for agreement between people
praying (Matt. 18:19). But the general picture is that
of prayer as an open door. If we enter that door by faith,
then nothing at all is impossible.

Yet it is a commonplace of the devotional life that
even very godly souls experience failures in prayer. And
if this is so in the case of the spiritual giants, much
more is it the case with more ordinary mortals. All the
more remarkable is it then if we are not surprised by
what we read.

John supplements the Synoptic teaching in two ways:
he mentions qualifications that must be added to this
teaching, and he shows us in Christ that perfect faith
and union with God which produces prayer as it ought
to be. Thus under the first heading John tells us that
it is necessary that the praying man be in close com-

munion with Christ: "If ye abide in me, and my words abide in you, ask whatsoever ye will, and it shall be done unto you" (John 15:7). Several times we read that it is necessary to pray "in the name" of Jesus: "And whatsoever ye shall ask in my name, that will I do, that the Father may be glorified in the Son. If ye shall ask anything in my name, that will I do" (John 14:13f.; cf. 15:16; 16:23, 26; cf. also 1 John 5:14f., where the condition is that we make our requests "according to his will"). Such passages reveal that, while faith is necessary, it is not sufficient of itself. A readiness to do the will of God (or to act in accordance with "the name") is also important, as is a life in close communion with the deity.

The second way in which John supplements the Synoptists is in showing us in Christ the perfect faith and union with God which produces prayer as it should be. He speaks of Christ as living in the most perfect harmony with the Father. He shows us what it is to live the kind of life from which the right kind of prayer flows naturally. When we look at the portrait of the Johannine Christ we see that the absolute statements about prayer in the Synoptics are true. Christ demonstrated their truth in His own life. When we read the Synoptics we unconsciously make the required adjustments and qualifications. But the point of importance for our present inquiry is that it is John who supplies these qualifications.[58]

12. *The Theological Significance of Synoptic Incidents.* It has often been pointed out that the Synoptists have a good deal to say about demon possession, whereas John omits all reference to the phenomenon. For the first three writers demons were real. They took possession of men. They saw Jesus as in continual conflict with the

---

[58] Cf. J. E. Davey: "What is the explanation of the differences between Christ's teaching on prayer in the Synoptic records and the form it assumed in John and Paul and James? Surely that Christ meant it, but spoke it from the level of His own experience; He did know how to pray and He did not ask amiss. Thus the Johannine portrait of the abiding mystical communion of Christ with the Father is the key to the Synoptic teaching on prayer" (*op. cit.*, p. 144).

demons. Again and again He cast them out of sufferers.
His ministry began with a time of temptation by the chief
of all the demons, and from that point the battle was
joined. It is interesting that, in Bishop Cassian's words,
in John we have "a theology of the devil."[59] John does
not speak of exorcisms, but he depicts for us a continuing struggle between light and darkness, between Christ
and the forces of evil. He can say, "Did not I choose
you the twelve, and one of you is a devil?" (John 6:70),
and He characterizes His opponents as "of your father
the devil" (John 8:44). His whole ministry is one of
conflict with the evil one. This comes to its climax in
the passion. It was the devil who put it into the heart
of Judas to betray Him (John 13:2). The devil is three
times referred to as "the prince of this world" in this
last great struggle. He comes to Jesus but has nothing
in Him (John 14:30), nothing on which he can take
hold to defeat Him. On the contrary he himself is cast
out (John 12:31), and he is judged (John 16:11). The
exorcisms are not there,[60] but the conflict is there and
the theology is there. John is concerned with theological
significance through and through, and his words about
the devil help us to see the struggle in the Synoptics
in its right perspective.

Something similar is to be said about the Good Shepherd. He appears in a parable in both Matthew and
Luke. But in the Fourth Gospel the theology behind this
figure is brought out in a full and satisfying way. We
cannot do without the parable, but we cannot do either
without "the theology of divine pastorship" (Cassian)
which John sets before us.

---

[59] *Op. cit.*, p. 146.

[60] We should perhaps say three more things about the absence of
exorcisms from John. (i) It is possible that John saw the exorcists
as a class of well-known miracle workers, and that he did not wish
to put Jesus into that class.

(ii) John was writing according to a plan (John 20:31), and it
may well be that he did not see the exorcisms as fitting into that
plan.

(iii) John often speaks of the miracles as "signs." He uses both
Synoptic and non-Synoptic "signs." But he may well have thought
that there was little significance in casting out demons. He preferred to use "signs" that taught other spiritual lessons.

13. *Living Out Synoptic Precepts.* Hoskyns makes the point that in John there are many passages that dwell upon and enlarge the thought of a saying in the Synoptics.[61] Thus Mark records that Jesus said, "Whosoever would save his life shall lose it; and whosoever shall lose his life for my sake and the gospel's shall save it" (Mark 8:35). Hoskyns points out that in John this "no doubt underlies the discourse spoken in answer to the Greeks who wished to *see Jesus* (xii. 20-30) and becomes almost audible in *v.* 25. But it is in the Fourth Gospel not a Saying among other Sayings; in it, rather, is voiced the imperative of God from which no man can escape, be he Jew or Greek: *He that hateth his life in this world, shall keep it unto life eternal.* This is, moreover, the imperative accepted by Jesus Himself."[62]

It would not be true to say that we have to turn to John to see the meaning of the Synoptic saying. The crucifixion, which all the Evangelists record, shows this very plainly. But Hoskyns has put an important truth into words for us. John does bring out as a major, dominant theme what appears in the Synoptics as a saying.

The same is true of other sayings. Thus Mark 3:35 reads, "For whosoever shall do the will of God, the same is my brother, and sister, and mother." But it is John who really shows us what it means to live out a life of complete obedience to the divine will. Similarly Mark records the saying, "Ye shall be hated of all men for my name's sake" (Mark 13:13). But it is in the farewell discourse in John that the theme is really developed. F. N. Davey makes a similar point for the discourse attached to the feeding of the multitude: "... The Feeding of the Five Thousand is now seen to point to

---

[61] "These familiar Sayings are not so much quoted, or embedded in a discourse; rather, they constitute its theme. It is as though they had been so welded into the author's theology that they had ceased to be detached or even detachable. They lie no longer on the periphery, as though they were just Sayings; rather they have moved into the centre and have taken control, not merely of single discourses, but of the whole presentation of what Jesus was and is" (Edwin C. Hoskyns and F. N. Davey, *The Fourth Gospel*, London, 1947, pp. 73f.).

[62] *Ibid.,* p. 74.

Jesus as the ultimate answer to man's hunger."[63] He also reminds us that, while John records neither the transfiguration nor the agony in Gethsemane, "the heavenly glory of Jesus and His troubled humiliation are shown to condition every part of His life."[64]

14. *The Upper Room*. The events in the upper room on the eve of the crucifixion have always been held by Christians to be profoundly significant. But in Matthew and Mark what happened is described "with such reserve ... as to be almost unintelligible."[65] Mark tells us only that Jesus spoke of being betrayed, but without identifying the betrayer. Then in words of great obscurity He spoke of some bread as His body and of some wine as His blood. When the company had consumed it they went out. Matthew adds but little to this. Luke's narrative is a little fuller, but it still leaves obscurities.

John does two things. He provides us with a fuller account of what took place (though without mentioning the institution of the service of Holy Communion). And he records a long discourse which interprets the significance of it all. It is from this Gospel that we see what the upper room means.

15. *The Palm Sunday Enthusiasm*. The Synoptists record that Jesus entered Jerusalem on the first Palm Sunday riding on a donkey. They tell us that He was greeted with great enthusiasm, but they give no reason for it. It may be that their mention of the fact that Jesus fulfilled the prophecy of Zechariah is part of the explanation. If the crowd recognized this, the supporters of Jesus among them might well be enthusiastic. Yet it is not unlikely that others were entering Jerusalem on asses. It was a common mode of travel and there were many travellers coming up to Jerusalem for the feast. We seem to need something else. And if the Synoptists scarcely explain the enthusiasm of the crowds it is also the case that they do not account for the heightened animosity of Jesus' enemies, an animosity which was to lead to His death within a few days.

---

[63] *Ibid.*, p. 76.
[64] *Ibid.*, p. 81.
[65] *Ibid.* (Hoskyns), p. 432.

Some outstanding event seems required which would both fire the imagination of Jesus' supporters and arouse the ire of His enemies. John, by recording the raising of Lazarus, supplies such an event. And he specifically tells us that this goaded Jesus' enemies into consulting together to find a way of countering Him. He goes on to link this with the triumphal entry (John 11:47ff.; 12:17).[66]

16. *The Greatness of John the Baptist.* The Synoptists assure us that John the Baptist was truly great. They record Jesus' words that he was more than a prophet, and that none born of women was greater than he (Matt. 11:9ff.; Luke 7:26ff.). But they give us very little from which we may discern in what this greatness consisted. The John of the Synoptists was a good and courageous man but, most would feel, not conspicuously so. John, however, makes the situation clearer. He shows us a John the Baptist who possessed an insight into the person of Jesus that was unmatched among His followers. John the Baptist spoke of Jesus' preexistence (John 1: 15, 30). Consistently he bore witness to what Jesus was. Indeed, in the Fourth Gospel he appears constantly in this capacity of witness. In this Gospel on the first occasion when he saw Jesus he is recorded to have greeted Him as "the Lamb of God, that taketh away the sin of the world" (John 1:29). We see real greatness in words like "He must increase, but I must decrease" (John 3:30), words that surely must rank among the most noble ever uttered by mortal man. And they are words that show a true understanding of who and what Jesus was. It is the Fourth Evangelist who really depicts John's greatness,[67] for he shows him as penetrating

---

[66] H. E. Edwards is so impressed by this point that he can say, "... It is not an exaggeration to say that, if the Fourth Gospel had not been written or had not come down to us, historians would have found in the Marcan account of the first Holy Week either an insoluble problem or else they would have been obliged to invent some event as public, as impressive and as provocative as the raising of Lazarus in order to account for what S. Mark tells us" (*op. cit.*, p. 178; cf. also pp. 183f.).

[67] C. F. Nolloth can say, "No grander figure of a man, nor a more pathetic, appears on the scene of the Old and the New Testa-

quickly to such an understanding of the person of Jesus as the disciples did not attain for quite a long time.

17. *Minor Points.* A number of small points, proving nothing individually but strengthening the general impression, might also be adduced. Thus while John does not report the accusation of blasphemy made at Jesus' trial, he does record the fact that the Jews accused Jesus of this crime much earlier than do the Synoptists (John 10:33; this is not to overlook the fact that an occasional such accusation is made earlier still, both in the Synoptics and in John; what is in question is the accusation made specifically with a view to bringing about Jesus' death and which in the end did just that). The Johannine incident forms an intelligible prelude to the Synoptic account.

There is a further interesting link with the Synoptists in John's reference to Jesus as going into Perea before the final visit to Jerusalem (John 10:40). Matthew and Mark both tell us that Jesus took His final journey to Jerusalem through this region (Matt. 19:1; Mark 10:1).

A rather curious minor point is the hesitation of Philip in bringing the Greeks to Jesus when they made their request to him (John 12:21f.). It is clear that Philip was dubious about this. But why? It is difficult to see on the basis of the Fourth Gospel alone. From early times the suggestion has found favor that the reason for his hesitation was the instruction of Jesus, recorded in Matthew 10:5, "Go not into any way of the Gentiles."[68] This works the other way round from the points we have so far been considering, for it explains John from the Synoptics. But it certainly points to an interrelated tradition.

There are other indications of an interlocking tradition. C. K. Barrett in his discussion of John 8 draws attention to several points of contact between John and

---

ment history. And it is here in the Fourth Gospel, rather than in the others, that the explanation of his greatness is to be found. They give Christ's pronouncement of the fact; St. John gives the ground of it" (*The Fourth Evangelist*, London, 1925, p. 212).

[68] M. F. Wiles cites Theodore, Chrysostom, and Cyril as subscribing to this point of view (*The Spiritual Gospel*, Cambridge, 1960, p. 20).

the Synoptists. The theme of light is found in both (Mark 4:21f.; Matt. 4:16; 5:14; Luke 2:32; John 8:12). The Jews' claim that they were not born of fornication (John 8:41) may well show knowledge of the Virgin Birth and point to Jewish slanders with this as the starting point. The argument about the descent of the Jews from Abraham reminds Barrett of a saying of John the Baptist (Matt. 3:9; Luke 3:8), while the accusation that John is a Samaritan and has a devil (John 8:48) is reminiscent of the Beelzebub controversy (Mark 3:22-30; Matt. 12:24-32; Luke 11:15-22; 12:10). Jesus is greater than Old Testament worthies (John 8:53; cf. Matt. 12:39-42; Luke 11:29-32). The treatment of the descent from Abraham, "which Jesus minimizes in comparison with something greater, recalls his question about the Messiah and David's son (Mark 12:35-7; Matt. 22:41-6; Luke 20: 41-4)."[69]

All this indicates a relationship to the tradition in the Synoptics, but not, I think, one of dependence. Another point Barrett makes elsewhere is that the division of men into two classes, those who are Christ's sheep and those who are not, is made in the Synoptics as well as in John. But in John it is clearer "that the ground of this distinction lies ultimately in the Father's will"; and further, "John brings out the point that the issue between Jesus and the Jews is in the last resort Christological."[70] The two traditions supplement one another, and we need John to clarify certain things in the other three Gospels.

MacGregor brings out another aspect of this interlocking tradition. He is dealing with John 11:48, "If we let him thus alone, all men will believe on him: and the Romans will come and take away both our place and our nation." He comments, ". . . This fear of revolution fits in better with Jesus' claim (as in the Synoptics) to be 'Messiah' than with the Johannine claim that he is 'the light of the world,' 'resurrection and life.' "[71] We

---

[69] Barrett, *op. cit.*, p. 276. Barrett goes on to suggest that John "is working with primitive Christian material, but he has deepened it, and sharpened its edge."

[70] *Ibid.*, p. 315.

[71] MNTC, *ad loc.*

need both traditions to get the full flavor of the words.

As we are thinking of the interlocking tradition this may be the place to draw attention to a study by J. Coutts, "The Messianic Secret in St. John's Gospel."[72] We have long been familiar with St. Mark's "messianic secret" and Coutts is concerned to show that the secrecy motif is to be seen also in John, though not necessarily at the same places. Thus in John "the supreme title, Son, is fully and publicly expounded. In Mark, it is hedged about with secrecy until after the Crucifixion."[73] By contrast, in John the nature of the passion is not revealed as it is in Mark. But though there are differences Coutts sees a most important resemblance: "It is clear in Mark, and underlined in John, that the motive behind the reserve with which Jesus communicates revelation, and the reason which governs the lack of understanding of the disciples, and ultimately of the crowd and his enemies, is theological. The events of the Passion, Resurrection and the coming of the Spirit provide the only key to the teaching, and the power which can bestow sight on the believer."[74] This is not exactly a case of one clearing up the other, but rather of an intermeshing of the traditions. We need both for the full picture.

*   *   *

SUCH POINTS AS THESE INDICATE THAT THE RELATIONSHIP between John and the other Gospels is complex. I do not think that they can fairly be cited to show direct literary dependence. But they do indicate that John had knowledge of some things that are recorded in the Synoptics, and that his knowledge is fuller than theirs, at least as they have recorded it. The traditions with which he was familiar and the traditions with which they were familiar at many points supplement each other. Each requires the other for its full understanding.

My conclusion is that John is independent of the Synoptics, but that he is in essential agreement with them. The evidence is such, I think, that literary de-

---

[72] SE, III, pp. 45-57.
[73] *Op. cit.*, p. 53.
[74] *Op. cit.*, p. 56.

pendence not only cannot be established, but is highly unlikely. His Gospel is too different from the others for that. But he is not speaking about a different Jesus. It is the same Saviour that he depicts. And what he writes in many places serves to fill out and explain what they have written. There is an interlocking tradition and we need all of it. We should be immensely impoverished without either John or the Synoptics.

Chapter Two

History and Theology in the Fourth Gospel

THAT THE AUTHOR OF THE FOURTH GOSPEL WAS A THEO-
logian no one can doubt. This truth has been recognized
ever since this Gospel was first studied seriously. But
John does not simply give us a theological treatise, dealing systematically with his chosen topics. Rather, he tells
a story. He tells us of things that happened as well as
giving us discourses and comments of his own.

But because he is a theologian and undoubtedly presents theology in his book, questions arise: What are
we supposed to make of the incidents he relates? Are
these meant to be stories of things that actually occurred?
Or is he simply manufacturing incidents (as the Master
composed parables) that will serve his purpose of edification? Perhaps he is taking a basis of fact and erect-
ing upon it a superstructure which, while sound the-
ologically, is questionable when it comes to matters of
historical fact.

Some have said that there ought never to have been
any question of taking the Johannine history seriously.
Typical of these is P. W. Schmiedel, who in a well-known
statement contended, "A book which begins by declaring Jesus to be the *logos* of God and ends by representing
a cohort of Roman soldiers as falling to the ground at
the majesty of his appearance (18.6), and by represent-

ing 100 pounds of ointment as having been used at his embalming (19.39), ought by these facts alone to be spared such a misunderstanding of its true character, as would be implied in supposing that it meant to be a historical work."[1] Those who see the Fourth Gospel in this light have no problems. There is no history in the strict sense, though there may be statements here and there that are literally and factually true. But the book is to be judged simply as a work of theology.

Views such as this are widely held. Thus E. Käsemann thinks that John, unlike the Synoptists, had no intention of giving us "authentic tradition."[2] And G. Bornkamm maintains that "The Gospel according to John has so different a character in comparison with the other three, and is to such a degree the product of a developed theological reflection, that we can only treat it as a secondary source."[3] Recent German theology would mostly agree with such points of view[4] (though with some distinguished exceptions), and, of course, such views are not confined to Germany.[5]

But discussions elsewhere have often shown more respect for John's grasp of and reverence for the facts of history. Most, I think, would agree that on some points

---

[1] *Encyclopedia Biblica*, Vol. II, col. 2542.

[2] He says, "It can hardly be doubted that the Synoptists intended in all good faith to give their readers authentic tradition about Jesus. But it is impossible to ascribe the same intention to the fourth Evangelist, at least in the same sense.... It is now widely acknowledged that for him the merely historical only has interest and value to the extent to which it mirrors symbolically the recurring experiences of Christian faith" (*Essays on New Testament Themes*, London, 1964, p. 22).

[3] G. Bornkamm, *Jesus of Nazareth*, London, 1960, p. 14.

[4] A. J. B. Higgins has some striking citations to this effect: BJRL, 49, 1966-67, pp. 363f.

[5] Cf. Neville Clark: "Enquiry begins with the recognition that the predominantly theological nature of the Fourth Gospel renders it useless as a primary source for the immediate purpose. Though St John may be cautiously used in supplementary and confirmatory fashion, it is the Synoptic Gospels which provide the material on which reconstruction depends" (*Interpreting the Resurrection*, London, 1967, p. 32; Clark's immediate preoccupation is with "the self-understanding of Jesus," but clearly he has no high opinion of the Fourth Gospel's historical worth).

at any rate the Johannine account should be accepted as giving us the facts.[6] But John's relation to strict historical accuracy is regarded as a live question. Does he in the last resort allow his history to be dominated by his theology? Granted that he makes use of certain facts, does he at the critical moment give his vote for theology and distort the picture or even manufacture incidents in order to make his theological points? Such questions must be faced by all who study the Fourth Gospel seriously.[7]

These questions ought to be determined in the light of the facts, not in accordance with some *a priori* consideration of what John is or is not likely to have done.

---

[6] G. W. Broomfield goes further: "An eye-witness, writing many years after the events described, might easily make mistakes. Nobody's memory is infallible. Nevertheless, there does not seem to be any case in which the Fourth Gospel is demonstrably wrong" (*John, Peter, and the Fourth Gospel*, London, 1934, pp. 96f.). See also below, pp. 108ff., 125ff.

[7] J. Ernest Davey sees three varieties of opinion: "those who hold, like Westcott, that the book is a historical account of Christ's ministry written by the Apostle John (son of Zebedee) or, possibly, by 'the elder John', a disciple of Jesus or of the Apostle John; secondly those who hold, like Réville, that the book is a complete fiction, a sustained attempt to depict the Logos of philosophy as incarnate; thirdly those who believe, like Macgregor, that the Gospel is based on the memoranda or the preaching of an apostolic figure, whether the son of Zebedee or another disciple of Jesus, but that the present form of the Gospel represents a very considerable process of development by reflection and preaching, i.e. it is an editorial amplification of selected material from tradition, worked up and filled out to present a universalistic and philosophical Greek Gospel" (*The Jesus of St. John*, London, 1958, p. 10). He himself espouses the third position, in which he is a typical representative of the modern approach. Elsewhere he says: "In view of the completeness, thoroughness and unity of the presentation in *John*, there seem to be no real alternatives to declaring it either to be a fiction *in toto*, or to be based essentially upon a historical substratum throughout" (p. 153). Davey's work is interesting and valuable. But it is marred by a steady refusal to take seriously the contributions of conservative scholars. This comes out clearly in his summary of recent literature on the subject (pp. 174ff.), where he takes it as axiomatic that more conservative works are of little worth and more radical ones are to be welcomed.

It is not difficult to find scholars who err either by telling us that John must have written accurate history or that he must have done nothing of the sort. We have already noticed some who deny that John had any intention of being factual. This seems to mean that he has composed fictional narratives in order to bring out theological truth. Those who take up such positions usually assume them. They make little attempt to prove them. They assert that in antiquity this was a recognized and respected procedure. If we wanted to bring out the truth about Jesus, they might say, we would distinguish carefully between, for example, what Jesus actually said and what we deduce from His words. But in the first century a man would regard it as perfectly acceptable, for example, if he were quite convinced that Jesus thought of Himself as the Messiah, to report that Jesus had claimed this. Thus we must expect that John would compose "sayings" of Jesus, and manufacture incidents in which Jesus' character and claims are made plain.

It is this kind of *a priori* approach against which I wish to protest. Though it is widely assumed that this procedure was rife in the ancient world little evidence can be found for it. That is to say, little evidence can be found that careful and serious writers practiced it. There are examples of people, like the authors of the apocryphal gospels of a somewhat later time, who valued edification above fact, and who did not hesitate to manufacture their incidents. And there are careless and bungling historians, who took little care to be accurate. But these should not be regarded as the standard. Specifically John should not be classed with either. Whatever else is to be said of his writing it is plain that his Gospel is well and carefully written, and that it gives evidence of a high moral purpose. We ought not lightly to assume that he has fallen below the better of the accepted standards of his day.

A. W. Mosley has examined "the influences which must have shaped the attitude of people in the first century to the question of accuracy in historical reporting. These influences came from the cultures of Greece, Rome and

Judaism."[8] He shows that some widely accepted assumptions ought to be discarded. Some of the historians of antiquity tell us plainly how they conceived their task. In the process they show a reverence for truth, and they have worked out high standards which the historian should strive to attain, and which their histories show they did strive to attain. Mosley notes that they did not hesitate to compose speeches when necessary and put them into the mouths of historical characters. But they did this only when necessary. If they had reliable reports of what was said they used them. And when they did compose speeches they did not regard themselves as having unlimited freedom in this matter. They tried to confine themselves to what the original speakers were likely to have said. Mosley further makes the extremely important point that, while they composed speeches in this way, they did not compose stories of events.[9] The widespread modern view that the men of antiquity were quite ready to distort the facts if only they could bring out the truth, is not supported by the statements of the men themselves. It is simply assumed. But only the second-rate did this (for that matter the second-rate in modern times are not exempt from guilt in this matter; but we do not therefore argue that this is standard practice). The express statements of the ancients make it plain that we must take seriously the historical statements of any careful writer who purports to give us facts.

This does not, of course, mean that without further

---

[8] "Historical Reporting in the Ancient World," NTS, 12, 1965-66, p. 11.

[9] Mosley can say: "Several scholars have already studied this matter and the general conclusion has been that sometimes ancient historians felt at liberty to compose speeches for their reports. Even this is now being questioned. But our survey has shown that these same historians did not feel free to invent stories of past events. . . . Several writers (especially Herodotus, Thucydides, Polybius, Dionysius, Lucian, Cicero and Josephus) had set out plainly the standards by which historical reports should be judged, and in each case it is emphasized that events should be described as they happened" (*ibid.*, p. 25). He also lists writers who saw "that 'mere tradition' and 'accurate history' are two different things" (*ibid.*).

ado we must assume that John is to be accepted as factually accurate. That is a matter for further examination. But it does mean that we must not make the facile assumption that he must have been careless about his facts, for that was the way men wrote in the first century. That was not the way men normally wrote in the first century. And if we are to convict John of doing this we must produce some clear evidence. In view of established historical procedure the probabilities are all the other way.

FACT AND INTERPRETATION

IT MUST BE ACCEPTED UNHESITATINGLY THAT JOHN IS not attempting to set forth an objective, unbiased account of certain historical events. He is a convinced believer, and he wants his readers to see the saving significance of what he narrates. He makes not the slightest attempt to conceal this, but says plainly, "These are written, that ye may believe that Jesus is the Christ, the Son of God; and that believing ye may have life in his name" (John 20:31). He is trying to persuade. He is not recording facts for facts' sake. We completely miss his purpose if we assess his work on narrowly historical lines.

There is no question then as to whether John is giving us interpretation. That is undisputed. The question is whether his interpretation is a good one, and soundly based, or whether he allows his presuppositions to dominate the facts in the interests of buttressing up a dogmatic position.

It must be emphasized that there is no need to apologize for an element of interpretation. It is an outdated view of history that "facts" can be established quite apart from the interpretation of the historian. Alan Richardson quotes some words of the historian Carl Becker, as important as they are emphatic: "The facts of history do not exist for any historian until he creates them, and into every fact that he creates some part of his individual experience must enter."[10] The past is gone.

---

[10] Alan Richardson, *History, Sacred and Profane*, London, 1964,

The historian can never work with the original materials. Even if he is so close to the events that he has testimony from an eyewitness he must face the fact that the eyewitness has already interpreted what he has seen. Further, the eyewitness cannot report every minute detail. He makes his selection from what he saw, thus introducing his personal judgment of what is important and what is not. The historian must now interpret what the eyewitness tells him. And he must adopt a similar procedure with all his sources, written and otherwise, recent and ancient. He must interpret them all as he is able. He can never escape the obligation of interpreting his data. Indeed, it can be said that this interpretation is the very stuff of history. "Facts" in isolation from interpretation simply do not exist.[11] And if they did, they would, by definition, have no meaning.

The element of interpretation is at a minimum in a journal or a chronicle. But these are not history. "Simply to record and catalogue (the evidence) is hardly to write history; the result, says Karl Barth, 'is not history: it is photographed and analysed chaos.' "[12] For history

---

p. 192. Richardson also says, "Today it would seem to be widely understood that historical facts are simply judgments of evidence: 'objective' facts are nothing more than judgments of evidence which have been agreed upon by a large number of historians; they do not seem as objective in one age as in another, not (as a rule) because the evidence alters or is significantly enlarged, but because of changes in 'the climate of opinion' " (p. 193).

[11] We must bear in mind Nietzsche's often quoted dictum, "Not facts, but only interpretations exist." Cf. also E. C. Rust, "...It is an open issue whether we can even speak of a bare historical event. All the data of the historian is a composite of fact and evaluation. Contemporary eyes and records have added a subjective element to what reaches us. We may try to sift the evidence, but we have to make our own judgment of significance. The historian's evidence for a period may be limited, but he still has the task of estimating the relations between the facts which he can delineate and of answering satisfactorily, in the particular mode he chooses, the question 'Why?' The past matters insofar as it comes alive to us through an intelligible form. A mere chronicle of the past is dead and meaningless" (*Towards a Theological Understanding of History*, New York, 1963, p. 5; cf. also R. G. Collingwood, *The Idea of History*, Oxford, 1963, pp. 131-3).

[12] R. L. Shinn, *Christianity and the Problem of History*, New York, 1953, p. 7.

there must be the exercise of judgment, a critical approach to the data. A history is more selective than these others. And a history treats what it selects in such a way as to bring out its significance. "History deals not with events, but with situations which are of significance to somebody."[13] We must be on our guard against the fallacy that the scientific historian is concerned only with facts whereas the theologian is incurably involved in working his interpretation into the facts. The truth is that there is no history without interpretation. Therefore as we approach the Gospels the question is not whether an element of interpretation enters into them. It is rather whether the interpretation that is undoubtedly there enables us to account for the data in a satisfactory manner.[14]

THE VALUE OF INTERPRETATION

LET US EXAMINE MORE CLOSELY THIS ELEMENT OF INterpretation. It is not something to be looked down on, and endured with as good a grace as we can muster. It is not a distasteful, but unavoidable, ingredient in the writing of history. It is the element of interpretation that leads us to the significant truths. An absence of interpretation (if that were possible) would be downright misleading where the facts are significant facts. C. D. Dodd has pointed out that there are some events "which can take their true place in an historical record only as they are interpreted." He gives as examples the beginning of the Reformation at Wittenberg, the fall of the Bastille, and the abdication of King Edward VIII. He proceeds, "The events are such that the meaning of

---

[13] Victor Murray, cited in John Baillie, *The Idea of Revelation in Recent Thought*, London, 1956, p. 67. He also cites F. W. Maitland, "The essential matter of history is not what happened but what people thought and said about it" (*ibid.*).

[14] G. E. Wright points out that "real historical events are here [i.e. in the Bible] involved, but in themselves they do not make the biblical event. In the Bible an important or signal happening is not an event unless it is also an event of revelation, that is, unless it is an event which has been interpreted so as to have meaning" (G. E. Wright and R. H. Fuller, *The Book of the Acts of God*, London, 1960, p. 19).

what happened is of greater importance, historically speaking, than what happened."[15] I do not see how this can be disputed. Unless we include interpretation we will certainly give a false impression, for example, of the events that took place at the Bastille on that July day in 1789. To content ourselves with a purely "factual" account of what took place is to miss the path and to fail *as historians*. Fact and interpretation are inextricably interwoven, and neither may be neglected.[16]

This is certainly true of those events in Galilee and Jerusalem of which John writes. Pilate and Caiaphas, for example, were intimately concerned in some of them, but nothing is more sure than that they did not realize what was really happening. They did not understand the significance of the events that were taking place, even though they themselves were taking leading parts. They would have been quite capable of giving "factual" accounts of what "happened" when Jesus of Nazareth came before them. But had either of them left us a description of the events as he knew them, we can be sure that it would have been a distorted and meaningless account.[17] For an account that is not to mislead, some-

---

[15] C. H. Dodd, *History and the Gospel*, London, 1938, pp. 104f. He says further, "There are even events of outstanding historical importance in which practically nothing at all happened, in the ordinary external sense of happening. It was simply that the meaning of the whole situation changed for an individual or a group, and from that change of meaning a chain of happenings ensued. Such events were the call of the prophet Mohammed, and the conversion of Ignatius Loyola, and the mysterious inward process that made the housepainter Adolf Hitler into the hope or the terror of Europe." T. A. Roberts criticizes Dodd, maintaining that "events happened in the past, and events are what they are, no more, no less. They cannot be divided by some process of division, mental or otherwise, into occurrences and meaning. An event strictly has no meaning" (*History and Christian Apologetic*, London, 1960, p. 92). This seems impossible to maintain, and it is contradicted by his own contentions in other places, e.g. his account of the significance of the Battle of Britain (pp. 89f.).

[16] Cf. A. Richardson, "The facts of history cannot be disentangled from the principles of interpretation by which alone they can be presented to us *as history*, that is, as a coherent and connected series or order of events" (*Christian Apologetics*, London, 1963, p. 150).

[17] Sir Edwyn Hoskyns protests against the view that John "has

thing of the significance of those events must be brought out.

If then John introduces interpretation in his Gospel, that does not rule it out *as history*. Of course, though it introduces an indispensable qualification, it does not make it history either. Conceivably his interpretation may be all wrong and distort rather than reveal the significance of the facts. That is a matter for further examination. At this point all that I am saying is that the nature of the events he is describing is such that for justice to be done to them there must be interpretation.

Perhaps this is the place to notice the dilemma in which the Christian historian finds himself. Roger Shinn puts it this way: "If man's destiny is superhistorical as St. Paul affirmed, if history is a province of the Kingdom of God as Toynbee says, the fact makes a major difference for our understanding of history. No historian simply *qua* historian can say so; he lacks evidence. Yet, if the belief be the truth, its omission vitiates the history which is written without it."[18] John had not thought through the problems of scientific historiography in the modern sense. But it is plain that he had a firm grasp on the truth that to omit the spiritual dimension is to vitiate history. He made no attempt to write without giving his history an interpretation, and a religious interpretation at that. And if Christianity is true, anything less would be completely unjustified. John's clear sight of the hand of God in the events associated with Jesus of Nazareth may not commend itself to the modern scientific historian. But it does not make John's account any less true.

simply equated what any observer might have seen or heard of Jesus with that which eye hath not seen nor ear heard of the glory of God" (*The Fourth Gospel*, London, 1950, p. 18).

[18] *Op. cit.*, p. 11. Hans Urs von Balthasar is another who maintains that the Christian understanding of things must place the spiritual at the center. He sees Christ as the norm of history and all history is to be seen in His light (*A Theology of History*, London and New York, 1964). It is significant that in working out his thesis he appeals frequently to the Fourth Gospel.

THE LIMITS OF HISTORICAL METHOD

WE MUST ALWAYS BEAR IN MIND THAT THERE ARE LIMITS to what the method of the scientific historian can elicit. Sometimes scholars write as though we can accept what the historian says but when the man of faith speaks we must immediately introduce a heavy discount. M. Goguel has a salutary warning: "The rôle of the historian is to recognize facts and organize them in relation to others. Yet he cannot fully explain history, because history has to do with personalities, and every personality is a mystery which it needs human sympathy and comprehension to understand."[19] The warning is timely. And if the historical method is limited in dealing with persons, much more is this the case when it comes to the great realities of faith. These take us beyond the mysteries of human personality. But they do not take us into the world of the unreal. Persons and personalities are real. Information about them may well be factual, even though the historian, *qua* historian, cannot come to grips with it. So is it with faith. The ultimate truths of faith are nonetheless real because the historian cannot prove or disprove them. Faith is a reality just as certainly as personality is a reality. The inability of the historian to explain either of them fully must be recognized. But it casts no doubt on the reality of either.

By definition the historian works with the purely human. As D. E. Nineham puts it, "It is of the essence of the modern historian's method and criteria that they are applicable only to purely human phenomena, and to human phenomena of a normal, that is a non-miraculous, non-unique character."[20] Theology is not confined

---

[19] Cited in ET, 75, 1963-64, p. 296. Also, "We cannot reconcile the postulates of faith with the findings of science including historical science. We have to determine their relations by an entirely different method." To the question, "What method?" the answer is, "... The formulas of religion are of another order than those of science, and neither can confirm or disprove the other" (*ibid.*).

[20] D. E. Nineham, *Historicity and Chronology in the New Testament*, S.P.C.K. Theological Collections, no. 6, London, 1965, p. 3. He proceeds to say, "It followed that any picture of Jesus that

to the purely human. The spheres covered by the two disciplines differ markedly.[21] But it does not follow from this that either can invalidate the other. The fact that the historian cannot, as a historian, reckon with the basic theological concepts does not make them untrue. Nor does it render unreliable the work of a theologian who writes history. The historian simply cannot pronounce in this case.[22]

This must be emphasized in view of the fact that some who approach the New Testament are so anxious to be good historians that they appear to forget that it is even more important to be good Christians. Let me repeat some words of J. V. Langmead Casserley, which I quoted in the Preface: ". . . Modern biblical scholarship has proved itself so insipid and unstimulating. We are confronted with the paradox of a way of studying the word of God out of which no word of God ever seems to come, with an imposing modern knowledge of the Bible which seems quite incapable of saying anything biblical or thinking biblically."[23] The fact is that to treat

---

could consistently approve itself to an historical investigator using these criteria, must, a priori, be of a purely human figure and it must be bounded by his death."

[21] C. F. Evans makes the point that "The best history in the Bible, as we understand history, is to be found in the first book of Maccabees, but it would be a hardy theologian who would contend that the core of the revelation was to be found in that book" (On the Authority of the Bible, S.P.C.K. Theological Collections, no. 1, London, 1960, p. 29). There are limits to what history can do. Evans proceeds to point out that the book of Daniel is more important from the point of view of revelation.

[22] D. E. Nineham elsewhere reminds us that "the scientific historian's whole procedure rests on the basic assumption that the universe, and society within it, possess sufficient uniformity to exclude the possibility of any pronounced deviation." The Bible claims that certain events did in fact involve such a pronounced deviation. "That means that though any given historian may, as a Christian, believe that they occurred, he cannot, as an historian, pronounce in their favour, because he has been robbed of the only criterion by which he could judge" (The Church's Use of the Bible, London, 1963, pp. 154f.).

[23] Toward a Theology of History, London, 1965, p. 116. He also says, "The fundamentalists have tried to react against a real scandal, a method of interpreting a supremely great religious-historical

the Bible as no more than a piece of secular history is to miss the wonderful thing the Bible is saying. The Christian historian has a duty to all the facts, including the fact that God has spoken and acted. To fail to reckon with this may bring acclaim from the purely secular, but it is not being true to all the evidence. As E. K. Lee puts it, "Whatever the secular historian may say, I do not think that the whole truth of an historical event can be disclosed by the employment of secular techniques of investigation; part of the truth, no doubt, is disclosed but not the whole truth."[24] John was endeavoring to do more than bring out that element of truth which is apparent to the secular historian. But that does not mean that he was distorting or obscuring the facts. He was endeavoring to bring out the truth so dear to the secular historian, but also to go beyond it.

Admitting then that the Fourth Gospel contains interpretation and that it is other than a catalogue of facts or a theological treatise, the question that arises is not, "Is an element of interpretation permissible?" but rather, "What kind of interpretation are we faced with? Is it an interpretation that sits loose to the facts or one that is bound up with the facts and rests securely on them? Does it distort the historical situation or does it meaningfully bring out the significant elements?"[25]

---

document like the Bible out of which no word from God ever seems to come" (p. 25); "I regard the contemporary fundamentalist protest against the comparative spiritual poverty and theological sterility of modern biblical scholarship as justified," though he adds, "but I think the protest is made in the wrong way and on the wrong grounds" *(ibid.).*

[24] E. K. Lee, CQR, 167, 1966, pp. 292f. He goes on to liken this to "the scientific explanation of a human being, which would leave many things unsaid."

[25] Cf. H. Cunliffe-Jones: "The presentation of the ministry of Jesus in the Fourth Gospel is markedly different from that in the other three, and yet it leads to the same result. If the right way to think of the Fourth Gospel is to think of it as an interpretation rather than a simple narrative, and that the independent factual historical traditions which it may contain are to be discerned through that interpretation rather than picked out from it as plums from a cake, can we not go on from there to ask whether we agree with the interpretation, and whether that interpretation expresses

As we proceed with the discussion it will, I think, emerge that John's interpretation must be regarded as a good one, soundly based. But let us round off this section by drawing attention to three factors that impressed Vincent Taylor, so that he could say:

> That his interpretation is legitimate, as compared, say, with the fantastic developments in the Apocryphal Gospels, is shown by three things: (1) our knowledge of the Synoptic sayings with which he so often begins, (2) the many points of contact between the picture of the Johannine Christ and that presented by the Synoptics, and (3) the response his interpretation has evoked throughout the centuries, so that many Christians find themselves peculiarly 'at home' with John, while appreciative of the worth of the Synoptics and the Pauline Epistles as a whole.[26]

I am not sure that I would put his first point in quite this way. Earlier in this book I have argued that John is independent of the Synoptics. But if we can take Taylor's point to mean that these sayings came to John through oral tradition I have no quarrel with it. And certainly his other two points are very relevant. Neither can be overlooked in a balanced estimate.

THE FOUR GOSPELS AND HISTORY

THE QUESTION OF HISTORICITY CANNOT BE CONFINED TO one Gospel. There is theology in all of them. It is increasingly accepted in modern writing that all four Gospels are basically theological documents. None is an objectively written piece of history. In the modern cliché, all are written "from faith to faith." No one can prove by the accepted canons of historical research that Jesus is the Christ, the Son of the living God. Nor that His death brings life to men. But it is with such truths, and not with the writing of biographies, that all four Evangelists are concerned. For long enough it

---

something that was true of the life and death and resurrection of Jesus as it happened? If our answer is in any way positive to these questions, then it should be possible to think together what we have accepted as true of the ministry in all four Gospels" (SE, I, p. 22).

[26] Vincent Taylor, *The Life and Ministry of Jesus*, London, 1955, p. 24.

has been clear that there is a profound theological purpose behind the Fourth Gospel. Recent writers lay in-
creasing emphasis on the fact that this is true of the
Synoptists also. All the Evangelists are primarily theologians. All are interested in the *kerygma*. The problem
of history and the gospel is perhaps more acute in the
case of the Fourth Gospel than in that of any of the other
three. But it is essentially the same problem. It is the
problem of whether the history can be accepted as true
history or whether the theological concern of the Evangelists has so warped their view of the facts that they
are not to be taken seriously as historical sources.[27]

It must, of course, be borne in mind in assessing this
problem that the Gospels may well be valuable historical
sources even though they were not originally intended
as such. The intention of the original writer never completely circumscribes the freedom of the modern reader.
It may make him wary. But it does not prevent him
from looking for something the Gospels do not explicitly
set out to supply. It may be there as a by-product. This
truth is not always borne in mind by New Testament
critics, though it appears to be a commonplace among
the historians. And it means that the concentration of
the Evangelists on their theological purpose does not fore-
close the question of whether what they write is or is
not good history.

This must be maintained in the face of the fact that
many modern scholars, especially among the Bultmanni-
ans, hold that the Evangelists' preoccupation with the
kerygma renders them practically useless as historical
sources. Such scholars often deny outright the possibility
of writing a life of Jesus.[28] The materials, they say, are

---

[27] The question must be faced honestly and not treated as fore-
closed as it is by those critics whom B. Gerhardsson castigates
when he refers to "an extremely tenaciously-held misapprehension
among exegetes that an early Christian author must *either* be a
purposeful theologian and writer *or* a fairly reliable historian"
(*Memory and Manuscript*, Lund, 1964, p. 209).

[28] Actually there is considerable disagreement among those who
follow Bultmann. As is well known, James M. Robinson in his book,
A New Quest of the Historical Jesus (London, 1959), argued that
the old "Quest" was doomed. It was trying to do something impos-

simply not there. Instead of historical documents we have religious writings from which we can learn much about the Christ of faith, but little or nothing about the Jesus of history. The Gospels were written by convinced believers who, as they looked back, saw the Christ of faith, not Jesus of Nazareth as He would have appeared to the historian. Jesus as He really was cannot be discerned from the Gospels. We may agree that He was in some way associated with the salvation event, but not that He was as the Gospels portray Him. This is to take up the curious position that there is salvation in the Christ, but we cannot know anything really significant about Him. Why should God save men in such a curious fashion? We are not told.

We may get a little help with the problem of the historicity of the records of Jesus of Nazareth by considering the way the matter stands with another personality of a past age. If we can agree in principle on a solution there, this may be of significance in our handling of the gospel material. In the face of the contention that the Gospels cannot give us a reliable picture of Jesus, Stephen Neill considers the somewhat parallel case of St. Patrick. He draws attention to the work of Zimmer in criticizing the accepted picture. "By the time that Zimmer has completed his 'Form-critical' investigations, all that is left of poor Patrick resembles a heap of small fragments on the floor." But at about this time the historian J. B. Bury engaged in research into the life of the same saint. His competence was beyond dispute, and, since he was an unbeliever, he had no interest in supporting any particular religious view. On purely critical grounds he rejected Zimmer's theories. They were seen, "when critically handled, to be as full of inconsistencies as the documents they so ruthlessly tore to

sible with the materials at its disposal. But he points to a new way forward for scholarship. Van A. Harvey and Schubert M. Ogden, however, maintain that Robinson has misunderstood Bultmann and that basically the new "Quest" is identical with the old one (see their article, "How New is the 'New Quest of the Historical Jesus'?" in *The Historical Jesus and the Kerygmatic Christ*, ed. Carl E. Braaten and Roy A. Harrisville, New York, 1964, pp. 197-242).

pieces." In the end Bury's picture "is much more like the Patrick of Christian recollection than we might have expected."[29] F. F. Bruce is another who draws attention to the case of St. Patrick. He points out that "Our sources for reconstructing Patrick's career are unpromising enough, and much scantier than our sources for the ministry of Jesus." Then he looks at the material and concludes, "Yet what is the result of historical criticism of this material? Not only are the main outlines of Patrick's career reasonably clear, but we get a convincing and attractive picture of the humble, kindly and powerful personality of the man himself."[30] Similar comments could be made about many historical personages. The fact is that while we should not ignore the difficulties in the way of a historical reconstruction we should not exaggerate them either. Though the Gospels are religious documents they are written by men with an interest in what happened and how it happened. Only utter scepticism can prevent us from seeing good historical material here.

FORM CRITICISM

THE CONVICTION THAT WE CANNOT KNOW THE HISTORICAL Jesus is often allied to a dependence on the results of form criticism. It is held by the form critics that a good deal in the Gospels arose, not out of the life of Jesus of Nazareth, but out of the circumstances of the early church. As questions arose, charismatic leaders felt that they knew what Jesus would have done and said. Under the inspiration of the Spirit accordingly they affirmed that He had said and done those things. Incidents and sayings were evolved to meet the need. The Gospels are accordingly more instructive for the con-

---

[29] Stephen Neill, *The Interpretation of the New Testament 1861-1961*, London, 1964, pp. 284f. Neill goes on to point out that "In the whole history of modern scholarship, only two great historians have concerned themselves with the events of the first Christian century — J. B. Lightfoot and Eduard Meyer." Both are much more respectful of the New Testament than are the form critics. Clearly other motives than the desire for good history have been at work.

[30] F. F. Bruce, *Faith and Thought*, 93, Summer, 1964, pp. 121f.

ditions of the early church than for information about Jesus.[31]

Despite the popularity of this kind of approach and the great names that can be ranged in support of it, it is difficult to see how it can be substantiated. I have never seen any real answer to the criticism Vincent Taylor made quite a few years ago, that this demands from the community an unusual degree of creativity. His words still merit careful attention:

> It is evident that I have done Bultmann no injustice in speaking of his regard for possibilities: no tendency which conceivably might have corrupted the tradition is missed; no power of the mind to forget, to transform, and to create is neglected. For Bultmann, the personality of Jesus is faint and remote; but the community is alert, full-blooded, ready for every enterprise of corruption and creation. I have no doubt that he lays a just finger on tendencies which do darken the tradition; but several considerations show that his position as a whole is one of violent exaggeration.
>
> 1. In the first place ... Bultmann takes no account of the existence of eye-witnesses. The orphaned Christian community has no leaders to whom it can appeal for an account of what Jesus said: it might have been marooned on an island in the Greek Archipelago! This attitude is due to Bultmann's preoccupation with forms, but it vitiates a study of the question of genuineness from the beginning.
>
> 2. Again, the creative power of the community is too easily assumed. Do communities produce matchless sayings like those of Jesus? Easton rightly maintains that sayings are created by individuals, not by communities. . . .[32]

---

[31] This approach takes too lightly the tremendous emphasis in antiquity on the handing down of the tradition in correct form, as is made plain, for example, by B. Gerhardsson, *op. cit.*

[32] *The Formation of the Gospel Tradition*, London, 1935, pp. 106f.; cf. also pp. 41, 86f. Similarly Donald Baillie says, "... It seems seldom to occur to them that the story may have been handed on simply or primarily *because it was true*, because the incident had actually taken place in the ministry of Jesus, and was therefore of great interest to His followers, even if they sometimes failed to understand it. Yet surely we should expect those men, believing what they did about Jesus, to be immensely interested in recalling

Surely these strictures are well merited. The form critics do not do justice to the fact that all our knowledge goes to show that it is great individuals, not communities, that are creative. Nor do these critics seem to reflect that their approach is in the extreme largely self-defeating. Their contention is that very little in the Gospels is original. The Gospels do not go back to Jesus, but to the community, which distorted and proliferated His teaching. Now if everything is secondary we have no yardstick whereby to discern it. We cannot tell whether the narrative somewhere on its way to us has not been affected by another line of tradition that is authentic.[33]

Bultmann and his allies assume the existence of the myth-manufacturing community. Where did it come from? On their premises there appears to be no answer. They reject the Easter message and thus cut away any basis from the Easter faith. But the community and its faith were realities. They existed. To say that there is a historical basis for their characteristic affirmations gives a satisfying explanation. After all they were near enough to their origins to have some worthwhile idea of what had happened. To reject the historical basis while admitting the fact of the community (and the reality of the saving event) is not a scientific or historical procedure.[34] It is

anything that He had said or done, simply because He had said or done it, however remote they might be from the modern 'biographical' interest" (*God Was in Christ*, London, 1955, p. 57).

[33] Cf. R. P. C. Hanson: "The extraordinary thing is that it has not yet dawned on many New Testament scholars that, in respect of the materials in the Gospel, if nothing is certainly original then we cannot be sure that anything is certainly secondary. If Matthew has modified Mark, and Mark's materials are themselves all modified, how do we know that Matthew is not modifying Mark in the interests of a genuine tradition? This is not to say that Matthew is in this case disposing of a genuine tradition; but on these premises we cannot know that he is not. If *all* the material has been altered from an original condition which is itself unknown and unknowable, how do we know that the larger part of the material is not authentic? In other words, when Form Criticism is pushed to extremes and compelled to dominate entirely the historical criticism of the Gospels, it destroys its own presuppositions" (*Vindications*, ed. Anthony Hanson, London, 1966, p. 40).

[34] One is reminded of R. P. C. Hanson's words, "Form Criticism explains all the phenomena presented by the Gospels — except the reason why there should be any phenomena at all" (*ibid.*, p. 38).

to abdicate responsibility at the critical point, that point above all where a responsible judgment is called for. What was it historically that called this community into existence?[35]

C. F. D. Moule has a powerful argument on this point.[36] He points out that the case is not in all respects equivalent to that of movements that have flourished though having "a mistaken view of things." Professor Moule makes the important point that such movements succeed not because of their error, but because of the truth that they retain. They succeed only provided "that the mistake contains enough of truth, or corresponds sufficiently to basic human needs or to the needs of the moment, or has a leader forceful enough, for it to gain momentum." He adds, "But it is precisely here that Christianity is different."[37] He sees this difference in the fact "that what is alleged to have been a delusion was the first Christians' sole *raison d'être*: they had nothing else to lend momentum to the launching, or to prevent their simply losing their identity thereafter."[38] He later says, "... The birth and rapid rise of the Christian Church therefore *remain an unsolved enigma for any historian who refuses to take seriously the only explanation offered by the Church itself.*"[39] I do not see how this

---

[35] J. S. Bezzant is scathing about form criticism. He regards its assumptions as "often plainly theological or based on a scepticism that is sceptical of nearly everything except scepticism itself, which is swallowed in one gulp almost as uncritically as the assumptions of 'Fundamentalism' and on grounds which, when any are alleged, are often guesswork." He further says, with reference to the Gospels: "But break them down into an assemblage of originally unconnected anecdotes and sayings, assign their origin to some interest and problem of the Church and regard them as invented to be relevant to these, and is it not surpassingly strange that there should have emerged the depiction of a Figure which has compelled the reverence of mankind? It is as much so as if a magnificent cathedral were reduced to small heaps of stones, rubble and disjointed timbers, originally separate, leaving the cathedral still visible" (CQR, 164, 1963, p. 244).

[36] Ch. I of his *The Phenomenon of the New Testament*, London, 1967.

[37] *Ibid.*, p. 10.

[38] *Ibid.*, p. 11.

[39] *Ibid.*, p. 13 (Moule's italics).

can fairly be disputed. The Christians were different from the Jews only in respect of their convictions about Jesus, and specifically about the resurrection. They were quite open in proclaiming this as their essential message. Take it away and you take away the reason for their existence and the only serious explanation of their origin.

I find it extremely difficult to accept the extreme scepticism of scholars of this school of thought.[40] The interest of the community in the tradition is clear. But so is a determined refusal on some recorded occasions to manufacture "sayings" of Jesus when it would have been very convenient to have had them. For example, in 1 Corinthians 7 Paul carefully distinguishes between sayings he has from the Lord and his own opinion. It would have suited him very well to have had sayings of Jesus for each of the problems with which he deals. But he does not produce them, which seems to show a respect for the tradition.

Again, according to the form-critical view the church was busy manufacturing sayings of Jesus at and after the time when, say, the Epistle to the Romans was written. This Epistle contains some admirable material for this purpose, but it does not seem to have been used at all. Not one saying in any of the Gospels can be shown to have been hewn from this quarry. A similar comment may be made about other New Testament epistles.[41] If the

---

[40] This scepticism is not rendered any more attractive by the dogmatism that so often accompanies it. For example, H.-W. Bartsch dismisses E. Stauffer in these words: "Stauffer merely conceals his failure to reflect with any precision on the proper starting point for historical research, while at the same time, by repudiating the form-critical method, he rejects the literary-critical starting point it chooses" (Braaten and Harrisville, *op. cit.*, p. 122, n. 48). Form criticism is thus regarded not merely as a useful tool, a valuable line of inquiry. It is the one proper approach: "historical research" "chooses" it as "starting point."

[41] B. Gerhardsson makes the point that the Evangelists are interested only in Jesus, whereas if the church was manufacturing sayings some at least of the manufacturers might be mentioned: "The Evangelists are only interested in mediating the words and works of *Jesus;* the traditionists have nothing to say — not even in passing — about any creative contribution made by a Peter, a James or a John to the teaching of Jesus Christ. So great is the concentration on the words and works of Jesus that even the con-

church stubbornly refused to manufacture sayings out of material we know to have been in its possession and to be suitable, why should we postulate this process in cases where it cannot be checked?[42]

In this connection we should also notice that the New Testament contains one important group of sayings ascribed to the risen Jesus, namely those in the letters to the seven churches in Revelation. The interesting thing about these sayings is that they address themselves without ambiguity to the local and contemporary situation. There is no pretense of fitting them into some time and place in the earthly life of the incarnate Jesus. They are quite unlike the sayings in the Gospels. It would be fair to say that the only sayings of Jesus that we *know* to refer primarily to the life-situation of the early church are openly described as such. There is no attempt to read them back into the ministry of Jesus of Nazareth.

A RECORD OF EVENTS

THE FACT IS THAT THERE IS AMONG THE NEW TESTAMENT writers a much greater respect for what really happened than many modern students allow. C. K. Barrett points out that, "Like the theological tradition, the historical tradition of the words and deeds of Jesus is thus rooted

---

tribution of these 'three pillars' is without interest" *(Tradition and Transmission in Early Christianity*, Lund, 1964, p. 42). If the church was active in creating sayings and attributing them to Jesus it is curious, to say the least, that none at all is attributed to the church's outstanding leaders, those men who were to the fore in producing the sayings. This is quite contrary to the practice in Judaism where the sayings of leading Rabbis were treasured by their disciples and others.

[42] T. W. Manson examines and rejects the basic contentions of the form critics, saying, "I submit that what is long overdue is a return to the study of the Gospels *as historical documents* concerning Jesus of Nazareth, rather than as psychological case-material concerning the early Christians"; "... We must ask that (the Gospels) should be taken seriously as evidence for the events they purport to describe; and in the first instance as evidence for *those events* rather than for the states of mind of first-century Christians" *(Studies in the Gospels and Epistles*, Manchester, 1962, pp. 8, 10).

in the *event*." He goes on, ". . . It is worthwhile to note that it is sometimes its sheer historical accuracy, its recounting things that Jesus said and did simply because he said and did them, that leads to a measure of diffuseness, of failure to concentrate upon the focal point."[43] The form critics appear to overlook this aspect of the New Testament entirely. Yet it is there. There are many things in the Gospels that appear to have no great theological point and to be inserted simply because they happened. To overlook this is to fail to deal with all the evidence.

The present Archbishop of Canterbury draws attention to this aspect of the New Testament. Dr. Ramsey notices the tendency to make the *kerygma* the absorbing preoccupation of the early church to such an extent that interest in the historical Jesus is minimal or even nonexistent. Against this he is able to show that, in writings like the Pauline Epistles, 1 Peter, and Hebrews, there is a large amount of information about the life of Jesus that is not related to the *kerygma* at all. The same thing is true of the Gospels. There are limits to the extent to which the *kerygma* controls the writers. Dr. Ramsey asks two questions: "(1) Is it true that the Church was not interested in the order of events, and that therefore it is idle to try to shew an order of events from any of the Gospels? (2) Is it true that the Church — and therefore the evangelists — had no interest in Jesus as a human figure?"[44] He answers both in the negative. As to the first, "It seems impossible for the Church to have had the interest in Jesus in his life on earth, which the evidence shews that it had, without a concomitant interest in the 'before and after', the stages in the movement of the story. The onus of proof would seem to rest heavily on those who think otherwise."[45] He concludes his discussion of the second question with some words of T. W. Manson: "It is conceivable that he [i.e. Jesus] was at least as interesting,

---

[43] *The Church's Use of the Bible*, ed. D. E. Nineham, London, 1963, p. 21.

[44] SE, I, p. 40.

[45] *Ibid.*, p. 41.

for his own sake, to people in the first century as he is to
historians in the twentieth."[46]

It is also worth noticing that there is quite a stress in
the New Testament on the place of the eyewitness. Thus
when Matthias took the place of Judas as an apostle he
was chosen from those men "that have companied with us
all the time that the Lord Jesus went in and went out
among us." He was marked out to be "a witness with
us of his resurrection" (Acts 1:21, 22).[47] The thought
that the Christian preachers were witnesses is stressed
in Acts. It appears in Peter's first sermon (Acts 2:32),
and recurs in his second (Acts 3:15), and in his words in
the house of Cornelius (Acts 10:39, 41). It was even
plain to the opposition that Peter and John "had been
with Jesus" (Acts 4:13), and these apostles explained
that they were constrained to "speak the things which
we saw and heard" (Acts 4:20). In the same strain Peter
defended them before the council by saying, "We are
witnesses of these things," adding, "and so is the Holy
Spirit" (Acts 5:32).

Paul was in a different position as an apostle, in that
he had not been a follower of Jesus during His lifetime.
But he gives his own commission in terms of witness.
He tells Agrippa that the Lord said to him, "To this
end have I appeared unto thee, to appoint thee a minister
and a witness..." (Acts 26:16). In his first recorded
sermon he refers to the resurrection appearances to men
"who are now his witnesses unto the people" (Acts
13:31). We should not overlook in this connection the
careful way he lists eyewitnesses who could testify to the
resurrection and indicates that this was part of his

---

[46] I take the quotation from T. W. Manson, *op. cit.*, p. 6 (there
are slight differences in Ramsey). A. Wikgren's examination of
the New Testament leads him to see "a strong undercurrent of
concern for the Jesus of history as a fundamental part of the
authors' faith" (SE, I, p. 123). Specifically he sees this in the case
of the Fourth Gospel.

[47] D. E. Nineham reminds us that μάρτυς "has wider connotations
than αὐτόπτης .... But the qualifications for the μάρτυς in this
passage seem to show that here at least μαρτυρία was felt necessarily to involve αὐτοψία, and that also appears to be the implication
in other passages in Acts" (JTS, n.s., 9, 1958, p. 14, n. 1).

preaching when he first went to Corinth (1 Cor. 15:5-8).

Luke's appeal to eyewitness testimony is well known (Luke 1:2 — "who from the beginning were eyewitnesses and ministers of the word"). There are references also in both Epistles of St. Peter. The writer of the first letter claims to be "a witness of the sufferings of Christ" (1 Pet. 5:1). In the second we read: "We did not follow cunningly devised fables, when we made known unto you the power and coming of our Lord Jesus Christ, but we were eyewitnesses of his majesty" (2 Pet. 1:16).

When then it is claimed that the author of the Fourth Gospel is a "witness" (John 21:24), and when we have definite appeal to the testimony of an eyewitness in his Gospel (John 19:35), this should not be understood as an isolated thing. It is reinforced by the firm statements in 1 John that the writer is testifying to what he has seen (1 John 1:1, 2), and by all the passages we have here noted. There are probably others. But these are sufficient to indicate that the writers of the New Testament valued the testimony of eyewitnesses. We should not treat them as though they were interested only in edification and were prepared to manufacture statements and incidents which they felt must have happened. Again and again they appeal to the fact that they are bearing witness to what they have seen.

It is important to be clear that the Evangelists had a strong interest in the historical Jesus, and that this was a controlling factor in their writing. When systems like Docetism and Gnosticism appeared they were rejected. Those who evolved these systems put all their emphasis on theology and paid scant attention to the historical. They were interested in ideas, not facts. But the orthodox could never take a similar line. They felt that what they taught was bound up with the actual person of Jesus of Nazareth, and with the things He said and did. They could not substitute their sanctified imaginations for the traditions that had been handed down to them.

GOD AND HISTORY

THIS IS OF THE ESSENCE OF THE MATTER AS THE NEW Testament writers understood the faith. It was a bold, and

for most of the ancient world a novel doctrine that God
had willed to reveal Himself in history. In fact so bold a
conception is this that sometimes men still shrink from
its implications. It is difficult to resist the conclusion that
some scholars have feared to trust God to history. The
world of history is such an uncertain world. We can never
be sure what the historian will bring forth. If behind the
kerygma there is a genuine historical Jesus then (we are
told) we are at the mercy of the historian. If he comes
up with something new the basis of our faith is gone. And,
even if in fact he never does this, in principle it is always
possible that he will. Our faith then is built on a shaky
foundation. It is safer to rescue God from the whole
world of history.

In the first place, however, God has not chosen to give
us this kind of security. He has preferred to reveal Himself in the historical, and it is there that we must find
Him. Unless we affirm that Jesus has come "in the flesh"
we are not on God's side. We align ourselves with the
antichrist (1 John 4:2f.). And the denial that Jesus is the
Christ is a denial of the Father as well as of the Son
(1 John 2:22f.). We cannot flee history into a safe world
of ideas and still remain authentically Christian.[48]

Christians can never avoid the challenge of the historian. There seems no reason why God could not, had He
so chosen, have continued to reveal Himself in the New
Testament as He did in the Old, through prophets and the

---

[48] Cf. E. M. Sidebottom: "Modern theology, beginning in the Mar-
burg tradition which lay behind both Barth and Bultmann, reinforced by the discovery of Kierkegaard, tended to fear that the
facts if discovered might undermine the faith.... But this flies in
the face of essential Christianity. The 'ends of the world' have
come upon us because we have met God in the flesh. We indeed
no longer know Christ 'after the flesh', but this in itself implies
the importance of knowing who he was in the flesh. He who denies
that he has come 'in the flesh' is anathema. If we may so put it,
God became subject to the ambiguities of history while not ceas-
ing to be God: the Word 'became flesh' and so 'overcame the world'.
If therefore it were possible to show that Jesus was not in fact
such as to be congruous with this claim, our faith would be in jeop-
ardy. There is no security from this possibility on Christian premises. It is itself part of the setting for the 'existential' decision"
(*The Christ of the Fourth Gospel*, London, 1961, p. 184).

like.[49] That instead He chose to reveal Himself in the Son, and what is more to reveal Himself in a life and death and resurrection and ascension which have saving significance, means among other things that He has chosen to give new dignity to the historical. As Jeremias put it, "We may not avoid the offence of the Incarnation. And if it be objected that we fail to apprehend the essential nature of the act of faith if we make historical knowledge the object of faith, and that faith is in this way sacrificed to such a dubious, subjective, and hypothetical study, we can only reply that God has sacrificed Himself. The Incarnation is the self-sacrifice of God, and to that we can only bow in assent."[50]

I do not think that by this Jeremias means that we submit the faith to the historian, so that we believe only if the historian gives us leave. That would be an intolerable situation, all the more so since the judgments of the historian may change. We need only refer to the widely divergent pictures of Jesus given by the various participants in the "Quest of the Historical Jesus" of the last century for the point to become clear. No thinking Christian could bind himself to the latest pronouncement of the technical historian. But Jeremias is emphasizing the fact that God did choose to enter this world of time and space in the person of His Son, and in this way to become involved in the historical. There is a problem here and its solution is not simple. But we must recognize that for Christians God has set His seal on the importance of the historical.

Again, it may be fairly contended that in the Gospels there is history and there is faith. The history does not necessarily lead to faith. Many have read the Gospels for information about the ancient world and have not come to the place of faith. The historian is not necessarily a believer. To faith the significance of Jesus shines through the history. It is not the accuracy of the history, a con-

---

[49] I realize that this is not to deal with the question of redemption. For that it was necessary that something more than prophecy should take place. But we are concerned here with revelation.

[50] ET, 69, 1957-58, p. 336.

viction of historical truth, that produces faith.[51] It is a
religious conviction, the witness of God's Spirit with
that of the believer. The history did not produce the faith
and the history cannot destroy the faith.[52] But that does
not mean that it is not genuine history. It is real history,
and it is open to question like all other history. But the believer is confident that it will survive the question, for
God is in it. He, and no one less, has spoken through the
holy men of old.

THE APOCRYPHAL GOSPELS

THERE IS AN INTERESTING COMPARISON BETWEEN THE
canonical Gospels and the apocryphal gospels spawned in
the early church.[53] These "gospels" are not really concerned with fact, though they purport to relate events.
They are concerned with edification as their authors
understand it, and the result is a curious hotchpotch of

---

[51] Yet we must bear in mind Conzelmann's rejection of "the way
the attempt is made to grow a systematic Christ-rose from the soil
of historical skepticism" (Braaten and Harrisville, op. cit., p. 56).
If the history is completely unreliable then it is more than difficult
to see how it can ever lend support to faith, let alone originate it.

[52] Cf. M. Kähler, as summarized by C. E. Braaten: "Faith cannot
be made dependent upon the fluctuating, incalculable, and always
problematic results of historical science. Neither the basis nor the
content of faith can be secured by the always more or less probable findings of historical research. Historical facts may be established with a high degree of probability, but with respect to
faith's access to the living Christ the highest degree of probability
is insufficient to guarantee for faith saving knowledge of its object" (ibid., p. 89). We cannot make the faith depend on the latest
findings of the scholars. But neither can we surrender the firm
historical basis of the faith. Therein lies the paradox which all
Christians must face.

[53] Cf. F. Godet's comment on John, "The more closely the narrative of John is studied, the less is it possible to see in it the
accidental product of tradition or of legend." He goes on to say,
"Instead of the juxtaposition of anecdotes which forms the character of the Synoptics, we meet at every step the traces of a
profound connection which governs the narrative even in its minut-
est details. The dilemma is therefore, as Baur has clearly seen,
real history profoundly apprehended and reproduced, or a romance
very skillfully conceived and executed" (Commentary on the Gospel of John, II, Grand Rapids, 1956, p. 216). In a similar situation
the authors of the apocryphal gospels have settled for romance.

piety and wonder tales and superstition. Without handing
over our faith to the mercy of the historian we yet can
say that it is impossible to conceive of Christianity ever
having come into existence on the basis of what is contained in these writings. The canonical Gospels are
essentially different. As A. Wikgren puts it, they "show
a qualitative difference, and are by comparison set within a definite historical matrix and are redolent of the
times and places which they treat. The one is clearly
imaginative writing; the other might be called appreciative reporting."[54]

This last expression seems to me to sum up the Gospels
beautifully. Appreciative they certainly are. But the
writers are engaged in reporting, and that should not be
overlooked. They never break out into expressions of
praise or adoring wonder or the like. They give us sober
narratives of events. We need not doubt that a selection of
incidents and sayings has been made, nor that the selection has been carefully arranged to produce the desired
effect. But the writers do not lose touch with the world
of reality. Their feet are on the ground. They do not give
way to the temptation to manufacture traditions that will
fit their doctrines.[55]

It must also be borne in mind that the Gospels are early
writings. Some scholars pay so much attention to the
time between the occurrence of the events and the com-

---

[54] *Op. cit.*, p. 120.

[55] This seems to me to make such a verdict as that of T. A. Roberts unduly sceptical: "... There seems to be sufficient evidence to
establish the fact of the existence of Jesus as a historical person,
but there may be insufficient evidence to say very much more than
this" (*op. cit.*, p. 164). The evidence we have does seem to enable
us to say much more than this. Roberts is concerned to point out
that Christianity's claim is not subject to the consent of historians,
and this may be freely conceded. He says that Christianity's
claim about the act of God in Jesus "cannot be proved or disproved by the historian, using the techniques of historical criticism, for the claim goes beyond the bounds of what is within the
historian's power to assert to be either true or false" (*ibid.*). He
insists that theological language "is not historical language and
is not entirely supported by appealing to historical considerations.
Our main criticism of historical theologians is that all too frequently they seem unaware of this distinction" (*ibid.*, p. 171).

position of the Gospels that they do not notice that this interval is not great enough for very much in the way of development. The wonders of the apocryphal gospels took much longer to appear.[56]

FACT AND FAITH

THIS POINT AMONG OTHERS IS BROUGHT OUT BY A. M. Sherwin-White in an important concluding section of his Sarum Lectures.[57] As an example of what can happen he cites Herodotus, writing on the Persian wars and the preceding generation after an interval of forty to seventy years. This historian wrote with enthusiasm, and used his history as the vehicle of a moral or religious idea. "Yet the material of Herodotus presents no intractable difficulty to a critical historian. The material has not been transformed out of all recognition under the influence of moral and patriotic fervour, in a period of time as long, if not longer, than can be allowed for the gestation of the form-myths of the synoptic gospels."[58] We may ask: If

---

[56] Wikgren contrasts Christianity with the religions of Egypt and of Greece: "Osiris may have been an ancient Egyptian king; Orpheus was very possibly a reformer of the Dionysiac religion. But there is nothing in the way of written records from the period concerned which remotely approaches our gospels in authenticity, and the myth has completely taken charge of what if any historical events may have been involved. It is difficult to imagine that proponents of the view that the myth is all-important, to the exclusion of the historical events, will be ready to place Christianity and these cults on the same level in this respect. If they do not, they must suppose that the christology arose from the events and sustains some vital connection with them" (*op. cit.*, p. 122). The point of all this is that the lapse of time between the events and the writings in the case of Christianity is too short for the kind of development to take place that many radical critics postulate.

[57] A. M. Sherwin-White, *Roman Society and Roman Law in the New Testament*, Oxford, 1963, pp. 186-193.

[58] *Ibid.*, p. 190. Elsewhere he says, "... It is astonishing that while Graeco-Roman historians have been growing in confidence, the twentieth-century study of the Gospel narratives, starting from no less promising material, has taken so gloomy a turn in the development of form-criticism that the more advanced exponents of it apparently maintain — so far as an amateur can understand the matter — that the historical Christ is unknowable and the history of his mission cannot be written. This seems very curious" (p. 187).

this can happen with Herodotus why can it not happen with John?

In a good deal of modern writing that discounts the historicity of the Gospels on the grounds that they are the products of faith, there appears to be the implication that the narratives of events written by men who firmly believed the *kerygma* cannot be accepted as historical. One may fairly ask, "Why not?" It is true that people who believe strongly sometimes give way to the temptation to twist the facts so that they may have stronger support for their views. But it is also true that this is not invariable. A man with a case to argue may be scrupulously fair to the facts, strong in the assurance that his case is so unassailable that all that he has to do is to set forth the facts and let them speak for him. We must always bear in mind that such an attitude was possible in antiquity also.

C. H. Dodd brings this out with regard to the fulfilment of prophecy, which figures so largely in the New Testament. He examines in some detail the Old Testament passages referred to in the passion narrative in the Fourth Gospel and rejects the view that John was manufacturing incidents to fit previously selected prophecies. "It was not to provide documentation for a previously formulated theology that the early Church searched the scriptures; it was to find an explanation for attested facts, many of which appeared to run counter to their inherited beliefs and even counter to the scriptures as they were currently understood. The facts themselves exerted pressure upon their understanding of prophecy and fulfilment, and dictated the selection of testimonies."[59] What is true of the selection of prophecies is true also on a wider canvas. The men of the early church were interested in theology, but they were also interested in facts. They did not confuse the two.

It is also worth reflecting on the fact that the Evangelists attained their purpose by writing *gospels*. C. Braaten speaks of the view "that the intention of the

---

[59] HTFG, p. 49. A little later he says, "Fundamentally, the framers of the tradition were in bondage to facts, although here and there they strained at their bonds."

Gospels is not to transmit historical information about Jesus, but to portray him as God's eschatological deed of salvation."[60] But if the Evangelists had this intention why did they not write epistles? The New Testament affords ample evidence both that this form was congenial to the early Christians and that it was an efficient way of conveying teaching. Most scholars agree that there are some New Testament documents in the form of epistles that are not genuine "letters" in our sense of the term. In the light of this it is fair to ask, What is the point of writing gospels at all unless to convey historical information?[61] And if the intention of the Gospels is "not to transmit historical information" why do they contain so many precise notes of locality, time, etc., which appear to serve no theological purpose?

It is further to be borne in mind that the first Christians, for all their interest in the Christ of faith, never took their eyes off history. The Gospels are sober, factual accounts. They are not historical romances. What gave the peculiar quality to Christian faith was that the believers saw it as securely rooted in historical events. They were not like the Greeks and Romans, whose religions were replete with mythological stories which nobody credited. The Christians were not concerned with ideas, but with a Person. They maintained that that Person had lived and died and risen. It was "that which we have heard, that which we have seen with our eyes, that which we beheld, and our hands handled, concerning the Word of life" (1 John 1:1) that they declared to their hearers.

J. V. Langmead Casserley puts emphasis on the preoccupation of the early Christians with history. A faith that is not concerned with historical events may produce an interesting form of religion, and may even depict an attractive Christ. But it is not the historic *Christian* faith.

---

[60] Braaten and Harrisville, *op. cit.*, p. 102.

[61] Cf. Neville Clark: "In order to bear their testimony, they [i.e. the Evangelists] create an entirely new literary form — the 'Gospel'. Thereby they make plain that they are seeking to ground the life of the Church to which they belong in the words and deeds, the life and death and resurrection of Jesus of Nazareth. They must write *in this way* precisely because their faith is ineluctably tied to historical events" *(op. cit.,* p. 92).

He says, "No doubt there was something about the *Jesus of history* which compelled his most intimate followers to see and interpret him as the *Christ of faith*, but much more certainly there is something about the *Christ of faith* which compels Christians to identify him with the *Jesus of history*, and this is because Christian and biblical faith is essentially historical faith, a uniquely biblical kind of faith which is willing, when necessary, to make even historical affirmations on the ground of faith alone."[62] The Christian passion for history is a distinctive thing. The early Christians differed from the Gnostics and from the writers of the apocryphal gospels (and shall we add, from Bultmann?) in their insistence on the importance of what happened. They saw men as saved, not by their faith, nor by any ideas they held, but by what God did in Jesus. This preoccupation with the historical must never be overlooked as we study the Gospels.[63]

The Evangelists were concerned to write history as well as theology. We cannot dismiss the history on account of the theology. The element of interpretation in the Gospels does not disqualify them from being good history. It raises the question whether the interpretation is a good one, and one that enables us to account for the data in a satisfactory manner, or whether it is not. But in this the believer is in precisely the same position as the unbeliever.

---

[62] J. V. Langmead Casserley, *Toward a Theology of History*, London, 1965, p. 208. He has already said, "The real difficulty about the trite distinction between the *Jesus of history* and the *Christ of faith* is the failure to see that it is of the essence of the faith which affirms the *Christ of faith* to be indeed the *Christ of faith* to declare that the *Christ of faith* is the *Jesus of history*" *(ibid.).* If "the Christ of faith" is not in fact "the Jesus of history," then we are not dealing with Christianity.

[63] Cf. H. Butterfield's view that Christianity "confronts us with the questions of the Incarnation, the Crucifixion and the Resurrection, questions which may transcend all the apparatus of the scientific historian ... but which imply that Christianity in any of its traditional and recognisable forms has rooted its most characteristic and daring assertions in that ordinary realm of history with which the technical student is concerned" *(Christianity and History*, London, 1960, p. 12). He later says, "Traditional Christianity ... claims to be an historical religion in a more technical sense; for certain historical events are held to be a part of the religion itself" *(ibid.*, p. 156).

Both must justify their approach. The believer with his theological approach is not one whit worse off than the unbeliever with his nontheological approach. No objective rule of procedure assures us that a nontheological approach will necessarily yield superior history. The nontheological approach may as easily be vitiated by prejudice as the theological approach. Neither side has the advantage here unless it be that the believer can claim with justice that he is in a better position to approach the Gospels sympathetically.[64] It is true that he cannot establish history as he sees it beyond all doubting. But then that is true of all history. There is nothing from the past (and very little from the present!) that is so surely established that it cannot possibly be doubted by the utterly sceptical. J. R. Lucas can say, "Since there is nothing that cannot on some occasion be reasonably doubted, there can be no truths established beyond doubt to all comers, no elemental facts which we just have to accept and on which all else is based. . . . Facts are not sacred: they are not worth worshipping: they do not exist: they are not even things."[65] Since we can doubt anything it is not surprising that some have been found who doubt all that the Evangelists wrote. But, since we can also have our certainties, we may well feel that the Gospels attest certain facts as well as could be.

Many of the objections to the Gospel narratives at base amount to this, that the Gospels speak of happenings like the incarnation and the miracles which we do not see at other periods of history and which historians accordingly cannot take seriously. But this is precisely the point of the Gospels. They do not purport to tell us the kind of thing that takes place from time to time in the history of men,

---

[64] G. B. Caird can say, ". . . In the past the probing of the New Testament by the methods of the secular historian has led not to deeper understanding but to complete scepticism" (*The Scope of Theology*, ed. Daniel T. Jenkins, Cleveland and New York, 1965, p. 41). A little later he says, "Historical criticism of the New Testament ends in scepticism only when it starts with scepticism as one of its presuppositions" (p. 42). The sceptic is not the best interpreter of the New Testament.

[65] Cited in *Authority and the Church*, S.P.C.K. Theological Collections, no. 5, London, 1965, p. 68.

but of something that happened once for all. They are written to describe unique events. As J. Jeremias reminds us, "... Every sentence of the sources bears witness of it to us, every verse of our Gospels hammers it into us: something has happened, something unique, something which has never before come into existence.... The more we multiply analogies, the clearer it becomes that there are no analogies to the message of Jesus."[66] We can find parallels to this or that aspect of Jesus' teaching, and to this or that incident in the Gospels. But there is no parallel to the authority with which Jesus spoke, nor to the impact of His life as a whole. The Gospels must be understood in terms of their claim to describe a unique series of happenings. It is no criticism of them to point this out. It simply highlights their claim.

There is, of course, a sense in which everything in history is unique. History never repeats itself exactly. There is only one Napoleon. There is only one Black Death. Every happening is unique. The historian is always dealing with the unique. But there is a difference. While all events are in a sense unique, the events that concern the technical historian are recognizably of the class of human happenings, whereas those in the Gospels are not (or at least some of them are not). This difference must be recognized. But when full allowance is made for it, it is plain that the uniqueness of the gospel events is no reason for ruling them out historically.

CONTINUITY AND DISCONTINUITY

IN THIS CONNECTION WE MUST NOT OVERLOOK THE continuity of the church with its Founder. There is another problem here, for the preaching of the early church is not the same as the preaching of Jesus. There is an element of discontinuity, as well as one of continuity. The death and resurrection of Jesus were critical. It was these events which were decisive for the formation of the Christian community. The more we insist on them as central the clearer it becomes that there was a discontinuity. Jesus could not, as the early church could and

---

[66] *Op. cit.*, p. 338.

did, appeal to men on the basis of His death and resurrection. There was a new thing at the end of His earthly
ministry.

This discontinuity is emphasized in much modern
writing. This is, of course, the point of the contention
that we can know the Christ of faith but not the Jesus of
history. Those who urge this so strongly are impressed
with the difference that the critical end to Jesus' life
made. Indeed, they are so impressed by it that they maintain that we cannot know what that critical end really
was. All that we can know is how the early church
preached it.

I have already suggested that this is unduly sceptical,
and that it is the abdication of critical responsibility. The
early church is a fact, and the critical historian must have
something to say about the church's own account of the
way it came into being. Even if he cannot agree with the
theological affirmations made by the first Christians he
can note them and give a judgment on whether they form
a reasonable explanation of the existence of the community.

For the fact is that there is continuity between Jesus
of Nazareth and the early church as well as discontinuity.
Why was it Jesus and not someone else to whom the first
Christians gave their allegiance? Why was it that they
recounted sayings and incidents concerning *Him* and not
another teacher? There is no evidence in the New Testament that any Christian teacher thought he was seriously
distorting the teaching of Jesus as he preached the gospel
or sought to edify the church. Whence did the early
Christians derive the idea that they were being faithful
to the teaching of Jesus? Or even the idea that they ought
to be faithful to it? These are questions that cannot be
simply shrugged off.

In an earlier and less sophisticated day it was possible
to maintain that there is a continuity between the tempo-
ral and the eternal. Sometimes the illustration of the iceberg has been used. The iceberg has by far the most
significant part of its being out of sight under the water.
But the underwater part and the abovewater part form
one continuous whole. So may we conceive of reality.

Part, and the most significant part, is the unseen, eternal world. We see only this world of time and sense, but this world is constantly influenced by the unseen. But on occasion it may also influence the unseen world, and that is what happened in the coming of Jesus. This means, of course, that the events told about Jesus, or at least the most significant of them, really happened. Unless they really happened in the one world they could not have any effect in the other.

This way of understanding things is not as widely held these days as it once was. But have we any valid reason for denying that it may well point us to a reality? At the very least we are in no position to deny that there is another world than the one we see and know. Nor can we affirm dogmatically that what goes on in our world does not influence what goes on in the other.

Gerhard Ebeling sees the element of continuity between the Jesus of history and the first church in the faith of the early Christians in Jesus. "To belong to Jesus means to believe, and to believe means to belong to Jesus. Faith is not a form that can be given any content at will, but is the very essence of the matter, the thing that came with Jesus Christ, the content of revelation, the gift of salvation itself."[67] This must be taken with full seriousness. For Christians it is not a matter of faith as such, of faith in any object or person. For Christians there is but one faith, and that is faith in Jesus Christ. As Ebeling says, "Faith is not a form that can be given any content at will." Jesus is essential to faith.

This means that being a Christian is being a committed person. And it means being committed to Jesus. But it does not mean that the historical explanation the committed Christian gives of the basis of the Christian experience that has transformed him is necessarily wrong, or, for that matter, necessarily right. The assumption that it is wrong is far too often made by the unbeliever and the sceptic. Yet it should surely be obvious that faith and commitment are not the same thing as error. Whether the historical account given by the committed Christian is valid or not is not given in these premises. That is a

---

[67] G. Ebeling, *Word and Faith*, London, 1963, p. 303.

matter for further consideration. But the point I wish to emphasize is that the very reality of the salvation the believer experiences demands that the historical behind it be taken seriously. Of course, if a secular historian denies that there is any reality corresponding to the Christian's experience of salvation we must part company with him. But we do so, not as those who are so deluded that they cannot face facts. Rather we do so as those who regret his inability to reckon with *all* the evidence. We insist that Christian experience must be taken as one of the facts of life, to be explained as best we can.

Now it is no explanation to say that Christian experience can be divorced from Jesus of Nazareth. As D. E. Nineham has said,

> If this Jesus never lived, or if he was totally different from, or incompatible with, the picture of him presupposed in the kerygma, then the kerygma form of the Gospel seems to me such a senseless paradox as to make the Gospel itself incredible. For what conceivable reason should God proclaim salvation through a series of false statements about the life of a man who either never lived or was in fact *toto caelo* different from the statements about him? I could not ask anyone to believe that God acted in this way.[68]

This may not be a complete and final answer to those who divorce the Jesus of history from the Christ of faith, but it is at the very least an important consideration. And it is all the more important if we refuse to believe in an irrational God. Anyone who thinks seriously of God must think of Him as One who acts rationally and who in His dealings with men takes their history seriously.

If God does enter history we must expect that the result will be unusual. That is the whole crux of our problem. Could we explain everything in the Gospels in the usual historical fashion, we would have purely human events, not a divine intervention. If we once grant the possibility of a divine intervention in the affairs of man we concede that unusual, even miraculous events may well take place.

---

[68] D. E. Nineham, *Historicity and Chronology in the New Testament,* S.P.C.K. Theological Collections, no. 6, London, 1965, p. 13.

That is the crux of the whole Christian case. Everything depends on whether we are ready to concede the possibility of an incarnation. And we should not overlook the truth that the refusal to concede the possibility is just as dogmatic and theological a position as that which accepts it.

William Lillie has an apt comment. "What the student of history has the right to demand is not that the Christian should abandon his pattern of thinking for one more congenial to twentieth-century secularism, but that he should demonstrate that this Christian pattern of thinking gives a more coherent interpretation of the facts than any other that has been suggested."[69] That is the position the Christian maintains. The Gospels will not necessarily convince everybody. As Lucas says, it is possible to doubt anything. But there were certain things which happened in first-century Palestine and which have been recorded in the Gospels of which it can be said that the approach of the Evangelists gives us a coherent interpretation, and one that is eminently satisfying. This is more than can be said for the reconstructions of their critics, at least as so far put forward. All other approaches so far suggested come short in some way. Commonly they fail to account for the formation of the Christian community or for its continuance. The answer of the New Testament writers makes sense and it fits the facts. The Christian may well feel that he has good grounds for his position.

THE GOSPEL

QUITE OFTEN THE ATTEMPT IS MADE TO SEPARATE THE Fourth Gospel from the Synoptics in such a way as to compel us to choose. The picture of Christ we get in the one, it is said, is incompatible with the picture of Christ we get in the other. If Christ was like the Synoptists depict Him, then He could not be as shown in the Fourth Gospel and vice versa.

It is probably significant that from the earliest times the church has thought of the four Gospels as being essentially in harmony. The manuscripts are entitled, significantly, not "The Gospels," but "The Gospel." The

---

[69] William Lillie, *Historicity and Chronology in the New Testament*, S.P.C.K. Theological Collections, no. 6, London, 1965, p. 120.

four are then differentiated with "according to Matthew," etc. [70] The church proceeded from a deep-seated conviction that there is no cleavage between one and another of the four, but that they must be taken together in any attempt to understand the Christian gospel. We have need of this insight still.

Cullmann has an interesting comment on the fourfold Gospel. "Four *biographies* of the same life could not be set alongside one another as of equal value, but would have to be harmonized and reduced to a single biography in some way or other. Four Gospels, that is, four books dealing with the content of a faith, cannot be harmonized, but require by their very nature to be set alongside one another."[71] There is more than one thing in this passage with which I would disagree, but the suggestion that the Gospels should be set side by side is most valuable. It is possible to struggle vainly seeking better and better ways of harmonizing difficult passages, and in general wrestling with the difficulties posed by the fact that we have a multiplicity of Gospels. It is better to let each speak for itself and give its own picture. We can then absorb the contribution made by each of the Evangelists and rejoice in the enlarged understanding that fourfoldness brings.[72]

---

[70] Oscar Cullmann thinks that at first the multiplicity of Gospels was a problem to the church: "When the need to possess a New Testament canon alongside that of the Old Testament gradually emerged and apostolic authorship was required as the criterion for canonicity, it was inevitable that the combination of our four Gospels should give offence" *(The Early Church,* London, 1956, p. 41). But his attempt to show that the "offence" existed is not in my judgment particularly convincing. I see no evidence that the church did other than welcome the Gospels, perhaps hesitating a little over John. And in any case Cullmann can say, "The description of the Gospels as εὐαγγέλιον κατὰ Ματθαῖον, κατὰ Μάρκον, κατὰ Λουκᾶν, κατὰ Ἰωάννην, which had probably become current by the middle of the second century, best does justice both to the true unity of the four Gospels and the necessity of having a number of different authors. It is a question of combining different witnesses to the one Gospel" *(ibid.,* p. 53).

[71] *Ibid.,* p. 54.

[72] Cunliffe-Jones quotes B. F. Westcott: "The real harmony of the Gospels is essentially moral and not mechanical. It is not to be found in an ingenious mosaic composed of their disjointed fragments, but in the contemplation of each narrative from its proper point of view" (SE, I, p. 20).

For we need all four, and we would be immeasurably impoverished without any of them.

It is possible to be taken up with the differences between the Fourth Gospel and the Synoptics. These differences are real. We should not shut our eyes to them. But neither should we be hypnotized by them.[73] The church was surely right in detecting an essential harmony among the four. They agree among themselves in a way that sets them off from all their competitors.[74] A lot here depends on what we are emphasizing. Traditionally the church has been more impressed by the resemblances than with the differences. The church has not worshipped two Christs, the Christ of St. John and the Christ of the Synoptists. It has worshipped one Christ, the Christ of the gospel — the fourfold gospel. It has acted on the assumption that, for all their obvious differences, the four Gospels are basically in harmony. In line with this, H. Cunliffe-Jones has asked an interesting question: ". . . Can we think with full integrity of mind, and without diminishing the persistent analytic study of the New Testament documents, that whatever the intimacy of relation between the first three Gospels, and, even though we realize that it is quite impossible to compose a formal harmony between the Gospels, can we think that we have in fact for our thinking as well as for our devotion, four synoptic Gospels, because all four contribute to a common under-

---

[73] J. A. T. Robinson regards as "a dangerous habit" the practice "of treating the fourth Gospel in separation from the other three and indeed from the common proclamation behind them all" (*Jesus and His Coming*, London, 1957, p. 162).

[74] I recall that when I first went to America I horrified some of my hosts by saying that I could not tell northern speech from southern. Then they proceeded to return the compliment by referring to my "English" accent! I could, of course, tell that not all Americans spoke alike. But what impresses the outsider at first is what is common to all American speech and sets it apart from, say, English or Scottish or Australian speech. I heard Americans, not primarily Northerners or Southerners. In the same way sometimes Americans do not distinguish easily between the speech of a Londoner and that of a Yorkshireman. There are unities that mark the groups of those who speak English as well as diversities. Much depends on what we are looking for.

standing of a common Lord?"[75] "Four Synoptic Gospels"!
It is an intriguing phrase for a valuable idea. And, though
the church has never used this terminology, it has always
acted on the idea that underlies it.

There is no question but that the language of the
Fourth Gospel is different from that of the Synoptics. But
it is important to penetrate beneath the surface of the
words to the meaning they are expressing. Some years
ago A. M. Hunter stressed this in a well-known study,[76]
in which he pointed out that it is quite possible to have an
essential unity in the realm of ideas even though the
form of words employed in different writings may be
very different. Thus "when Jesus said, 'The Kingdom of
God has come upon you' (Luke x.9) and Paul 'If any man
is in Christ, there is a new creation' (2 Cor. v.17) and
John 'The *Logos* became flesh and dwelt among us' (John
i.14), they were not making utterly different and unrelated announcements; on the contrary, they were using
different idioms, different categories of thought, to
express their common conviction that the living God had
spoken and acted through his Messiah for the salvation of
his people."[77] What each of these writers is saying in his

---

[75] SE, I, p. 24. He has earlier noted Dodd's point that the Farewell Discourses in the Fourth Gospel have a good deal of matter
in common with the Synoptic Gospels, and goes on, "If this is so,
then the possibility of integrating together the teaching of Jesus
in all four Gospels is not so remote as it might at first sight seem.
If the teaching of Jesus as given to us in the Fourth Gospel is in
fact in large measure a true interpretation of the actual historic
teaching of our Lord, then while for other purposes we need to
stress the analysis of the differences between the different traditions as to the teaching of our Lord, for many theological and
pastoral purposes the unity and coherence of the teaching in all
four Gospels is a stress of enormous practical importance" (p. 23).

[76] A. M. Hunter, *The Unity of the New Testament*, London, 1943.

[77] *Ibid.*, pp. 14f. He has preceded these words by pointing out
that a concentration on differences may lead us astray. "The Synoptic Gospels speak of the advent of 'the Kingdom of God'; Paul of
'being in Christ'; John of 'the Logos becoming incarnate.' Now,
isolate each of these phrases, and observe what is likely to happen.
Your study of the Kingdom of God may take you back through
Judaism to the Old Testament and perhaps even (as it did Otto)
to primitive Aryan religion. Your study of the Pauline formula 'in
Christ' may take you back to Hellenistic mysticism (as it did Deiss-
mann). Your study of the *Logos* may take you back through Philo

own idiom is that in Jesus Christ we see God's action for the salvation of all mankind. It is this breadth of vision that we need if we are to compare the Fourth Gospel with the other three. There are differences indeed, but there is not a different message and there is not a different Christ. John is speaking about the same Lord and the same salvation. His different way of expressing it should not hide this from us.

Jesus is such a gigantic figure that we need all four portraits to discern Him. And we must bear in mind that, for all their differences, the four Evangelists had the same Person in mind. It was the one Jesus who inspired the four Gospels. While we must be on our guard against trying to conform one of the Gospels to another, yet we must also bear in mind that it is our task to look for Him who could cause such Gospels to be written. Allan Barr has some wise words to say in this connection. He reminds us that "When we have gleaned from it [i.e. the Fourth Gospel] all that we may feel should be added to the Synoptic account of events we are still left with a Johannine portrayal of Jesus in act and word which we cannot dismiss as unhistorical *except by theological judgments of our own*."[78] This is a most important consideration. The reasons so many reject the Johannine portrait are primarily theological, not historical. Of course this does not mean that they are not to be treated with respect. They should be seriously weighed. But it is an error to hold that the Johannine picture is to be dismissed on purely historical grounds.[79]

Barr further makes the point that there was one historical Jesus who inspired both the Synoptic and the

---

to Plato and the Stoics. At the end of your investigations you may be left wondering what conceivable connexion there is among them all." But as we have noted in the text Hunter goes on to demonstrate the basic unity. This is a case where too close attention to language to the neglect of ideas can lead one widely astray.

[78] S.P.C.K. Theological Collections, no. 6, London, 1965, p. 24 (my italics).

[79] Perhaps I should make it clear that I do not mean that those who reject the historicity of John have no historical grounds for this. All that I am saying is that I think Barr to be correct in maintaining that the primary considerations are usually theological.

Johannine portraits.[80] We should keep this in mind and work steadily toward trying to secure such an understanding of Jesus as will account for both pictures. It is too simple to accept one and to reject the other. And if we do, as Barr has pointed out, we do so on theological, not historical grounds. It would be better to work toward a more adequate theology, one that can allow for both portraits.

SOME JOHANNINE ACCURACIES

ATTENTION HAS OFTEN ENOUGH BEEN DRAWN TO THOSE facets of the Fourth Gospel which make it difficult for many scholars to hold it to be a factual record — the differences from the Synoptic accounts, the advanced Christology, elements that are claimed to be Hellenistic and so on. These are real. But they need to be balanced by other facts.

One is that on a number of points John appears to be remarkably accurate. Consider, for example, his topography. John has many references to places, and quite often it is apparent that he knew what he was writing about and has described it with precision. R. D. Potter has carried out a survey of the topographical references in this Gospel and has shown that, as far as our present information goes, they are accurate. He concludes that John must have known Palestine.[81]

---

[80] "It is a different kind of history, indeed, as there are different kinds of portrait painting, and it may remain the wiser course to keep the portrait separate from the Synoptic one. Yet there was in history one Jesus, and ideally there should be ultimately one historical portrait of him, for which the modern historian will be obliged to judge and to use the theological concepts both of the Synoptics and of John" (Barr, *loc. cit.*).

[81] See his article, "Topography and Archaeology in the Fourth Gospel," SE, I, pp. 329-337. *Inter alia* he can say, "... Time and again, it will be found that those who have lived long in Palestine are struck by the impression that our author did so. He knew the Palestine that they have learned to know" (p. 335). He concludes that "we have in this gospel not only the Word of God, but also the narrative of a reliable witness, a Palestinian Jew" (p. 337). W. F. Albright also stresses the accuracy of the topographical references in this Gospel. See *The Archaeology of Palestine*, Pelican Books, 1949, pp. 244-8; *The Background of the New Testa-*

A feature of John's work is the way he employs notes of time. Again and again he tells us that such and such a thing happened on such and such a day, or at a given hour of the day, or the like. These details often appear to have no significance for the point of the story. Thus in John 1:39 there does not seem to be any importance attaching to the fact that it was at about the tenth hour that Jesus invited two disciples of John the Baptist to come and see where he was staying. This is the case over and over again. We are driven to conclude that John tells us these things only because he had information that enabled him to fix the time when certain events took place. It is impossible to find a dogmatic motive for the inclusion of these notes of time.

It is all of a piece with this that John has many references to the feasts of the Jewish year, far more than we find in the other Gospels. This raises the questions of why John did this, and of what significance he sees in the feasts. But the way he uses the Jewish calendar has convinced many that he knew what he was talking about. He referred to the Passover, for example, in chapter 6 because the events in question took place at Passover time. E. Stauffer is insistent that John is the only Evangelist who enables us to fix the chronology of Jesus' life, and he sees this done through the various references of this kind scattered through John's Gospel.[82]

---

ment and its Eschatology, ed. W. D. Davies and D. Daube, Cambridge, 1956, pp. 158-160.

[82] Cf. the following statements: "The fourth evangelist, John, has cleared up the chronology of Jesus' story" *(Jesus and His Story*, London, 1960, p. 15) ; "It is clearly impossible to fit the chronological structure of John's gospel into the narrow frame of the synoptic presentation. *But it is easily possible to insert the synoptic frame into the Johannine construction.* This is one argument, besides very many others, for the correctness of the Johannine chronology" (p. 17). J. Ernest Davey, by contrast, thinks that John's chronology "seems secondary and suspect, and cannot easily be accepted against the Marcan scheme without independent corroboration of some kind to make it probable" *(op. cit.*, p. 42). But Davey goes on to reject the Marcan scheme also. He maintains that Jesus came up to Jerusalem not just a week before His death but some considerable time earlier. Davey thus puts us in the curious position of rejecting John's chronology because it does not agree with Mark's, a chronology which is itself regarded as unreliable.

JOHN THE BAPTIST

VERY ILLUMINATING IS THIS EVANGELIST'S HANDLING OF John the Baptist. He tells us in his first reference to him that this man came "for witness, that he might bear witness of the light" (John 1:7). This sets the stage. He sees John in no other character. Always he depicts him as a witness, bearing his witness to Jesus so that men might believe in Him. We hear nothing of the Baptist's ethical teaching. For that we must turn to Luke. We hear nothing of his denunciation of the "offspring of vipers" (Luke 3:7). We hear nothing of the eschatological judgment, or the wrath to come. We do not even read that John baptized Jesus, though there can be little doubt but that this Gospel refers to the occasion when this took place. From first to last the Baptist is depicted as a witness, that and nothing more. The writer allows nothing to distract us from seeing John in this role.

Since this is undeniable we might well feel that John's portrait of the Baptist is unreliable. Here surely John must be thought of as allowing his interpretation to dominate the facts, of letting us see the Baptist not as he was, but as he would have liked him to be? Such indeed is the conclusion of some exegetes.[83] But in recent times the discovery of the Qumran scrolls has altered all that. These show us that the portrait of John the Baptist is remarkably accurate. At point after point there are resemblances, and so many are the points of contact that some have thought that John must at one time have been a member of the Qumran community. This seems to me too much to affirm, though the possibility must be allowed. But we are told that he was in the deserts until the time that he was manifested to Israel (Luke 1:80), and there is nothing improbable in the suggestion that during this

---

[83] P. Gardner-Smith thinks that the Fourth Evangelist knew little about the Baptist. "What is not so often recognized," he says, "is that there is little evidence that he knew more of the John of history than what he might have learned from the vague traditions of the churches before these traditions became crystallized in the Synoptic Gospels" (*Saint John and the Synoptic Gospels*, Cambridge, 1938, p. 4). How the picture has changed since 1938!

period he developed an acquaintance with the teaching of Qumran or of a sect resembling it.

It must be stressed that the contacts with Qumran teaching are not occasional.[84] J. H. Brownlee maintains that almost every point in the teaching of John the Baptist, in the Fourth Gospel as in the Synoptics, has its contact with the teaching of the scrolls. He can say, "The most astonishing result of all is the validation of the Fourth Gospel as an authentic source concerning the Baptist."[85] With this we should take the verdict of J. A. T. Robinson, no friend of conservative opinions:

> ... One of the most remarkable effects of the Scrolls has been the surprising vindication they appear to offer of ideas and categories attributed to John by the fourth Evangelist which recent criticism would never have allowed as remotely historical. Indeed, nothing, I prophesy, is likely to undergo so complete a reversal in the criticism of the Gospel as our estimate of its treatment of the Baptist, and therefore of the whole Judean ministry of Jesus with which it opens. This treatment has almost universally been assumed to spring from purely theological motives of a polemical nature and thus to provide evidence for a very minimum of historical foundation. ... On the contrary, I believe that the fourth Evangelist is remarkably well informed on the Baptist, because he, or the witness behind that part of his tradition, once belonged to John's movement and, like the nameless disciple of 1,37 'heard him say this, and followed Jesus.'[86]

---

[84] Here I am stressing the fact that the scrolls have links with the teaching of John the Baptist. But it is worth noting that they have more points of contact with the Fourth Gospel than with any other book of the New Testament. See further Ch. VI.

[85] *The Scrolls and the New Testament*, ed. K. Stendahl, London, 1958, p. 52.

[86] SE, I, p. 345. A. Wikgren is another who is impressed by John the Baptist. "The enigmatic figure of John the Baptist is one which no early Christian apologist is likely to have invented and which most would like to have forgotten. Certainly he constitutes an insurmountable stumbling-block to any purely mythological interpretation of Jesus. ... The Qumran scrolls have now also released a flood of new light upon the total background against which John and Jesus began their ministries. Whatever one may think of the bearing of this upon the question of Christian origins, the

This is most important. There is not the slightest doubt but that the Baptist is depicted in a certain way in order to attain a theological end. This is conceded by all and is plainly stated by the Evangelist. But it now appears that when he writes about the Baptist John is accurate. If on this point where he has been so often and so confidently assailed the Fourth Evangelist is now seen to emerge with flying colors, this gives us confidence in other passages.[87] The doctrinal and polemical motives are there. Few would deny it. But John has been able to effect his aim without distorting the facts. He took what actually happened, made his selection of the facts and recorded them in such a way as to bring out his (and their) meaning. Now if John could do this in one place he could do it elsewhere. If his facts are right while he is painting the portrait of the Baptist why should they not be right also when he is depicting Jesus?

FACT AND THEOLOGY

It should further be noted that John does not introduce his theology indiscriminately. While on occasion he certainly brings out the theological meaning of the things he narrates, it is also the case that sometimes he does nothing of the sort. For example, in the trial narrative John relates that at one point the Jews told Pilate

---

effect is nevertheless to set them both more firmly than ever within a definite historical situation, and to facilitate a more accurate appreciation and evaluation of the religious factors which constituted the milieu in which messianic thought had its most important pre-Christian development" (*op. cit.*, p. 124).

[87] It is interesting to notice how opinion has changed on such a subject as the raising of Lazarus. Cf. Bishop Cassian, "The Lucan parable (16) ends with Abraham's answer to the request of the Dives (v. 31) that Lazarus might be sent in his father's house. For the liberals of the XIX century the resurrection of Lazarus in John was a fiction intended as an answer to this request. The contemporary scholars would not deny its historicity" (SE, I, p. 145). As an illustration of this W. H. Cadman in an article called "The Raising of Lazarus" (SE, I, pp. 423-434) discusses the story without casting doubts on its historicity. J. E. Davey does raise grave doubts about it (*op. cit.*, pp. 119, 126f.), but he thinks there is some history here and that it gives the explanation of Jesus' return to Jerusalem (p. 46).

that Jesus ought to die because "he made himself the Son of God ($\upsilon\iota\grave{o}\nu$ $\Theta\epsilon\hat{o}\hat{v}$)" (John 19:7). This is an expression that surely invites theological treatment. But all that John tells us Pilate did was to ask Jesus, "Whence art thou?" for he was greatly afraid. That is to say, Pilate is taking $\upsilon\iota\grave{o}\nu$ $\Theta\epsilon\hat{o}\hat{v}$ in the sense, "son of a god." He is inquiring whether Jesus is a demigod (in the usual Greek and Roman sense). John does not correct this, nor dwell on the true meaning of "Son of God." He does not even make this central to the charge against Jesus. Rather he emphasizes that Jesus was condemned as "King of the Jews," dangerous though this admission was politically for Christians when the Gospel was written. In other words, John has deliberately passed over an opportunity of bringing in his distinctive view of the Person of Jesus, and that in a place where it would have made things easier for Christians confronted with the Roman might. It would have been good tactics to have stressed the religious motif. Instead he has emphasized a politically dangerous thought. I do not see how we can well conclude other than that he has chosen to be faithful to the facts.[88]

---

[88] C. H. Dodd draws attention to the words of the Jews, "We have no king but Caesar" (John 19:15), and comments: "This might very naturally be read as an admission that Jews were loyal subjects and Christians were not: a damaging admission, surely, in the situation in which Christians found themselves at the time when the gospel was published. If the evangelist set himself to reproduce with essential fidelity the ethos of the actual situation in which Christ was condemned, as it was handed down (however much he may have felt free to dramatize it), the preservation of these challenging traits could be understood; but I should find it difficult to imagine a Christian writer under Domitian (let us say), or even under Nerva or Trajan, going out of his way to introduce them into a relatively harmless account" (HTFG, p. 115). The same writer elsewhere sees the passion narrative as fixed in the tradition very early, and speaks of "the absence of any such theologizing of the story as might not unreasonably have been expected, in view of its theological importance. This is especially notable in the Fourth Gospel. That work is in general deeply penetrated with a distinctive theology, but if one reads its Passion-narrative it is difficult to find more than two or three points at which the narrative appears to have been influenced by that theology. As a whole it is singularly plain and objective" (*History and the Gospel*, London, 1952, pp. 83f.). On a very small point, the doubled "verily, verily" (against the single "verily" of

It is also worth noting, in view of the persistent claim that John presents us with a Christology too high for a first disciple,[89] that John also stresses the complete dependence of Jesus on the Father in a way incomprehensible if he were simply enunciating the doctrine of a divine Christ. He reports that Jesus said, "I can of myself do nothing" (John 5:30), and his Gospel is full of the thought. Jesus' message is not His own, for He could pray, "Now they know that all things whatsoever thou hast given me are from thee: for the words which thou gavest me I have given unto them" (John 17:7f.). Again and again Jesus refers to being "sent" by the Father, the frequency of mention rendering quotation superfluous.

Jesus' witness to Himself is not necessarily to be accepted, but God bears the decisive witness to Him (John 5:31f.). Jesus obeys the commandment of the Father (John 14:31); indeed, He tells us that His very meat "is to do the will of him that sent me" (John 4:34). Much more could be cited, but perhaps it will be sufficient to refer to the verdict of J. E. Davey, who has submitted the evidence to close scrutiny. He notices that in the Synoptics we see Jesus going about doing good, i.e. manifesting love, "and love is the Christian name for God." Likewise he sees in "dependence the essential mark of true human religion," and goes on, ". . . We have here a reversal of the usual formula of the theologians and find that it is in a real sense the Synoptics who show us the divinity, and *John* the humanity, of Christ."[90] Whether

the Synoptics), J. E. Davey draws attention to Jesus' habit of repeating words as shown in the Synoptics (Matt. 23:37, Luke 10: 41, 13:34, 22:31) and concludes, ". . . It seems probable that *John* has preserved in 'verily, verily' a trick of speech of Jesus Himself (at times), which is here supported by parallel, yet quite different, cases in the Synoptic Gospels" (*op. cit.*, p. 55).

[89] Some critics, of course, while admitting that the Christology is high, would repudiate the suggestion that it is too high. Thus Lord Charnwood can say, as the conclusion of a critical treatment of the material, "Make of it what we may, Jesus Christ of Nazareth did think and did speak as according to St. John He thought and spoke, concerning His Father, Himself, His followers, and that Spirit of His which should abide with them for ever" (*According to St. John*, London, n.d., p. 244).

[90] *Op. cit.*, p. 131. Davey devotes a long chapter to "The De-

this be accepted in its entirety or not, there can be no doubt but that John does stress the dependence of Jesus on the Father in a way the Synoptists do not. This is a major theme.[91] We cannot thus accept lightly the thesis that John's high Christology rules him out as unhistorical. We must also give account of the fact that he puts a stress on the dependence of Jesus which is inexplicable if his Gospel took its origin, in thought as well as date, at the time when Christians were putting all their emphasis on the divinity of Christ.

Another point, if a minor one, in which John's accuracy is in evidence is that in which he refers to the unbelief of Jesus' brothers (John 7:5). This time is evidently not so very long before the crucifixion and it is incredible that an inventor would go out of his way to manufacture such a lack of faith unless it were historical.[92]

---

pendence of Christ as Presented in *John*" (pp. 90-157). He deals with this under sixteen headings and his treatment of the subject should leave no doubt but that the concept is fundamental in John. He introduces the discussion with, "There is no more remarkable element in the Fourth Gospel than the consistent and universal presentation of Christ, in His life and work and words and in all aspects of His activities, as dependent upon the Father at every point" (p. 90). This he regards as indicating historicity. He does not claim that everything in John is history, but says, ". . . My real contention is that the unhistorical in *John* is the embroidery of what is historical, that the nucleus of the picture of Jesus and His teaching in John is in fact not fiction, history not doctrine, and that therefore the Fourth Gospel has not a little to contribute to a historical reconstruction of the ministry and personality of Jesus" (p. 91). He maintains that "we have much to learn from *John*, not only regarding details of the life of Jesus but regarding the content of His consciousness, much which is independent of the Synoptic Gospels and which constitutes a real gain for a historical study of the life of Christ" (p. 131). What we might call the normal critical view is put succinctly by Wernle, "Here [in the Synoptics] the Man; there [John] the God" (Nolloth, *op. cit.*, p. 149).

[91] F. C. Burkitt, though he rejects out of hand any suggestion that John should be taken seriously as a historical source, yet can say, "In no early Christian document is the real humanity of Jesus so emphasised as in the Fourth Gospel" (*The Gospel History and its Transmission*, Edinburgh, 1907, p. 233).

[92] Cf. Lenski, "The complete openness with which John reports their unbelief as continuing as late as six months before Jesus' death is noteworthy in various ways. John tells the true facts; a

We should also bear in mind the use of terminology
that shows what Brownlee calls "a historical sense on
John's part."[93] Thus he refers to Jesus as the Logos,
but does not put this term on the lips of Jesus or John
the Baptist. Jesus uses "the Son of man" or "the Son
of God" to refer to His preexistence, never "the Logos."
In the Gospel Jesus calls Himself "the Son of man"
as in the Synoptics, but the term does not occur in
the Johannine Epistles. This does not look like a lack
of concern for the facts.

I am not, of course, arguing that John is concerned
only or primarily to set before his readers a bare factual
recital of events. As Hoskyns so well says, for John
the problem of history "is not solved ... by depressing
his gospel to an exact historical narrative of Palestinian
events." There is much more to it than that. But, as
Hoskyns goes on, it is not solved either "by escaping
from them into a veiled description of the ideas and experiences of Greek-speaking Christians a century later."[94]
It is too readily assumed these days that John did not
hesitate to manipulate the facts in the interest of his
theology. The evidence shows that John had a profound
respect for the facts. He was able to set forward his
theological purpose without doing despite to his facts.
He had a deep concern for the truth.

It must be insisted that some at any rate of the modern radical criticism looks suspiciously like a dogmatic
refusal to face the facts. To select one example, H.
Braun maintains that the value of the Qumran texts
in relation to John is limited: "... The possibility that the
description of Jesus' activity in the Fourth Gospel is
the work of an eye-witness at an early date is still excluded. The results of decades of research which have
observed in this Gospel an advanced stage in the formation of primitive Christian theology, especially an ad-

---

fabricator would omit at least a fact like this if he knew of it,
or would alter it in some way" (*The Interpretation of St. John's
Gospel*, Columbus, Ohio, 1956, p. 532).

[93] *Op. cit.*, p. 47.
[94] *Op. cit.*, p. 227.

vanced christology, still retain their full weight."[95] He further maintains that "The discoveries of Qumran modify our previous view concerning the possible site of the composition of John's Gospel, but they do not affect the insights of decades of traditio-historical work on the syncretistic character of the Johannine texts."[96]

I find this a fascinating example of the way in which some radical scholars refuse to let facts interfere with a beautiful theory. Decades of scholars have decided that John is late and that it cannot be the work of an eyewitness. Its history is not to be accepted. The evidence of the scrolls must not be allowed to shake this position.

Yet Braun's position appears to be refuted by even the very limited value he allows to the Qumran material (and it must be borne in mind that many give it a much greater value). He admits that the scrolls show that Palestine had been penetrated by the "syncretistic material" which he finds also in John.[97] He is ready to concede on this basis that John may possibly have been written in Palestine. But he does not even consider the question of date. Since the Qumran monastery was destroyed before AD 70, and since no one dates the characteristic ideas of the scrolls in the community's declining years, what Braun calls "syncretistic material" must have been present in Palestine at a very early date, probably before the Christian era. There is therefore, on the face of it, no reason at all why John's "syncretism" should not also be early.[98] But Braun does

---

[95] Braaten and Harrisville, *op. cit.*, p. 72.

[96] *Ibid.*, p. 73.

[97] *Ibid.*, p. 72.

[98] Thus Raymond E. Brown says, "The critical import of the parallels between the Scrolls and John is that one can no longer insist that the abstract language spoken by Jesus in the Fourth Gospel *must* have been composed in the Greek world of the early second century A.D. What Jesus says in John would have been quite intelligible in the sectarian background of first-century Palestine" (ET, 78, 1966-67, p. 22). Brown is not dogmatic. He immediately goes on to say, "Yet this observation does not in itself establish that Jesus actually did speak in the way He is quoted by John, for it remains perfectly possible that much of the Qumrân colouring came from the Evangelist." It is this readiness to allow the possibility that those of another opinion may be right that one misses in Braun.

not face this possibility, let alone refute it. I do not wish to be harshly critical. But is there any reason for this other than a dogmatic conviction that "the insights of decades of traditio-historical work" cannot be wrong?

It is true that Braun does speak of John as having an advanced theology, and that he implies that it must be late. But neither Braun nor anyone else known to me has ever produced a convincing reason for holding that on this score John need be any later than, say, Romans. There is no question but that Romans has a weighty theology, and an advanced Christology. And there is no question either but that it is early. It must be dated before the Neronian persecutions, and probably some years before them. On the score of development of theology, then, there is no reason to postulate a late date for John. It always seems to me that radical scholars tend to live in an unreal world when they come to this matter of the time needed to develop a theology. In the case of great theologians of our own time like Barth or Bultmann we have before our very eyes evidence that development can take place much more quickly than these critics commonly allow. If the author of the Fourth Gospel were an original disciple of Jesus (though the very raising of the possibility must be very near to heresy these days!) his theology would have reached something like its fully developed form thirty or forty years after the crucifixion at the latest. This could still place his Gospel quite early. The development of a mature theology certainly takes time. But the time required should not be exaggerated. On this particular ground it does not seem to me that we are required to date the Fourth Gospel very late or to deny that it could have come from an eyewitness.[99]

---

[99] Bultmann notices and rejects the view that John "must be regarded as the culmination of the development that leads out beyond Paul" (*Theology of the New Testament*, II, London, 1955, p. 6). But he does not consider whether John may not, in view of this, be early. He is firmly of the opinion that it was written some time after the Synoptic Gospels, though probably within the first century (p. 10).

JOHN AND "THE TRUTH"

ONE OF JOHN'S MAJOR THEMES IS "THE TRUTH." HE USES the word ἀλήθεια twenty-five times, as against one occurrence in Matthew and three each in Mark and Luke. Similarly he uses the adjective ἀληθής fourteen times (once each in Matthew and Mark, not at all in Luke), and ἀληθινός nine times (not in Matthew or Mark, once in Luke). The very recital of these statistics shows that John is unusually interested in "truth."

He sees truth not only as a quality of words, but also of actions, for it is possible to "do" the truth (John 3:21).[100] Moreover he sees truth as especially connected with Jesus, who indeed may be said to be "the truth" (John 14:6). S. Aalen, in a very important article, sees John's concept of truth as central.[101] It contrasts the true way to God with the false and inadequate ways outlined by other religions. Consequently it constitutes both a rejection of those ways and an invitation to men to walk in the right path.

The fact that truth is one of John's key concepts should not be overlooked. While it is true that he is more concerned to show us the consequences of seeing Jesus as the truth than with any other aspect of truth, yet we cannot let the matter rest there. It would be strange in the extreme if a writer who placed unusual stress on the truth were to sit loose to the truth in a book written about Jesus as the truth. This does not mean, of course, that it would be completely impossible for John to have put down anything that was not strictly true. He might, for example, have held something to be true which in fact was not true. Indeed this is the gravamen of the charge often made against him. He was so sure of the truth of the gospel that he dramatized incidents to bring out this truth. He put down what must have happened in order to show the reality he knew in his heart. But this I question. John's stress on the truth serves as a warning against seeing him as

---

[100] This idea is found also in the Old Testament, namely in Gen. 32:10; 47:29 (in each case see the Hebrew text).

[101] "'Truth', a Key Word in St. John's Gospel," in SE, II, pp. 3-24.

an incurable theological romancer. He does not see truth as comparatively unimportant. On the contrary, for him it is of a critical importance. It is unlikely accordingly that he will tamper with the facts with a view simply to edification. It is the *truth* he is seeking. No one could make truth a central concept in a writing like this Gospel if he knew that the facts were other than he was reporting them. He must have held firmly that his writing expressed the truth as nearly as he could make it.

It is, of course, possible that I have too limited a conception of truth. Certainly some recent writers think that an author might have a regard for "truth" that is perfectly compatible with a readiness to narrate "incidents" that lack factual basis. They suggest that John is like this, and that he is more interested in the truth than in the facts. They may be right; but I cannot see it that way. It is not that the idea shocks me. I see that a writer may take up such a position and that he may make some very telling points. What I cannot see is any real evidence that this is what John is doing. As far as I am able I have thought through all his references to truth, and they do not seem to allow such an interpretation. He may well mean more than we normally mean by truth. I think he does. But he does not mean less.

One point in favor of John's accuracy in narrating incidents, and one that is usually overlooked, arises from a consideration of the speeches in this Gospel. It is a matter of common knowledge that they are all in a uniform style, with no attempt to differentiate the way Jesus spoke from the way anyone else spoke.[102] It is notoriously difficult to be quite sure in some passages

---

[102] On this point Cardinal Newman long ago pointed out that the practice of distinguishing between direct and indirect speech by the use of the first person and the third person is quite modern and was unknown in antiquity. "And so every clause of our Lord's speeches in S. John may be in S. John's Greek, yet every clause may contain the matter which our Lord spoke in Aramaic. Again, S. John might and did select or condense (as being inspired for that purpose) the matter of our Lord's discourses, as that with Nicodemus, and thereby the wording might be S. John's, though the matter might still be our Lord's" (cited in A. Plummer, *The Gospel according to S. John*, Cambridge, 1882, p. 100).

whether we are dealing with a continuation of a speech by Jesus or with the Evangelist's own comments. This, of course, is often used as an argument that the speeches are the literary creation of the author (an argument which must be taken with full seriousness).[103] But this uniformity of style also forms an argument for something quite different. It shows that John was not interested in creating verisimilitude. It would not have been difficult for him to make his narrative appear life-like by making his characters speak in different styles. The fact that he has not done this is reason for holding that he was not interested in verisimilitude. This being the case we are justified in asking on what grounds it can be urged that he created incidents or parts of incidents to give verisimilitude to his Gospel. As he has set down the speeches just as they came to him so we must expect is it with the incidents. In neither case is there a striving for effect.

With this we should take John's stress on witness. He uses the noun μαρτυρία fourteen times (not in Matthew, three times in Mark and once in Luke), and the verb μαρτυρέω thirty-three times (once each in Matthew and Luke and not in Mark). Obviously this is another of his characteristic concepts. He sees witness as borne by deity: the Father (John 5:31f., etc.), the Son (John 8:14, 18), and the Spirit (John 15:26). Jesus' works bore witness (John 5:36; 10:25), as did the inspired Scripture (John 5:39). There was testimony also from a variety of human witnesses, which in this case could, of course, be verified and interrogated by normal human processes. Among such witnesses are the Samaritan woman (John 4:39), the disciples (John 15:27), John the Baptist (John 1:7, etc.), and even the multitude (John 12:17).

This emphasis on witness is noteworthy. Witness is a legal term. It points to valid testimony, to that which will carry conviction in a court of law. It is incompatible with hearsay or with a romantic elaboration of a theological kind based on the barest minimum of fact.

---

[103] See below, pp. 128f., 135f.

At the very least, John's habitual use of the category of witness shows that he is quite confident that his facts cannot be controverted. There is perhaps significance in the fact that the Synoptics have nothing like this. The confident appeal to witnesses is John's own.

In this connection we must protest against a good deal of the method of those scholars who assume that John simply wrote out of the needs of the church of his day. The thought is that John is not trying to tell us what Jesus said and did, but what He would have said and done had He been trying to deal with the situation in which John and his readers found themselves. The discourses and incidents are thus regarded as the author's more or less free compositions to meet the needs he saw.

To deal with this kind of thing at all fully would be to embark on a lengthy examination. But we may take an example, namely Cullmann's treatment of John 4:38, "I sent you to reap that whereon ye have not labored: others have labored, and ye are entered into their labor." He sees this saying as taking its origin not from any situation in the life of Jesus but from the missionary situation posed by the spread of the gospel to Samaria. Cullmann takes the "others" of this verse to mean the Hellenists of Acts 8 who took the Christian gospel to Samaria. The apostles did not come until later and they thus entered into the fruits of the labors of their predecessors. Cullmann thinks that John's aim is "to show that the Christ of the Church corresponds to the Jesus of history, and to trace the direct connection between the life of Jesus and the varied expressions of Church life."[104] In John 4 in pursuance of that aim he thinks that John is concerned to show that the mission of the Hellenists to Samaria was not a private venture, but "was intended by Christ."[105] In other words, though the passage purports to tell of an incident in the life of our Lord it actually refers to no such incident, but to a situation in the life of the church.

But Cullmann has come short of demonstrating his thesis. J. A. T. Robinson has subjected his contention to

[104] *Op. cit.*, p. 186.
[105] *Ibid.*, p. 192.

a close scrutiny in an article called, "The 'Others' of John 4, 38," with the significant subtitle, "A test of exegetical method."[106] He is able to show without much difficulty that Cullmann's thesis, that there is no satisfactory historical situation in the life of Jesus to which these words can be applied, is not accurate. There is the ministry of John the Baptist and his followers, for example (and other suggestions have at times been made with a greater or lesser show of plausibility). The point is that when we put to the test the suggestion that John was in the habit of manufacturing incidents on which to hang his instruction for the church of the day, it is found wanting. Robinson's conclusion is worth noticing: "It is, I believe, by taking the historical setting of St. John's narrative seriously, and not by playing ducks and drakes with it, that we shall be led to a true appreciation of his profound reverence for the history of Jesus as the indispensable and inexpendable locus for the revelation of the eternal *Logos* itself."[107]

In point of fact John was scarcely in a position to manufacture his incidents and his sayings. It is agreed by nearly all students that one of the aims of this Evangelist was to deal with opponents of a Docetic type.[108] In effect these men denied the reality of the incarnation. They denied the reality of the experiences attributed to Jesus, or at least they denied their reality as having happened to the Christ of God. John affirms that "the Word became flesh" (1:14) and writes his Gospel so as to bring out the truth of this affirmation. The Docetists just as emphatically denied it. For them the Godhead could not defile itself with any contact with sinful flesh.

---

[106] SE, I, pp. 510-515.

[107] *Ibid.*, p. 515.

[108] Cf. Conzelmann: "... We also cannot eliminate the identity of the risen Lord with the earthly Jesus without falling prey to docetism and robbing ourselves of the possibility of distinguishing the community's Easter faith from a myth" (quoted in Braaten and Harrisville, *op. cit.*, p. 116). This warning must be borne in mind in connection with John's whole method. Incidentally it is curious to see the way in which some scholars emphatically repudiate Docetism, but refuse to see any solid grounds for refuting it.

All here was "seeming." In the face of such teaching John
stressed the actuality of the incarnation.[109] But he could
do this only by keeping strictly to historical events. He
was on safe ground only as long as he kept to the facts.
The moment he made use of a fabricated incident he
laid himself open to the accusation that he was proceeding
along exactly the same lines as did the Docetists. If his
"incidents" had no reality outside his fertile brain then
in fact he was not basically different from them. They
could accept "incidents" and indeed a whole "incarnation"
of this type. In fact this was their essential position. It
was the factuality of what Jesus did (and specifically of
his contact with matter) that they denied. They had no
interest in denying edifying stories that had no factual
basis but were only a teaching medium. They could fairly
claim that they were stressing the spiritual reality while
they denied the physical events of the life of Christ.
Whatever his personal inclinations may have been, John
was thus compelled by the nature of the opposition he
faced to stick to events that both he and his readers could
recognize as factual. The moment he departed from such
a practice he gave his case away. A general respect for
history was not enough. He had to carry this over to the
concrete examples he used.[110] In the face of those who
assert that to John the spiritual significance is everything
and the historicity immaterial, the question must be
pressed, "What is the theological meaning of something
that never happened?" The very idea of bringing out
theological significance seems to imply respect for the
facts. What did not happen can scarcely be called redemptive.[111] But John was concerned with the large issue of

---

[109] Cf. Hoskyns: ". . . His whole conscious intention is to force his
readers back upon the life of Jesus in the flesh and upon His death
in the flesh, as *the place of understanding:* he is therefore guilty
of gross self-deception if he is inventing or distorting the visible
likeness of Jesus to further his purpose" (*op. cit.,* p. 117).

[110] Cf. J. A. T. Robinson: "It is astonishing how readily critics
have assumed that our Evangelist attached the greatest importance
to historicity in general and had but the lightest regard for it in
particular" (*op. cit.,* p. 344).

[111] Cf. Braaten's account of Kähler: "The meaning of the kerygma is nullified if the redemptive events attested — including in-

the way God saves men and brings them to everlasting life.

It is worth mentioning here that many historians are not as sceptical about the value of the Gospels in general and of John in particular as historical sources as are some New Testament scholars. It would be preposterous to suggest that they feel that all is well in the Johannine garden. They are more than a little hesitant, and that at a number of points. All that I am pointing out here is that John has convinced some very hardheaded scholars that he has access to good tradition, and that there are many points in his Gospel which must be unhesitatingly accepted as factual. Schleiermacher is a well-known example of one who looked to John to provide material for a life of Jesus. And M. Goguel, though sceptical about much in all the Gospels, has found Johannine teaching of great importance. There is much from the Fourth Gospel in his *The Life of Jesus*.[112]

Perhaps more important is the thorough examination made by C. H. Dodd in his book, *Historical Tradition in the Fourth Gospel*.[113] Dodd is not arguing for a conservative position, and he freely concedes that theological motives have been at work in the Fourth Gospel, sometimes resulting in distortion. But the main drift of his argument is that behind this Gospel there lies a very early tradition,[114] and one independent of that behind the Synoptic Gospels. This is a serious historical judg-

---

carnation, life and teachings, cross and resurrection — never happened. Faith cannot appropriate the meaning of events if there are no events in the first place" (Braaten and Harrisville, *op. cit.*, p. 101).

[112] London, 1958. E. Stauffer is another to make a good deal of use of John (*Jesus and His Story*, London, 1960).

[113] Cambridge, 1963. In this book Dodd dissents from the view that the religious interests of the Evangelists disqualify them from being seriously considered as historical sources. He reminds us that "It was not for nothing that the early Church repudiated gnosticism, with all its speculative breadth and subtlety and its imaginative mythology" (*op. cit.*, p. 2). Facts were too important for that, and this should be remembered when assessing the Gospels.

[114] Bent Noack holds that the entire Fourth Gospel arose directly from oral tradition (see D. M. Smith, *The Composition and Order of the Fourth Gospel*, Yale, 1965, pp. 74f.).

ment, and is not lightly to be rejected. The work of P. Gardner-Smith already referred to had already convinced many that this Gospel must be thought of as independent. But Dodd's book is much more detailed and thorough. It is difficult to see how the main conclusion can be disputed. But if we accept it then it follows that part, at any rate, of this Gospel must be held to be very reliable.[115]

SYNOPTIC AND JOHANNINE IDEAS

THE QUESTION OF THE HISTORICITY OF THE FOURTH GOSPEL has often been pursued by concentrating on the incidents and the words it has in common with the Synoptics. Since, apart from the passion narrative, the number of incidents common to the two is very small, and since there are striking differences in vocabulary, it has been widely held that John's narrative must be viewed with the gravest suspicion. But it is not necessary for us to concentrate all our attention on minutiae. It is possible to give attention to the great ideas of this literature, and when we do it appears that John is not as dissimilar from the Synoptics as is sometimes thought. B. Balmforth has subjected the structure of the Second and Fourth Gospels to close scrutiny and finds that they are much the same. As an example of his method let us take the following reference to John 2—4:

> There is a miracle that Mark never mentions, a cleansing of the Temple that Mark puts at the end of the story, not at the beginning, and two long discourses, with a certain Nicodemus about new birth, and with an anonymous Samaritan woman about water and worship. Mark had given a short, straightforward

---

[115] Sometimes John is even reproached for being too accurate to be true! Thus A. J. B. Higgins points out that the saying about the temple being forty-six years in building would make the date of the saying 27 or 28 A.D., since Herod began building in the eighteenth year of his reign (20-19 BC). He comments, "If the ministry according to John lasted about two years, and A.D. 30 is taken as the year of the crucifixion, A.D. 28 as the year of Jesus' first visit to Jerusalem would fit perfectly his placing of the saying. But this is probably too neat" (*The Historicity of the Fourth Gospel*, London, 1960, p. 46, n. 4).

narrative of how Jesus came proclaiming the advent
of the Kingdom of God and making its presence known
by mighty words and mighty works. Yet is not John
doing precisely the same thing? The Kingdom is the
dominant theme of the tradition about Jesus' teaching, its leading motif from the beginning, when Jesus
came declaring that the time was fulfilled and men
must repent and believe the good news. And here
John takes this theme and, as his manner is, unfolds
the underlying meaning of the tremendous phrase
βασιλεία θεοῦ. At Cana of Galilee the waters of Judaism
are changed into the wine of the new age of the
Kingdom. The cleansing of the Temple is seen as more
than an explosive act of prophetic indignation; it
signifies the passing of the old worship 'through
the blood of goats and calves' and the coming of
the new worship in 'the temple of his body', the messianic community. In both these signs we are to see
the new age of the Kingdom bursting forth from the
old order. The two discourses reinforce and expound
the truth shown in the signs. In the discourse with
Nicodemus we have the theme of spiritual rebirth
ἄνωθεν. In the discourse with the woman of Samaria
we hear of new life given, new and true worship
made possible: the life and worship of the citizens
of the Kingdom.[116]

Balmforth concludes that the main lines and the struc-
tural themes in these two Gospels are the same. John
was not trying to put before men a different gospel.
This is, of course, essentially the point made years ago
by A. M. Hunter, when he argued that John was not
saying something different from the Synoptists or from
Paul or other New Testament writers when he used
his characteristic terminology, but conveying the same
basic Christian message in his own way.[117] It is important not to see things too small. There can be basic
unity even where the terminology is strikingly different.

A slightly different twist can be given to this by pointing out that there is an interrelationship between the
Synoptic Gospels and John. I have elsewhere argued
that there are many points where the Synoptic teaching

[116] SE, II, pp. 28f.
[117] See the passages quoted on pp. 106f. above.

is difficult or impossible unless we interpret it in the light of John.[118] Occasionally the reverse is true. There is the impressive evidence that the traditions represented in the Synoptic Gospels on the one hand, and in John on the other, supplement and illuminate each other.

From all this it appears that the ideas in the Synoptics and John are not in conflict. It is the one Christ that lies back of both portraits. We should recognize the differences, but that should not blind us to the fact that the underlying unity is real.

THE ORIGIN OF THE JOHANNINE TRADITION

PROBABLY WHAT LOOMS LARGEST IN MANY MINDS WHEN people think of the problem of history in John is the difference in tone between this Gospel and the Synoptics.[119] We have seen in this study that although there is certainly interpretation in the Fourth Gospel this is no barrier to historicity, since it is interpretation of the kind that we can accept. We have seen also that this is in its measure true of all the Gospels. There is evidence that John is in essential harmony with the Synoptists, and that he is in essential harmony with the facts. Can we go further and say that this Gospel is to be rooted basically in the thought and teaching of Jesus and not in that of the Evangelist? Despite the difficulties, I believe we can.

It is true that, while there is no conflict in the world of ideas, the difference in expression between this Gospel and the other three is such that many people instinctively feel that if the Synoptics give us an authentic picture then John can scarcely be other than erroneous. It is true that in this Gospel it is hard to tell where

---

118 See above, pp. 42ff.

119 Lord Charnwood sees John's concern for Jesus' rejection by the Jews as an adequate explanation of the differences. He says, "The discrepancies between this Gospel and the others are, I think, seen, upon fuller study, to amount to less than they appear to do when first observed. But, if they were more profound than they are, the Evangelist's passionate interest in the Rejection would account for them, in a way which casts no doubt upon his real knowledge of what our Lord was to His disciples" (*According*

118 See above, pp. 42ff.

the words of Jesus end and those of the Evangelist begin. The whole is in a uniform style with no distinction between the words of one and another. It is also true that the style is quite different from that which we see in the Synoptics. One must have sympathy with those who say, "If Jesus spoke in the style with which He is credited in the Synoptics He cannot have spoken as the Fourth Gospel says He did. You cannot have it both ways." This is a very natural reaction. But I doubt whether it expresses all the truth.[120]

There is a difference between the two pictures. But it is possible to account for this difference. The church traditionally has not thought the problem insoluble, for it has adopted this Gospel as well as the other three. There are two considerations that I wish to adduce as significant.

The first is that to many who have a deep understanding of things Jewish the Fourth Gospel rings true. Thus Israel Abrahams can say, "My own general impression, without asserting an early date for the Fourth Gospel, is that that Gospel enshrines a genuine tradition of an aspect of Jesus' teaching which has not found a place in the Synoptics"; and he speaks of "the Fourth Gospel's close acquaintance with Hebraic traditions."[121] Some scholars have failed to discern this, as in F. C. Burkitt's view that "It is quite inconceivable that the historical Jesus of the Synoptic Gospels could have argued and quibbled with opponents, as He is represented

---

[120] R. E. Brown maintains that "it is time to liberate ourselves from the assumption that Jesus' own thought and expression were always simple and always in one style, and that anything that smacks of theological sophistication must come from the (implicitly more intelligent) evangelists" (*The Gospel according to John (i-xii)*, New York, 1966, p. LXIV).

[121] I. Abrahams, *Studies in Pharisaism and the Gospels*, First Series, Cambridge, 1917, pp. 12, 135. Bernard also cites Abrahams: "Most remarkable has been the cumulative strength of the arguments adduced by Jewish writers favourable to the authenticity of the discourses in the Fourth Gospel, especially in relation to the circumstances under which they are reported to have been spoken" (ICC, *St. John*, I, p. lxxxii, n. 3). S. Neill also reports him as saying, "To us Jews the Fourth Gospel is the most Jewish of the four" (*op. cit.*, p. 315).

to have done in the Fourth Gospel."[122] But Burkitt is not typical. To most it seems clear that, wherever it came from, there is an authentic Jewish note in the Fourth Gospel, and that it is in harmony with the spirit of Jesus. The reality behind Burkitt's words is not that Jesus "quibbled" (it is a pity that this great scholar chose to use such a loaded word), but that He met His opponents on their own ground.[123] R. V. G. Tasker reminds us of an important truth when he says, "It is very true that the portrait of the Johannine Christ does not at all square with the portrait that has often been drawn of Him by liberal theologians. But we have to remember that Jesus was put to death not because He was inoffensive, but because He struck at the roots of the pride, the prejudices, and the self-satisfaction of mankind."[124] It simply will not do to say that we know enough about Jesus from the Synoptists to know that He could not have been as John depicts Him. The Johannine portrait is lifelike. There is that in it which is not typical of the Synoptists, but we cannot without further ado put this down to a Hellenist or to some other who did not know Palestine. The teaching of this Gospel is redolent of the Holy Land. This does not, of course, mean that it is necessarily authentic. But it is a first step in that direction.

It should not be overlooked that the Synoptics contain at least one snippet of teaching that is definitely of a Johannine type: "I thank thee, O Father, Lord

---

[122] F. C. Burkitt, *The Gospel History and its Transmission*, Edinburgh, 1907, p. 228.

[123] Cf. R. V. G. Tasker: "Though at times the utterances of Jesus in this Gospel sound harsh, particularly to those who overemphasise the gentleness of Jesus' nature, there is no valid reason for supposing that, when dealing with the Rabbis at Jerusalem, Jesus did not debate with them in rabbinical fashion the nature of His claims; and it may well be just this side of the Lord's ministry that the Galilean disciples knew little about, but with which the Fourth Evangelist was more familiar, particularly if, as has already been suggested, he was himself a Jerusalem disciple" (*The Nature and Purpose of the Gospels*, London, 1962, pp. 96f.).

[124] Tasker, *The Gospel according to St. John*, London and Grand Rapids, 1960, p. 31.

of heaven and earth, that thou didst hide these things
from the wise and understanding, and didst reveal them
unto babes: yea, Father, for so it was well-pleasing in
thy sight. All things have been delivered unto me of my
Father: and no one knoweth the Son, save the Father;
neither doth any know the Father, save the Son, and he
to whomsoever the Son willeth to reveal him" (Matt. 11:
25ff.). That more of this type of teaching is not recorded is not really surprising. Even assuming that they
had access to it in their tradition, setting it down is
not easy (try recalling these exact words!). Nor is it
congenial to all. The minds of the Synoptists appear to
have moved rather differently. And they record the things
in which they are interested and which have relevance
to their purpose. They omit what is not. But what they
omit is not necessarily unauthentic. To affirm the contrary is to make the gate far too narrow.[125]

MEMORIZATION IN THE FIRST CENTURY

THE SECOND CONSIDERATION I WISH TO ADDUCE IS THE
point made by H. Riesenfeld that the methods of teaching in the first century featured memory work.[126] Every
Rabbi required his followers to commit to memory the
essentials of his teaching. The very word κατηχέω, which
is frequently used of the teaching process, reveals what
was done. The verb means "to sound down upon." The
teacher "sounded down" upon the class, and the class
echoed back his words. This continued until the lesson
was learned. The good teacher would, of course, set out
his teaching in forms that could be memorized easily.
It is well known that the Mishnah was not committed to

---

[125] C. H. Dodd regards this saying as one of those which serve
"as warning against a hasty assumption that nothing in the
Fourth Gospel which cannot be corroborated from the Synoptics
has any claim to be regarded as part of the early tradition of
the sayings of Jesus" (HTFG, p. 431). He has already pointed
out that "If [Matthew and Luke] had not happened to include
this one isolated saying, we should never have suspected that we
had before us anything but a purely Johannine theologumenon"
(ibid.).

[126] H. Riesenfeld, "The Gospel Tradition and its Beginnings,"
SE, I, pp. 43-65.

writing for many years after New Testament times, for it was held that a scholar ought to know and not simply to read what he had been taught. Any student worth his salt would remember things accurately and not require such aids as books. Some phenomenal feats of memory are on record.[127] There is nothing improbable in the suggestion that Jesus perpetuated the essential features of His teaching by getting His followers to learn them by heart. Indeed, much of the teaching in the Synoptic Gospels looks like this kind of teaching. It is the sort of thing that might stick in the memory, and it is of set purpose put in such memorizable form. It is Riesenfeld's contention that it is essentially this kind of activity that lies behind the traditions recorded in the Synoptic Gospels. He can say, "And this implies that Jesus made his disciples, and above all the Twelve, learn, and furthermore that he made them learn by heart"; ". . . What was essential to his message he taught his disciples, that is, he made them learn it by heart."[128]

The stories of Jesus' deeds may well have been embodied in the tradition in much the same way. As the

---

[127] Thus R. Meir, on discovering that there was no copy of the book of Esther in a city he was visiting, promptly wrote one out (Meg. 18b). This kind of practice was not encouraged except in an emergency. Thus R. Ḥisda urged R. Ḥananel to desist when he found him writing scrolls without a copy, though he admitted, "You are quite qualified to write the whole Torah by heart" (Meg. 18b). A *tanna* must know "law, Sifra, Sifre and Tosefta" (Kidd. 49b). There is a story of R. Ḥiyya that he wrote out the five books of Moses and taught one to each of five children, and taught one of the six orders (of the Mishnah? the Talmud?) to each of six other children (Ket. 103b says he was ready to do this; BM 85b that he did it). Gerhardsson quotes a saying of R. Ishmael b. Jose, "I can write out the whole Scripture from my memory" (*Memory and Manuscript*, Lund, 1964, p. 46, n. 4). Bruce M. Metzger lists a number of places where not outstanding scholars, but every humble candidate for ordination to the Christian ministry was required to have memorized whole books of the Bible (*The Text of the New Testament*, Oxford, 1964, p. 87, n. 1).

[128] *Op. cit.*, pp. 59, 61. Also, "The essential point is that the outlines, that is, the beginnings of the proper genus of the tradition of the words and deeds of Jesus, were memorized and recited as holy Word. We should be inclined to trace these outlines back to Jesus' activity as a teacher in the circle of his disciples" (p. 63).

Master taught His disciples to pass on His sayings, what was more natural than that they should commit to memory and pass on accounts of outstanding and important deeds, especially if they led up to memorable sayings? What was thus begun by our Lord and His apostles would then have been carried on in the oral tradition of the early church (this may allow the form critics to have their say). But Riesenfeld's contention is that the origin of it all is in the instruction given by Jesus and memorized by the disciples, not in the preaching of the church. Those who affirm otherwise do not always keep in mind the methods of first-century Jewish teachers. When this is done the Synoptic teaching is seen to have all the hallmarks of the kind of teaching that must go back ultimately to the Master.

INFORMAL INSTRUCTION

BUT A RABBI DID MORE THAN SELECT EPIGRAMS FOR HIS disciples to memorize. In addition to his formal teaching, systematically committed to the memories of his students, there would be instruction of a more informal kind. There is an informality back of every teacher where the real man is revealed in a way different from that which we see when he is engaged in public teaching. He will engage in "table talk," that intimate intercourse when teaching as such is not primarily in mind at all (nor wholly out of mind!), and when one mind takes fire from another. There must have been something of this in Jesus' relationship to His followers, and there is no reason why it should not have led to a quite distinct type of tradition. Riesenfeld thinks that the starting point of the Johannine tradition is to be found in this sort of thing, "in the discourses and 'meditations' of Jesus in the circle of his disciples, such as certainly took place side by side with the instruction of the disciples proper, with its more rigid forms."[129] It is plain

---

[129] *Ibid.*, p. 63. Riesenfeld's work has been subjected to expansion by B. Gerhardsson in *Memory and Manuscript*, and to criticism by many (see, for example, C. F. Evans in *Theology*, 61, 1958, pp. 355-362). A useful short account is that by J. J. Vincent, SE, III, pp. 105-118. Ned B. Stonehouse criticizes certain features of

enough that there is a meditator behind the Fourth Gospel. But why should we insist that the meditator is John?
Why should it not be Jesus?[130]

A record of "table talk," where no attempt was made
by Jesus to lay down what must be remembered and to
differentiate it from what is less important, will necessarily reflect something of the recorder as well as of
the Speaker. His own interests will account for the
selection, and he will reproduce both words and sayings as they have been stored in his mind. But this
element of personal interpretation does not mean error,
nor a failure to give due regard to testimony.[131]

It is also worth reflecting that the teaching recorded
in the Synoptics is small in quantity. It is impossible to
hold that it represents the entire teaching of a great

Riesenfeld's position (see *Origins of the Synoptic Gospels*, Grand
Rapids, 1963, pp. 138-145). But he quotes approvingly Riesenfeld's
words, "Jesus is the object and subject of a tradition of authoritative and holy words which he himself created and entrusted to his
disciples for its later transmission in the epoch between his death
and the parousia" (*ibid.*, p. 148).

[130] Notice that this is not the view that "the synoptic sayings
contained Jesus' public teaching, while the Johannine were drawn
from his secret instruction addressed to the disciples — an ancient
Gnostic view" (F. C. Grant, *The Gospel of John*, New York and
London, 1956, p. 6; Grant points out that this theory is refuted
by John 18:19-21). There is no question of the Fourth Gospel as
representing an esoteric teaching, carefully hidden from all but
an inner circle. What is contended is rather that it differs from
teaching intended from the first for memorization and couched in a
style suited thereto. It is less premeditated utterance, and more
the reaction to opponents and quiet reflection among friends.

[131] H. E. Edwards sees evidence that the Gospel is a record of
what John actually said (rather than wrote): "... We have preserved for us no general impression of what 'S. John' said, but a
trustworthy reproduction of his actual words" (*The Disciple Who
Wrote These Things*, London, 1953, p. 31). He draws attention to a
note of G. Milligan which demonstrates the existence of shorthand.
Milligan cites a papyrus concerning the apprenticing of a slave to
a shorthand writer, for a payment of 120 drachmae. The teacher
has received 40 drachmae; he is to receive a similar sum when the
boy has learned the whole system and the final instalment when
he "writes fluently in every respect and reads faultlessly" (*Here
and There among the Papyri*, London, 1922, p. 46). Since the art
was known there is no reason why it should not have been used
for the recording of St. John's words.

religious figure. Moreover, much of it is spoken either in the hearing of or with a view to those outside the circle of the disciples. In other words, it is the kind of thing Jesus meant for public circulation. It does not preclude other teaching of a different type.

F. L. Godet long ago stressed this point. "The general tradition, which forms the basis of the three Synoptical Gospels," he wrote, "was formulated with a view to the popular preaching, and to serve the ends of the apostolic mission.... Now, it was in Galilee, that province which was relatively independent of the centre, that the ministry of Jesus had especially displayed its creative power and produced positive results." Godet goes on to suggest that at Jerusalem "the hostile element by which Jesus found Himself surrounded, forced Him into incessant controversy. In this situation, no doubt, the testimony which He was obliged to give for Himself took more energetic forms and a sterner tone. It became more theological, if we may so speak; consequently less popular."[132] A Gospel that gives greater attention to Jerusalem is bound, if there is anything in what Godet says, to differ markedly from those which concentrate on Galilee.

Admittedly this approach does not explain everything. It does not explain, for example, the uniform style of the Fourth Gospel whether it is Jesus or anyone else who is speaking. Yet we must bear in mind that Jesus and the other participants in the Gospel activity spoke in Aramaic, whereas the Gospel is written in Greek. If we can hold that John entered more fully than most into a sympathetic understanding of the Master,[133] then we may well feel that when he reported His words in an alien tongue he is likely to have been faithful to the original thrust of the words, even though he took no trouble to reproduce the nuances of style.[134] This process of trans-

---

[132] Op. cit., I, pp. 448f.

[133] In quite another connection P. H. Boulton says, "Thus to be a διάκονος in the mind of S. John — and, I would submit, he presents us with the mind of Christ..." (SE, I, p. 422). Such a comment might often be made.

[134] Cf. Westcott: "... It is quite conceivable that the meaning and effect of a long discourse, when reduced to a brief abstract, may be

lation may in fact be the basic reason for the fact that John gives us no differences of style. He was not reporting the words as originally spoken, but giving his version of them in his own translation.

The thought that this Gospel brings us a picture of Jesus not taken from the public ministry may help us also with the disputations that John records. We have already noted the opinion of Abrahams and others that this Gospel rings true to the Hebraic background.[135] May it not be that John reports with accuracy certain disputes which Jesus had with His enemies and which were not transmitted in the Synoptic tradition at all?[136] A few disputes are included there, but in view of the manner in which Jesus met His death we cannot feel that it is anything like the total number. John's account is certainly lifelike.

William Temple reminds us that we should not overlook the personalities of the Evangelists. He reminds us that John was called "Son of Thunder," and suggests that something of this temperament survived till the writ-

---

conveyed most truly by the use of a different style, and even, to a certain extent, of different language from that actually employed"; "Compression involves adaptation of phraseology" (*The Gospel According to St. John*, I, Grand Rapids, 1954, pp. cxv, cxvi). Hoskyns notices these passages and goes on, "The final question is, therefore, not whether the Evangelist has or has not employed his own style and language, but whether the words were fitted to convey to us the meaning of the Lord" (*op. cit.*, p. 44).

[135] A. Corell finds in this Gospel "teaching presented in the form employed by the Jewish rabbis, which was doubtless the form also used by Jesus himself. Now if this latter proves to be true, our confidence in the historical value of the Fourth Gospel will be greatly increased; for, thanks to the teaching technique employed here, many sayings of Jesus will have been preserved in their original form" (*Consummatum Est*, London, 1958, p. 47). Since Corell is speaking of certain units and not the Gospel as a whole, this is not a contradiction of Riesenfeld's position.

[136] Cf. R. H. Strachan: ". . . We must remember that, in the Synoptic Gospels, we have few occasions on which Jesus and the ecclesiastical authorities meet in controversy within the synagogue" (*The Fourth Gospel*, London, 1955, p. 211). Strachan goes on to notice the sternness with which Jesus speaks of the blasphemy against the Spirit (Matt. 12:31), the "prophetic passion" with which He denounces the Pharisees (Matt. 23:1-36), etc., as evidence that the temper of the disputes in the Fourth Gospel is in accordance with the Synoptic picture.

ing of this Gospel. "St. John records no saying of the Lord which shews sympathy for the difficulty which the Jews had in recognising Him, such as that which very characteristically St. Luke reports, 'No man having drunk old wine desireth new: for he saith, The old is good' (*St. Luke* v, 39)."[137] We should not reason as though the Evangelists were mechanical reporters. They were human, perhaps at times all too human. The kind of teaching and acting they recorded depended on a number of factors, e.g. their memories, their aims in writing, and not least the kind of men they were.

It is not necessary to agree with everything said by Riesenfeld and his supporters to see that theirs is a very suggestive approach. *A priori* there seems no reason why Jesus should not have made His disciples learn certain things, nor that this should have formed the starting point of the Synoptic tradition. Other teachers relied heavily on the memory work of their disciples and it is highly probable that Jesus also made use of the method. But if He did, it is not in the least improbable, in fact it is quite certain, that He would also have engaged in more informal conversations with His friends and disputes with His enemies. We have no reason for thinking that all this would either have been lost or gathered into the Synoptic tradition. We are not in a position to deny that it led to the emergence of the Johannine tradition. We are not in a position either to assert that the Johannine tradition emerged in this fashion, but we can say that there is a reasonable probability. And if this was indeed the way things happened, many things are explained. This will preclude us from denying the historicity of John simply because the tradition embodied in this Gospel is in some ways markedly different from that in the Synoptics.[138]

*   *   *

MY CONCLUSION IS THAT MANY RECENT SCHOLARS HAVE

---

[137] William Temple, *Readings in St. John's Gospel*, London, 1947, p. 105.

[138] It is perhaps worth adding that A. Richardson thinks that historical perspective is important. He sees John as written late, and regards this not as historically disadvantageous but rather the reverse. The historical significance of great events cannot be

been too hasty in denying that John is to be taken seriously when we look for history. There are several factors
that indicate that this history is reliable. John does not
sit loose to facts.[139] And there is one way, at least, of
accounting for the differences from the Synoptic Gospels.
I do not say that this is necessarily the right way, but at
least it opens up a possibility. This being so, the indications of accuracy that we noted earlier must be given
their full weight. John is not careless about the factual-
ness of his narrative. On the contrary, he seems determined to make it clear that his work is to be trusted.
And in this twentieth century there is still good ground
for agreeing.

Perhaps we could say, "especially in this twentieth
century," for it is worth noting that there is more
evidence now to support conservative scholars than at
any previous time. Green-Armytage says forthrightly
that conservative students of John "can claim with justice
that every new discovery, literary or archeological, made
in the past hundred years has always proved favourable
to their side, never to that of their opponents."[140] Those
who hold to radical positions at the present time do so
not because they have any more evidence than their
predecessors had, but because of their subjective evaluation of the evidence.

---

discerned by those who are too close to them. We must allow the
passage of time for perspective to develop. But histories with
perspective are not for this reason to be distrusted. John he
thinks to be a later interpretation than the Synoptics, based on no
new evidence, "but it may give us a profoundly illuminating repre-
sentation of the truth of history. In this most important sense the
Fourth Gospel is thoroughly historical" (*History, Sacred and
Profane*, London, 1964, p. 239).

[139] Hoskyns draws attention to the uneasiness of some of the
older scholars to whom it seemed that "the critics were tumbling
over the precipice into the abyss, chanting a hymn in praise of the
nobility of free and unfettered debate and research and investigation" (*op. cit.*, p. 39). These words are still worth pondering. It is
possible to be so caught up in the delightful critical problems that
John poses, so sure that we can fault him here and here, that we
miss the great thing that he is saying.

[140] *Op. cit.*, p. 19. He further cites Vincent Taylor: "In the case
of John, the whole history of radical criticism is the story of a
continual retreat."

Chapter Three

Was the Author of the Fourth Gospel an "Eyewitness"?

TRADITIONALLY, CONSERVATIVE THEOLOGIANS HAVE affirmed emphatically that the evidence shows that behind the Fourth Gospel is the testimony of an eyewitness of the scenes described. This is held to give the Gospel much of its value. This is not an invention of the conservatives. J. A. T. Robinson has said, "The narrative is patently presented as that of an eye-witness and if that claim is groundless it affects our total assessment of it."[1] Some radical critics find little of value in the thesis. They are more impressed by the evidence they discern that the author lacked exact knowledge at least in some particulars. In my opinion there is more to be said for the former position. But the evidence is rarely marshalled these days, and it may be profitable to assemble some of the indications that are urged for and against the thesis.[2]

Let us begin with the notes of time in the first chapter. Various things are said to have happened on a certain day (John 1:19-28). The next day is mentioned in v. 29, and a third day in v. 35. Most see a reference to a further day in v. 41, though this is not explicit (unless we accept

[1] SE, I, p. 349.
[2] Estimates of what are and what are not the touches of an eyewitness are very subjective, so in this discussion I have relied for the most part upon those passages in which responsible commentators have expressed an opinion.

the reading "early" instead of "first"). The fifth day comes to the surface in v. 43. It would take two days to travel from the Jordan in chapter 1 to Cana of Galilee, which explains "the third day" of 2:1 (according to the inclusive method of counting in vogue among the Jews). All this seems to Strachan to point "ultimately to someone who remembered the happenings of one momentous week before the public ministry began, and whose recollections, probably in written form, were available."[3] He puts this in a form that indicates that the observer was not the Evangelist. But this is not a necessary deduction. The point is that this opening chapter gives evidence of the reminiscences of someone who knew what had happened. The alternative would be to see these time references as simply a dramatic framework, perhaps paralleling the seven days of the first creation in Genesis 1. Against this is the fact that the "framework" is so little emphasized that some have doubted its existence. And nothing is said about what was done on one of the days. Personal reminiscence is a more likely explanation.

This first chapter affords an example of John's habit of noticing the time of day when events happened. Andrew and his companion came to Jesus at "about the tenth hour" (v. 39). This indication of the precise time at which events took place recurs (see 4:6, 52; 18:28; 19:14; 20:19). There seems no point in this kind of thing if the writer is late and without personal knowledge of what happened. There is no symbolical meaning in these references (or at least none that I can discern).[4] On the hypothesis that the writer did not know Palestine these time notes are an enigma. But they are natural touches if the author had been there and remembered when things took place. It is important to notice that this happens often enough to be significant, but not so often that we

---

[3] Strachan, *The Fourth Gospel*, London, 1955, p. 121. He goes on, "That he should thus preserve the chronological arrangement of his source indicates that the stories of the Baptist and of the call of the various disciples have an historical basis."

[4] Bultmann, it is true, sees symbolism: ". . . The tenth hour is the hour of fulfilment" (*Das Evangelium des Johannes*, Göttingen, 1956, p. 70). This seems farfetched to me, and it does not account for the fact that John has other such time notes.

may say, "This is a touch added to give verisimilitude." Were the latter the case it would be reasonable to expect that it would take place fairly consistently.

Toward the end of the first chapter some titles of Jesus are of interest. Thus Nathanael, after asking scornfully, "Can any good thing come out of Nazareth?" was persuaded by Jesus' greeting and saluted Him in the words: "Thou art the Son of God; thou art King of Israel" (John 1:46-49). It is not without its interest that Nathanael has "King of Israel" as his climax. More important is the fact that he uses the title at all. After the fall of Jerusalem in AD 70 it is difficult to see how the expression could have been used. It must go back to early days.[5] This is the kind of touch which is natural enough in someone who remembered what took place, but which is difficult to explain in a late writer, composing freely without factual basis. N. E. Johnson says of this incident, along with those dealing with Nicodemus and Lazarus, ". . . They should be taken at their face-value and treated as historically accurate. If we do this, their vivid characterizations cannot be overlooked, and we may quite reasonably suppose that the details come from an eyewitness source."[6] Johnson's view is all the more significant in that he accepts the view that the Gospel as a whole was not written by the apostle. Agreeing with this modern view he yet cannot overlook the fact that some passages, at least, bear the stamp of an eyewitness.

William Temple makes an important point in connection with the "confessions" in this chapter. He accepts the Marcan framework, and he thinks that the confession of Peter at Caesarea Philippi "is both a novelty and a

---

[5] Cf. A. Plummer: ". . . It points to hopes of an earthly king, which since the destruction of Jerusalem even Jews must have ceased to cherish. How could a Christian of the second century have thrown himself back to this?" (CGT, John, p. 87). C. H. Dodd also sees in this "a primitive title," and one which "smacks of a messianism more Jewish than Christian" (HTFG, p. 155). Elsewhere he reminds us that claims made for Jesus with political aspects "are not late accretions upon the tradition" but early, belonging in fact "to a stage of affairs in Palestine which soon lost interest for the Church in its mission to the world" (*op. cit.*, p. 216).

[6] CQR, 167, 1966, p. 280.

turning point." Nevertheless he is impressed by the
indications of authenticity in this chapter. "So much of
this chapter has the 'feel' of exact memory that I am
uneasy about an interpretation which involves a view of
it as pervasively influenced by an imagination stimulated
by later beliefs." He solves his dilemma by thinking of
"the striking confessions here" as "outbursts of an exalted
hope rather than formulations of settled conviction."[7] The
important point for us is not the way Temple solves his
problem, but the fact that the problem exists for him. He
thinks that the recognition of Jesus as the Christ did not
come about until Caesarea Philippi. But there is so much
in John 1 that "has the 'feel' of exact memory" that he
cannot pass it by. In the judgment of one competent
scholar there is an authentic ring about this section of
the Gospel.

"HIS" DISCIPLES

IN THE SECOND CHAPTER THERE IS A SMALL TOUCH. JOHN
says that Jesus was invited to the wedding in Cana, "and
his disciples" (v. 2). The use of the expression "his
disciples" rather than "the disciples" is characteristic of
John (also incidentally of Mark), and it points to an
early period. At first, the followers of Jesus were called
"His" to distinguish them from the disciples of other
Rabbis. But as the Christian movement developed the first
followers of Christ by a natural process were elevated to
a unique place in the Christian scheme of things. The
term "disciples" no longer aroused memories of many
Jewish teachers with the necessity for distinguishing
between the followers of Jesus and those of others. "The"
disciples now stood for Jesus' followers only. John's usage
is the early one.

A little later in the chapter John records that Jesus,

---

[7] William Temple, *Readings in St. John's Gospel*, London, 1947,
p. 32. Cf. also the verdict of Theo Preiss on one of the titles used
here, "the Son of man" (v. 51): "The title which Jesus himself
prefers and remarkably enough, as in the Synoptics, is found only
on his lips — is that of Son of Man. Do we not see there another
proof, indirect, but very substantial, of the definitely ancient
character of the Johannine tradition?" (*Life in Christ*, London,
1954, p. 24).

His family, and His disciples went down to Capernaum (v. 12). This looks like a reminiscence from one who recalled the event. The visit to Capernaum is sandwiched in between the story of the marriage in Cana and the account of the cleansing of the temple. It is neither prepared for nor followed up. It is difficult to imagine why a late writer should introduce such an apparently irrelevant remark into his narrative. From the Synoptists we know that Jesus spent a lot of time at Capernaum. It was even called "His" city (Matt. 9:1). Thus there is nothing at all improbable in John's statement. But its introduction by someone who was composing a fictional gospel is difficult to account for.

John adds a time note, "The passover of the Jews was at hand" (v. 13), which he reinforces a little later, when he tells us that Jesus "was in Jerusalem at the passover" (v. 23). C. H. Turner sees these as the first of six such time notes which he regards as resting on accurate knowledge. He speaks of this Gospel as distinguished from the other three "by its careful enumeration of six notes of time, five of them Jewish festivals, between the Baptism and the Crucifixion," and he goes on to speak of "these precise and detailed recollections of an eyewitness."[8] These notes are hard to explain symbolically. They come in naturally enough if, as Turner suggests, they are part of the recollections of an eyewitness who noted things carefully and accurately.

In the story of the cleansing of the temple we read that "His disciples remembered that it was written, Zeal for thy house shall eat me up" (v. 17). But after the saying about the raising of the temple in three days the situation is different. "When therefore he was raised from the dead, his disciples remembered that he spake this; and they believed the scripture, and the word which Jesus had said" (v. 22). The different attitudes of the disciples in the two cases invite comment. It looks as though we have here someone who recalls what happened. In the case of the first passage Plummer asks, "Who could know this but a disciple who was present? Who would think of

---

[8] HDB, I, p. 407. The other five time notes are at John 4:35; 5:1; 6:4; 7:2; 10:22.

inventing it?"[9] And if the first statement rings true so does the second. It represents the disciples as failing to understand a saying of Jesus. If this is not what happened how are we to explain it? We would need to postulate someone who invented the disciples' lack of understanding of a saying that he himself had ascribed to Jesus. Moreover the misunderstanding is expressly not permanent, but lasts only until the resurrection. I suppose that it is not impossible to conceive of a *falsarius* who did all this. But it is far simpler to think of a disciple who remembered.

Next let us notice the words of the Jews, "Forty and six years was this temple in building" (v. 20). This does not mean that the temple was completed in the period named. We know that it took far longer. But this points us to a time forty-six years after the commencement of Herod's work on the structure. This dates the saying in the right period for the public ministry of Jesus, and is a point in favor of its authenticity.[10] The alternative is more than a little difficult. All told it took about eighty-four years to build the temple, and it was destroyed in AD 70. It is very improbable that a writer of pious fiction at the end of the century would have been able to locate a pause in the building with such accuracy. MacGregor quotes Drummond, "It is most unlikely that a Greek teased himself with this troublesome investigation, and then allowed his antiquarian knowledge to slip out in such a way that no one would take any notice of it."[11]

---

[9] *Op. cit.*, p. 95.

[10] W. F. Howard says, "Herod's temple was begun in 20-19 B.C. Forty-six years would bring the date to A. D. 27-28. As the temple was not finally completed until A.D. 64, this saying sounds like an early Christian tradition preserved by the evangelist, and is a point in favor of the place given to this incident in the Fourth Gospel" (IB, *ad loc.*).

[11] *John*, MNTC, p. 60. J. B. Lightfoot has a valuable note on this passage (E. Abbot, A. P. Peabody, and J. B. Lightfoot, *The Fourth Gospel*, London, 1892, pp. 158ff.). He shows that for a late writer research would have been necessary into both the life of Jesus and the details of the building of the temple. "When he has taken all these pains, and worked up the subject so elaborately, he drops in the notice which has given him so much trouble in an incidental and unobtrusive way. It has no direct bearing on his

This puts the matter neatly. The figure comes in happily enough if it is a genuine reminiscence of one who recalled what was said. But it was too hard to discover in later times for a man to slip it in so unobtrusively. A guess would have had to be a very lucky one indeed. A researcher might legitimately be expected to have made more of his discovery.

The chapter concludes with many believing in Jesus on account of the signs that He did. "But Jesus did not trust himself unto them, for that he knew all men . . . he himself knew what was in man" (vv. 24f.). This is in striking contrast with Jesus' attitude to those who were earlier said to have believed in Him, namely the disciples. F. Godet sees in the passage evidence of both insight and knowledge.

> It is a profound observer initiated into the impressions of Jesus' mind, — this man who has laid hold of and set forth this delicate feature of His conduct. If he was himself one of the disciples whose call is related in chap. i., he must indeed have felt the difference between the conduct of Jesus towards these persons, and the manner in which He had deported Himself towards himself and his fellow-disciples. Let one picture to himself such a feature invented in the second century![12]

The story of Jesus' interview with Nicodemus in chapter 3 is Jewish through and through. It is not easy to see a Greek inventor of such a scene and such a conversation. Take for example the mention of "the kingdom of God" (vv. 3, 5). This is a thoroughly Jewish expression, occurring often in the Synoptic Gospels, but here only in this Gospel.[13] Perhaps even more important is the obscurity of some of the conversation. If Jesus did talk with a learned Pharisee this might be expected, especially since the conversation is recorded by neither

---

history; it does not subserve the purpose of his theology. It leads to nothing, proves nothing" (p. 160).

[12] F. Godet, *Commentary on the Gospel of John*, Grand Rapids, 1956, I, p. 372.

[13] Godet cites Meyer as drawing attention to the use of the expression only here in the Fourth Gospel and adds, "and rightly finds in this fact a proof of the truly historical character of the narrative" (*ibid.*, pp. 377f.).

of the participants.[14] But if the whole is a brilliant piece
of fiction why has not the author made his meaning
plain?[15]

A WOMAN OF SAMARIA

THE FOURTH CHAPTER RAISES SOME FASCINATING PROB-
lems. Put simply, though the chapter gives every evidence of being factual (there are many touches which
seem to indicate the presence of an eyewitness), it speaks
of a conversation from which, in the opinion of many
scholars, all but the two participants were absent. Moreover, in it Jesus tells a Samaritan woman that He is
the Messiah, a fact which according to the Synoptic
Gospels, especially Mark, He made a point of keeping
secret.

For the first point we might cite the verdict of Renan:
"Most of the circumstances of the narrative bear a strikingly impressive stamp of truth."[16] For details we might
instance, with MacGregor, "the great high-road passing
through Samaria through which 'he must needs go' on
his way from Judaea to Galilee, the deep well, the reference to the overhanging heights of Gerizim, the illus-
trations drawn from the ripening corn, for which the
locality is noted."[17] Such small touches as the statement
that Jesus was weary (v. 6) bear the stamp of truth.

Then there are some points of a psychological nature.
Thus Godet rejects Baur's idea that the event is unhistorical and should be understood as "an *idea* presented
in action by the author of our Gospel." He asks, "If the
Samaritan woman was nothing but a personification

---

[14] This does not of itself mean that the narrative is fictitious.
It is not said that Jesus and Nicodemus were alone (cf. v. 11).
And if they were it is not impossible that Nicodemus should
subsequently have told others what was said.

[15] Cf. Westcott: "If the narrative were a free composition of a
late date, it is inconceivable that the obscure allusions should not
have been made clearer; and if it were composed for a purpose,
it is inconceivable that the local colouring of opinion and method
should have been what it is" (*The Gospel According to St. John*,
Grand Rapids, 1954, I, p. 118).

[16] Cited in Godet, *op. cit.*, p. 416.

[17] *Op. cit.*, pp. 115f.

of the Gentile world, how would the author have put into her mouth (ver. 20f.) a strictly monotheistic profession of faith, as well as the hope of the near advent of the Messiah (ver. 25; comp. ver. 42)?"[18] The narrative bears all the marks of genuineness in this respect, and it is difficult to see it as a story manufactured for a Gentile audience.

Against this kind of approach some critics have countered that the vividness belongs to the mind of the writer (any good writer of fiction is vivid!), not to the circumstances of the narrative.[19] I imagine that this cannot be ruled out as impossible. But the argument is not convincing, if only for the reason that writers of fiction in antiquity did not normally insert the kind of detail that carries conviction here. At the very least we cannot simply dismiss Renan's estimate, but must take it with all seriousness.[20]

Attention has often been drawn to the questions that the disciples did not ask: "They marvelled that he was speaking with a woman; yet no man said, What seekest thou? or, Why speakest thou with her?" (v. 27). Even Wright, who as we have seen is somewhat sceptical about the historical value of this chapter, says of these words, "Such a record seems to spring from some transmitted personal recollection of the impression of the inscrutable which the disciples had in the presence of Jesus."[21] It is very difficult to see them as coming from

---

[18] *Loc. cit.*

[19] Cf. C. J. Wright: "Those who point to the 'vividness' of the narrative, in proof of its 'actuality,' forget that this dramatic vividness pervades the Gospel: it is evidence of the character of the author's mind, and not of the precise historicity of his narrative" (*Jesus the Revelation of God*, London, 1950, p. 145). Wright's argument is, of course, double-edged. The vividness that "pervades the Gospel" may be due to the fact that there is eyewitness testimony throughout.

[20] J. A. Findlay comments, "... The story is so true to human nature and to what we know of the character of our Lord, that it must surely have been taken from life, and told to His friends by Jesus Himself" (*The Fourth Gospel*, London, 1956, p. 66).

[21] *Op. cit.*, p. 148. Bernard similarly sees in these questions "the reminiscence of some one who was of the company" (*John*, ICC, I, p. 152).

a fabricator. A little later in the story the disciples are recorded as grossly misunderstanding what Jesus means. Jesus says to them, "I have meat to eat that ye know not." But they do not understand. They "therefore said one to another, Hath any man brought him ought to eat?" (vv. 32f.). On this Plummer comments, "These candid reports of what tells against the disciples add to the trust which we place in the narratives of the Evangelists."[22]

A further point made by Plummer is that the words "salvation is from the Jews" (v. 22) rule out a late Gnostic origin of the Gospel. "This verse is absolutely fatal to the theory that this Gospel is the work of a Gnostic Greek in the second century.... That salvation proceeded from the Jews contradicts the fundamental principle of Gnosticism, that salvation was to be sought in the higher knowledge of which Gnostics had the key."[23] I do not think that very many would nowadays assign the Gospel to a second-century Gnostic, so Plummer's words may perhaps not be as pertinent as when first written. But there are still those who maintain that "the Gnostic myth" had a great place in the thinking of the author, so Plummer's point is still of some relevance.[24]

From a different standpoint R. D. Potter thinks that the topographical references are significant. He takes us through a number of such in this chapter and concludes, "No passage could show better that our author knew this bit of Samaria well."[25]

A couple of points at the beginning of the chapter may well claim our attention. One is that the writer introduces the Pharisees rather abruptly. He simply says that the Pharisees had heard that Jesus was making

---

[22] *Op. cit.*, p. 124.

[23] *Ibid.*, pp. 120f.

[24] Bultmann, for example, cannot fit the words into his understanding of the Evangelist, so he assigns them to a Redactor (*op. cit.*, p. 139, n. 6).

[25] SE, I, p. 331. He proceeds to remind us that this part of the country is not southern Palestine. Some scholars such as Dodd and Barrett think that the author was a southern Palestinian, or at least was familiar with that region. These Samaritan references indicate something more.

and baptizing more disciples than John, and that Jesus, on being informed of this, left Judea and went to Galilee. He has not previously made any mention of the hostility of the Pharisees to our Lord, but here he assumes it. This is natural enough in a writer who was familiar with the people of whom he writes. But why should a romancer adopt this course? He would surely indicate that there was hostility between Jesus and the Pharisees, if only briefly. Otherwise there is no reason for Jesus' departure. The narrative is very compressed, and is intelligible only to those who know the situation.

Another point in the same passage is John's usage of "the Lord" (v. 1). Bernard notes that the Western text has good support here for the reading "Jesus," and he feels that the text has been tampered with. Though he accepts the reading "the Lord" he goes on to make the point that this is not John's usual custom. In the days of His flesh Jesus was apparently usually called "Teacher" ("Master"), though "Lord" was not impossible. In Luke in direct narrative the expression "the Lord" is common, but this is not the case in Mark. There "Jesus" is the term. The interesting point is that John habitually follows this Marcan usage rather than the Lucan. In other words, John has the earlier rather than the later use.

Thus there are not wanting indications that the chapter is factual. But against this we must set the fact that the conversation recorded is between two people, neither of whom is the writer, and there is moreover a disclosure of Jesus' messiahship which is out of character. As to the first point there is no insuperable difficulty. This very chapter shows that the woman was not averse to a little chatter (vv. 28f., 39), and there is not the slightest reason for thinking that she kept the conversation a secret. Indeed v. 29 appears to mean that she immediately told others of it. There is no difficulty in thinking that the author of the Gospel got his information from the lady. Nor is there much more in thinking that he got it from Jesus. The conversation is very instructive and Jesus might well have disclosed it to His intimates. And in any case we must bear in mind

that we are never told that the two were alone. They
may have been. But there is nothing to be said against
the possibility of John's having stayed behind with the
Master while the others went off. He could have been
present, though saying nothing, while Jesus talked with
the woman. It is true that v. 8 says that "his disciples" had gone away, but this need not mean that every
one of them was absent (though admittedly that is the
easiest interpretation).

The real difficulty here is with Jesus' disclosure of
His messiahship. When the woman says, "I know that
Messiah cometh," Jesus says, "I that speak unto thee am
he" (vv. 25f.). MacGregor puts the objection strongly
when he speaks of "the inherent improbability that Jesus
would reveal to a flippant woman a secret which he with-
held for long even from his closest friends."[26] MacGregor
goes on to notice other objections, e.g. Jesus' revelation
of the spirituality and universality of the gospel would
not be understood by the woman, the subtle allusions of
vv. 35-38 could not be understood by the disciples, etc.
These seem to me of little weight. We have no means
of knowing how much or how little the woman was capable of comprehending, and a dogmatic assertion that she
could not have understood what Jesus said is in my
opinion of little worth. The "subtle allusions" depend
on the relevant verses having the significance that Mac-
Gregor assigns to them, namely that "we have not so
much the actual words of Jesus spoken at the time in
question, but rather a comment by the Evangelist, put
indeed upon the lips of Jesus, but really spoken from the
point of view of his own day."[27] If in fact the words are
those of Jesus then they are not "spoken from the point
of view" of the Evangelist's own day. There are then no
"subtle allusions" and the difficulty does not exist. Mac-
Gregor has to assume his point in order to raise the
difficulty.

But the point about messiahship remains and it certainly is an obstacle. At first sight it is difficult to see
why Jesus should disclose to this woman a truth He

---

[26] *Op. cit.*, p. 115.
[27] *Ibid.*, p. 112.

revealed to nobody else until the trial. V. H. Stanton may give us part of the explanation: "There was not indeed among the Samaritan population, cut off as it was from the life of the Jewish people, the same danger that mischief would arise from false expectations as there was in other districts where He preached."[28] To have announced Himself as Messiah in Jewry would have been to invite misunderstanding. To do so in a Samaritan village may well have been much less hazardous. To this we should probably add the point that the Physician of souls discerned that in this particular case this disclosure was needed. This may well be so. But there is nothing in the narrative that convinces us.

In the end I am left to conclude that this remains a difficulty. I do not find any of the suggested explanations completely satisfying. If the disclosure were by itself the problem could be more easily solved. But it is not by itself. There are all the circumstances dealt with earlier. These make it more difficult to reject the story on account of this one difficulty than it is to accept it with some such explanation as that of Stanton.

HISTORY AND IDEAS

GODET INTRODUCES HIS DISCUSSION OF CHAPTERS 5 – 12 by saying, "The progress of this narrative is purely historical. The attempt, often renewed — even by *Luthardt* — to arrange this part systematically according to certain *ideas*, such as *life, light* and *love,* is incompatible with this course of the narrative which is so clearly determined by the facts."[29] I am not sure that his point is well taken. That is to say, the ideas might well have controlled the Evangelist's selection of material. Without denying the historicity it is possible to hold that this whole section of the Gospel is arranged in such

---

[28] *The Gospels as Historical Documents,* Part III, The Fourth Gospel, Cambridge, 1920, p. 227.

[29] *Op. cit.,* p. 450. A little later he says, "We must go with Baur, to the extent of claiming that the facts are invented in order to illustrate the ideas, or we must renounce the attempt to find a rational arrangement in the teachings of which these events are, each time, the occasion and the text" (p. 451). This seems an oversimplification.

a fashion as to put emphasis now on one and now on another of the ideas that Godet mentions. It does not appear that his consideration is at all decisive.

Chapter 5 begins with the healing of the man at the pool of Bethesda. John locates the miracle with the words, "Now there is in Jerusalem by the sheep gate a pool" (v. 2). This looks as though the writer means that Jerusalem is still in existence at the time of writing and thus brings him close in time to the events of which he writes.[30] There may be something in this but we must bear two things in mind. The one is that it is quite possible for a person who is engaging in reminiscence to use the present of a town which does not in fact continue to exist. The other is that John uses the past tense of Jerusalem or Bethany, or both, in 11:18. The point retains some value, but it cannot be pressed.

The story of the miracle is told simply, but effectively. William Barclay points out that many have seen allegorical meanings in the story and he is ready to concede that it is now possible to read such meanings into the story. He goes on, ". . . But it is highly unlikely that John wrote it as an allegory. The whole story has the vivid stamp of truth and of fact."[31] It is most lifelike. Some have discerned this also in the discourse that follows. Thus Wright, who is not over-prone to seeing early touches, rejects the contention that there is developed theology in v. 17, "My Father worketh even until now, and I work." He says, "It is expressive of the religious consciousness of Jesus," and he further points out that "The saying does not stand alone."[32] Similarly a little later Jesus says, "The Son can do nothing of himself, but what he seeth the Father doing" (v. 19). This ex-

---

[30] Godet cites Lange and Bengel as exegetes who conclude from the present tense that Jerusalem was still standing when this Gospel was written.

[31] W. Barclay, *The Gospel of John*, I, Edinburgh, 1956, p. 176. As one small example of this, Westcott says of the words Ἆρον . . . καὶ περιπάτει (v. 12), "The words are given with great naturalness in an abrupt form" (*op. cit.*, p. 185).

[32] *Op. cit.*, p. 160. Shortly afterward he says, "Nowhere more clearly than in this Gospel is the complete dependence of Jesus on the Father more emphatically and continuously expressed" (p. 161).

pression of subordination, Strachan thinks, comes from Jesus Himself rather than the Evangelist. The words "do not strike one as an utterance which would spring spontaneously from the mind of a writer who thinks of Jesus as the Eternal Logos made flesh."[33] All in all it seems that we have every reason for thinking that this chapter rings true. There are touches that point to accurate knowledge of what was said and done, and there is no good reason for thinking of the incident or the discourse as manufactured for doctrinal purposes.

THE MIRACULOUS FEEDING

THE FEEDING OF THE FIVE THOUSAND IS THE ONLY MIRA-cle (apart from the resurrection) that is narrated in all four Gospels. Some have seen in the Johannine narrative evidence for dependence on the Synoptics, and thus have discounted any apparent indications of an eyewitness. They simply affirm that these are due to the sources on which this Evangelist drew. But, as we have already seen, there are good grounds for holding that John is independent of the Synoptics here as elsewhere.[34] And in the second place, some of the lifelike touches occur in those parts of the story which are peculiar to John. Thus, he alone mentions the parts played by Philip and Andrew. Bernard points out that "Philip was of Bethsaida (144), and presumably he knew the neighbourhood; he was thus the natural person of whom to ask where bread could be bought. This is one of those reminiscences which suggest the testimony of an eyewitness."[35]

---

[33] Op. cit., p. 169.

[34] See above, pp. 28ff.

[35] Op. cit., p. 175. He goes on, "The Synoptists, in their accounts of the wonderful Feedings of the Multitudes, do not name individual disciples; but Jn. names both Philip and Andrew, and their figures emerge from his narrative as those of real persons, each with his own characteristics." For Barrett's point that John's use of names is a sign of lateness, see the discussion on pp. 238ff. below. Barrett does, however, notice that this miracle is certainly not invented by John, as is proved by its occurrence in the Synoptics, and he remarks that this creates a presumption that John's other miracles were not created by him (op. cit., p. 226).

Throughout this story John's account rings true. Mc-Clymont cites Sanday as comparing John's account with those in the Synoptics and concluding, ". . . The superiority in distinctness and precision is all on the side of St. John."[36] Godet takes up a similar position. He points out that "John's account contains altogether peculiar features which attest the narrative of an eye-witness; thus the part of Philip, of Andrew and of the lad, and the character of the bread *(of barley)*. But above all the narrative of John is the one which, as we have seen, makes us penetrate most deeply into the feeling of Jesus and the true spirit of this scene."[37] The freshness and general air of authenticity in John's account have impressed many.

This is true for the story that follows also, the story of the disciples' crossing of the lake and of their seeing Jesus "walking on the sea" (v. 19). An interesting feature of this little episode is that several commentators who reject the miracle, preferring to think that Jesus was walking on the shore at the edge of the lake, nevertheless see in the vivid narrative evidence that it is told by an eyewitness. Thus William Barclay says forthrightly, "Now John was actually there, and, if ever there was an eye-witness account this is one. This is clearly an incident in which John took part"; and again,

> Here is just the kind of story that a fisherman like John would have loved and cherished and remembered. Every time he thought of it he could feel that night again, the grey silver of the moonlight, the rough oar against his hand, the flapping sail, the shriek of the wind, and the sound of the surging water, the astonishingly unexpected appearance of Jesus, the sound of His voice across the waves, and the crunch of the boat as it reached the Galilaean side.[38]

---

[36] McClymont, *The Century Bible, St. John*, Edinburgh, 1901, p. 175.

[37] *Op. cit.*, p. 9. Earlier, commenting on vv. 8, 9, he says, "We can believe that we hear him telling the story" (p. 7).

[38] *Op. cit.*, pp. 211, 212. Temple also says, "Certainly the story is vivid, and bears all the marks of an eye-witness who, as a fisherman, was familiar with that Lake, its distances and its squalls" (*op. cit.*, p. 77). Wright sees the story as "incorporating . . . some of the reminiscences of John the son of Zebedee" (*op. cit.*, p. 170).

There is certainly an element of imagination in this comment, but Barclay leaves us in no doubt as to how the narrative strikes him. It is very obviously a convincing story.

John 6:22ff. is a very complicated little section and it has given the commentators a few headaches as they tried to sort out the Greek. But in the process not a few have found themselves convinced that it must come from someone who was there — no one else would have left us with such a tangle of words! Godet gathers up his impressions in this fashion: "Thus there are described with an astonishing precision, in this long sentence, all the impressions, fluctuations, various observations of this multitude, up to the point of the decision which brings them to Capernaum, and gives occasion to the conversations of the next day. Let one imagine a Greek writer of Alexandria or of Rome, in the second century, narrating after this fashion!"[39] Godet is surely right. The crowded nature of this passage is evidence of someone who knew what he was talking about but who was trying to compress his statement to the limit. Anyone else would surely have produced a more tidy sentence.

THE FEAST OF TABERNACLES

THE EVENTS AT THE FEAST OF TABERNACLES COME BEfore us in John 7. Of this chapter Westcott says,

> No section in the Gospel is more evidently a transcript from life than this. It reflects a complex and animated variety of characters and feelings. Jerusalem is seen crowded at the most popular feast with men widely differing in hope and position: some eager in expectation, some immovable in prejudice. There is nothing

---

[39] *Op. cit.*, pp. 16f. Similarly Temple comments, "We notice the vivid and crowded recollection of the eye-witness. Such writing is the expression of personal memory" (*op. cit.*, p. 82). So also Plummer, "A complicated sentence very unusual in S. John ... but its very intricacy is evidence of its accuracy. A writer of fiction would have given fewer details and stated them with greater freedom" (*op. cit.*, p. 152). J. O. F. Murray takes up much the same position: "This little note, which is curiously cumbrous in expression, must surely embody an historic reminiscence" (*Jesus according to S. John*, London, 1936, p. 147).

of the calm solemnity of the private discourse, or of
the full exposition of doctrine before a dignified body,
such as has been given before. All is direct, personal
encounter.[40]

This is the way the chapter strikes many. It is vivid
and true to life.[41] And if this is true of the chapter as
a whole it is true also of details. Thus Bernard points
out that the discussion between Jesus and the brothers
"which is reported in vv. 3-8, could only have been
known to one who was in intimate relations with the
family; and there could be no motive for setting it down
in narrative, if it had not actually taken place."[42] The
latter point is important, for sometimes when attention
is drawn to the lifelikeness of a scene in this Gospel
the retort is that this shows no more than the skill of
the author as a dramatist. But what could be his motive
for setting down this kind of conversation? To reply
that this gives an air of verisimilitude scarcely meets the
case, for authors in the first century were not given to
that kind of verisimilitude. It was foreign to their
methods, and we should not read back our ideas into
their day.

There is another feature of this conversation that
deserves notice, namely the fact that the brothers of
Jesus do not come out very well. It is even said that
they did not believe on Him (v. 5). But at the time
this Gospel was written they were highly esteemed in
the church, especially James. It is most unlikely that at
that time anyone would manufacture a story that put
James and his brothers in such a bad light.[43]

---

[40] *Op. cit.*, p. 260. He goes on to notice language like the use of
"brethren," "the Jews," "the multitudes," "the people of Jerusalem,"
"The Pharisees," etc., who "appear in succession in the narrative,
and all with clearly marked individuality" *(ibid.)*. Then he
notices actions and feelings, and proceeds, "All is full of movement,
of local colour, of vivid traits of conflicting classes and tendencies"
(p. 261).

[41] "The chapter is a remarkable piece of reporting by an eye-
witness" (Vacher Burch, *The Structure and Message of St. John's
Gospel*, London, 1928, p. 80).

[42] *Op. cit.*, p. 266.

[43] Cf. J. E. Davey: ". . . When we remember that James, the brother
of Jesus, became head of the Church in Jerusalem and that Christ's

When we move on to the scene at Jerusalem at the Feast, the same lifelike touches continue. For example, the Jews there were astonished at Jesus' teaching, since they knew that He had not been through the schools. "How knoweth this man letters, having never learned?" they asked (v. 15). Plummer reminds us that "Their questions and comments throughout this section are too exactly in keeping with what we know of the Jews in our Lord's time to be the invention of a Greek a century or more later."[44] This is a feature that recurs throughout the Gospel. The controversies recorded are those of first-century Palestine, not those of second-century Asia.

A number of points are raised as the dialogue unfolds. Bernard finds it "a lifelike touch" that the people are incredulous about a plot to kill Jesus (v. 20). "It was not the 'people,' but the 'Jews,' who had begun the plot; the people knew nothing of it."[45] J. E. Davey is impressed by the sabbath regulation cited in v. 23 ("If a man receiveth circumcision on the sabbath, that the law of Moses may not be broken"). He disputes the contention that John has borrowed this from contemporary Rabbis, pointing out that the Synoptists independently attest Jesus' knowledge of rabbinical teaching and His humane application of it. "The argument here in *John* regarding circumcision, which is not in the Synoptics, is therefore probably an additional historical ut-

family was highly honoured by the Christians for generations, we recognize that *John* here is not voicing the views of the earthly Church, which tended to forget the defects of their heroes, except where anchored firmly in tradition, like Peter's denial; but that we have here probably a primitive and independent piece of tradition regarding the family attitude to the ministry of Jesus" (*The Jesus of St. John*, London, 1958, p. 48). Bultmann, by contrast, asserts that the brothers here "represent the world" (*op. cit.*, p. 218). But there is no evidence to support this, and it looks like a refusal to face the plain meaning of the words.

[44] *Op. cit.*, p. 171. On the specific question Plummer comments, "Their question is so eminently characteristic, that it is very unlikely that a Greek writer of the second century would have been able to invent it for them; he would probably have made them too cautious to commit themselves to any expression of astonishment about Him" (*ibid.*).

[45] *Op. cit.*, p. 262.

terance of Jesus."[46] Similarly Wright sees in the reference to the idea that no one would know where Christ
comes from (v. 27) evidence of genuineness. "A rabbinical saying confirms the Evangelist's accurate knowledge of the popular Jewish expectation."[47] Lenski is impressed with John's choice of verb when he says that
Jesus "cried" in the temple (v. 28), thinking that it is
evidence of the scene as vividly present to the writer.[48]
Plummer seizes on the same point: "S. John well remembers that moving cry in the midst of Christ's teaching in the Temple."[49] Barrett, it is true, finds in the
conjunction of "the chief priests and the Pharisees"
(v. 32) reason for casting doubt on John's knowledge.
He reminds us that the chief priests were Sadducees:
". . . We should not in general expect to find them acting
in concert with the Pharisees."[50] He contrasts John, who
several times associates the chief priests with the Pharisees, with Mark, who links them only in the passion
narrative. This would be a more impressive argument
if cognizance had been taken of the fact that Mark does
not mention any action in Jerusalem until the end of
his story. He thus has little scope for mentioning the
chief priests. In fact he does not speak of them, apart
from references in predictions of Jesus, until 11:18.
It would accordingly be impossible for Mark to link the
chief priests with anyone as early as does the Fourth
Evangelist. The point under discussion is not to be
taken in isolation from the whole Jerusalem ministry
of which John writes. If that is historical we have no
reason for denying that the chief priests linked up with
the Pharisees in opposition to Jesus from quite early
times. This would mean the action of the sanhedrin, and

---

[46] *Op. cit.*, p. 49.

[47] *Op. cit.*, p. 193. He cites the saying: "Three things are wholly
unexpected, Messiah, a god-send, and a scorpion."

[48] Lenski, *The Interpretation of St. John's Gospel*, Columbus,
Ohio, 1956, p. 560. He says, "In this loud cry we are still to hear the
teacher and speaker engaged in his Temple work."

[49] *Op. cit.*, p. 174. He proceeds to note that neither ἐν τῷ ἱερῷ
nor διδάσκων is needed for the narrative. They proceed from the
memory of the man who was there, not from the exigencies of the
writer's craft.

[50] *Op. cit.*, p. 268.

the sanhedrin would be much more likely to act in Jerusalem than in Galilee. In view of all this it seems rather much for Barrett to say, "It seems that, either in ignorance or with no concern for accuracy in such matters, he simply takes οἱ Ἰουδαῖοι as a general term for the enemies of Jesus, analyzing it on occasion into οἱ ἀρχιερεῖς (or οἱ ἄρχοντες) together with οἱ Φαρισαῖοι."[51]

In contrast with Barrett, Bernard has a long note on this verse in which he outlines the composition and some of the activities of the sanhedrin, but he raises no difficulties about the passage at all.[52] Nor does Wright, no friend of conservative opinions. He notices that this is the first reference in this Gospel to the chief priests, and that the Pharisees are traditionalists. He goes on, "The significant point to note in this passage is the nature of the cause which unites the 'chief priests' and 'the Pharisees' in their common action. Life brings strange bedfellows together."[53] The last words indicate that, far from finding in this passage evidence that John was writing "either in ignorance or with no concern for accuracy," Wright finds this touch exceedingly lifelike. With all respect, I do not think that Barrett's doubts spring naturally from the passage at all. To many, and some who are far from being conservative, the passage is realistic. The evidence seems to me to favor this conclusion.

A little later in this scene Jesus quotes Scripture as follows: "He that believeth on me, as the scripture hath said, from within him shall flow rivers of living water" (v. 38). There are several problems about this passage. One is the notorious difficulty of knowing what passage of the Old Testament Jesus had in mind. But the very fact that the difficulty can arise is, of course, evidence for the genuineness of the passage. As Bernard points out, ". . . The fact that we cannot precisely fix the quotation makes for the genuineness of the reminiscence here

---

[51] *Ibid.*

[52] *Op. cit.*, pp. 277f.

[53] *Op. cit.*, p. 194. Similarly Godet says of the same incident, "There are in this story shadings and an exactness of details which show an eye-witness" (*op. cit.*, p. 72).

recorded. A writer whose aim was merely to edify, and who did not endeavour to reproduce historical incidents, would not have placed in the mouth of Jesus a scriptural quotation which no one has ever been able to identify exactly."[54] This must be taken with full seriousness. It is intelligible that Jesus cited Scripture in an unusual fashion. It is not intelligible that someone who was manufacturing the incident would affirm that Jesus ascribed certain words to Scripture, but do it so badly that no one has been able to find the passage.

The discussion continues. In vv. 40-44 we have recorded some of the impact made on the crowds. These glimpses of people's reactions are extraordinarily realistic, and provoke Godet into saying, "These brief descriptions of the impressions of the people, which follow each of the discourses of Jesus serve to mark the two-fold development which is effected and thus prepare the way for the understanding of the final crisis. These pictures are history taken in the act; how could they proceed from the pen of a later narrator?"[55]

Of the following section, vv. 45-52, Wright says, "As we read these verses we seem to be in that company of priests and doctors, watching the expressions of surprise, of suspicion mingled with fear, of incredulous anger, and of vehement scorn which sweep over their Semitic faces as they confront their 'officers' and Nicodemus."[56] This may possibly be meant to indicate that the passage is genuine. That, it seems to me, is the conclusion that ought to be drawn from the narrative, and for the reason that Wright suggests. However, he goes on, "A writer who can in a few lines suggest such a picture is one of the geniuses of literature. With a few sure strokes of the brush an impressionistic picture is unforgettably drawn." It may well be accordingly that Wright is thinking of no more than John's dramatic power. Be Wright's view what it may, the words seem to me to indicate that the scene was before John as he wrote.

---

[54] *Op. cit.*, p. 281.
[55] *Op. cit.*, p. 80.
[56] *Op. cit.*, p. 198.

At the end of the chapter comes a retort of the Pharisees to Nicodemus, "Art thou also of Galilee? Search, and see that out of Galilee ariseth no prophet" (v. 52). Barrett is rather scornful about the statement made by the Pharisees. He finds it without parallel in Jewish literature, and goes on, "John's words raise the question whether he had any first-hand knowledge of Palestinian Judaism in the first century."[57] But Barrett overlooks some of the possibilities. For example, he pays no attention to the possibility that the Pharisees are simply speaking in haste. After all, few prophets *did* come from Galilee, and in their angry and excited state they may well have overlooked the origins of Jonah. We ought not to take these as the considered words of calm and dignified men who are giving their verdict in the light of a careful scrutiny of the facts. But in any case the sentence need mean no more than, "From your knowledge of Galilee, do you consider it the kind of district to produce a prophet!"[58] Anything Barrett says must be weighed seriously. But this particular objection would be more convincing had he taken notice of the alternative possibilities.

THE LIGHT OF THE WORLD

JOHN PROCEEDS TO THE GREAT DISCOURSE ON THE LIGHT of the world. This is a connected piece of teaching, but Jesus' words are punctuated with interjections of the Jews. The whole is vivid and forceful. For a summary of chapter 8 we can scarcely do better than draw attention to the words of William Sanday:

> The whole of the Jews' reasoning is strictly what we should expect from them. These constant appeals to their descent from Abraham, these repeated imputations of diabolic possession, this narrow intelligence bounded by the letter, this jealousy of anything that seemed in the slightest degree to trench on their own rigid monotheism — all these, down to the touch in *v.* 57, in which the age they fix upon in round numbers is that assigned to completed manhood, give local truth

---

[57] *Op. cit.*, p. 275.
[58] Hoskyns, *op. cit.*, p. 326.

and accuracy to the picture; which in any case, we
may say confidently, must have been drawn by a
Palestinian Jew, and in all probability by a Jew who
had been himself an early disciple of Christ.[59]

This could scarcely be improved on as a summary of the
impression made by the chapter as a whole.

Attention might be drawn to some of the details. The
saying of Jesus in v. 12, "I am the light of the world,"
has evoked a good deal of comment. J. E. Davey thinks
that in the light of Matthew 5:14 this cannot be regarded as unhistorical.[60] Barrett maintains that a review
of the background of the verse "shows that John stands
within the primitive Christian tradition."[61] However, he
adds, "Nevertheless, it remains very probable that in
the formulation of his statement he was influenced both
by Hellenistic religion and by Jewish thought about
Wisdom and the Law."

There is reference to "walking" in darkness. Bernard
points out that this use of the verb "to walk" is found
once only in the Synoptics (Mark 7:5) but that it occurs
often in both Paul and John. He remarks, "It is, in fact,
a Hebraism."[62] This is of course a small point favoring
the genuineness of the remark. While it would not be
impossible to a Greek, it is much more natural with a
Hebrew.

A little later John notes that Jesus was teaching "in
the treasury, as he taught in the temple" (v. 20). Strachan finds here "one of those unexpected notes of locality which occur in this gospel."[63] It impresses Godet
also. He thinks that the words uttered by Jesus were
regarded by the Evangelist as words of great gravity.
He proceeds, "Even the recollection of the locality in
which they had been uttered had remained deeply en-
graved in the memory of the evangelist."[64]

---

[59] Cited in Plummer, *op. cit.*, p. 203.

[60] *Op. cit.*, p. 49.

[61] *Op. cit.*, p. 278.

[62] *Op. cit.*, p. 293.

[63] *Op. cit.*, p. 208.

[64] *Op. cit.*, p. 96. Godet also finds in this chapter one of these
passages "where we can make palpable the fact that the discourses
of Jesus in the fourth Gospel are not compositions of the writer,

It is worth noticing that Jesus is recorded as referring to Himself as "a man that hath told you the truth" (v. 40). This rings true. Jesus of Nazareth would have said it. But would a late writer, at a time when the deity of Christ was being stressed, have manufactured such a saying?

Hugo Odeberg puts stress on the accuracy of the rabbinical knowledge displayed in this chapter. Of 8:30-59 he says, "It might be urged that the utterances in the present section laid in the mouth of the Jews not only reproduce exactly the early Rabbinic conceptions but also constitute a picture, artistically drawn of the Rabbinic mode of reasoning. The section postulates a real first-hand knowledge of and familiarity with the Tannaitic mind as well as the Tannaitic world of ideas."[65]

The healing of the man born blind occupies our attention in chapter 9. Temple says that in this chapter the story does not demand "specially close thought or deep meditation." But he characterizes it as "a chapter of vivid movement, disclosing the spiritual outlook of those concerned with singular clearness.... Once more, as at the beginning of Chapter VII ... we notice the qualities which only the narrative of an eye-witness would show."[66]

---

but real discourses of Christ" (p. 104). The three points that seem to him especially significant are (1) the impossibility of inventing the communion of Jesus with God which is described: "If it were not in the experience, it would not be in the thought." (2) The allusion to the Jewish law (vv. 17, 18), and (3) the locality indicated with such precision (v. 20): "A perfectly accurate historical recollection; otherwise, there would be here a piece of charlatanism, which it would be impossible to reconcile with the seriousness of the whole narrative" (ibid.).

[65] H. Odeberg, *The Fourth Gospel*, Uppsala, 1929, p. 301. He goes on, "The utterances ascribed to J [i.e. Jesus] also take as starting-point current Rabbinic notions, although — and this is in accordance with the whole trend of the Gospel — at the same time the J-utterances serve to underline the constitutive differences between Jewish ideas and the teaching of J."

[66] *Op. cit.*, p. 153. Such a discussion as that of Bultmann (*op. cit.*, pp. 250ff.) overlooks this. Bultmann sees the whole as symbolically setting forth the truth that Christ is "the Light of the World." But this is to ignore the many indications that, whatever spiritual lessons may be discerned in the chapter, the story is drawn from life.

These qualities of an eyewitness are manifest throughout, but especially when the man who has received his
sight is himself in action. The vivid narrative gives a
clear impression of the character of the man and we
see the scenes before our eyes. Thus on v. 8 Bernard
remarks, "The lively account which follows, of the experiences of the blind man who had recovered his sight,
may go back to the evidence of the man himself."[67]

McClymont sees significance in the retort of the man
to his neighbors when he was asked, "How then were
thine eyes opened?" (v. 10). His reply includes the
words, "The man that is called Jesus" (v. 11). McClymont sees in this "one of many tokens of freshness and
originality in the narrative."[68] Plummer draws attention to the gradual development of faith in the man as
outlined in this chapter, and asks, "What writer of fiction in the second century could have executed such a
study in psychology?"[69] It must be borne in mind in
considering many passages in this Gospel that psychological studies belong to the modern, not the ancient
world. The study of ancient writing shows that occasional touches were sometimes added to give an air of verisimilitude, but it is clear that a consistent essay in psychology was never thought of. In other words, a portrait
such as John paints for us in this ninth chapter may
perhaps be conceivable in a modern writer of fiction.
But we have no reason for thinking that an ancient
writer would go to the trouble of manufacturing this,
or for that matter that he could have done it if he had
wanted to. Godet maintains that "The whole scene here
described has an historical truthfulness which is obvious. It is so little ideal in its nature that it rests, from
one end to the other, upon the brute reality of a *fact*."[70]

---

[67] *Op. cit.*, p. 329. Cf. A. P. Peabody: "This man is painted to the
life. He must have told the story himself" (E. Abbot, A. P. Peabody,
and J. B. Lightfoot, *The Fourth Gospel*, London, 1892, p. 120).

[68] *Op. cit.*, p. 215.

[69] *Op. cit.*, p. 207. Wright has this to say: "The play and inter-
play of the divergent motives of different minds give striking
realism to the scene" (*op. cit.*, p. 225).

[70] *Op. cit.*, p. 135. He is scornful of the position of Baur. He cites
him for the statement, "The reality of the fact is the point against

THE GOOD SHEPHERD

THE GOOD SHEPHERD AND HIS SHEEP ARE BROUGHT BE-
fore us in chapter 10. It is, of course, possible to discern
shepherd imagery in the literatures of many countries,
ancient and modern. Some critics have suggested that
accordingly there is no great significance in it. It arises,
they feel, out of the general stock of man's ideas or perhaps should be explained in terms of ideas current in
various religions in the Roman Empire of the time.
But, as Hoskyns reminds us, "To place the parable in
the Fourth Gospel upon the background of such general mysticism is to obscure the delicate allusions to
the Old Testament, and to destroy that vigorous sense
for history which it is the main purpose of the Evangelist to expose as the ground of Christian truth."[71] To
explain this chapter as genuine reminiscences of Jesus'
teaching is much simpler than to postulate "explanations" borrowed from the mystery religions or the like.
Such raise more difficulties than they solve. On one
small but significant point, the reference to Jesus as
"the door" (v. 9), Davey draws attention to the recurring theme of the doorkeeper in the Synoptic Gospels
(Matt. 7:22, 23; 25:10f.; Luke 13:25, 27).[72]

A little later in the chapter we are told that "it was
the feast of the dedication at Jerusalem: it was winter;
and Jesus was walking in the temple in Solomon's porch"
(vv. 22f.). As Bernard puts it, "This vivid touch suggests that the writer is thoroughly familiar with the
place and the conditions in which instruction was given

---

which the contradiction of the adversaries is broken." Godet proceeds, "And yet this fact, according to him, is a pure invention!
What sort of man must an evangelist be, who describes, with greatest detail, a whole series of scenes for the purpose of showing how
dogmatic reasoning is shattered against a fact in the reality of
which he does not himself believe?"

[71] *Op. cit.*, p. 368. Hoskyns also points out that a commentator
who thinks in terms of mysticism is obliged to find some explanation for the thieves and robbers and hirelings in both the parable
and its interpretation.

[72] *Op. cit.*, p. 49. Davey further explains his point with this
definition of the doorkeeper: "the Messiah or Son of Man who
decides the destinies of those who knock."

there."[73] Bernard proceeds, "At the time when the Fourth
Gospel was written, the Temple had been for some years
in ruins; but the note of time and circumstance is easily
explicable, if we have here the reminiscence of an eye-
witness of the scene."[74]

The discussion led the Jews to bring stones to stone
Jesus.[75] The expression "brought" rather than "took up"
is a little touch of one with exact knowledge. Certainly
it is not easy to see how someone writing at a distance
from Palestine at a time subsequent to the destruction
of the temple would have been able to produce an effect
like this.

The argument throughout the section is thoroughly
Jewish. Plummer draws attention to the significance of
the reasoning in vv. 34f., "Jesus answered them, Is it
not written in your law, I said, Ye are gods? If he called
them gods, unto whom the word of God came (and the
scripture cannot be broken)...." This is a thoroughly
Jewish way of arguing, so much so that Plummer could
say, "But how incredible that any but a Jew should
think of such an argument, or put it in this brief way!"[76]
Barrett finds an error in the statement in v. 31 that the
Jews took up the stones to stone Jesus. He agrees that
the penalty for blasphemy was stoning so that this part
of the statement fits in well enough. He goes on, "... But
stoning was not a matter of lynch law, though that is
what seems to be in operation here. John's apparent
unfamiliarity with the Jewish practice (though this was

---

[73] Bernard, *op. cit.*, p. 343.

[74] See also Westcott, *op. cit.*, p. 64.

[75] This appears to be the force of the verb ἐβάστασαν. Stones
would not be lying around in Solomon's porch. We do not know how
far the Jews would have had to go to find them but they "brought"
them along. Godet states, "Shades of expression like this reveal
the eye-witness, whose eyes followed anxiously this progress of
hatred" (*op. cit.*, p. 163).

[76] *Op. cit.*, p. 227. Plummer adds, "These last eight verses alone
are sufficient to discredit the theory that this Gospel is the work
of a Greek Gnostic in the second century." Bernard similarly points
out that "The argument is one which would never have occurred to
a Greek Christian, and its presence here reveals behind the narrative a genuine reminiscence of one who remembered how Jesus
argued with the Rabbis on their own principles" (*op. cit.*, p. 367).

probably but rarely carried out) fits ill with the view that he was himself a Jew who had lived in Palestine before A.D. 70."[77] The curious thing about this comment is that there is no reference to the stoning of Stephen. This is all the more curious in that elsewhere Barrett recognizes that parts of Acts 6, 7 "read like the story of a lynching."[78] In that place he gives no hint that he believes that that stoning "is not a matter of lynch law." Many competent authorities are of opinion that Stephen's death was the result of a lynching.[79] Even if it were not, it was certainly the result of a very summary court procedure. On the face of it there is no reason for thinking that the procedure envisaged in John 10 is noticeably different from that carried out in Acts 7. To talk about John's "apparent unfamiliarity with the Jewish practice" without discussing this almost contemporary example of Jewish practice is somewhat strange. The case of Stephen, in my opinion, proves that John's statement here fits in with the current situation. It is a mark of his acquaintance with Palestinian conditions, not of his unfamiliarity with them.

Godet says that the whole discourse recorded in this chapter is evidence that John is recording that which was actually said:

> It is absolutely impossible to suppose that a later writer, the inventor of the theory of the Logos, should have imagined an argument such as this passage contains. How could such a man have thought of ascribing to Jesus an argument which, superficially under-

---

[77] *Op. cit.*, p. 318.

[78] *Ibid.*, p. 446.

[79] Cf. the discussion in *The Beginnings of Christianity*, ed. F. J. Foakes Jackson and K. Lake, IV, London, 1933, p. 85. The writer finds difficulty in coming to a conclusion and in the end thinks that Stephen was actually executed, but that one of Luke's "subordinate purposes was to suggest that Stephen was put to death by the violence of a mob, not by the legal sentence of a court." J. Klausner is firmly of opinion that Stephen was lynched (*From Jesus to Paul*, London, 1946, pp. 292f.) ; and M. Wilcox, as though there were no doubt at all on this point, characterizes Acts 7 as "a simple, natural, and direct story of the preaching of Stephen, his ultimate trial, and lynching" (*The Semitisms of Acts*, Oxford, 1965, p. 159).

stood, seems to contradict everything which he had
made Him affirm hitherto with relation to His divinity? This mode of discussion evidently bears the
character of immediate historical reality. It testifies,
at the same time, of the most lively understanding of
the Old Testament. Evidently this whole discourse
can be attributed only to Jesus Himself.[80]

This will seem to many modern scholars to be too confident. Yet it must be borne in mind that if this Gospel
is late it was written at a time when the deity of Jesus
was receiving some stress. It is highly unlikely that at
such a time the inventor of sayings would make Jesus
defend himself with such a tortuous line of argument
as we see in vv. 32-38. It is much simpler, with Godet,
to see here an authentic account of Jesus' own teaching.

The end of the chapter takes Jesus beyond Jordan,
"into the place where John was at the first baptizing"
(v. 40). Wright notices "a psychological fitness in such
a retiral.... This visit to Peraea is recorded in the Synoptic Gospels, and is doubtless historical."[81]

LAZARUS

WHEN WE MOVE ON TO CHAPTER 11 WE COME TO ONE OF
the most difficult problems in the whole Fourth Gospel,
that of the raising of Lazarus. The story is told at some
length. It is clear that the raising of a man who had
been dead four days is regarded as especially significant
and as having made a deep impression on both the

---

[80] *Op. cit.*, p. 168.

[81] *Op. cit.*, p. 243. Plummer cites Sanday to the same effect:
"The chapter ends with a note of place which is evidently and
certainly historical. No forger would ever have thought of the
periphrasis 'where John at first baptized'... 'John did no miracle:
but all things that John spake of this man were true.' It would
be impossible to find a stronger incidental proof that the author
of the Gospel had been originally a disciple of the Baptist, or at
least his contemporary, and also that he is writing of things that
he had heard and seen. A Gnostic, writing in Asia Minor, even
though he had come into relation with disciples of John, would not
have introduced the Baptist in this way. In circles that had been
affected by the Baptist's teaching, and were hesitating whether
they should attach themselves to Jesus, this is precisely the sort
of comment that would be heard" (*op. cit.*, p. 229).

friends and the enemies of Jesus. It stirs up the latter into violent opposition and leads on to the sequence of events that brought about Jesus' death. Yet none of the other Evangelists mentions this miracle. It is usually said that the silence of Mark in particular is very significant, for if he did not mention such a stupendous miracle, it must have been only because he did not know about it. And he has a fairly close and accurate knowledge of what went on in and about Jerusalem in the days that led up to the passion. Sometimes it is felt that the silence of Luke is more significant even than that of Mark, for Luke shows special knowledge of the little family at Bethany.

The silence of the Synoptists is undoubtedly a difficulty but it is not decisive. We do not know what would have made one of the Evangelists include a given story in his book. We do know that the Synoptists record the raising of the daughter of Jairus, and it may well be that they do not want another story of resurrection, especially so close to the resurrection of Jesus Himself. It is also worth noting that Mark has nothing about Jesus' ministry in Jerusalem before the final week. It may have been outside his plan or even outside his knowledge, to include matters that took place earlier. On this point Temple can say, "All I contend is that the origins of *Mark* are such that the omission of this story there is not at all decisive; and to accept, as I do, the Johannine narrative is in no way false to the principles of evidence. The story is singularly vivid and has all the characteristics of the record of an eye-witness."[82] R. F.

---

[82] *Op. cit.*, p. 177. Godet cites Deutinger to the same effect: "This narrative is distinguished among all the narrations of the fourth Gospel by its peculiar vivacity and its dramatic movement. The characters are drawn by a hand at once firm and delicate. Nowhere is the relation of Christ to His disciples set forth in so lifelike a manner...." He continues with other points made by Deutinger, showing that "invented stories are not of this sort." Godet adds the pertinent point, "And especially, it was not thus that invented stories were formed in the second century; we have the proof of this in the Apocryphal narratives" (*op. cit.*, pp. 196f.). Westcott maintains that those who deny the historicity of this narrative "are sooner or later brought to maintain either that the

Bailey adds the point that, if it is difficult to see why the Synoptists omit this story, John does give a reason for the enthusiasm on Palm Sunday. The Synoptists speak of the enthusiasm on that day but there is nothing in their narratives to account for it. If the miracle raises one difficulty at least it helps to solve another. Bailey agrees that it is strange that St. Mark should either not know or not mention the raising of Lazarus, but proceeds, "On the other hand I find it still more difficult to believe that the fourth evangelist is either misinformed about, or deliberately misplacing or inventing an incident which bears such strong evidence of personal observation."[83]

The lively narrative has impressed very many.[84] Even those who reject entirely the miracle involved in the raising of Lazarus are usually impressed with the life-likeness of the story. They ascribe it to the Evangelist's dramatic power. It seems better, however, to take such evidence as pointing to a vivid recollection of what actually happened. The story is lifelike because it is taken from life.

The information given about Martha and Mary (vv. 20ff.) is very true to life and has impressed many. Wright brings this out when he says,

> The portrayal of Martha and Mary by the Evangelist is true to what from the Lucan story in Lk. 10[38f.] we should expect. The first is the busy mistress of the house, eager in homely service, quick to express in speech what she thinks. It is she who goes to meet Jesus, and expresses to Him with precipitation her thoughts. The second is meditative and self-distrustful; of deep feeling not easily expressed in speech. She stays at home to await the coming of Jesus. Nor

---

scene was an imposture, or that the record is a fiction. Both of these hypotheses involve a moral miracle" (op. cit., p. 78).

[83] R. F. Bailey, Saint John's Gospel, London, 1957, pp. 141f. Bailey, like many others, thinks the explanation of St. Mark's omission of the story is that he "confines himself to incidents based on S. Peter's personal memories, and that S. Peter was not present during any part of the Jerusalem ministry."

[84] A. P. Peabody describes it as a "self-authenticating narrative, which could have been written only by an eye-witness" (op. cit., p. 120).

was it until the Master sent to call her that she 'rose quickly and went unto Him,' without telling her purpose to those with her.[85]

This writer has more to say to the same purpose. He is quite clear that the characterization of the sisters is magnificently done and that it fits in with the story in Luke. He goes so far as to say that the contrast between them is "mainly true to historical fact." But he still insists on "the allegorical nature of the narrative."[86] The conviction that the narrative is allegorical, however, is one that is reached from another premise than the language about Martha and Mary. If we confine our attention for the moment to them the impression is that of being true to life.[87]

Another touch of a psychological nature is afforded by the question of the Jews, "Could not this man, who opened the eyes of him that was blind, have caused that this man also should not die?" (v. 37). Since Lazarus was at this point dead one might perhaps think that it would have been more apposite to recall the raisings from the dead of the daughter of Jairus and the son of the widow of Nain. Indeed, precisely this objection is sometimes made. If the narrative were historical, it is argued, appeal would certainly have been made to miraculous raisings of the dead, not to healings of the blind.[88] But surely the reverse is the case. It is intelligible that people near Jerusalem would have appealed back to the healing of the blind man which had taken place in their own city. This was the last evidence of Jesus' great powers in their midst. It would be natural for them to appeal to it. They may not even have known of raisings from the dead that took place in remote Galilee. But

---

[85] *Op. cit.*, p. 256.

[86] *Ibid.* He goes on, "It is, indeed, psychologically most natural to suppose that the author will weave his allegory out of the strands of history."

[87] Thus Plummer can say, "It is incredible that the coincidences between S. John and S. Luke as regards the characters of the sisters should be either fortuitous or designed. It is much easier to believe that both give us facts about real persons" (*op. cit.*, p. 239).

[88] Godet cites Strauss as one who takes this position (*op. cit.*, pp. 185f.).

it is not intelligible that a second-century writer, composing freely in a time when the Synoptic narratives were well known, should have overlooked those raisings from the dead, which were more than ever appropriate to this occasion. It is perhaps worth noting also that the Jews were not talking about a resurrection. They were thinking of the power of Jesus to save Lazarus from dying, which is not the same thing.

Another touch which it is difficult to think of a later writer as ascribing to Jesus, is the activity described in vv. 33, 38 and which the ARV renders, "groaned" and "groaning." The Greek verb is a very down-to-earth one and may be used, for example, of horses snorting. It is not the kind of word that one could easily imagine a pious fabricator applying to Jesus. Indeed Murray maintains that this little section "cannot be attributed to creative imagination."[89]

The end of the chapter refers to the effect that the miracle had, especially on Jesus' enemies. Barrett recognizes that this is a dramatic event but he regards it as "of dubious historical value." Thus in the reference to the "Pharisees" in v. 46, he thinks John seems to speak of "an official body, like priests, magistrates, or councillors." Barrett adds, "If he did so speak of them he was ignorant of Judaism."[90]

Concerning the latter point little need be said. Barrett says no more than, "if he did so speak of them." It has not occurred to most commentators that John may have been speaking of the Pharisees as a body of officials; there is no need for us to import this into the narrative. There is scarcely more to be said for Barrett's first point. The fact that the narrative is dramatic does not mean that it is erroneous. This is not proof that John intends this section to be a substitute for the accounts of the Synoptic Gospels of the trial before the high priests. There is no semblance of a trial here and the equivalent in the Synoptics is to be seen in the plot, not the trial.[91]

[89] *Op. cit.*, p. 210.
[90] *Op. cit.*, pp. 337f.
[91] In one small point, the prophetic utterance of Caiaphas, Plummer sees evidence that the writer is a Jew. "None but a Jew

THE ANOINTING AT BETHANY

CHAPTER 12 BEGINS WITH THE STORY OF THE ANOINTING at Bethany. There are intricate questions in the relationship between this account and those of anointings in the Synoptic Gospels, which need not concern us here. One tiny detail, peculiar to John, is the statement that "the house was filled with the odor of the ointment" (v. 3). This has seemed to many to be a personal reminiscence.[92] It is one of those small things which mean much to a participant in the original happenings and which stick in the memory. But there is no real reason for ascribing this kind of detail to the imagination of the narrator.

Another small touch in the same passage is that in which we are assured that Judas was a thief (v. 6). This is sometimes rejected. It is said that when Judas proved false the natural reaction on the part of some was to invent harsh sayings about him like this one. This overlooks the fact that the Gospels do nothing of the sort. Indeed their reserve when they refer to Judas is noteworthy. We should expect that he would have been criticized in the severest of terms. He is often referred to in words like, "who also betrayed him." But that is all. The statement is not elaborated. Nor is Judas reviled. The writers of the Gospels simply state the fact and leave it at that.

Moreover, the very fact that the writer on this point is obviously emotionally involved as he narrates what Judas was and did, is evidence that the remark comes from an early disciple. Bernard points out that "the bitterness of the words about Judas in this verse is easily explained if they go back to one who was a former comrade in the inner circle of the Twelve, who had had

---

would be likely to know of the old Jewish belief that the high-priest by means of the Urim and Thummim was the mouthpiece of the Divine oracle. The Urim and Thummim had been lost, and the high-priest's office had been shorn of much of its glory" (*op. cit.*, p. 247).

[92] E.g. Westcott, *op. cit.*, p. 111; Bernard, *op. cit.*, p. 418; McClymont, *op. cit.*, p. 248.

no suspicions even at the end . . . and whose indignation, when disillusioned, was all the more severe."[93]

Some see significance in the statement that people came to Bethany "not for Jesus' sake only, but that they might see Lazarus also, whom he had raised from the dead" (v. 9).[94]

THE TRIUMPHAL ENTRY

JOHN PROCEEDS TO TELL THE STORY OF THE TRIUMPHAL entry. His account differs from those in the Synoptics on certain points, one of which concerns the way in which Jesus obtained the ass on which to ride into the city. John says simply, "And Jesus, having found a young ass, sat thereon" (v. 14). This is in somewhat of a contrast with the Synoptic account, which tells us that Jesus sent two of His disciples to a certain village expressly to obtain a donkey. The entry into Jerusalem on a donkey was considered the fulfilment of the prophecy in Zechariah 9:9, and MacGregor thinks that John has altered the story a little in order to get a more striking fulfilment of the prophecy: "John makes the fulfilment of the prediction seem even more striking by suggesting that Jesus 'came across' the ass by a providential chance."[95] Everything here depends, of course, on whether the ass was in fact obtained "by a providential chance." Moffatt does indeed translate at this point "came across." But it is at least arguable whether this is a fair rendering of εὑρών. MacGregor draws attention to the use of the verb in John 1:43, to which he adds "etc." It is not easy to see why he adds this "etc.," for John often uses the verb to denote a purposeful seeking with a definite object in view from the very first. Thus it is used in this way in John 1:41 of Andrew's finding of Peter, and again in v. 46 of Philip's finding

---

[93] *Op. cit.*, p. 420. Godet also points out that to maintain that John shows "a special hatred to Judas" means "to affirm beyond question the authenticity of the Gospel; for what writer of the second century could have cherished a personal hatred against Judas?" (*op. cit.*, p. 210).

[94] E.g. Westcott, *op. cit.*, p. 114; see also Plummer, *op. cit.*, p. 253.

[95] *Op. cit.*, p. 262.

of Nathanael. It is used of Jesus' finding of the man He had healed from his lameness (5:14), and other passages can be readily found. It does not seem as though the turn of expression will bear the weight MacGregor places upon it. In other words John's way of putting it is no necessary indication that he was telling us anything other than what happened.

Barrett finds a mixture of hoary tradition and gross error. In the assertion that the disciples did not understand the significance of what was happening (v. 15) he sees John as reproducing "intentionally or unintentionally, old and reliable tradition." But since the crowds hailed Jesus as King (v. 13) John has contradicted himself.[96] This, however, does not appear to be the case. The multitude greeted Jesus as King, but John does not say that they recognized the fulfilment of the prophecy of Zechariah 9:9 either then or later. There could be other reasons for enthusiasm and for regarding Jesus as "the King of Israel" than this prophecy. In any case, the way John tells it the enthusiasm was there before Jesus rode the ass and thus fulfilled the prophecy. In other words he does not connect the crowd's enthusiasm with the prophecy. What he does connect with it is the later understanding of the disciples (not the crowd). The contradiction has to be read into John; it is not of his making.

In the next section of this chapter we have some thoughts on the meaning of the death of Jesus. They are introduced by the coming of some Greeks to Philip with the request that they might see Jesus. Wright objects to the authenticity of this passage on the grounds of its dramatic quality. He says, "The scene has a peculiar dramatic fitness in the whole setting of the Gospel; and this forbids our building too much on its historicity."[97] This kind of reasoning seems to me a little precarious. It is true that if we are faced with a storymaker we may expect him to have a sense of drama.

---

[96] *Op. cit.,* p. 349.

[97] *Op. cit.,* p. 275. Wright adds, "Though some such incident may well have happened in the closing days of the Ministry in Jerusalem." But it is clear that he does not take the section seriously.

But even so it is fair to comment that the essence of "dramatic fitness" is the quality of being true to life. Otherwise we have melodrama, not drama. Wright's objection is interesting, but subjective.

If it is a question of the subjective possibility we might as well adopt Renan's position, "Here are verses which have an unquestionable historical stamp."[98] Or, perhaps a little less subjectively, we might draw attention to a point made by J. E. Davey. He notes that in this passage, as in the Gethsemane story, "A limitation in Christ's knowledge is essential . . . as the essential perplexity in them cannot otherwise be understood." He goes on to point out that "This psychological difficulty, so created for the modern reader, is a mark of the historicity of the passages."[99] This is an interesting point. It would never have occurred to men of an earlier day that there was a psychological problem in connection with Christ's perplexity on these occasions. But the psychological knowledge made available in modern times reveals the perplexity in which Jesus stood, as Davey points out, as another mark of historicity. This kind of thing means a great deal to Davey. He recognizes that it is possible for early writers to manufacture ideas and incidents, but only such as are in character. It is not in character for them to picture Christ as perplexed. We might do so, but not first- or second-century writers. The fact that Jesus is here said to be uncertain is in itself evidence that John is recording faithfully what happened. Perhaps the same might be said of the statement with regard to the voice from heaven that "The multitude therefore, that stood by, and heard it, said that it had thundered" (v. 29). This is not the kind of interpretation of a voice from heaven that first-century man would readily evolve. It is a mark of John's faithfulness to the facts that he records it.[100]

---

[98] Cited in Godet, *op. cit.*, p. 219.

[99] *Op. cit.*, p. 128.

[100] Cf. McClymont, "It may be regarded as an evidence of the writer's honesty and freedom from dogmatic prejudice that he gives such prominence to the popular impression that the sound was nothing but a peal of thunder, while at the same time the minute-

Toward the end of the chapter John records Jesus as saying, "For I spake not from myself; but the Father that sent me, he hath given me a commandment, what I should say, and what I should speak" (v. 49). The implication of this verse should not be overlooked. It would be a rather unusual person who could manufacture it. He would be saying that Christ could speak only as the Father tells Him while at the same time he himself has been manufacturing sayings of Christ and is manufacturing this one![101]

THE UPPER ROOM

CHAPTER THIRTEEN OPENS WITH THE EPISODE OF THE foot-washing. This has struck a number of commentators as being extremely lifelike. Thus M.-J. Lagrange,

> The story is moreover, extremely natural. The calm of Jesus persisting in His charitable purpose without any ostentation and the liveliness of Peter, impressionable and changing, form a striking contrast but one which corresponds well to the character of the people concerned. The dialogue unfolds itself without obscurity unless one introduces mysteries. There is nothing in John which more closely resembles a page out of Mark.[102]

---

ness of his narrative bespeaks a personal knowledge of the facts" (*op. cit.*, p. 256).

[101] Godet asks, "Are there not enough impossibilities here? Let us remark also how this retrospective glance, interrupting the narrative, fails of appropriateness if we suppose it to have been composed in the second century, at a time when the question of the rejection by the Jews was no longer an actuality; on the contrary, how natural it is on the part of a man who was himself an eye-witness of this abnormal and unexpected fact of Jewish unbelief" (*op. cit.*, p. 239).

[102] M.-J. Lagrange, *Évangile selon Saint Jean*, Paris, 1936, p. 359. Godet also refers to the scene as "simple and life-like" and he thinks that Schweizer "has admirably brought out the stamp of historical truthfulness impressed upon this whole story" (*op. cit.*, p. 254). McClymont speaks of the laying aside of Jesus' garments as "the first of a number of graphic touches that bespeak an eye-witness" (*op. cit.*, p. 265). Westcott maintains that "The form of the narrative is marked by extreme minuteness and vividness of detail (*vv.* 4ff.), and by directness of recollection (*v.* 11). The portraiture of St. Peter is instinct with life" (*op. cit.*, p. 144);

Similarly William Hendriksen, when he comes to comment on v. 5, notes that "The details of the action are pictured one by one. The scene had left an indelible impression on the mind of the evangelist John, who was present. Hence, the record is very graphic."[103]

A number of the details in the narrative have aroused comment. It is obvious that the whole is very realistic and produces an impression of authenticity. Thus Plummer reminds us that Peter's impetuosity (v. 9) fits in with what is known of his character from the Synoptic Gospels. He thinks that it "comes out very strongly in his three utterances here." He goes on, "It is incredible that this should be invention; and if not, the independent authority of S. John's narrative is manifest."[104]

At the end of this incident Jesus said, "Ye are clean, but not all" (v. 10). John goes on to explain why Jesus said this: "He knew him that should betray him." On this Westcott comments, "The addition is quite natural if the writer's vivid recollection of the scene carries him back to the time when the words arrested the attention before they were fully intelligible. Otherwise it is difficult to account for the obvious explanation. No one who had always been familiar with the whole history would have added them."[105]

The prediction of the betrayal is evidence to many of the exact knowledge possessed by the writer. This is not universal. C. J. Wright, for example, thinks that the dramatic fitness of the narrative makes it difficult to think of it as historical. He says, ". . . There is a dramatic quality in the passage which suggests that the Evangelist was dealing with his source or sources with the freedom of the artist bent on emphasising the allegorical significance of the scene."[106] We have noticed a similar objection

---

". . . Each step in the act of service is noted with the particularity of an eye-witness" (*op. cit.*, p. 147).

[103] W. Hendriksen, *Exposition of the Gospel according to John*, II, Grand Rapids, 1954, p. 230. Marcus Dods similarly comments, "Each step in the whole astounding scene is imprinted on the mind of John" (EGT, John, p. 815).

[104] *Op. cit.*, p. 265.

[105] *Op. cit.*, p. 151.

[106] *Op. cit.*, p. 291.

raised by Wright in dealing with an earlier passage. We saw then that dramatic fitness is a subjective consideration which appeals in different ways to different minds. If we take the function of drama as holding a mirror up to life then it is a little hard to complain on these terms. And in any case it must be borne in mind that Wright in the same passage can say, ". . . If, as is here suggested, his teaching [i.e. that of John, son of Zebedee] forms one of the main sources for the presentation of the Evangelist, it is very probable that such personal reminiscence is at the basis of this narrative." To many commentators this seems to convey the truth of the matter. Thus Murray thinks that "the incident is described from within,"[107] which accords with the estimate of T. D. Bernard, "The details of the incident are before us as spectators of it, or rather as sharers in it. We receive the impressions of the moment from gestures and movements, and changing looks, and little tokens of the terms on which the persons are with each other."[108]

Some of these details are very impressive. Take, for example, the reaction to Jesus' prediction of the betrayal: "The disciples looked one on another, doubting of whom he spake" (v. 22). Hendriksen comments, "The vivid description of the reaction among the disciples shows that the author of the Fourth Gospel was one of the company. He never forgot that dramatic moment. As he was writing, it was as if the soul-terrifying words of Jesus regarding the betrayer were still resounding through the Upper Room."[109] The means whereby the identity of the betrayer was communicated to Simon Peter gives us several lifelike touches. Thus, of Peter's beckoning to the beloved disciple[110] that he should ask Jesus who it was,

---

[107] *Op. cit.,* p. 234.

[108] T. D. Bernard, *The Central Teaching of Jesus Christ,* London, 1900, p. 79. Cf. also Plummer, "It is the artless story of one who tells what he saw because he saw it and remembers it. The lifelike details which follow are almost irresistible evidences of truthfulness" (*op. cit.,* p. 268).

[109] *Op. cit.,* p. 243. McClymont sees in these words "a fine touch in the narrative of an eye-witness" (*op. cit.,* p. 269).

[110] N. E. Johnson says, of the passages which refer to the beloved disciple, ". . . In the five passages where he is mentioned, it is interest-

Bernard says, ". . . It may at least be claimed that Jn.'s narrative is peculiarly vivid,"[111] and D. Guthrie thinks it one of those details which leave the impression that the writer was present in person.[112] Again Strachan refers to the statement that the beloved disciple leaned back on Jesus' breast as a "realistic detail," and thinks that it "suggests the touch of one who was present."[113]

On the other hand some have difficulty in accepting certain aspects of the story. Barrett is very scathing about v. 26, in which Jesus gives the sop to Judas. He says, "It is plain from the narrative that the beloved disciple must have understood that Judas was the traitor. To say that he failed to grasp the meaning of the sign is to make him an imbecile. His subsequent inactivity is incomprehensible, and . . . casts doubt on John's narrative."[114] Alan Richardson similarly regards it as difficult to see why the disciples did not stop Judas when his identity was made clear. He says that John notices the difficulty, "but his attempt to explain it away is not entirely convincing. Again we must note that St John's dramatic scenes are theological parables rather than historical reminiscence or biographical reportage."[115]

Such positions are commonly argued. But I find this

---

ing to note the great amount of detail, which must have come only from an eyewitness account or source" (*op. cit.*, p. 280).

[111] *Op. cit.*, p. 472.

[112] D. Guthrie, *New Testament Introduction, The Gospels and Acts*, London, 1965, p. 228.

[113] *Op. cit.*, p. 270. R. V. G. Tasker thinks that if οὕτως was in the original text (and the textual evidence convinces most critics), "its presence here suggests that we are reading the personal evidence of the actor concerned in the incident. The disciple remembers that without moving his position he leaned back further, till he actually touched the breast of Jesus and was thus in a position to whisper to him" (TNTC, *John*, p. 162). Plummer cites Lightfoot: "This is among the most striking of those vivid descriptive traits which distinguish the narrative of the Fourth Gospel generally, and which are especially remarkable in these last scenes of Jesus' life, where the beloved disciple was himself an eye-witness and an actor" (*op. cit.*, p. 269). Westcott also sees in this "the recollection of an eye-witness" (*op. cit.*, p. 155); so does Bailey (*op. cit.*, p. 178).

[114] *Op. cit.*, p. 373.

[115] TBC, *John*, p. 160.

line of approach completely unconvincing. In the first place it means reading back into "betray" the full meaning that the term has for us. On this side of Calvary we can scarcely fail to understand it to mean something like "deliver up to death." But there are many degrees of betrayal. Few Christians will feel that they are completely guiltless of betraying their Master in one way or another. There is absolutely nothing in John's narrative up to this point to indicate the content of the betrayal of which Jesus spoke. Then, in the second place, betrayal can be involuntary. That it was this kind of betrayal that was in the disciples' minds seems clear from the fact that, as the Synoptists report, when Jesus prophesied betrayal the disciples asked, "Lord, is it I?" This can be understood only as indicating that the thought of a voluntary betrayal did not enter their minds. It would accordingly be completely relevant that Judas left the feast shortly after. If the disciples thought of an involuntary act of betrayal there was no particular reason for stopping him, even if they all caught the reference to Judas (which is certainly far from clear; the evidence seems against it). This is all the more the case in that there is nothing in Jesus' words to show that the betrayal was to take place immediately. If we confine ourselves to what He said and do not read anything into His words, the betrayal may have lain well in the future, perhaps even the distant future. In short, unless we read into the story of the upper room our fuller knowledge of what Judas was about to do and what Jesus was about to suffer, there is not the slightest reason for doubting the statement, "Now no man at the table knew for what intent he spake this unto him" (v. 28). The suggestions that John makes, namely the buying of something for the feast and the giving of money to the poor, are the things that may well have occurred spontaneously and naturally to the disciples. The scepticism of Barrett and Richardson can, it would seem, be justified only when we read back into the narrative something it does not contain.

The farewell discourses give little scope for the touch of the eyewitness, naturally enough. One or two things, however, have impressed commentators. For example,

Plummer notices the interjection of Judas, "Lord, what is come to pass that thou wilt manifest thyself unto us, and not unto the world?" (14:22). On this he remarks, "Judas supposes with the rest of his countrymen that the manifestation of the Messiah means a bodily appearance in glory before the whole world, to judge the Gentile and restore the kingdom to the Jews. Once more we have the Jewish point of view given with convincing precision."[116] By contrast MacGregor says that the passage contains "an indissoluble mingling of Jesus' own teaching, daring reinterpretations of that teaching under the guidance of the Spirit, and the recollections of the Evangelist and his associates also enriched by long years of spiritual experience."[117] In the words of 14:26, "But the Comforter, even the Holy Spirit, whom the Father will send in my name, he shall teach you all things, and bring to your remembrance all that I said unto you." But this must be understood as a subjective impression. MacGregor cites no evidence. This is the way the passage appears to him. It is not the way it appears necessarily to other people.

Jesus' words about "a little while" in connection with the disciples' seeing him and not seeing him, have impressed many. Thus Strachan can say, "The way in which the changes are rung on the expression *a little while*, suggests that the Evangelist has before him the actual expression used by Jesus."[118] A little later in the same chapter the words of Jesus are recorded, "These things have I spoken unto you in dark sayings" (16:25). This is noteworthy as forming one of the passages in which Barrett sees evidence of Johannine accuracy. He draws attention to the contrast made also in Mark between those who understand the teaching of Jesus and those who do not (Mark 4:11). Barrett proceeds, "John is well aware of this radical division brought about by the teaching and work of Jesus; but he is perhaps truer to the facts than

---

[116] *Op. cit.*, p. 280.

[117] *Op. cit.*, p. 312.

[118] *Op. cit.*, p. 296. This also impresses Westcott, who thinks it records "a distinct impression on the mind of the Evangelist as to the actual scene" (*op. cit.*, p. 227).

Mark when he suggests that even the Twelve remained to the end among the mystified."[119]

The great prayer recorded in chapter seventeen is regarded by many as clearly authentic. Thus Wright, who is often ready to espouse solutions which leave John in error, and who asserts that "this 'Prayer' is not an exact report of *one* prayer of Jesus. The language throughout is Johannine," yet goes on to say, "it is not possible to believe that the whole prayer is an original composition of the Evangelist himself. The certitude of the Father's presence and of the Father's will which throbs through the whole prayer is the certitude of Jesus Himself." Wright notices other points of a similar character and then says, "All this, we cannot but feel, is a transcript from the consciousness of the historic Jesus. . . . What we do wish to maintain is that *in substance* the prayer is a true transcript of the mind of Jesus when confronted with His approaching death on the Cross."[120]

Similarly Bernard is impressed with the parallels to verses in the Lord's Prayer. He cites a number of examples and proceeds, "None of these coincidences or parallels is likely to have been invented by one setting himself to compose a prayer for the lips of Christ on the eve of His Passion; but, when taken together, they show that the spirit which breathes through c. 17 is similar to that with which we have been made familiar when reading Jesus' words as recorded by the Synoptists and elsewhere in Jn."[121]

It is this kind of thing that impresses most people. The prayer as a whole is convincing and it is not unlike what we have read elsewhere. Now and then, however, other points receive mention. Thus J. C. Ryle comments on the words, "lifting up his eyes to heaven" (v. 1). He points out that this is a reverent gesture and that it "seems clearly to show that the prayer was prayed before witnesses. John writes as one describing what he saw and heard."[122] Again, Plummer is impressed by the later

---

[119] *Op. cit.*, p. 413.
[120] *Op. cit.*, p. 323.
[121] *Op. cit.*, p. 559.
[122] J. C. Ryle, *Expository Thoughts on the Gospels, St. John*, III, London, 1957, p. 194.

statement that some of the words of Jesus uttered in this prayer were fulfilled, namely, "Of those whom thou hast given me I lost not one" (18:9). He points out that "If the prayer were the composition of the Evangelist to set forth in an ideal form Christ's mental condition at the time, this reference to a definite portion of it would be most unnatural."[123] The implication is that, since there is a later appeal to the fulfilment of the words, their first utterance must in fact have taken place.

THE ARREST OF JESUS

WITH CHAPTER EIGHTEEN WE RETURN TO NARRATIVE, AND the lifelike details recur. There is much in this chapter to which significance has been attached. Perhaps we may begin with the criticism made by many and voiced clearly by MacGregor, namely that John, son of Zebedee, would certainly not have omitted to mention the agony in Gethsemane. He is explicitly said by the Synoptists to have been one of the three that Jesus took to pray with Him. So it is impossible that he was ignorant of it. This argument is plausible, but it fails to do justice to the fact that on any showing this Gospel has some extraordinary omissions. It is impossible to think, for example, that anyone who knew enough about Jesus to write a gospel should not know of the institution of the Holy Communion. Yet, though this Evangelist has far and away the longest narrative of what took place in the upper room he does not mention it. I am not aware of anyone who has given a convincing explanation for this omission. We may engage in guesses, more or less plausible, but we do not know why John did this. And we do not know why he omitted the story of Gethsemane. But since he demonstrably omitted some important things of which he had full knowledge, it is impossible to maintain that the omission of the Gethsemane story shows that he did not know it and that therefore he could not have been the apostle John. The most we can say is that we would have expected him to mention it. It seems to us that it would have been congenial to his purpose. But against this

---

[123] *Op. cit.*, p. 309.

some have suggested that John depicts Jesus' whole life as one of lowliness and humble dependence on God. He would not, accordingly, have found congenial an incident that might give the impression that all the lowliness was found here. I do not find this convincing. But some thinkers evidently do.

Other suggestions have been made. Thus P. Gardner-Smith holds that "dogmatic interests would provide a sufficient explanation here,"[124] while D. Lamont "hazards the opinion" that the omission of the agony and recording of the betrayal are because "John intends the betrayal to suggest one cause of the Agony."[125] C. H. Dodd comments, "John, it might be said, has drawn a veil over the scene from motives of reverence, and, omitting the inward struggle, has turned the final acceptance into an overt declaration."[126] Whatever our view of the merits of such suggestions it is plain that MacGregor's argument from silence is being asked to prove too much. Minds both reverent and profound have interpreted John's silence very differently.

Chapter 18 begins with the statement that Jesus went with His disciples "over the brook Kidron" (v. 1), a statement which to Wright "seems a clear indication of his knowledge of the locality."[127]

In v. 3 we have mention of the arresting party which Judas led. It includes Roman soldiers, a statement MacGregor rejects on the grounds that "if Roman soldiers had effected the arrest Jesus would almost certainly have been led direct to Pilate."[128] However, MacGregor is not supported by all in this opinion. Wright, for example, maintains that "The whole historical situation, however, makes it much more probable that the Evangelist here is stating historic fact."[129] W. F. Howard feels the strength

---

[124] *Saint John and the Synoptic Gospels*, Cambridge, 1938, p. 57.
[125] *Studies in the Johannine Writings*, London, 1956, p. 99.
[126] HTFG, p. 68.
[127] *Op. cit.*, p. 336.
[128] *Op. cit.*, p. 324. The reason for the mention of Roman soldiers, MacGregor thinks, is "for dramatic and symbolical reasons."
[129] *Loc. cit.* Wright notes that the fact "would have its own dramatic and symbolical significance for his mind." Plummer, commenting on v. 3, says, "The details which follow are minute and accurate as of an eyewitness" (*op. cit.*, p. 307).

of the objection, but decides in favor of the authenticity. He says, "The introduction of a Roman officer and a band of Roman soldiers into the story of the arrest is at first sight an improbable embellishment. On closer examination, however, it is not unlikely that, if the Sanhedrin, or its most active spirits, had resolved on delivering Jesus up to the Roman authority as a dangerous stirrer up of sedition, they would take the precaution of seeking some help from the officer whose special duty at the feast it was to prevent dangerous disorder from arising in the Temple court."[130]

It was Judas who led the soldiers, and John records that after Jesus had told the military men that He was Jesus of Nazareth, "Judas also, who betrayed him, was standing with them" (v. 5). This impresses Temple. He points out that Judas "can do nothing but stand there with the rest, and the Beloved Disciple saw him."[131]

At the point when the soldiers were about to arrest Jesus, "Simon Peter . . . having a sword drew it, and struck the high priest's servant, and cut off his right ear. Now the servant's name was Malchus" (v. 10). Barrett notes the use of the names Kidron, Peter, and Malchus and thinks that it may be supposed "either that John possessed other valuable sources of traditional material in addition to the synoptic gospels, or that with the lapse of time the earlier tradition came to be enriched with such personal details. Comparison with the apocryphal gospels (cf. e.g. Gospel of Peter 31, where the name Petronius, of the centurion is given; Acts of Pilate 1.1) suggests that the latter is the more probable alternative."[132] However, neither here nor elsewhere does Barrett produce evidence to show that this Gospel is of the same type as the apocryphal gospels. It is much simpler to think that John put in the names because he knew them. The addition of names is sometimes evidence of access to

---

[130] FGRCI, pp. 134f. He goes on to cite the later collaboration between Claudius Lysias and the sanhedrin when the peace of the city seemed imperilled.

[131] *Op. cit.*, p. 338.

[132] *Op. cit.*, p. 431. For a discussion of the use of names see below, pp. 238ff.

reliable tradition. Thus Mark does not name the high priest to whom Jesus was taken (Mark 14:53), whereas Matthew tells us that his name was Caiaphas (Matt. 26:57). Matthew's insertion of the name is usually accepted as reliable and not as due to a tendency to insert names on no historical basis. Why should we think otherwise with John? Barrett does not tell us. He only says it is so. By contrast with Barrett, Hendriksen sees in the name "the touch of eyewitness."[133]

THE "TRIAL" BEFORE THE JEWS

AFTER THE ARREST JESUS WAS TAKEN TO ANNAS FIRST (v. 12). John does not give as much prominence to Jesus' "trial" before the Jewish authorities as do the Synoptists. He prefers to concentrate on proceedings before Pilate. Moreover there are difficulties in what he tells us: for example, he is the only one to mention the appearance before Annas. However, Barrett seems to go too far when he says, "In John's own account great difficulties appear at once. The most notable is the impossibility of combining the statements made about the high priest; why should Jesus be sent to Caiaphas (v. 24) when the high priest (who, John tells us (v. 13), was Caiaphas) has already questioned him (v. 19)?"[134] It will be noticed that this depends on our understanding "the high priest" in v. 19 to refer to Caiaphas. There is no difficulty at all if it refers to Annas, as the context seems to require. In v. 13 Jesus was brought to Annas, and it was then explained that Annas was father-in-law to Caiaphas (13b-14). A paragraph referring to Peter follows (15-18), so that when we return to Jesus we expect to

---

[133] *Op. cit.*, p. 382. W. Milligan and W. F. Moulton are likewise impressed with this; "His name was Malchus, and the mention of this fact, as well as of the minute circumstance that the ear cut off was the right ear, illustrates the personal knowledge possessed by John of what he describes" (*Commentary on the Gospel of St. John*, Edinburgh, 1898, p. 198). So also Bernard (*op. cit.*, p. 589). Bailey sees in the name of Malchus "one indication of his [i.e. John's] familiarity with priestly circles" (*op. cit.*, p. 207). Even MacGregor can speak of "this appearance of inside information" (*op. cit.*, p. 326).

[134] *Op. cit.*, p. 437.

find Him with Annas. He does not come before Caiaphas
until v. 24. It is true that there was only one "high
priest" and that at this time Caiaphas held the position,
having been placed in office by the Romans. But there
is nothing strange in Annas' also being called "high
priest." He had held the office until the Romans deposed
him, and in the eyes of those Jews who denied the right
of aliens to depose God's high priest he was still the
legitimate holder of the office. He is specifically referred
to as high priest (Luke 3:2; Acts 4:6), and this is implied
also in the use of the plural in this very chapter (v. 35).
It is curious that Barrett takes no notice of the fact that
Annas is elsewhere called "high priest," for if both men
can be described by this title the difficulty disappears. It
is not without its interest that Barrett sees "no historical
difficulty in the statement that Jesus first appeared before" Annas.[135] If there is no difficulty in this, one wonders why the difficulty should be raised about a point of
nomenclature which in any case is independently attested
by Luke.[136] Renan, who was not noticeably conservative,
could say of this incident, "Our author alone represents
Jesus as brought to the house of Annas, the father-in-law
of Caiaphas. Josephus confirms the correctness of this
account. . . . This circumstance, of which the first two
Gospels give no hint, is a beam of light. How should a
sectary, writing in Egypt or in Asia Minor, have known
this? It is a strong proof of the historical value of our
Gospel."[137] Lord Charnwood is another who finds the
Annas incident significant: ". . . There is no doctrinal
purpose served, but it is a scene full of character and

---

[135] *Op. cit.*, p. 438.

[136] Wright draws attention to the fact that we commonly do
much the same sort of thing. He says, "If, for example, we could
imagine a very famous 'Archbishop of Canterbury' being alive when
his successor is enthroned in Canterbury, we should not be surprised if an author were to call each of them by the same title
'Archbishop.'" He concludes his discussion of this point with,
"What, therefore, has been regarded as an 'astonishing contradiction' and 'self-stultification' on the part of the Evangelist, will not
appear so to those who exercise the historical imagination" (*op. cit.*,
p. 341).

[137] Cited in Godet, *op. cit.*, p. 357.

life, which really enriches the history which we obtain as a whole when we take the Gospels together."[138]

It is well known that John records the three denials of St. Peter in a way different from the Synoptists. He places an interval between the first denial (v. 17) and the second and third denials (vv. 25ff.). Sometimes it is alleged that this shows that John was not aware of the true sequence. It is much more likely, however, that he was giving us what actually happened and that the Synoptists have grouped the denials. Godet is quite sure of this, for he says, "This better articulated narrative certainly reproduces the true course of things, and nothing more clearly reveals in the author of our Gospel the witness of the facts."[139] MacGregor regards John as unreliable here. He draws attention to the fact that in v. 25 Peter is warming himself at the fire as he was in v. 18, though there has been a change of scene to the house of Caiaphas in v. 24, and in the light of this maintains that "the Redactor by prematurely changing the scene has reduced Peter's position to absurdity."[140] Quite apart from the fact that this states as fact an activity by a redactor whom some of us regard as mythical, this is going too fast. The writer does not say that the happenings of v. 25 took place after those of v. 24. He has been outlining the examination before Annas, and when he comes to an end he says that Annas sent Jesus on to Caiaphas. This rounds off the narrative nicely. That done, the writer returns to Peter. But there is not the slightest reason for thinking that Peter is affected by the change of scene. He is standing by the same fire. The difficulty appears to be created by the commentator. It does not spring out of the narrative.

John tells us that that night "it was cold" (v. 18). Barrett sees in this in all probability an inference from Mark 14:54, a verse which does not mention the temperature but says that Peter was "warming himself." But

---

[138] Charnwood, *According to St. John*, London, n. d., p. 99.
[139] *Op. cit.*, p. 358. Godet proceeds to cite Renan to the same effect. Milligan and Moulton likewise see this as history (*op. cit.*, p. 203).
[140] *Op. cit.*, p. 328.

he is constrained to admit that it is equally possible that the detail arises from the recollection of an eyewitness.[141] Bernard is more certain of John. He reminds us that this mention of the cold is peculiar to this Gospel and he thinks that it "suggests that the story has come from one who was present, and who shivers as he recalls how cold it was in the open court."[142]

The interrogation of Jesus before the high priest (vv. 19ff.) is recorded in a way very different from anything in the Synoptics. This does not mean that John is manufacturing the incident. C. H. Dodd points out that there are undoubtedly early features in this account and he concludes that John's account of this interrogation "is drawn from some source, almost certainly oral, which was well informed about the situation at the time, and had contact with the Jewish tradition about the trial and condemnation of Jesus."[143] On one detail in this examination, the smiting of Jesus by one of the officers and Jesus' calm reply (vv. 22f.), Dods says, "The calmness and reasonableness of Jesus' retort to this blow impressed it on the memory of John, whose own blood would boil when he saw his Master struck by a servant."[144]

When John returns to the story of the denial he says that one of the questions was asked by "One of the servants of the high priest, being a kinsman of him whose ear Peter cut off" (v. 26). This does not impress Barrett. He reminds us that no one else gives the name of the man who was struck or the name of the questioner, and proceeds, "We must conclude either that behind the Johannine passion narrative there stands a first-hand source, or that John is himself elaborating details in the manner of the apocryphal gospels." His conclusion is, "The general lack of coherence in the narrative does not confirm the former alternative."[145] Others, however, do not view the narrative in the same way. McClymont sees

---

141 *Op. cit.*, p. 440.

142 *Op. cit.*, p. 598. Murray thinks that John, "having also been out that night, had special reason to remember how cold it had been" (*op. cit.*, p. 328).

143 HTFG, pp. 95f.

144 *Op. cit.*, p. 849.

145 *Op. cit.*, p. 442.

in the mention of the relationship "another token of independent knowledge on the part of the writer,"[146] and Plummer exclaims, "How natural that an acquaintance of the high-priest (v. 15) known to his portress (v. 16) should know this fact also as well as Malchus' name (v. 10)."[147]

JESUS BEFORE PILATE

WHEN WE COME TO THE NARRATIVE OF THE TRIAL BEFORE Pilate we again have diverse interpretations of the evidence.[148] Barrett, for example, thinks that most of John's material "is based upon the Marcan narrative." It is true that John has quite a number of things that Mark has not, but of this Barrett says, "John's additions and alterations do not inspire confidence in his historical reliability." Ivor Buse, however, as we saw earlier, has a very different picture. He accepts Vincent Taylor's division of the Marcan passion narrative into two strands, the basic narrative A, and the Petrine and other Semitic material B, and proceeds to show that while John has parallels with B he has none with the basic narrative A. This shows that John did not have Mark either before him or in mind.[149] Under these circumstances he can scarcely be said to base his narrative on that of Mark. It is possible that not all of Buse's arguments will be accepted. But he has made it clear that the position is not as simple as Barrett claims.

Barrett refers details to the notes but as a general comment maintains that "it is highly improbable that reliable information respecting private conversations between the prisoner and the judge (if any took place) should have reached the evangelist."[150] As to these conversations Plummer thinks that "we seem to have the

---

[146] *Op. cit.*, p. 315.

[147] *Op. cit.*, p. 313. Westcott also sees in this detail evidence of "an exact knowledge of the household" (*op. cit.*, p. 278).

[148] On a very small point, the fact that "it was early" (John 18:28), Bultmann says, "... The day of Jesus' victory over the world has dawned" (*op. cit.*, p. 504). But it needs the eye of faith to see such a symbolical reference in so simple a statement.

[149] Ivor Buse, NTS, 4, 1957-58, pp. 215-219.

[150] *Op. cit.*, p. 443.

evidence of an eyewitness."[151] It is, moreover, doubtful whether any private conversation is recorded, private, that is to say, in the sense that no one other than the participants was present. There are certainly conversations in which no one is mentioned as saying anything other than Pilate and Jesus. But there is not the slightest reason for affirming that no one else was present. We are explicitly told that the reason that the Jews did not enter the Praetorium was not that they were not permitted to enter, but that they chose to stay out lest they be defiled and not able to eat the Passover (v. 28). It is impossible to imagine such a scruple deterring any of the friends of Jesus at such a time. And nothing in the narrative leads us to think that John would not have been allowed to enter the Praetorium. By contrast with Barrett's sceptical estimate, Strachan is of the opinion that John's account "everywhere shows traces of an independent and first-hand source of information." Strachan sees the reason for this in John's ecclesiastical background: "If the Evangelist was originally a member of the Sadducean party, and had access to ecclesiastical circles, his extraordinarily vivid and accurate account, not only of the happenings, but of the motives of the ecclesiastical authorities and the hesitation in the mind of Pilate, can be explained."[152]

John informs us that the Jewish leaders "entered not into the Praetorium, that they might not be defiled, but might eat the passover" (v. 28). This information is given by nobody else and Barrett regards the statement as very important. He notes the Jewish dictum, "The dwelling-places of Gentiles are unclean." But he maintains that the uncleanness incurred by the Jews would last only until the end of the day, when it could be removed by a bath. He maintains that John is accordingly in error in holding that the entering of a Gentile dwelling would have prevented the priests from keeping the Passover. He also notices the provision whereby "if the priests were unclean but the congregation clean, the Passover may be kept in uncleanness." Barrett goes on, "John's

---

[151] *Op. cit.*, p. 134.
[152] *Op. cit.*, p. 311.

statement, therefore, that the Jews acted as they did in order that they might be able to eat the Passover, seems very questionable. This is an important example of the way in which some of John's detailed historical notes, which add verisimilitude to his narrative and have led to the view that he was an eye-witness, break down when they are subjected to criticism."[153]

Barrett describes this as "an important example." It will thus bear looking into. Barrett's case sounds very convincing. But he has not given attention to the fact that there were different kinds of uncleanness. It is true that some types of uncleanness were removed at the end of the day by a ritual bath. But it is also true that there was another type of uncleanness, that contracted by contact with a dead body, which lasted for a week (see Num. 19:11). This did not require actual physical contact with the dead body. To enter the tent in which a man had died was quite sufficient to convey this kind of defilement (Num. 19:14). It is relevant to the present inquiry because the reason that Gentile houses conveyed uncleanness was that the Gentiles were held to throw abortions down the drains.[154] It is thus clear that a seven-

---

[153] *Op. cit.*, p. 444.

[154] See S Bk, II, pp. 838ff. They say plainly, "The house was thus regarded as defiled by a corpse and according to Num. 19:14 it made the Israelite who entered unclean for seven days" (p. 839). See also H. Danby, *The Mishnah*, Oxford, 1933, p. 675, n. 10. The Mishnah tractate *Oholoth* provides that "The dwelling-places of Gentiles are unclean." In answer to the question, "How long must a gentile have lived in them so that examination becomes needful?" the reply is, "Forty days" (*Ohol.* 18:7). The reason for this period was apparently the belief that it takes forty-one days for the embryo, to become human young (a miscarriage on the fortieth day need not be dealt with as for human young; see *Nidd.* 3:7). *Ohol.* 18:9 joins regulations about the houses of Gentiles with references to graveyards, which probably indicates that they are regarded as of the same class as concerns uncleanness. Similarly Gentiles and those polluted by contact with a corpse are classed together as ineligible to enter the Rampart (*Kel.* 1:8). Josephus tells us that when the Romans retained the high priest's vestment it was handed to the priests seven days before each of the great festivals and the fast (Ant. XVIII. 94; elsewhere he speaks of handing it back the day before, Ant. XV. 408; possibly this was considered sufficient for most occasions, but at the great festivals no risks were run and the full seven days were required). Clearly this was to give

day uncleanness and not a one-day uncleanness was what the priests feared. To enter the governor's residence would have involved them in such uncleanness as would have prevented them from keeping any part of the feast.

Nor is the concession referred to by Barrett of much relevance. It was a concession to enable the Passover to be held when all the priests were defiled. It was a remedy for a desperate situation which would otherwise prevent anyone from keeping the Passover. It is irrelevant to the present passage for two reasons. First, there is no question of the entire priesthood entering the Praetorium. Only a delegation is meant. There would still be some priests clean and this would enable the Passover to be held. Only those who were defiled would have been debarred. It is of importance that John does not say that they refused to enter the Praetorium "lest no passover be held" or the like, but "that they might not be defiled, but might eat the passover." It is the priests who might have entered the Praetorium who are in mind. The second consideration is that even had the whole priesthood been involved we have no reason for thinking they would have regarded with equanimity the prospect of keeping the Passover "in uncleanness." That was a desperate remedy for desperate circumstances, only to be used as a last resort. It would be on all counts greatly preferable (and much simpler) to induce Pilate to come out to them. This would enable the Passover to be held on the normal fashion.

Barrett calls this "an important example." As in this "important example" our best evidence seems to show that John is right (and his modern critics wrong) we have all the greater confidence in his reliability.

---

the time necessary for purifying the robe after a corpse pollution. A. Büchler maintains that the schools of Hillel and Shammai differed on the kind of uncleanness conveyed by Gentile dwellings, with the Hillelites certainly holding the view that it was corpse uncleanness (JQR, 17, 1926-27, pp. 18f.). Büchler holds that many thought that the lighter form of uncleanness only was involved. But nothing that he says indicates that in as weighty a matter as the cleanness of the priests at Passover time any chances would be taken with the laws of uncleanness. The evidence cited above forms a solid argument that the uncleanness conveyed was corpse uncleanness.

After Pilate had spoken with the priests he returned to the Praetorium and spoke with Jesus (v. 33). This is one of the places where a number of critics complain of John's inaccuracy, maintaining that he describes a private conversation at which he could not possibly have been present. We have already noticed that this is more than doubtful. As Bernard points out, "The priestly accusers of Jesus could not follow Him inside the house, because of their scruples about ceremonial uncleanness (v. 28); but it is not likely that admission to the chamber of inquiry was forbidden to others duly introduced who wished to hear what was going on."[155] This is important. There is not the slightest reason for thinking that Pilate was engaging in Star Chamber methods. To maintain that the writer of this Gospel could not have been present in the Praetorium is sheer assumption. There is not one shred of evidence for it.

The mockery of Jesus by the soldiers (19:1ff.) impresses different critics in different ways. Thus McClymont thinks that "The Apostle seems to have preserved a vivid recollection of the whole scene."[156] By contrast, Barrett thinks the scene "highly dramatic but equally improbable,"[157] and MacGregor holds that "it is much more likely" that "the mockery by the soldiers took place only after Jesus had been handed over for execution" (as in the Synoptics).[158] Neither Barrett nor MacGregor seems to have taken into account the character of Pilate as revealed by both biblical and nonbiblical sources. There is no reason for thinking of him as a firm, just man who would, in Barrett's words, "have released or executed his prisoner." This is undoubtedly what a Roman judge ought to have done and what many of them would have done. But all our evidence shows that Pilate was a weak man all too ready to be pushed by the mob into a course of action not of his own choosing. Thus on this occasion

---

[155] *Op. cit.*, pp. 608f. Bernard also thinks that "The disciple who seems to have been present at the examination of Jesus by Annas ... may also have been a witness of the scene in Pilate's palace which is here told so vividly" (p. 608).

[156] *Op. cit.*, p. 320.

[157] *Op. cit.*, p. 450.

[158] *Op. cit.*, p. 338.

he undoubtedly wanted to release Jesus. But to do so would have been difficult and unpopular. He was not prepared to face the consequences. So he tried to win others around to his point of view. John describes the mocking as though it were part of Pilate's plan. He wanted to show Jesus as a pitiable object, an object of mockery and derision, one who was in no sense a king and who might well therefore be released. Since Barrett and MacGregor give no attention to this possibility their comments have the less weight.

At the height of Pilate's attempt to release Jesus the Jews yelled, "If thou release this man, thou art not Caesar's friend: every one that maketh himself a king speaketh against Caesar" (v. 12). This was the critical point. The implied threat was to impeach Pilate if he failed to do as the Jews wanted. Pilate immediately condemned Jesus. Strachan sees in this evidence of John's acquaintance with the situation: "Here the Evangelist displays a remarkable knowledge of the popular feeling towards Pilate."[159]

It is more than a little difficult to ascribe the knowledge the Evangelist shows, both of Pilate and of the reaction of the Jews, to a writer of fiction in the second century. The whole is not only dramatic, but it also fits in very well with conditions and people as we know them.

Sometimes it is the small points in the narrative that carry conviction. In v. 14 John mentions that "it was

---

[159] *Op. cit.*, p. 317. Of the whole scene Godet says, "... The scene described by John is its own defence. It is impossible to portray more to the life, the astuteness, the perseverance and the impudent suppleness of the accuser, determined to succeed, at any cost, on the one side, and, on the other, the obstinate struggle, in the heart of the judge, between the consciousness of his duty and the care for his own interests, between the fear of sacrificing an innocent man, perhaps more formidable than He appeared to be outwardly, and that of driving to extremity a people already exasperated by crying acts of injustice, and of finding himself accused before a suspicious emperor, *one stroke of whose pen (Reuss)* might precipitate him into destruction; finally, between cold scepticism and the transient impressions of natural religiousness and even pagan superstition. *Reuss* acknowledges that it is 'the Fourth Gospel which gives the true key of the problem' of Pilate's inconceivable conduct" (*op. cit.*, pp. 381f.).

about the sixth hour." This leads Lenski to say, "He writes so many details that we conclude that he must have been present."[160] There are certainly plenty of them throughout the narrative, and they are not put in indiscriminately as though the writer did not know his facts but was trying to make it look as though he did. H. E. Edwards is impressed by "the quite superfluous detail that Pilate 'sat down in a place called The Pavement but in Hebrew, Gabbatha'. These small and gratuitous additions to the information given to us by the Synoptists, just because they are unnecessary, suggest the eyewitness. They are without significance in themselves. They are given because the speaker is telling us what he remembered."[161]

When Pilate made his final appeal, "Shall I crucify your King?" John tells us that the Jewish priests replied, "We have no king but Caesar" (v. 15). This introduction of the political note and of the Jews' profession of loyalty rings true. It is very difficult to see this saying as manufactured at some later time. It must always be borne in mind that the Christian church was not a popular institution in the late first and early second centuries. It was often misunderstood and always in danger of persecution. The standard Christian response in this situation was to make it plain that Christians were loyal subjects of the emperor. They might be theological nonconformists but they were not political rebels. It is unthinkable that in such a situation a Christian would introduce into any narrative sayings that purport to indicate that Jesus Christ had been killed as a claimant to the imperial throne. Still less would a believer have imported into a narrative the claim that Jesus' crucifixion was effectively brought about when his Jewish opponents proclaimed their loyalty to Caesar. The introduction of this politically dangerous motif is an indication of faithfulness to the facts. As C. H. Dodd says, "If the evangelist set himself to reproduce with essential fidelity the ethos of the actual situation in which Christ was condemned, as it was handed

---

[160] *Op. cit.*, p. 1272.
[161] H. E. Edwards, *The Disciple Who Wrote These Things*, London, 1953, p. 128.

down (however much he may have felt free to dramatize it), the preservation of these challenging traits could be understood; but I should find it difficult to imagine a Christian writer under Domitian (let us say), or even under Nerva or Trajan, going out of his way to introduce them into a relatively harmless account."[162]

THE CRUCIFIXION

JOHN IS THE ONLY EVANGELIST TO MENTION THAT JESUS set out carrying His cross, a fact that leads Milligan and Moulton to comment, "It is a trace of the accuracy of John both in observing and relating facts, that he is the only Evangelist who mentions the circumstance."[163]

When we move on to the story of the crucifixion itself there are many touches of the eyewitness. Bernard can say, ". . . Throughout the Johannine account of the Crucifixion (vv. 23-37), the fuller testimony of an eye-witness (see v. 35) reveals itself. This account is due to one who was near the Cross all the time."[164]

Sometimes objections are raised on minor points. For example, Barrett thinks it improbable that Jesus' friends stood near the cross.[165] This would be more impressive if we had evidence from antiquity as to how close to a cross the relatives and friends of the crucified were permitted to come. In a case like this, where there was no danger of rescue or riot, there seems no reason why they should not have been allowed as close as John says they were. In other words the objection is purely subjective.

Barrett also finds it difficult to think that Jesus would commend His mother to the care of the beloved disciple when there were brothers who had a legal claim.[166] This would be more cogent if Jesus were doing anything legal; but it is reading a lot into the simple words, "Woman, behold thy son!" "Behold, thy mother!" (vv.

---

[162] HTFG, p. 115.

[163] *Op. cit.*, p. 212.

[164] *Op. cit.*, p. 629. McClymont is also of the opinion that the narrative shows that John followed Jesus to the cross and thus speaks as an eyewitness (*op. cit.*, p. 315).

[165] *Op. cit.*, p. 458.

[166] *Op. cit.*, p. 459.

26f.), to see in them a legal statement giving John an official position. The writer appears to mean no more than that Jesus now gave to John the general responsibility of looking after Mary. And in view of the fact that up until this point the brothers lacked faith in Jesus there is nothing unlikely about this. N. E. Johnson, by contrast with Barrett, comments on "the obviously first-hand knowledge" shown in this statement.[167] Barrett's further comment, ". . . At Acts 1:14 the mother of Jesus appears in company with his brothers," is perhaps misleading. In that passage there is a list of the apostles, after which we are told that these all continued in prayer "with the women, and Mary the mother of Jesus, and with his brethren." In the Greek, Μαριαμ τῇ μητρὶ τοῦ Ἰησοῦ is linked with γυναιξίν under the one σύν, whereas καὶ σύν intervenes between it and τοῖς ἀδελφοῖς αὐτοῦ.[168] There is no reason for thinking of Mary as specially linked with the brothers at all. She is grouped with the women, not the brethren.

As He hung on the cross Jesus received vinegar from a sponge which someone raised to His lips (v. 29). There are some touches here that have impressed a number of scholars. Thus John knows more than that the means of raising the sponge to Jesus' lips was "a reed" (as in the Synoptics). He tells us that it was in fact hyssop, which indicates to Lenski "his presence as an eyewitness."[169] Plummer notices John's reference to the "vessel full of vinegar." He comments, "John's exact knowledge appears again. The Synoptists do not mention the σκεῦος but he had stood beside it."[170] When Jesus had received the drink thus supplied to Him, "he said, It is finished: and he bowed his head, and gave up his spirit" (v. 30). It is perhaps worth noting that none of the Evangelists says that Jesus "died." Each has his own way of referring to death. John speaks of His giving up His spirit, which perhaps points to some voluntary act of will. Be that as it may, the little detail "he bowed his head," which is

---

[167] *Op. cit.*, p. 281.

[168] Some MSS do omit the second σύν, but it seems to be part of the true text.

[169] *Op. cit.*, p. 1307.

[170] *Op. cit.*, p. 331. He also sees in the hyssop "another mark of exact knowledge" (p. 332).

not found in the other accounts, "suggests that the account depends on the testimony of an eye-witness."[171]

John goes on to tell us that certain things happened after Jesus died. The Jews wanted the bodies removed from the crosses, so they asked Pilate that the legs of the crucified should be broken. In the case of those still living this would hasten the onset of death. Accordingly the legs of the two people crucified with Jesus were broken, but when the soldiers saw that Jesus was dead they did not break His legs. Instead one of them pierced Jesus' side with his spear, whereupon "there came out blood and water" (v. 34). John evidently regarded this as very important, for he solemnly assures us that an eyewitness vouches for it (v. 35). Barrett, however, is not impressed. He says that "the presence of an eye-witness is not probable," and he goes on to refer to "the alleged fact," which he thinks "could conceivably have arisen out of John's theology."

Barrett also tells us that "John does not seem fully to have understood the Jewish reason for removing the bodies from the crosses before nightfall."[172] He does not tell us what he means by this remark, but it appears that what he has in mind is John's mention of the sabbath. The Jews objected to the bodies staying on crosses overnight on any day of the week. Barrett appears to think that John means that their objection referred only to the sabbath. This, however, is reading something into the narrative. It is not what John says. And the position is adequately covered by some words of Barrett on the same page: "Of course, it is true that what would have been objectionable on any day was doubly so on so important a day." That is clearly what John means. To impugn his accuracy by saying that it might perhaps be taken to mean something else is not being fair to him.

Barrett's rejection of the view that the passage is due to an eyewitness is based on his view that it fits in with and could have arisen out of John's theology. John is in-

---

[171] Bernard, *op. cit.*, p. 641. Plummer similarly comments, "Another detail peculiar to the Evangelist who witnessed it" (*op. cit.*, p. 332).

[172] *Op. cit.*, p. 461.

deed perfectly capable of selecting his facts so that they agree with his theology, but that does not mean that they are any the less facts. This is amply demonstrated and needs no further proof here. We need more than an affirmation that a statement is congenial to John's theological position before recognizing a historical inaccuracy. Other commentators have no great difficulty in discerning truth behind John's words here. Thus Murray can say, "S. John has another incident to record, which came under his own eye and to which he clearly attaches deep significance."[173] Others have similar statements. Lenski is impressed by the manner by which the breaking of the legs is described: ". . . The soldiers do their awful work. John saw it performed, first on the one, then on the other malefactor. . . . John tells the facts as he saw them."[174]

Finally in this chapter let us notice the mention of the weight of spices used in embalming the body of Jesus. Since it is so great ("about a hundred pounds," v. 39) some reject it out of hand. But Guthrie, for example, sees in it the touch of a man who was there.[175] How else should the figure be known?

THE RESURRECTION

WHEN WE COME TO THE RESURRECTION STORIES IN CHAPTER twenty we are on difficult ground. A good deal depends here on whether we believe the miracle of the resurrection to be historical or not. If we feel that the "resurrection" was nothing more than a profound spiritual experience of the disciples we will be more than a little sceptical about the way in which the story is recounted. We must be prepared accordingly for diverse estimates of the value of this chapter.

---

[173] *Op. cit.*, p. 346.

[174] *Op. cit.*, p. 1314. Lenski proceeds, "Why, since Jesus' cross stood between those of the malefactors, did the soldiers pass by his cross and go from the one malefactor to the other? Why do they leave Jesus as the last one? Already this is strange." It is rather curious that Jesus, though He was in the middle, was left until last. It is not what one would have imagined and it might be the recollection of an eyewitness.

[175] *Loc. cit.*

The impression made on many readers is that all is exceedingly natural and (apart from the great miracle at the center) lifelike. This point has been very well put by Percy Gardner: "... The graphic touches in regard to the disciple whom Jesus loved are noteworthy.... It is no doubt very difficult ever to judge from the naturalness and vividness of a story that it is really historic. But it is very hard for any reader not to think that we have here a simple piece of testimony, an uncoloured narrative of fact."[176] Such statements could be multiplied. The story is artlessly told and it has every appearance of being a simple narrative of what really happened.

Richardson gives it as his opinion that John "is setting forth the truth of history by means of stories which are not in their details intended to be literally true."[177] It is not easy to see how this can be substantiated. Indeed the contrary seems self-evident to many commentators, namely that John intended to tell the truth, whatever be their estimate of the extent to which he succeeded. Richardson's estimate is really not based on a study of the position in this chapter. It is a view of John's method throughout his Gospel. But we have already seen good evidence for holding that in many places we have the testimony of an eyewitness. If it is not substantiated elsewhere that John is trying to convey the truth by stories he did not intend to be understood as true, then this chapter will not supply the lack.

In contrast to Richardson's is the estimate of Wright. Of the first incident narrated in chapter twenty, for example, he says, "The story which follows has the vividness and realistic detail of historical reminiscence."[178]

---

[176] P. Gardner, *The Ephesian Gospel*, London & New York, 1916, p. 288.

[177] *Op. cit.*, p. 206.

[178] *Op. cit.*, p. 367. Wright goes on, "The Evangelist doubtless knew these details from the beloved disciple, who must often have told the story of that unforgettable morning when he outran Peter to the sepulchre, how he hesitated to enter though not to look, how the disciple he had outrun entered before him, and how he himself entered and saw and believed. Love lent wings to the beloved disciple's feet, though doubtless they were younger than Peter's."

Others are impressed with the specific details of the story. Thus Godet says of the behavior of the two at the tomb, "These details are so natural, and so harmonious with the personality of the two disciples, that they bear in themselves the seal of their authenticity."[179] Bailey sees in the detail that John beat Peter in the race "a natural touch, surely, of innocent pride typical of an old man's memory, and not, as has been suggested, an elaborate allegorical invention."[180]

Bernard is impressed by the fact that Peter entered the tomb ahead of John. "That the first disciple to note the presence of the grave-cloths in the tomb did not actually go into it first is not a matter that would seem worth noting, to any one except the man who himself refrained from entering. This strongly suggests that we are dealing with the narrative of an eye-witness."[181]

John tells us that when the disciples entered the tomb they saw the cloth that had been about Jesus' head rolled up in a place by itself (v. 7). This little detail has impressed very many. McClymont thinks that "We have in this remark the most striking of numerous tokens that the narrative embodies the observations of an eye-witness."[182] N. E. Johnson sees as "the significant detail" the words, "he believed." He proceeds, "If this is not eyewitness, it must be invention, but what is the point of inventing the race, and the hesitation, and then the

---

[179] *Op. cit.*, p. 414.

[180] *Op. cit.*, p. 224. On the same point Plummer asks, "Would a second century writer have thought of this in inventing a story? And how simply does S. John give us the process of conviction through which his mind passed: the dull unbelief beforehand, the eager wonder in running, the timidity and awe on arriving, the birth of faith in the tomb. This is true psychology free from all self-consciousness" (*op. cit.*, p. 339).

[181] *Op. cit.*, p. 660. J. C. Ryle also sees in this "precisely one of those little circumstantial details which bring out men's natural temperaments" (*op. cit.*, p. 404).

[182] *Op. cit.*, pp. 332f. Plummer also sees in this detail evidence of an eyewitness; "...He even remembers that the napkin was folded" (*op. cit.*, p. 339). Lagrange is also impressed by this detail. He notes that the distinction between the head cloth and the other cloths "proves only with what care Peter examined everything, and, on the other hand the precision of John's testimony" (*op. cit.*, p. 508).

belief of this disciple?"[183] The point is well taken that the many small details of this story are natural enough in a man recalling what he knows, but very difficult to explain as invention.

Godet is impressed by Mary's attitude during the conversation with the angels. "Mary answers the question of the celestial visitors as simply as if she had been conversing with human beings, so completely is she preoccupied with a single idea: to recover her Master. Who could have invented this feature of the story?"[184]

The story of this appearance impresses C. H. Dodd. He maintains that this story "never came out of any common stock of tradition; it has an arresting individuality." This leads to two alternatives, the one that it is an imaginative composition, the other that "the story came through some highly individual channel, directly from the source, and the narrator stood near enough to catch the nuances of the original experience." He registers his personal impression: "I cannot for long rid myself of the feeling (it can be no more than a feeling) that this *pericopé* has something undeniably first-hand about it."[185] This impression is one felt by others. Bernard, for example, is of the opinion that the story may go back to Mary herself.[186]

This appears in some of the details also. Thus Mary is asked by Him whom she believes to be the gardener, "Woman, why weepest thou? whom seekest thou?" But she ignores these questions and replies, "Sir, if thou hast borne him hence, tell me where thou hast laid him" (v. 15). Westcott sees in this concentration on the one thing that matters to Mary, "one of those direct reflections of life which mark St. John's Gospel."[187] Westcott also sees significance in the use of the form of address "Rabboni" (v. 16). "The preservation of the form is one

---

[183] *Op. cit.*, p. 281.
[184] *Op. cit.*, p. 416.
[185] HTFG, p. 148. Dodd persists, "It stands in any case alone. There is nothing quite like it in the gospels. Is there anything quite like it in all ancient literature?"
[186] *Op. cit.*, p. 664.
[187] *Op. cit.*, p. 344.

of those little touches which stamp the Evangelist as a Jew of Palestine."[188]

That Jesus appeared first to Mary Magdalene and not, say, to one of the apostles or to the Virgin Mary, is important to Plummer. "It confirms our trust in the Gospel narratives to find this stated."[189]

The difficulty Thomas found in believing that Jesus had arisen is a further mark of trustworthiness. It is possible to imagine an early writer of fiction presenting a picture of all the disciples as having difficulty in believing, and then all having these difficulties overcome. Or there might be an outstanding example of unbelief which is melted away to become an incentive to the others to believe. But it is very difficult to understand the mind of someone who would first record that the apostles in general came to believe in the resurrection and that then Thomas, who does not stand out in the apostolic band, should take up such a position as John tells us he did. We can understand John's reporting it if it happened. We cannot understand his making it up if it did not.[190]

BY THE LAKE OF GALILEE

THE FINAL CHAPTER IS THOUGHT BY MANY TO BE AN appendix added after the rest had been written. Be that as it may, as G. Appleton says, ". . . It has the same eye-witness touch about it as the earlier chapters of the gospel."[191] The first incident recorded is the story of the fishing expedition on the lake of Galilee. Barclay comments on this, "It was certainly someone who knew the fishermen of the Sea of Galilee who wrote this story."[192]

---

[188] *Ibid.*

[189] *Op. cit.*, p. 342. Plummer is able to cite a late and worthless tradition which does speak of the first appearance as having been to the Virgin Mary. This is the sort of thing that would naturally occur to a fabricator. We cannot imagine a reason for saying the first appearance was to Mary Magdalene unless this was the case.

[190] Cf. J. C. Ryle: "If imposters and deceivers had compiled the Bible for their own private advantage, they would never have told mankind that one of the first founders of a new religion behaved as Thomas here did" (*op. cit.*, pp. 453f.).

[191] G. Appleton, *John's Witness to Jesus*, London, 1955, p. 99.

[192] *Op. cit.*, p. 326.

H. E. Edwards points to the detail of the number of
fishermen. The author does not name two of them and
Edwards conjectures that he had forgotten who they
were when he came to write the story. But he remembers
the number and so includes them. There is no special
stress on the number, for the total is not mentioned (it
is seven). Edwards concludes that "we have here a
detail, like so many in the Gospel, which appears to
demand that the narrative is that of an eyewitness."[193]
Another small point which intrigues him is the form
of address, παιδία, "lads" (v. 5). Jesus nowhere else in
this Gospel uses this form of address, and an inventor
would surely have used τεκνία as in 13:33.[194] Again the
implication is that the story was written by someone
who was there.

The story is very lifelike. There is, for example, an
interesting passage between Peter and the beloved disciple in which the latter informs his comrade that the
figure on the seashore is the Lord. Immediately Peter
girds his coat about him and throws himself into the sea.
On this point of putting on his coat and fastening it
Plummer quotes Sanday, "No one but an eyewitness
would have thought of the touch in *v. 7*, which *exactly in-
verts* the natural action of one about to swim, and yet is
quite accounted for by the circumstances."[195] When we
reflect on it, it is a little strange that a man about to cast
himself into the sea should put on a coat. This can
scarcely be an invention. It indicates that the author
was there.

When the disciples got to land and counted their catch
they found 153 large fish. McClymont sees this as "a
simple matter of fact, being something which a fisherman
could not forget, and the mention of which (like other
particulars in the narrative) illustrates the writer's
position as an eye-witness."[196] Plummer also thinks that
"The details in this verse are strong evidence of the
writer having been an eyewitness: he had helped to count

---

[193] *Op. cit.*, p. 224.
[194] *Ibid.*, pp. 225f.
[195] *Op. cit.*, p. 350.
[196] *Op. cit.*, p. 343.

these 'great fishes' and gives the number, not because there is anything mystical in it, but because he remembers it."[197]

After breakfast Jesus talked to Peter. It is not without its interest that John puts the beginning of the conversation this way: "Jesus saith to Simon Peter, Simon, son of John, lovest thou me more than these?" (v. 15). Notice that John refers to the apostle as "Simon Peter." But, though "Peter" was the surname Jesus Himself had given to this apostle, He addresses him as "Simon, son of John." This is in accordance with the fact that, though the name originated with Him, Jesus very rarely, in fact only on one occasion, addresses Peter by it. The way in which the two names are used in this conversation has impressed a number of commentators. Plummer remarks that "This is in harmony not only with the rest of this Gospel, but with the Gospels as a whole." He goes on to point out that Jesus always addresses the apostle as "Simon" and that John usually gives the full name "Simon Peter." He proceeds, "Should we find this minute difference observed, if the writer were any other than S. John?"[198]

In the conversation which ensued there are some rather mysterious words of Jesus to Peter, "Verily, verily, I say unto thee, When thou wast young, thou girdedst thyself, and walkedst whither thou wouldest. But when thou shalt be old, thou shalt stretch forth thy hands, and another shall gird thee, and carry thee whither thou wouldest not" (v. 18). These words present problems. Their meaning is not at all clear. But perhaps for that very reason they must be held to be genuine. It is likely that an inventor of sayings would have made plain what he meant Jesus to say. Bernard comments, "But whatever the

---

[197] *Op. cit.*, pp. 350f.

[198] *Ibid.*, p. 352. McClymont also sees in this "another token of the genuineness of this part of the Gospel" (*op. cit.*, p. 344). Westcott similarly notes the way the names of Peter are used and says, "This varying usage, which exactly corresponds with the circumstances under which the title was substituted for the original name, is a striking indication of the exactness of the records, and specially of the exactness of the record of the Lord's words" (*op. cit.*, p. 366).

meaning of v. 18, the text clearly embodies a genuine reminiscence of words spoken by the Lord."[199]

EYEWITNESS TESTIMONY

FROM ALL THIS IT IS CLEAR THAT THERE ARE MANY touches in the Fourth Gospel which indicate the presence of an eyewitness.[200] In almost every case the indication is indirect, and it may be rejected. Indeed many writers do reject all such indications, holding that the Gospel was composed late by someone who had never been near the scenes he described.

But it is unreasonable to expect more. After all, the man who describes events he knows well will usually say in simple terms what happened. It is far from invariable to have him say explicitly, "I was there when this happened and I saw it." The most that one can expect is the insertion of unimportant details which would register with an eyewitness, but which are more difficult to think of as the creation of a writer of fiction. We have seen that, in the judgment of many scholars, there is a multitude of such touches right through the Fourth Gospel. Some of these carry more conviction than others. We have tried to take notice of the typical objections of some scholars of a sceptical turn of mind.[201] Their criticisms call us to discount some of the more optimistic estimates made by earlier scholars. It now seems that probably too much was claimed. But when full allowance is made for this, the most likely explanation of the facts is that this Gospel was written by

---

[199] *Op. cit.*, p. 709.

[200] Cf. C. H. Turner, "I have never faltered in the conviction that the testimony of an eyewitness lies behind this Gospel" (cited by C. F. Nolloth, *The Fourth Evangelist*, London, 1925, p. 87, n. 1).

[201] Sometimes the scepticism is scarcely well based. Thus E. F. Scott maintains that "the picturesque detail in John's narrative can be set down, not to the accurate memory of the eye-witness, but to the fine instinct of the literary artist" (*The Fourth Gospel*, Edinburgh, 1906, p. 19). This would be more convincing if he had really faced the evidence. But the only passages adduced are: "And it was night." "Jesus wept." "Behold the man!" "What is truth?" While these may impress Scott, they are not in fact the passages on which chief reliance is placed by those who see evidence for an eyewitness behind this Gospel.

someone who knew what he was talking about because he had been there. He describes what he had seen and heard.[202]

This would be widely disputed by most recent writers. Sometimes it is averred that the kind of evidence to which I have made appeal proves nothing, for it is even more abundant in the apocryphal gospels. To this it may fairly be retorted that this is simply not the case. There are some vivid touches in the apocryphal gospels, but the general impression they leave is of unreality. That is not the impression left by John. The extent of the evidence is greater and its quality better in John than in the apocryphal works.[203]

An interesting approach is that of D. E. Nineham in a series of articles under the title, "Eye-witness Testimony and the Gospel Tradition."[204] Prof. Nineham argues that, while *a priori* considerations, such as those advanced by Vincent Taylor, H. E. W. Turner, A. M. Hunter and others, lead us to hold "that the eye-witnesses of the Lord's life *must have* played a significant part in the development of the tradition about that life," it is also the case that "the form-critical approach, which is essentially *a posteriori*, starting from the characteristics of the finished Gospels," reaches "by what is generally agreed to be a fairly consistent internal logic, a view of Gospel development in which eye-witness testimony

---

[202] It is perhaps worth adding that the linguistic evidence caused C. F. Burney to say, "Even apart from a full acceptance of the theory propounded in the present volume, it must surely be admitted that the facts which have been brought together greatly strengthen the case for holding that the Gospel is the work of an eye-witness" (*The Aramaic Origin of the Fourth Gospel*, Oxford, 1922, p. 128).

[203] J. B. Lightfoot maintains that a study of the Protevangelium and the Clementine Homilies makes this clear (E. Abbot, A. P. Peabody, and J. B. Lightfoot, *The Fourth Gospel*, London, 1892, p. 143). He also points out that the Evangelist is accurate, but with more than the accuracy of a Jew who knew first-century Palestine: "... Unless I have entirely deceived myself, the manner in which this accurate knowledge betrays itself justifies the further conclusion that we have before us the genuine narrative of an eye-witness" (p. 164).

[204] JTS, n.s., 9, 1958, pp. 13-25, 243-252; 11, 1960, pp. 253-264.

played no very large part."[205] As he goes through the
evidence it is clear that Nineham's sympathies are with
the form critics. In each of the Gospels he sees evidence
for development, and he rejects any significant influence
from eyewitnesses. This does not, in his view, reduce
the value of the Gospels to any marked degree. "What
we have, incorporated in the gospels, is the insight into
the meaning of the events described which had been
given and tested in forty or fifty years of the Church's
experience of Jesus as the living Lord."[206] We should
accept the Gospels for what they are, and not see them
as the product of eyewitnesses or even as claiming to
be such.

Like many such treatments, that of Professor Nineham
is marred by what seems to many an uncritical attitude
to certain aspects of form criticism coupled with a sceptical attitude to more conservative positions. As regards
the first it would probably not be fair to complain that
he does not establish all his points, for his treatment
is necessarily short and a good deal must of necessity
be assumed. But that does not justify his claiming, for
example, that the simple occurrence of the pericope form
excludes the eyewitness. Thus he rejects Farrer's view
that Mark got his material from eyewitnesses but wrote
it down in anecdotal form, because "the *pericopae* in St.
Mark are not only *like* the anecdotes current in the community tradition, they *are* such anecdotes, however much
rephrased and reformulated by the evangelist."[207] To this
I would like to say two things. The first is that the
pericope form is no necessary indication of a community
activity. If I may cite an example: It was not my privi-
lege to know either of the gentlemen who were the first
two Principals of Ridley College. But I have often met
men who knew them intimately and who recount happenings in the early days of the college. Their stories
have a way of taking the pericope form. Indeed, that
form is practically universal. It is very, very rare indeed to have a connected recital. I cannot recall even

---

205 *Ibid.*, 9, p. 16.
206 *Ibid.*, 11, p. 263.
207 *Ibid.*, 9, p. 17.

one. But isolated incidents are constant. Frequently these bear all the marks of tales repeatedly told. This does nothing to impeach their character as the testimonies of eyewitnesses. It simply means that they are stories which the original eyewitnesses have told over and over again. Notice that I am not claiming that they are necessarily factually accurate. That may or may not be the case and is for decision on other grounds. The one point I am making is that eyewitness testimony to the sayings and doings of a revered teacher habitually takes the pericope form. The fact that a pericope bears every evidence of having been told and retold does not mean that it did not come, even in its finished form, from an eyewitness.

The second thing is that I have some scepticism of my own. I know it is highly unfashionable, but I am not at all convinced by the arguments of Nineham, or even Dibelius and Bultmann, that anybody reasoning in the middle of the twentieth century is able to say with tolerable certainty that in a certain pericope such-and-such elements are contributed by the community while so-and-so may perhaps be original. I know that this kind of reasoning is commonly accepted. But I find it totally unconvincing. I need more than a learned scholar's *obiter dicta* before I can accept this division into the product of the community and the residue of the original story (if any). I do not see how we can be sure, at this distance in time and with respect to narratives in a language not our own and which we know only from the outside, which are the touches a community would introduce.

When he deals specifically with the Fourth Evangelist, Nineham quotes from C. K. Barrett: "He sought to draw out, using in part the form and style of narrative ... the true meaning of the life and death of one whom he believed to be the Son of God, a being from beyond history. It is for this interpretation of the focal point of all history, not for accurate historical data, that we must look in John." This he does not regard as standing in need of demonstration. He assumes it, and proceeds, "In other words, John's motives for his reformulation

of the tradition were essentially theological and edificatory.... That means that, in order to develop the tradition in just the way he did, he will have had no need
of recourse to eyewitnesses; despite its narrative form,
his was not the *kind* of reformulation that needed fresh
eyewitness testimony as its basis."[208] This seems to me
suspiciously like the adopting of the *a priori* approach
that elsewhere Nineham imputes to his opponents. Instead of maintaining that John's method needs or does
not need the testimony of an eyewitness it is better to
look at what John has actually written. When we do, we
find that he claims eyewitness testimony for some of it
at least, and that he stresses concepts like "witness"
which point to the same thing. If his concern is not to
reproduce what actually happened but to bring out its
"true meaning," why are his topographical data so accurate? And why has he so many time notes? And
why is he so concerned for "the truth" ("doing" the
truth as well as "telling" it)?

Nineham goes on to ask, "For is it not paradoxical to
suggest that the early Christians, who pinned all their
hopes of salvation on the occurrence of certain specific
historical events, should have sat so loose to considerations of precise historical accuracy when they were framing the tradition of those events?" He admits that "By
our standards it *is* highly paradoxical."[209] He goes on
to suggest that John was not writing according to our
standards, and that by his there was nothing wrong
in bringing out the meaning by a narrative that was
not strictly accurate. He cites Origen, "... the true spiritual meaning being often preserved in what at the corporeal level might be called a falsehood."[210]

With all due respect, I submit that what is relevant
is not what our standards would demand, nor what those
of Origen demanded. The paradox to which Nineham
directs attention does exist. It would have been strange

---

[208] *Ibid.*, p. 246.

[209] *Ibid.*, p. 247.

[210] *Ibid.*, pp. 248f. A sentence later he says, "Nor is there really
any reason to think that Origen does in fact misrepresent the
evangelists."

if the Evangelists in general and John in particular had "pinned all their hopes of salvation on the occurrence of certain specific historical events" and then had sat loose to historical accuracy when recording those events. But the criterion is not what sounds strange (or plausible) to us. It is what the Evangelists did. John was certainly a creative thinker, but he was possessed of a greater ability than some of his critics have reckoned with. I have pointed out elsewhere that his portrait of John the Baptist affords us an important test of his method.[211] He depicts the Baptist in one capacity only, that of witness. He does not tell us of anything else that he did, not even of his baptism of Jesus. He gives us none of his ethical teaching. Always he shows him as a witness. But the Qumran scrolls have revealed that his portrait of the Baptist is remarkably accurate. J. A. T. Robinson's verdict I have quoted elsewhere.[212] He comments on the "surprising vindication" the scrolls appear to offer "of ideas and categories attributed to John by the fourth Evangelist which recent criticism would never have allowed as remotely historical."

Now if when admittedly he is depicting the Baptist from a single point of view he is yet able to preserve his accuracy, why not when he is depicting Jesus? It seems to me that John is a greater figure than has been reckoned with. He is so supremely master of the situation and the tradition that he is able to bring out his essential point without distorting the facts. Many recent critics have found it impossible to believe this. They have reasoned that he must have been ready to distort facts, for his concern was with the interpretation of the facts, not with historical accuracy. This *a priori* approach should be firmly rejected. John tells us that he is bearing witness and his testimony should be taken with the utmost seriousness.

*   *   *

My conclusion is that there is good evidence that the testimony of an eyewitness underlies the Fourth Gospel.

---

[211] See above, pp. 110ff.
[212] See above, p. 111.

As far as I am able I have seriously considered the objections raised. It is clear that there are difficulties, whichever view we finally adopt. But the balance seems clearly in favor of the eyewitness.

Chapter Four

The Authorship of the Fourth Gospel

FOR QUITE A LONG TIME BRITISH SCHOLARSHIP TENDED TO
be conservative in the matter of the authorship of the
Fourth Gospel. It was usual to hold to the apostolic
authorship or something like it (e.g. the view that, while
the apostle John may not have actually written the
words, he was the authority behind the Gospel, the "witness" whose words justify what is written). Continental
scholarship, by contrast, almost took it for granted that
there was no case for the apostolic authorship. It was
not considered as a serious option. Continental scholars
have regarded the problem as insoluble, or they have
gone straight to other solutions.

This has not been invariable. Men like T. Zahn have
had other ideas, and more recently E. Stauffer has sur-
veyed the evidence and concluded, "In view of all this
we have sufficient ground to ascribe these five writings
[i.e. the Fourth Gospel, the three Johannine Epistles,
and Revelation] to a common author of remarkable
individuality and great significance, and to identify him
as the apostle John."[1] But he does not stop here. He
thinks that the appendix (John 21) shows the work of
disciples of John. Since the style of this chapter bears

---

[1] E. Stauffer, *New Testament Theology*, London, 1955, p. 41.

a close resemblance to that of the other chapters he thinks it hazardous to decide definitely for John as the author of the whole. He concludes therefore: "It is impossible to separate the work of the Master from that of disciples in detail, indeed we cannot recognize traces of any individual disciple in the work. So we have to sum up our position in the cautious thesis: the Johannine writings of the NT are to be ascribed to the apostle John or to his influence."[2]

We cannot take Stauffer's position as typical. Continental scholars are usually much more radical, and in recent years most British scholars have followed them. There is usually in both camps a marked scepticism about too close a connection between the apostle and the Gospel. Barrett's position is probably typical. After speaking of the questions raised by this Gospel he goes on, "Some, particularly those regarding authorship, date, and composition, cannot now be answered with certainty, though much can be learnt by studying them."[3] Perhaps in the end we must be content with this verdict. Everything, of course, depends on what we mean by certainty. If we define it too narrowly we can scarcely be certain of anything in the modern, let alone the ancient world. But there are reasonable hypotheses, and it may not be too much to look for such even in the matter of the authorship of this Gospel. At any rate, with Barrett, we may all agree that there is much to be learned by studying the question.

An interesting aspect of much recent Johannine study is the refusal to take seriously the evidence that the apostle John was the author. Very few recent scholars make a sustained attempt to grapple with the evidence. They usually take some of it and show that it has been misunderstood or overstated by conservatives. Then they take other evidence that points away from John as author and proceed to accept it. But they do not, as a result, go carefully through such a massive argument as that of Westcott. It is widely assumed that only dog-

---

[2] *Ibid.*

[3] C. K. Barrett, *The Gospel According to St. John*, London, 1955, p. 4.

matic presuppositions could cause anyone to hold such a view these days. We still need C. F. Nolloth's warning:

> ... If opponents of the traditional authorship of the Johannine writings are not to be charged, *ipso facto,* with disloyalty to the cause of Christ, neither are upholders of that authorship to be accused offhand of an obscurantist apologetic. The matter does not admit of such an alternative presentation. It lies within the province of historical criticism, and by the laws which govern all historical investigation its treatment must be directed and ultimately judged.[4]

Unfortunately not all have shown this wide charity. And not all have regarded the matter as still open for discussion.

J. A. T. Robinson has indeed argued that for many people there has been no real possibility of considering the evidence. He points out that discussions on the Fourth Gospel have tended to be dominated by five presuppositions. These he lists as follows:

(1) That the fourth Evangelist is dependent on sources, including (normally) one or more of the Synoptic Gospels.

(2) His own background is other than that of the events and teaching he is purporting to record.

(3) That he is not to be regarded, seriously, as a witness to the Jesus of history, but simply to the Christ of faith.

(4) That he represents the end-term of theological development in first-century Christianity.

(5) That he is not himself the Apostle John nor a direct eye-witness.[5]

Bishop Robinson proceeds to discuss these presuppositions in order, and to show that there is not as much to be said for any of them as has usually been supposed. This is very important for the question of authorship, for it is these presuppositions rather than a careful weighing of the evidence that has usually been decisive. Robinson can say, "Indeed, the combination of the four preceding theses, all of which have the effect of set-

---

[4] C. F. Nolloth, *The Fourth Evangelist,* London, 1925, p. 3.
[5] SE, I, p. 339.

ting the Evangelist at a distance from the events, makes
the fifth conclusion of the reigning critics well-nigh
inevitable. Long before they train their guns on the
hapless Papias and Irenaeus and the ignorant Galilean
fisherman we know what the result will be."[6] Robinson
is not arguing for apostolic authorship. Indeed, part
of his purpose is to show that the question has been
wrongly posed, and that we should look not so much
for an author dating from the earliest days of Christianity as a tradition, continuous in a community of
Christians, and going back to very early days. But to
those interested in whether or not John the son of
Zebedee wrote this Gospel Robinson's contentions are
important. The fact is that for long enough it has
not been the evidence but the presuppositions that have
decided the matter. Now that this is clear we can make
a determined effort to set aside the presuppositions and
reexamine the question in the light of the evidence.
What I propose to do is to take Westcott's powerful
statement of the conservative case, and see, if we can,
what modern advance has done to it. Westcott considers
the internal evidence and the external evidence in turn.[7]

INTERNAL EVIDENCE

HE BEGINS WITH THE INDIRECT EVIDENCE.

(a) *The author was a Jew.* This Westcott sees demon-

---

[6] SE, I, p. 348.

[7] K. and S. Lake think these point in different directions. They
see the external evidence as strongly in favor of the traditional
position, but the internal evidence as against it. "Thus external
evidence, extremely good, is balanced by internal evidence pointing
the other way and equally powerful" (*An Introduction to the New
Testament*, London, 1938, p. 52). They summarize the case against
in this way: "The real reason for rejecting the tradition is purely
subjective, — the contents of the gospel seem irreconcilable with
the theory that it was written by a disciple who had been a companion of Jesus and an eye witness of his life. This view is based
on the theory, now widely held, that the Gospel of Mark gives a
true account of the ministry, and the Gospels of Matthew and
Luke a true account of the teaching of Jesus. Thus, since the
Johannine narrative is so different from them it must be largely,
if not entirely, fictitious and written by a Hellenistic Christian in
order to support the sacramental theology which finds a centre

strated on every hand. The author is familiar with Jewish customs, and with Jewish messianic expectations (John 1:21; 4:25; 6:14f.; 7:40ff.; 12:34, etc.). He can mention in casual fashion (but quite correctly) the popular estimate of women (John 4:27).[8] John knew the importance the Jews attached to the religious schools (7:15), the way the Dispersion was held in slight esteem (7:35), the idea that children might be punished for the sins of the parents (9:2). He knew the hostility between the Jews and the Samaritans (4:9), and "the supercilious contempt of the Pharisees for 'the people of the earth' (vii. 49)."[9]

Similarly he is at home with the observances of the Jewish religion. He knows that the sabbath is observed and that sabbath observance is overridden by the requirement of circumcision if the eighth day of a boy's life should coincide with a sabbath day (John 7:22f.). He knows the ceremonial pollution that may be conveyed by a Gentile court (18:28). The visit of Jesus to the temple at the Feast of Tabernacles "only becomes fully intelligible when we supply the facts at which the writer barely hints, being himself filled with the knowledge of them."[10] Thus we need to know something of the ceremony of pouring water from Siloam at the altar, and the lighting of the lamps in the court of the women, if

---

in the divine Jesus" (pp. 50f.). Contrast W. F. Howard, "The reason for the widespread abandonment of the full apostolic authorship of the Gospel is the clearer recognition that the external evidence is indecisive" (FGRCI, p. 7).

[8] Cf. the saying in S Bk, *ad loc.*, "A man shall not be alone with a woman in an inn, not even with his sister or his daughter, on account of what men may think. A man shall not talk with a woman in the street, not even with his own wife, and especially not with another woman, on account of what men may say." Or the words of *Ab.* 1.5, "Jose b. Johanan of Jerusalem said: Let thy house be opened wide and let the needy be members of thy household; and talk not much with womankind. They said this of a man's own wife: how much more of his fellow's wife! Hence the Sages have said: He that talks much with womankind brings evil upon himself and neglects the study of the Law and at the last will inherit Gehenna" (Danby's translation).

[9] Westcott, *The Gospel According to St. John*, Grand Rapids, I, p. xi.

[10] *Ibid.*

we are fully to comprehend the significance of the sayings about the "living water" and "the light of the world"
(7:38; 8:12). And a man had to know the details of
the feast to be able to speak of the last day of it as
"the great day" (7:37). A knowledge of the customs
in Jewish domestic life is seen in narratives as divergent
as the marriage feast at Cana of Galilee and the burial
of Lazarus (2:1-10; 11:17-44). Most early Christians
must have known of the stoning of Stephen. They must
have known that it took place on the initiative of the
Jews, quite without reference to the Romans, and at
the end of the trial before the sanhedrin. Under those
circumstances "clear information upon the point" was
required to report the words, "It is not lawful for us
to put any one to death" (18:31). Westcott deals with
the objection that no Jew could have spoken of Caiaphas
as "high-priest in that year," regarding the high priesthood as an annual office. He shows that John does not
make this error. He repeats the statement (11:49, 51;
18:13), and thus directs attention to it as significant.

> The emphatic reiteration of the statement forces the
> reader to connect the office of Caiaphas with the part
> which he actually took in accomplishing the death of
> Christ. One yearly sacrifice for atonement it was the
> duty of the high-priest to offer. In that memorable
> year, when all types were fulfilled in the reality, it
> fell to Caiaphas to bring about unconsciously the one
> sacrifice of atonement for sin.[11]

This argument from content still stands. Indeed, it
might be reinforced a little. For example, in 7:51 John
knows that in Jewish law the accused has the right to
speak before the judges. He knows that the agreement
of two witnesses is required (8:17). He knows that it
is illegal to carry a mattress on the sabbath (5:10). It is
possible that in some passages he shows a knowledge
of unusual rabbinic exegesis of the Old Testament. Thus
in 1:51, there is a reference to Jacob's ladder set up
to heaven with the angels ascending and descending.
The expression "on it" (i.e. the ladder) could be understood as "on him" (Jacob), the Hebrew בּוֹ being patient

---

[11] *Ibid.*, p. xii.

of either meaning; and R. Jannai accepts the latter meaning.[12] This scholar is too late to have influenced John, and much more, our Lord, but the saying shows that this exegesis existed and it may well have existed long before R. Jannai. The Rabbis were not noted for originality, and delighted to hand down sayings. The thought, then, of the angels ascending and descending on the Son of man might possibly owe something to a knowledge of this particular way of understanding the Genesis passage.

Peder Borgen has a sustained study of the discourse in John 6 which shows that this section of the Gospel is Palestinian both in its method and its content.[13] At point after point he is able to show that Jewish concepts lie behind this chapter. It is probable that a similar examination would yield a similar conclusion elsewhere in this Gospel. There is no reason for thinking that there is anything uncharacteristic about chapter 6.

Some also see a knowledge of Jewish exegesis in John 8:56, where Abraham is said to have rejoiced to see Messiah's day. There was a dispute between R. Johanan b. Zakkai and R. Akiba. One maintained that God revealed to Abraham the secrets of this world only, but the other held that God also revealed to that patriarch the age to come.[14]

I do not regard either of these last two examples as particularly convincing, but the point is that recent scholarship has done nothing to upset Westcott. On the contrary, it tends to reinforce him. The content of this Gospel is such that we should expect a Jew as its author. Its familiarity with Jewish customs is more than would be expected from someone outside the nation.

Westcott next turns to questions of style and vocabulary. "The vocabulary, the structure of the sentences, the symmetry and numerical symbolism of the composition, the expression and the arrangement of the thoughts,

---

[12] Gen. R. LXVIII. 12 (Soncino edn., p. 626).

[13] P. Borgen, *Bread from Heaven*, Leiden, 1965.

[14] Gen. R., XLIV. 22 (Soncino edn., p. 376). A similar dispute is recorded in the same passage between R. Leazar and R. Jose b. R. Ḥanina.

are essentially Hebrew."[15] He picks out words like "light," "darkness," "flesh," "spirit," "life," "this world," "the kingdom of God." I doubt that this list would carry the same conviction today. Our knowledge of Hellenistic religions shows that with the exception of "the kingdom of God" most of these terms can be found outside of Judaism. A similar statement might have to be made about pieces of imagery like "the shepherd," "the living water," "the woman in travail," at any rate as regards the first and the last. But if these expressions do not prove a Jewish environment at least they are consistent with it.

Westcott also draws attention to "the simplicity of the connecting particles: to the parallelism and symmetry of the clauses."[16] This has been tremendously reinforced by subsequent research. As is well known, scholars like Burney and Torrey have contended that this whole Gospel was written in Aramaic, and while they have not carried the scholarly world with them at least they have demonstrated that there is a good deal of Aramaic thought at the back of this Gospel. Barrett notes the following as significant among the points adduced:

(i) Parataxis, which "is as characteristic of Aramaic as it is rare in good Greek,"[17] and the adversative use of "and."

(ii) Asyndeton, which is common in Aramaic (though not in Hebrew, so this is an Aramaism, not simply a characteristic of Semitic languages).

(iii) John frequently uses epexegetic ἵνα and ὅτι, the frequency of ἵνα being especially noteworthy. These are rare in the rest of the New Testament. "Some of the unusual constructions of these words have been accounted for as mistranslations of the Aramaic ד *(de* or *di)*, which is used not only as a conjunction ($=$ ἵνα or ὅτι) but also as a mark of the genitive relation, and as a relative particle. It is claimed that these uses have

---

[15] *Op. cit.,* p. xii.
[16] *Ibid.*
[17] *Op. cit.,* p. 8.

sometimes been confounded by the writer of the Greek gospel."[18]

(iv) Then there are Aramaic words which appear in transliteration with translations or equivalents, as in John 1:38 ('Ραββεί, ὃ λέγεται μεθερμηνευόμενον Διδάσκαλε); 1:41, 42; 4:25; 9:7; 11:16; 19:13, 17; 20:16; 21:2; cf. 12:13.

(v) Again, John's language has Aramaic links. The lake of Galilee is called θάλασσα, not λίμνη, "a Semitic usage";[19] αὐξάνειν, "to increase," is used in 3:30 with the meaning "become great," and it is significant that the Aramaic רבי has both meanings. πιστικός (12:3) may be a transliteration of פיסתקא. John uses ὑψοῦν (3:14 etc.) in the double sense of "to exalt" and "to crucify," though this Greek word does not normally mean "crucify." But in Syriac and in Palestinian Aramaic the verb אזדקף has both meanings.

(vi) Constructions of an Aramaic type (e.g. the relative resumed by the pronoun in agreement).

(vii) Mistranslations have been urged, but Barrett does not find most of them convincing.

(viii) Traces of poetic structure such as parallelism, alliteration, etc.

Barrett points out that it is not easy to weigh the force of all this evidence and he agrees that different scholars will give different estimates. His own conclusion he puts in these words:

> It does however seem probable that John, though not translating Aramaic documents, was accustomed to think and speak in Aramaic as well as in Greek.... Perhaps it is safest to say that in language as in thought John treads, perhaps not unconsciously, the boundary between the Hellenic and the Semitic; he avoids the worst kind of Semitism, but retains precisely that slow and impressive feature of Aramaic which was calculated to produce the effect of solemn, religious Greek, and may perhaps have influenced already the liturgical language of the Church.[20]

---

[18] *Ibid.*
[19] *Ibid.*, p. 9.
[20] *Ibid.*, p. 11.

Many would be happy with this verdict. The Greek of
John is unusual Greek and the best explanation of it
appears to be that there is an Aramaic cast of thought
behind it.

Few modern scholars would contest the Jewish background to this Gospel. Admittedly the author was ver-
satile, and he may have been influenced by ideas and
language from other sources.[21] But this Gospel is basically
Jewish in its outlook. The linguistic argument has been
immeasurably strengthened since Westcott.

Westcott's third point under this heading is that "The
Old Testament is no less certainly the source of the
religious life of the writer. . . . From first to last Judaism
is treated in the fourth Gospel as the divine starting-
point of Christianity."[22] Thus Judea is "the home" (τὰ ἴδια;
cf. 16:32; 19:27) of the incarnate Word, and the people
"His own people" (1:11). The temple is "my father's
house" (2:16). References to "their Law" and to "the
Jews" do not really conflict with this. The Pharisees
tried to restrict to themselves the Law with all that
means (10:34; 15:25), and it is in this sense that it
is "their" law, while " 'the Jews' embodied just that
which was provisional and evanescent in the system
which they misunderstood."[23] "Side by side with the
words of Christ which describe the Law as the special
possession of its false interpreters (viii. 17, x. 34, xv. 25),
other words of his affirm the absolute authority of its
contents."[24] Scripture cannot be broken (10:35). What
is written in the prophets will come to pass (6:45; cf.
6:31). Moses wrote of Christ (5:46). Types of the Old
Testament are freely applied to Christ (the brazen ser-

---

[21] E. F. Scott sees value in John's use of Greek concepts: ". . . It
may fairly be argued that the Hellenic form is in some respects
more adequate than the Jewish" (*The Fourth Gospel*, Edinburgh,
1906, p. 7). In other words, where John uses Greek rather than
Jewish expressions to give the context of Jesus' teaching he "is
not necessarily unfaithful to the Master's teaching. On the contrary, he gives truer expression in many cases to the intrinsic
thought" *(ibid.)*.

[22] *Op. cit.*, pp. xii, xiii.

[23] *Ibid.*, p. xiii.

[24] *Ibid.*

pent, 3:14; the manna, 6:32; the water from the rock, 7:37f.; perhaps the pillar of fire, 8:12). Abraham saw His day (8:56). Judas' treachery and the hatred of the Jews are traced to Scripture (13:18; 15:25). Not only does the Evangelist record Christ as taking this attitude to the Old Testament, but he does the same himself. He sees the cleansing of the temple as reminding the disciples of Psalm 69:9, and the triumphal entry as fulfilling Zechariah 9:9 (2:17; 12:14ff.). So also with Israel's unbelief (12:37ff.) and certain details of the passion (the division of Christ's garments and the casting of lots, 19:23f.; the thirst, 19:28; the unbroken limbs, 19:36; the piercing of the side, 19:37). These fulfilments are brought forward as grounds for faith (19:35 — but it may legitimately be objected that this verse refers to the "witness," not to the Scripture). " 'The Law,' in short, is treated by the writer of the fourth Gospel, both in his record of the Lord's teaching, and, more especially, in his own comments, as only a Jew could have treated it."[25] His object was to show that Jesus was not only the Son of God, but the Christ (20:31; cf. 1:47).

The portraiture of the people accords with this. Though he writes as a Christian he records that "salvation is from the Jews" (4:22). He does not treat the whole nation as an undifferentiated unity. "The multitude" is the general gathering, mostly Galileans who received Christ in Galilee (4:45). They wanted to make Him King (6:15), they gathered round Him at feasts "in expectation and doubt," they were ignorant of the plot to kill Christ (7:20), and they were inclined to believe (7:40). They brought Him into the city in triumph (12:12) and "listen in dull perplexity to Christ's final revelation of Himself" (11:29, 34).[26] They do not appear in the story of the trial and crucifixion.

Contrasted with them is another group, which John calls "the Jews." These reflect the spirit of Jerusalem (1:19). "From first to last they appear as the representatives of the narrow finality of Judaism" (2:18;

25 *Ibid.*, p. xv.
26 *Ibid.*, p. xvi.

19:38).[27] They charge Jesus with sabbath violation (5:
10ff.; cf. 19:31), they "murmur" at Capernaum (6:41,
52), they silence the wavering multitude at Jerusalem
(7:11-13), they would stone Christ (8:59; 10:31), and
to them the crucifixion is attributed (18:12, 14, 31, 36,
38; 19:7, 12, 14). Even these may be struck with wonder
(7:15) or doubt (7:35; 8:22); they are divided (10:19),
and seek a clear enunciation of Christ's claim (10:24).
The defection of many of them marks the last crisis
(12:10f.). Within this group John distinguishes two
tendencies associated with the Sadducees and the Pharisees. The former are never mentioned by name in this
Gospel, but they are there. The two groups are pictured
as acting together in the sanhedrin (7:32, 45; 11:47, 57;
18:3; cf. 7:26, 48; 12:42, 'the rulers'), but only in 7:45
are they so grouped as to form a single body. The "chief
priests" are always first as "taking the lead in the
designs of violence."[28] "The Pharisees are moved by the
symptoms of religious disorder: the high-priests (Sadducees) by the prospect of ecclesiastical danger."[29] For
the Pharisees see 1:24; 4:1; 7:47; 8:13; 9:31ff.; 12:42,
19. Always their interest is in religion. But after chapter
12 they are never mentioned alone. The chief priests
"take the direction of the end into their own hands. Five
times they are mentioned alone, and on each occasion
as bent on carrying out a purpose of death and treason
to the faith of Israel."[30] They plotted the murder of Lazarus (12:11); they delivered Jesus to Pilate (18:35);
they were first to cry "Crucify" (19:6); they said, "We
have no king but Caesar" (19:15); they protested against
the title on the cross (19:21).

Recent writers have not dealt at length with this
aspect of the Fourth Gospel, but I do not see how Westcott is to be refuted here. John does know the condition of the Jews at the time of Christ and he writes
out of knowledge.

[27] *Ibid.*, p. xvii.
[28] *Ibid.*, p. xviii.
[29] *Ibid.* The distinction refers to occasions when they are mentioned separately.
[30] *Ibid.*

On all this first point, then, that the author of the Gospel was a Jew, it appears that there is nothing to disturb Westcott's case. Recent work has modified minor points here and there, but it has also produced new points to reinforce the case. The evidence is strong that the writer was a Jew.[31]

(b) *The author was a Jew of Palestine.* Westcott feels that the facts so far adduced show more than that the author was a Jew.

> It is inconceivable that a Gentile, living at a distance from the scene of religious and political controversy which he paints, could have realised, as the Evangelist has done, with vivid and unerring accuracy the relations of parties and interests which ceased to exist after the fall of Jerusalem; that he could have marked distinctly the part which the hierarchical class — the unnamed Sadducees — took in the crisis of the Passion; that he could have caught the real points at issue between true and false Judaism, which in their first form had passed away when the Christian society was firmly established; that he could have portrayed the growth and conflict of opinion as to the national hopes of the Messiah side by side with the progress of the Lord's ministry.[32]

It must be borne in mind that the destruction of the city destroyed "the old land-marks, material and moral," and also "revealed the essential differences of Judaism and Christianity, and raised a barrier between them."[33]

To this we must add the Evangelist's topographical knowledge. He mentions "Cana of Galilee" (2:1, 11;

---

[31] I am not certain that J. A. Bailey has given sufficient consideration to the evidence adduced in this section. He argues that the beloved disciple was not John the son of Zebedee, among other things, on the grounds that in Gal. 2:9 John is one of the leaders of "the Jerusalem Jewish-Christian party, whose theology, from what Paul tells us of it, was in the sharpest conflict with the theology of the fourth evangelist" (*The Traditions Common to the Gospels of Luke and John*, Leiden, 1963, p. 32n.; he goes on to suggest as the reason for the absence of all mention of John in this Gospel that the author disagreed with John's theology). This, it seems to me, reads a good deal into the Pauline reference while turning a blind eye to the Jewishness of the Gospel.

[32] Westcott, *op. cit.*, p. xx.

[33] *Ibid.*

4:46; 21:2), which is not thus noticed by any earlier writer. "Bethany beyond Jordan" (1:28) was forgotten by the time of Origen. Bethany near Jerusalem is precisely located as "about fifteen furlongs" away (11:18). Ephraim "near the wilderness" (11:54) may be the same as Ophrah (1 Sam. 13:17), but is not otherwise named in Scripture. Aenon (3:23) is not known from other sources, but the addition "near to Salim" shows that John was not hazy as to its location (despite our uncertainties). Sychar has not been identified in such a way as to satisfy all the authorities, but John's accuracy is not usually impugned. The implied dimensions of the lake of Tiberias (6:19; Mark 6:47 speaks only of the middle of the lake), and the reference to descending from Cana to Capernaum (2:12) are further incidental revelations of John's knowledge.

Even more conclusive are the notices about Jerusalem itself. John speaks of Bethesda, describing it as near the sheep-pool (or gate), and mentioning its five porches (5:2). He refers also to the pool of Siloam (9:7), and to the "winter torrent" Kidron (18:1), none of which is mentioned by the other Evangelists. They do mention the Praetorium and Golgotha, but John sees them "with the vividness of an actual spectator. The Jews crowd round the Praetorium which they will not enter, and Pilate goes in and out before them (xviii. 28ff.). Golgotha is *'nigh to the city,'* where people pass to and fro, and *'there was a garden there'* (xix. 17, 20, 41)."[34] John alone mentions Gabbatha (19:13), and Bethesda also is mentioned nowhere but in this Gospel. The cleansing of the temple shows familiarity with the scene, and there is a precise chronological note that the temple had been in building for forty-six years (2:20). The events at the Feast of Tabernacles, as already noted, show a familiarity with what went on in the temple; and there is a note in 8:20, "These things Jesus spake in the treasury, as He taught in the temple." At the Dedication Jesus walked in Solomon's porch in winter, "a part of the great eastern cloister suiting in every way the scene with which

---

[34] *Ibid.,* p. xxiii.

it is connected."[35] Westcott rounds off this section of his argument with this summary:

> ... It is inconceivable that any one, still more a Greek or Hellenist, writing when the Temple was rased to the ground, could have spoken of it with the unaffected certainty which appears in the fourth Gospel. It is monstrous to transfer to the second century the accuracy of archaeological research which is one of the latest acquirements of modern art. The Evangelist, it may be safely said, speaks of what he has seen.[36]

Most scholars have been impressed by this. Not so C. K. Barrett. He lists thirteen places mentioned in this Gospel but not in the Synoptics.[37] Then he decides that anyone might know the Praetorium, while the sheep-pool, Siloam, and Kidron might be known from the Old Testament, and Solomon's porch is mentioned in Acts. Tiberias did not receive its name until AD 26, so a reference to it does not look like early information. Six of the remainder are in southern Palestine, and knowledge of the south "does not suggest a close dependence of the gospel on John the son of Zebedee."[38] Barrett concludes, "Its value cannot be checked, but it may be observed *(a)* that tradition tends to add, even without authority, the names of places as of persons; *(b)* that the peculiar Johannine names may be due to the use of Palestinian sources by an author himself of different origin."[39]

Now with every desire to be fair to a great scholar I cannot see that Barrett has really faced the conservative position here, let alone answered it. Imagine the scorn with which a conservative would be treated who dealt with a critical position in this cavalier fashion! I find it very difficult, for example, to believe that John's

---

[35] *Ibid.*, p. xxv.

[36] *Ibid.*

[37] Lagrange, by contrast, lists twenty-four places (*S. Jean*, p. cxxiv). He includes some rather doubtful ones such as διασπορὰ τῶν Ἑλλήνων. When these are deducted, however, his list still has nineteen names, so that it is clear that Barrett is presenting us with a rather conservative list. It is not easy to see, for example, why he omits Jacob's well (he includes Solomon's porch), or "this mountain" (4:20; the reference is to Mt. Gerizim).

[38] *Op. cit.*, p. 102.

[39] *Ibid.*

knowledge of the pool of Siloam may be accounted for on the ground that it is mentioned in the Old Testament (it is found there but once). Are we to think that the writer searched the Old Testament for obscure place names, selected a handful and by a happy coincidence they all happen to be used aright? Moreover, Barrett gives the Evangelist no chance of being vindicated at all. If a place of which he speaks is mentioned anywhere else (even one reference tucked away in Nehemiah), he shows no great knowledge. If it is not, then we cannot be sure he is right.

R. D. Potter has much more respect for the Evangelist. He surveys briefly all the texts in this Gospel that admit of some archaeological or topographical reference. He points to a number of accuracies in John 4, for example, and points out that "our author knew this bit of Samaria well. Note too that all the setting of the chapter, its cadre, its place-names are not in Southern Palestine."[40] He does not find John in error at any point, and is highly appreciative of the accuracy that investigation reveals. He says, for example, with respect to the number of places where archaeology and topography verify statements on this Gospel, "The total is impressive, even when we allow fully for the debatable and uncertain results. For the moment it is another point which I would like to stress — time and again, it will be found that those who have lived long in Palestine are struck by the impression that our author did so. He knew the Palestine that they have learned to know."[41] He concludes his survey by giving expression to the opinion that "we have in this gospel not only the Word of God, but also the narrative of a reliable witness, a Palestinian Jew."[42] Such a conclusion will, I think, be found much more typical of the modern position than Barrett's rather perfunctory verdict. The writer of this Gospel knew Palestine, and it seems to me to be special pleading to deny this.

Westcott follows his argument from topography with

---

[40] SE, I, p. 331.
[41] Ibid., p. 335.
[42] Ibid., p. 337.

one from the way the Scriptures are used, which he finds points us to Palestine. He points out here that the people, the Evangelist, and our Lord Himself assume the messianic interpretation of the Old Testament, that the quotations are distributed over the three divisions of the Hebrew Scriptures, that about half of them are peculiar to this Gospel (including all but one of the quotations in our Lord's discourses), that the use of the LXX and also the Hebrew is "unquestionable."[43] Thus he finds quotations in John 19:37; 6:45; 13:18 which agree with the Hebrew against the LXX. Other quotations agree with both Hebrew and LXX where these agree, one with LXX against the Hebrew, one differs from the consent of the Hebrew and LXX, two differ from both Hebrew and LXX where these differ, and four are free adaptations. We cannot always be sure when there is a quotation, and thus some modern discussions differ somewhat from Westcott's. But most would agree that at least on occasion this Evangelist gives evidence of knowledge of the Hebrew. This favors a Palestinian origin (though it comes short of proof), for the LXX was widely used outside that land.

At first sight it is somewhat surprising that Westcott adduces the Logos doctrine of the Prologue as a further indication that the Gospel is Palestinian, for this has often been urged as showing that the writer was indebted to Greek philosophy.[44] But we must not confuse terminology and ideas. When he asks what the terminology means, Westcott finds that the idea of the Gospel is not Greek but Hebrew. He examines the thought of Philo, but does not think that we have the source of John's idea here, for Philo thinks rather of the divine Reason than the divine Word when he uses the term.[45] Westcott contrasts this with the Targums where both מימרא and דבורא are used in connection with the deity.

---

[43] Op. cit., p. xxvii.

[44] W. F. Howard agrees with Westcott: ". . . Whereas at one time it was usual to trace the leading ideas of the Prologue to Greek philosophy, it is now more commonly recognized that we do not need to go beyond Judaism for the idea of the Logos" (FGRCI, p. 11).

[45] Westcott, op. cit., p. xxxiv.

Thus the affinities of John are with these Palestinian sources rather than with Philo. "The whole scope of the writers of the Old Testament is religious. . . . The whole scope of Philo on the other hand is metaphysical."[46]

I do not see that there is anything in recent writing that overthrows Westcott's essential point here. The argument from topography seems to stand, as most will agree. So does that from the use of the Old Testament. Many recent students are more respectful of the place of Philo in John's background than was Westcott. Thus A. W. Argyle and C. H. Dodd, to name but two, insist that we should find some place for Philo if we are to understand John. But few would think that Philo is the source of John's essential thought. Many are recommending that we turn our attention to the wisdom literature of Palestine, so that Westcott is receiving a strong reinforcement. Raymond E. Brown has recently argued very convincingly that the Logos as John uses the concept "is far closer to biblical and Jewish strains of thought than it is to anything purely Hellenistic."[47] An even stronger reinforcement is that which comes from the Qumran scrolls. Whatever be the explanation, the fact is indisputable that these early documents, rooted in Palestine as they are, have more points of contact with the Fourth Gospel than with any other part of the New Testament. In my opinion the connection between these documents and our Gospel must be indirect, but a connection of some sort there must surely be (see Ch. V).[48] This means that the background to this book

---

[46] *Ibid.*, pp. xxxvif.

[47] R. E. Brown, *The Gospel according to John (i-xii)*, New York, 1966, p. 524. See his whole discussion, pp. 519-524. Certain aspects of Hellenistic thought had penetrated Palestine (cf. the Qumran scrolls), so that it is not enough to show that there are affinities with Hellenism. It must be indicated that the Hellenism in question is non-Palestinian.

[48] E. K. Lee puts together the reference to the unnamed disciple in John 1:35, and the connection between the teaching of John the Baptist and the Qumran scrolls. He sees it as likely "that the Baptist before his preaching in the wilderness was in some relationship with the community at Qumran." He proceeds, "If this is true and if the unknown disciple was John the Apostle, we can understand both the accuracy of the Fourth Gospel as a source for

is to be found in Palestine.[49] Westcott's point about the
Jewish controversies is also valid. We know something
about the controversies which exercised the Christian
church in the second century. They were matters like
episcopacy (cf. the letters of Ignatius), speculations about
Gnostic emanations, the date of keeping Easter, and
others. The controversies dealt with in the Fourth Gospel are not these but, as Westcott said, those concerning
the true and false Judaism.

I cannot but feel that the argument that the author
of the Fourth Gospel came from Palestine is stronger
now than it was. Raymond E. Brown sums up a very
judicious discussion of the influences to be discerned
behind this Gospel in these words: "In sum, then, we
suggest that into Johannine theological thought patterns
has gone the influence of a peculiar combination of various ways of thinking that were current in Palestine during Jesus' own lifetime and after his death."[50] This I
think is a fair statement of the position in the light
of our present knowledge.

Where I would be inclined to differ from Westcott is
in seeing also other strands in his background. The
Evangelist seems to have points of contact with Hellenism as well as with Judaism. While we need not doubt
that the Judaism is fundamental, the Hellenism is there.
The writer is surely from Palestine, but he is *from* Palestine. But for our present purpose the important thing
is the fundamental background. And this seems plainly
enough to be Palestine.[51]

(c) *The author of the Fourth Gospel was an eyewitness*

---

the ministry of the Baptist and also the special theological emphasis of the Gospel" (CQR, 167, 1966, p. 300).

[49] Cf. A. J. B. Higgins: "All this means that there is much
more reason than there was before for believing that, if not the
Fourth Gospel as a completed product, at any rate the traditions
or sources employed by the evangelist are Palestinian in origin and
of relatively early date" (*The Historicity of the Fourth Gospel*,
London, 1960, pp. 17f.).

[50] *Op. cit.*, p. LXIV.

[51] Cf. W. F. Howard: "... Nothing has ever really discounted the
weighty evidence of the Gospel itself that the writer understood
the topography, the manners and customs, the religious ideas and
expectations of Palestine in our Lord's own time" (FGRCI, p. 12).

of what he described. Westcott maintained that this narrative "is marked by minute details of persons, and time, and number, and place and manner, which cannot but have come from a direct experience. And to these must be added various notes of fact, so to speak, which seem to have no special significance where they stand, though they become intelligible when referred to the impression originally made upon the memory of the Evangelist."[52]

Thus as to persons we have information about Philip (6:5, 7; 12:21f.; 14:8), Thomas (14:5) and others. Nicodemus (3:1ff.; 7:50; 19:39), Lazarus (11:1ff.; 12:1ff.), Simon the father of Judas Iscariot (6:71; 12:4; 13:2, 26), and Malchus (18:10) are mentioned in this Gospel only. This writer alone tells of the relationship of Annas to Caiaphas (18:13) and of the relationship between Malchus and one of those who pointed to Peter (18:26). "The first chapter is crowded with figures which live and move: John with his disciples, Andrew, Simon Peter, Philip, Nathanael."[53]

As to time, the seasons are mentioned frequently: the first Passover (2:13, 23), the feast of the New Year (5:1), the second Passover (6:4), Tabernacles (7:2), and the Dedication (10:22). Then there are the indications of two marked weeks at the beginning and end of the ministry (1:29, 35, 43; 2:1; 12:1, 12 (13:1); 19:31; 20:1), the week after the resurrection (20:26), the enumeration of the days before the raising of Lazarus (11:6, 17, 39), the length of the stay in Samaria (4:40, 43; cf. 6:22; 7:14, 37). Even the hour or time of day are often mentioned: the hour at 1:40; 4:6; 4:52; 19:14; night, 13:30; early morning, 18:28; 20:1; 21:4; evening, 6:16; 20:19; by night, 3:2.

John often gives numbers. "It is unnatural to refer to anything except experience such definite and, as it appears, immaterial statements as those in which the writer of the fourth Gospel mentions the *two* disciples of the Baptist (i.35), the *six* waterpots (ii.6), the *five* loaves and *two* small fishes (vi.9), the *five-and-twenty*

---

[52] *Op. cit.*, p. xxxix.
[53] *Ibid.*, p. xl.

furlongs (vi.19), the *four* soldiers (xix.23. Cf. Acts xii.4), the *two hundred* cubits (xxi.8), the *hundred and fifty and three* fishes (xxi.11)."[54] Note also five husbands (4: 18), thirty-eight years sickness (5:5), three hundred pence (12:5; cf. Mark 14:5), a hundred pounds weight (19:39). Of these only the numbers of the loaves and fishes and the worth of the ointment (Mark has more than three hundred pence) can be paralleled in the Synoptics. It is clear that this Evangelist is interested in precision.

So it is with place. We have already noticed the topographical accuracy of this Gospel. Here we notice in addition that place names are brought in very naturally. They are used in such a way that it is difficult to account for them except on the hypothesis that they tell us where certain incidents occurred. Thus the scenes of John's baptism were Bethany and Aenon (1:28; 3:23). The nobleman's son was sick at Capernaum while Jesus was at Cana (4:46f.). Jesus found the healed paralytic in the temple (5:14). Toward the end of His ministry He gained adherents when He went "beyond Jordan to the place where John was at first baptizing" (10:40ff.). Mary came to Him when He had not yet reached the village, but was still in the place where Martha met Him (11:30). Jesus spent the interval between the raising of Lazarus and His return to Bethany in the country near the wilderness in a city called Ephraim (11:54). The people as they stood in the temple speculated about Him (11:56). Christ spoke certain words *"in a solemn gathering* [ἐν συναγωγῇ] *at Capernaum"* (6:59), others in the treasury (8:20), or in Solomon's porch (10:23), or before crossing the Kidron (18:1).

Under the heading "Manner" Westcott says, "More impressive still are the countless small traits in the descriptions which evince either the skill of a consummate artist or the recollection of an observer. The former alternative is excluded alike by the literary spirit of the first and second centuries and by the whole character of the Gospel. The writer evidently reflects what he had

---

[54] *Ibid.*, p. xli.

seen."[55] Westcott sees the marks of an eyewitness in such narratives as the call of the first disciples (1:35-51), the foot-washing (13:1-20), the scene in the high priest's court (18:15-27), and the draught of fishes (21:1-14). Thus of the first he says,

> ...We cannot but feel the life (so to speak) of the opening picture. John is shown standing, in patient expectation of the issue, as the tense implies ($\iota\sigma\tau\acute{\eta}\kappa\epsilon\iota$ comp. vii.37, xviii.5, 16, 18, xix.25, xx.11), with two of his disciples. As Christ moves away, now separate from him, he fixes his eyes upon Him ($\dot{\epsilon}\mu\beta\lambda\acute{\epsilon}\psi\alpha s$ comp. *v.* 43), so as to give the full meaning to the phrase which he repeats, in order that his disciples may now, if they will, take the lesson to themselves. Each word tells; each person occupies exactly the position which corresponds with the crisis.[56]

Similarly he notices that the loaves at the miraculous feeding are of barley (6:19), that Mary fell at the feet of Jesus (11:32; contrast vv. 20f.); when the ointment was poured out the house was filled with fragrance (12:3); branches were taken from the palm trees (12:13); it was night when Judas went out (13:30); Judas brought Roman soldiers as well as some temple police (18:3); Jesus' tunic was without seam, woven from the top throughout (19:23); the napkin which had been around His head was wrapped together in a place by itself (20:7); Peter was grieved because Jesus asked the third time, "Lovest thou me?" (21:17). Sometimes a mysterious saying is left unexplained where the obscurity refers to some previous but unrecorded conversation, as with, "Behold the Lamb of God" (1:29; cf. 6:36; 12:34), or unknown local circumstances (1:46), or personal revelation (Nathanael, 1:48). Apparent contradictions are left without comment (5:31 with 8:14; 13:36 with 16:5; 14:19 with 16:19).

In all this Westcott sees the marks of one who knew what had gone on and knew it from personal experience. This is the kind of thing that comes naturally enough from an eyewitness, but not from a fabricator.

---

[55] *Ibid.*, p. xlii.
[56] *Ibid.*, pp. xliif.

We could add to them one or two more. Thus, as we have already seen, the Gospel refers to a number of controversies, and these not the controversies of the second century, which concerned such subjects as episcopacy, and the Gnostic and Ebionite positions. They are those of Palestine before the destruction of Jerusalem. The mood of the Jews is that of those who look for the promised Deliverer who would rescue them from the Romans (6:15; 11:47-50). It is hard to see how the late product of someone far removed from Palestine could catch the mood of the times so well.

This part of Westcott's case is vigorously disputed in recent times. C. K. Barrett approaches the evidence of an eyewitness, as he himself says, "with some scepticism."[57] He sees three main lines of evidence. First, the names John mentions that are not found in the Synoptic Gospels. But he thinks that there is "little force in this argument. The apocryphal gospels contain yet more names, but we do not therefore accept them as eye-witness authorities. There was in fact a tendency to insert names into the tradition on no authority at all. It has also been held that John adds life-like details of characterization to the figures that appear in his story; but they are not perceptible to every reader."[58] Barrett's second point is the recording of the exact time. This, he says, is true but does not prove that we have the testimony of an eyewitness. The third point is details such as numbers. The Evangelist might have derived these from sources, and in any case "such features are precisely what a writer adds to his work in order to give it verisimilitude. An interesting example is to be found at 6:1-13, the feeding of the multitude, where John is in all probability following Mark. Some striking details are drawn from the source, others are elaborating additions to it."[59] This last point, of course, falls to the ground if John is not dependent on Mark at this point, or if he has other material to supplement Mark.

---

[57] *Op. cit.*, p. 104.
[58] *Ibid.*
[59] *Ibid.*

In this fashion, then, Barrett justifies his initial scepticism. He concludes,

> The most the evidence that has now been surveyed can prove is that here and there behind the Johannine narrative there lies eye-witness material. It is certainly not proved, and is perhaps not provable, that the gospel as a whole is the work of an eye-witness. And the evidence already given of the Hellenistic side of John's thought suggests that the final editor of the gospel was not an eye-witness.[60]

With Barrett's approach the elimination of the possibility of an eyewitness behind the Gospel seems inevitable. Everything that looks like the touch of someone who had seen what he describes is ascribed either to some hypothetical source utilized by the Evangelist or to the desire to give verisimilitude to a narrative that lacked it.[61] The only surprising thing is that Barrett speaks of it as "perhaps" not provable that there is an eyewitness behind the narrative. If this is to be our method it will seem to most that it is absolutely impossible to prove it.

But it will also seem to many that such a treatment of the evidence does not really face the facts of the situation. Let us take, for example, John's use of names. This clearly matters to Barrett, for several times in his commentary he reverts to it. Thus when he comes to the name "Philip" in the miraculous feeding story he says, "Names are often added in the later forms of New Testament narratives (and in the apocryphal gospels); they sometimes lend an appearance of verisimilitude, but are in fact a sign of lateness."[62] Similarly he

---

[60] *Ibid.*

[61] One is reminded of R. P. C. Hanson's words with respect to form critics: "If there are no details of place or name or time in any piece of material, then it clearly does not go back to an eye-witness. If there are details of place or name or time, or any other vivid touch suggesting an eye-witness, then these owe their origin to later elaboration" (*Vindications*, ed. Anthony Hanson, London, 1966, p. 44). In both cases it is difficult to see how the original writer stands any chance of being vindicated. Whatever he does he is condemned.

[62] *Op. cit.*, p. 228.

thinks that the names Kidron, Peter, and Malchus in the story of the arrest invite comparison with the apocryphal gospels,[63] and he can say in his comments on the use of Peter in this narrative, "It is characteristic of the later tradition to add names and make identifications which are not in the earlier sources."[64] It will be seen that two points have a way of recurring: the use of names is late, and it is like that in the apocryphal gospels. What I do not think Barrett ever does is to examine either of these presuppositions.

Let us look first at the idea that the use of names points us to lateness. It is true that sometimes later documents have more names than earlier ones, and it is this which enables Barrett to make his generalization. But what he does not notice is that this is not an invariable tendency. It is in fact the case, as H. J. Cadbury notes, that there was a tendency to omit names in later tradition as well as to insert them. He instances the omission by Matthew and Luke of the name Bartimaeus, which is given by Mark, in their accounts of the healing of the blind man.[65] It is also worth noticing that when a later document does include names not in the earlier this may be because the later has good reason, and not because it is striving for verisimilitude. Thus Matthew tells us that after the arrest, "they that had taken Jesus led him away to the house of Caiaphas the high priest" (Matt. 26:57), whereas Mark says only that "they led Jesus away to the high priest" (Mark 14:53; Mark never mentions Caiaphas by name, but cf. Matt. 26:3). No one, I think, argues from this that Matthew simply manufactured the name. He is later than Mark, and he supplies a name that Mark lacks, but he does so because he knows that this is the right name, not because he wants to give a name to a person not named in the tradition as it reached him. A. J. B. Higgins regards it as

---

[63] *Ibid.*, p. 431.

[64] *Ibid.*, p. 435.

[65] *The Making of Luke-Acts*, London, 1958, p. 53. He notices both tendencies, and sees John's naming of Malchus as an example of the tendency to insert names (p. 59). I do not agree with this, but Cadbury's clear recognition of divergent tendencies in the handing on of tradition is important.

"not inconceivable" that some of John's use of names "may actually be more primitive than their absence from the corresponding Synoptic passages."[66] It is not enough to point to John's names and say, "This is evidence of lateness." There was some use of names that was early and some that was late. My contention is that it is too easy to say that John's falls into the latter category. His careful use of names makes it more likely that his is the early and accurate use.

It is not the case that John introduces names freely, in the manner alleged to be characteristic of the apocryphal gospels. One of the well-known difficulties of this Gospel is that John the apostle is never named. It is incredible that the Evangelist did not know the name of the beloved disciple, whether or not that mysterious figure is to be identified with the apostle John. He could certainly have named the man by whose witness he sets so much store in 19:35. Again, he never names the Virgin Mary, referring to her as "the mother of Jesus." The unnamed disciple of 1:35ff. has aroused much speculation, and it is difficult to think that the Evangelist could not have named him had he so chosen. James the apostle is never named. And so we could go on. The omission of names is as striking a feature of this Gospel as is their insertion, and raises as many problems. Clearly, to say that John's habit of inserting names is a sign of lateness is an oversimplification.

It is also worth noting W. F. Albright's point that an examination of the ossuaries shows that the names in this Gospel (as in the others) "were characteristic of the period from Herod the Great to A.D. 70." He remarks, ". . . If the Gospel of John innovated as drastically as is often thought, we should expect to find at least a few names not taken from good tradition."[67] There is nothing improbable about any of the names that John uses.

Barrett's other point is that John resembles the apocryphal gospels in this matter of using names. This is, of course, only another way of saying that John is late and

---

[66] *Op. cit.*, pp. 55f.

[67] *The Background of the New Testament and its Eschatology,* ed. W. D. Davies and D. Daube, Cambridge, 1956, p. 158.

unreliable in this respect. But there are some unexplained omissions here. First, it is not the case that the apocryphal gospels always insert names. To select an example at random, in the nineteen chapters of *The Infancy Story of Thomas* there are only seven names. Three are taken from the New Testament, Jesus, Joseph, and his son James. Three are names found in the New Testament, but here applied to other people, namely Thomas, Annas, and Zaccheus. There is but one other, namely Zenon. This can scarcely be called an impressive list. I do not claim that all the apocryphal works are like this. But clearly not all of them insert names freely, and names that are not found in the tradition.

Higgins treats this point with greater insight than does Barrett. Thus he admits that in the feeding of the multitude, "The introduction of Philip, Andrew, and the lad is regarded by many as a sign of lateness, and there is certainly a tendency to bring in names and other details, as we see in the apocryphal gospels." He goes on, however, to make a very important even if rather obvious point: "The Fourth Gospel, however, is not an apocryphal book, nor does it bear the marks of the apocryphal books. These characters are an integral part of the tradition of the feeding utilized by the evangelist."[68] Barrett often refers to the apocryphal books when he is speaking of John's use of names. But if John is not an apocryphal book then their uses have little relevance to his. The fact is that to go from John to the apocryphal gospels is to move into a different world. Some cogent reason ought to be brought forward by anyone who classes John with these works.

It is true that some late writers add spurious details, such as names, to give an air of verisimilitude to their narratives. But is there any real reason for classing John

---

[68] *Op. cit.*, p. 31. Later he devotes a section to the topic of names generally (pp. 53-60). His conclusion is, "when due allowance is made for Johannine constructions, there is less to be said for attributing the use of personal names in the Fourth Gospel, both Synoptic names and those peculiar to it, to the evangelist's own inventiveness, than to sources or traditions which may claim a degree of reliability not inferior and sometimes even superior to the Synoptic tradition" (p. 60).

with them? Barrett keeps on classing John with the apocryphal gospels, but he never attempts to show that this classification can be justified. John does not read in the slightest degree like an apocryphal work. While it is certainly true that *falsarii* often manufacture details to embellish their narratives, it is also true that it is more than difficult to do this continually without tipping one's hand. Sooner or later (unless there are only one or two examples) the *falsarius* blunders. He puts in the detail which could not possibly be true and shows himself for what he is. Now John has much to say by way of specific detail, as we have seen. And the important thing is that he rings true. Where we can check him, as in topography, he emerges with flying colors. *Pace* Barrett, most people will feel that this Gospel reads like the writing of a careful man, one who delights in detail, and who inserts accurate comments from his own knowledge.[69]

R. A. Edwards points out that some details, like the woman of Sychar's leaving of her water-pot, could have been manufactured. But the strength of the case is not with such details but "in the fact that many of the details are so obviously contemporary as to be beyond the reach of a writer who was not himself present at the incidents he describes."[70] As examples he cites the reference to the bridegroom's friend, "an obscure and purely Judaean marriage custom which must have completely disappeared by the time the book came to be written"; the reference to "this mountain" rather than Gerazim (4:20) by a local patriot;[71] the progress of the crowd from the hills to

---

[69] Godet makes a not unimportant point about the character of the Evangelist. On the naming of Malchus (18:10) he says, "How can any one persuade himself that a serious Christian of the second century, writing at a distance from Palestine, at Alexandria, in Asia Minor, or at Rome, would have set up the claim of knowing the name of a servant of the high-priest's house, and, besides, the part played by a relative of this servant (ver. 26)! Is such pitiable charlatanism compatible with the character of the author of the Fourth Gospel?" (*op. cit.*, II, 353). Is it likely that a man who could write the sublime passages of this Gospel would manufacture this kind of detail?

[70] R. A. Edwards, *The Gospel according to St. John*, London, 1954, p. 7.

[71] J. B. Lightfoot takes as one of his examples of the naturalness

Capernaum (6:22ff.); the reference to the pool by the sheep-gate as still existing (5:2), "a mistake that no sub-apostolic writer could conceivably have made." He wonders what inventor would make the Jerusalem authorities call Jesus a "devil-possessed Samaritan" (8:48), and accuse Him of claiming to be Abraham (8:57); or create a difficulty for himself by making the crowd question the idea that the Son of man might be lifted up (12:34). He wonders what inventor would have dared doctrinal argument by representing the risen Lord as speaking of "My God and yours" (20:17). Then there are references to "torches and lanterns" and to "Jesus the Nazarene" at the arrest, and unexplained things like Mary Magdalene's use of "we" during the risen Lord's appearance to her, or the reference to the "dinghy" in the last story in the Gospel. "To ignore all this should be impossible for anyone of sincere literary perception."[72]

C. H. Dodd registers a caveat against a too ready acceptance of the view that there is an eyewitness behind this Gospel. "Some of the evidence which has been adduced in favour of authorship by an eyewitness is subject to a heavy discount," he writes. "For example, the convincing characterization and dramatic actuality of parts of the gospel are urged in its favour. But two of the passages which most powerfully display these features are represented by the evangelist himself as occasions when no eyewitness was present — the conversation with the Samaritan woman, and the examination before Pilate."[73] This is certainly an overstatement. The Evangelist does *not* say that no eyewitness was present on these occasions. He does not say whether anyone was

---

of this conversation: "Observe that there is no mention in the context of any mountain in the neighbourhood; and even here, where it is mentioned, its name is not given" (E. Abbot, A. P. Peabody and J. B. Lightfoot, *The Fourth Gospel*, London, 1892, p. 163). This would be a curious procedure in a late writer of fiction.

[72] Edwards, *op. cit.*, p. 8, from which all the points listed are also taken. Edwards goes on to say that all this, taken in conjunction with "the equally strong evidence of antiquity about the author," is bound to make us feel "that it is enough, and more than enough to warrant the assumption that the book was written by John the Apostle, the son of Zebedee."

[73] IFG, pp. 449f.

present or not, which is not the same thing at all. In the case of the Samaritan woman, there are at least three possibilities besides the position that Dodd assumes: (a) A disciple may have been present but not taking part in the conversation; (b) Jesus may have told the disciples what had happened: it would have been excellent instruction for them in the way of dealing with souls and He must have said *something* about how the woman was converted; (c) the woman may have been the Evangelist's informant. The narrative gives the impression that she was not averse to a little talking (John 4:28, 39, 42; cf. the use of λαλία in the latter verse). In the case of the examination before Pilate, it is unlikely that Jesus disclosed what happened, but I see no improbability in the suggestion that Pilate may have talked about it. More important, however, is the question, On what grounds is it alleged that no one else was present on this occasion? The only reason the enemies of Jesus were not in the Praetorium was that they feared ceremonial defilement (John 18:28). Nothing in the narrative indicates that either they or any other interested party was compelled to stay out. Roman officials would certainly have been present, and I see no reason why a Jew who was not concerned about ceremonial defilement should not have gone in, too. Neither of Dodd's examples is impressive. They do nothing to shake our conviction that an eyewitness is behind this Gospel as a whole.

(d) *The author was an apostle.* Westcott sees evidence for this in the character of the scenes the writer describes, the call of the disciples (1:19-34), the journey through Samaria (ch. 4), the feeding of the five thousand (ch. 6), the successive visits to Jerusalem (chs. 7, 9, 11), the passion, and the resurrection appearances. This is not really very strong evidence. Any disciple would be interested in these things and would have access to information about them. More significant is the Evangelist's "intimate acquaintance" with the feelings of the disciples. He knows their thoughts at critical moments (2:11, 17, 22; 4:27; 6:19, 60f.; 12:16; 13:22, 28; 21:12; cf. Luke 24:8; Matt. 26:75). He remembers words spoken among themselves (4:33; 16:17; 20:25; 21:3, 5), and to the

Lord (4:31; 9:2; 11:8, 12; 16:29). He knows "their places of resort" (11:54; 18:2; 20:19). He knows of "imperfect or erroneous impressions received by them at one time, and afterwards corrected" (2:21f.; 11:13; 12:16; 13:28; 20:9; 21:4).[74]

More than this: The writer "evidently stood very near to the Lord." He knew His emotions (11:33; 13:21). He knew the grounds of His action (2:24f.; 4:1; 5:6; 6:15; 7:1; 16:19). And especially,

> ... He speaks as one to whom the mind of the Lord was laid open. Before the feeding of the five thousand he writes, *This He* (Jesus) *said trying him, for He Himself knew what He was about to do* (vi. 6). *Jesus knew in Himself* the murmurings of the disciples (vi. 61); *He knew from the beginning who they were that believed not, and who it was that should betray Him* (vi. 64). *He knew the hour of His Passion* (xiii. 1, 3), and who should betray Him (xiii. 11); *He knew* indeed *all the things that were coming upon Him* (xviii. 4); *He knew* when *all things were accomplished* (xix. 28).[75]

Not much need, I think, be said about this. This evidence is not really discussed by modern scholars at all. It is simply assumed that the writer is not the apostle, and that therefore this information must have come to him from some source or other, or else be supplied from his own fertile brain as he filled in the gaps in his story. If we feel on other grounds that the apostle was not the writer, then we will have no great difficulty in accounting for these references.

But if we are not so convinced before we look at this evidence then it is different. While it would, perhaps, be too much to say that these passages prove that the writer was an apostle, at least they are not incongruous with that supposition. They are the kind of revealing detail that such a one might well have at his disposal. I do not think that more can be said. They are part of the evidence, and they fit in well with an apostolic author, should there be other evidence for postulating this. I cannot feel that this point is as strong as the preceding ones,

---

[74] Westcott, *op. cit.*, p. xlv.
[75] *Ibid.*

but it has some weight and should not be simply ignored.
(e) *The author of the Fourth Gospel was the apostle
John.* John 21:24 ascribes the Gospel to "The disciple
whom Jesus loved," an expression which occurs also in
13:23; 19:26; 21:7, 20; and, with the verb φιλέω in place
of ἀγαπάω, in 20:2. Westcott sees him as known to the
high priest (18:15)[76] and as standing in close relationship to Peter (13:24; 20:2; 21:7; cf. 18:15; Acts 3). From
21:2 he must have been one of the sons of Zebedee, or
one of the two unnamed. From the Synoptists we know
that Peter, James, and John were specially close to Jesus.
Peter is out of the question. James was martyred early
(Acts 12:2). "John therefore alone remains; and he completely satisfies the conditions which are required to be
satisfied by the writer, that he should be in close connection with St. Peter, and also one admitted to peculiar
intimacy with the Lord."[77] Support for this is found in
the absence of all mention of John in this Gospel, though
he is known in the Synoptics, in Acts (3:1; 4:13, etc.),
and in Paul (Gal. 2:9) as a central figure among the
Twelve. The nameless disciple fills the place we should
have expected John to fill. It might be inferred from
1:40f. that just as Andrew found his brother, so did
another find his brother, and a reference to 21:2 "leads to
the certain inference that these two brothers were the
sons of Zebedee."[78] It is clear that from the beginning of
this Gospel there is one disciple who is not named (John
1:35ff.). Why? Why mention him if he is to play no part
in the Gospel? This, of course, does not prove that he
wrote the Gospel. But the raising of the questions directs
us toward Westcott's view that he was the apostle John.

---

[76] Of the identification of this figure with the beloved disciple
Barrett says, "This view can be neither proved nor disproved; but
it can be said that if the beloved disciple, the son of Zebedee, be
intended, the description gives no ground for reliance upon the
author's accuracy. It is highly improbable that the Galilean fisherman was γνωστὸς τῷ ἀρχιερεῖ " (*op. cit.*, p. 99). To which one may
fairly retort, Why? What do we *know* (as against suppose) about
first-century Palestine which makes the statement improbable?

[77] Westcott, *op. cit.*, p. xlvi.

[78] *Ibid.*, p. xlvii.

While it cannot be proved beyond doubt it remains the most reasonable hypothesis.[79]

This is supported also by the peculiarity whereby this Evangelist never speaks of "John the Baptist" as the Synoptists do, but simply of "John." Yet he is usually very careful with names and habitually qualifies them carefully in a way the others do not. Thus he never speaks of Simon after his call, but always of Simon Peter or Peter. Three times out of four he identifies Thomas by calling him Didymus (11:16; 20:24; 21:2), a title not found in the Synoptics. Judas is the son of a Simon not elsewhere noticed (6:71; 12:4; 13:2, 26). The second Judas is expressly distinguished from Judas Iscariot (14:22). Nicodemus is described in the terms of his coming to Jesus (7:50; 19:39), and Caiaphas each time is "the high priest of that year" (11:49; 18:13). If the writer were himself called John his usage with John the Baptist is explicable, but if not, in view of his carefulness in distinguishing people, how shall we explain it?

It is perhaps worth adding the point that the beloved disciple must have been one of those present at the Last Supper. But according to Mark 14:17, it was the Twelve who were with Jesus then. Thus the beloved disciple appears to have been one of the Twelve.

Westcott proceeds to face two objections, the one that John would not have claimed by this title a preeminence above his fellows, and the other that specifically he would not have elevated himself above Peter. Taking the latter first, Westcott points out that John's question of Jesus at the Last Supper (13:24ff.), and the scenes in the court of the high priest and at the cross, "belong to details of personal relationship, and not to official position."[80] In any event Peter's primacy is just as clear in this Gospel as elsewhere: consider his surname (1:42), his confession (6:68), his prominence at the foot-washing (13:6), his defense of Christ (18:10), his waiting at the high priest's door (18:16), the facts that the resurrection

[79] J. B. Lightfoot has a valuable discussion of the passages concerning the unnamed disciple and the way they lead us to John (*op. cit.*, pp. 168ff.).

[80] *Op. cit.*, p. xlviii.

message is brought to him (20:2), that he first sees the signs that Christ has risen (20:7), that he directs the group fishing (21:3), that he is first to join Christ on the shore and chief in carrying out His command (21:7, 11), and that he receives the great commission (21:15ff.).

The writer is not trying to conceal his identity behind the expression "the disciple whom Jesus loved." He insists that his narrative is that of a witness and evidently takes it for granted that those for whom the Gospel is written will know who he is. Westcott puts a good deal of emphasis on the use of $\dot{\alpha}\gamma\alpha\pi\dot{\alpha}\omega$ rather than $\phi\iota\lambda\dot{\epsilon}\omega$ in 20:2, and understands the expression to apply to both Peter and the other. "St. Peter and St. John shared alike in that peculiar nearness of personal friendship to Christ (if we may so speak) which is expressed by the former word ($\phi\iota\lambda\epsilon\hat{\iota}\nu$ see xi. 3, 36), while St. John acknowledges for himself the gift of love which is implied in the latter; the first word describes that of which others could judge outwardly; the second that of which the individual soul alone is conscious."[81] Of the expression, "The disciple whom Jesus loved," he concludes, "... It is a personal thanksgiving for a blessing which the Evangelist had experienced, which was yet in no way peculiar to himself";[82] "The words express the grateful and devout acknowledgement of something received, and contain no assumption of a distinction above others."[83]

Westcott's examination thus rests heavily on the identification of the beloved disciple with the apostle John. It may be profitable to consider how Barrett deals with these references. He points out that they show that this disciple was at the Last Supper, that he is mentioned in close contact with Peter twice, and with the mother of Jesus once. There are no good grounds for thinking that merely an "ideal" figure is meant. Thus the evidence so far points to John, son of Zebedee. But all three passages "have secondary features."[84] The supper passage he sees

---

[81] *Ibid.*, p. li.
[82] *Ibid.*, p. lii.
[83] *Ibid.*, p. li.
[84] Barrett, *op. cit.*, p. 98.

as an attempt "to square the Matthaean tradition that the traitor was unmasked at the supper with the Marcan tradition that he remained unknown to the Eleven."[85] It is difficult to reconcile this with Barrett's contention elsewhere that it is likely that John used Mark and perhaps Luke, while the possibility that he used Matthew is so slight that it is not even examined.[86] We have no good reason for affirming that John knew the Matthaean tradition but not Matthew. Moreover, John's narrative at this point has all the marks of independence. It does not appear to be indebted to Matthew or to Mark. Further, the Fourth Evangelist is not conspicuous for harmonizing expedients. It is usually alleged that he "corrects" the Synoptists, not that he tries to harmonize them. There seems no good critical reason for suspecting this passage.

Barrett objects to the story of the beloved disciple and Mary the mother of Jesus at the cross, in these words: "It is both intrinsically improbable that friends and relatives of Jesus would be allowed to stand near the cross, and inconsistent with the Marcan tradition that all the disciples fled."[87] But is there any information from antiquity as to how near a cross relatives might stand? If there were no danger of riot or rescue there seems no real reason why friends as well as enemies might not be allowed to approach (and we know that enemies were near Christ's cross). I see nothing "intrinsically improbable" about it at all. That it is inconsistent with the Marcan tradition that all fled really looks like special pleading, for Mark is not speaking of what happened at the cross at all. He is referring to something that took place hours before, at the arrest. Exactly the same argument could be used against Peter's presence in the courtyard at the time of his denials. But no one, I think, would affirm that because all the disciples fled, the story of the denials must be unhistorical. The disciples fled at the time of the arrest (Mark 14:50), but that does not mean that they kept running. Sooner or later they had to stop. Peter came near enough to his Lord to deny Him, and

---

[85] *Ibid.*
[86] *Ibid.*, pp. 34ff.
[87] *Ibid.*, p. 98.

there is not the slightest reason for saying that John could not have come back to stand near the cross. Mark tells us that there were certain women there, though at a distance (Mark 15:40); and it is not at all impossible or unlikely that our Lord's mother and a close friend came closer. Barrett goes on to say that "in the early chapters of Acts, Mary is found not with John but with the brothers of Jesus (Acts 1:14)."[88] This is misleading. Acts does not tell us that Mary was with the brethren of Jesus at all. It tells us that a number of the believers were together, and it begins by listing the Eleven (including, of course, John). Then it adds others, some women, and Mary and the brethren.[89] It says nothing at all about whom she was with, and this passage cannot be held to tell against the Johannine passage.

Barrett objects to the third passage in these words: "The visit of Peter and John to the tomb is prompted by a message brought to them by one of the women; but in the earliest tradition the women said nothing to anyone (Mark 16:8)."[90] This is rather like the disciples running away. Did the silence of the women in this matter never terminate? If so, how do we know what was said to them? Sooner or later they must have spoken to someone, else these words could never have become part of the tradition. And we have no reason at all for holding that they did not get over their fear (at least one of them) in time to suit the conditions of John 20:2. Mark records the command of the young man in white that the women should tell His disciples "and Peter" (Mark 16:7), and it is incredible that Mark has simply recorded this as a command to be disobeyed.

Barrett proceeds to further points. "The beloved disciple appears only in Jerusalem, whereas the sons of Zebedee were men of Galilee."[91] This is true only provided that the beloved disciple is mentioned every time he was present. Westcott's case depends on the contention that

---

[88] *Ibid.*

[89] The Greek of Acts 1:14 gives a better reason for grouping Mary with the women than with the brethren. See the comment on p. 199 above.

[90] *Loc. cit.*

[91] *Ibid.*

he was not. "The beloved disciple is apparently ranked higher than Peter."[92] Westcott has dealt with this with some seriousness, but Barrett makes no attempt to reckon with the facts the earlier scholar adduced.

On the basis of this rather unconvincing discussion Barrett concludes, "Thus it must be admitted that, while the beloved disciple seems to be a designation of John the son of Zebedee, there is no evidence that the references to him were derived from him, and indeed no evidence that they rest on good historical tradition."[93] He proceeds to examine the references in John 21 and then says,

> We may for the present say, not with certainty but with at least some assurance, that the author of the gospel, whoever he may have been, described as the disciple whom Jesus loved, John, the son of Zebedee and one of the Twelve. The balance of probability is that a man would not so refer to himself; if this is true, the evangelist was not the son of Zebedee.[94]

I am inclined to be more respectful to this last objection than the earlier ones. Despite the assertions of Westcott and of other conservatives, "the disciple whom Jesus loved" does not seem to me to be a designation that a man would naturally use of himself. But this is a subjective estimate, and it is countered by the reflection that it is not a designation that a man would naturally use of someone else![95] Moreover, it must be admitted that in every age

---

[92] *Ibid.*

[93] *Ibid.*

[94] *Ibid.*, p. 99. W. F. Howard cites Eduard Meyer for the view that "the identification of the Beloved Disciple with the author of the Gospel, and, further, with John the son of Zebedee, is the manifest intention of the author." He proceeds to quote Meyer, "How this could be denied is one of the many things which remain incomprehensible to me in the assertions of modern criticism" (FGRCI, p. 70; Meyer, of course, rejects the apostolic authorship and regards the author as unknown).

[95] Green-Armytage admits that the writer appears to speak "a little boastfully." But he proceeds, "And, indeed, only a little. What is the total sum of his vainglory? That he was beloved. Has not many a lover also confessed that he was beloved, and is not this confession perfectly compatible with deep humility towards the beloved object? But the humility of saints often looks like its opposite in the eyes of the world" (*John Who Saw*, London, 1952, p.

some Christians have used expressions that are far from usual, to say the least. And it must be borne in mind that in this question of the authorship of the Fourth Gospel few will claim that all the evidence falls neatly into place. The problem is a complicated one, and it is a matter of estimating the probabilities and abiding by them. This subjective feeling cannot stand against the rest of the evidence which does seem to indicate that the beloved disciple was John the apostle.[96] Some modern writers have suggested other names, such as Lazarus (a clue being said to be given in John 11:3). But in early tradition there is no other name than John. And the evidence adduced in favor of any other is not as strong as that for the son of Zebedee.[97]

Green-Armytage mentions Delff's idea (derived from F. von Üchtritz) supported by Bousset, von Soden, Swete, and others, that the beloved disciple was "the owner of

---

86). Later he says, "But in any event, and however odd it may be to use such a periphrasis about oneself, is it not still odder to use it about anybody else?" (ibid.). "The fact is, John is in a dilemma. He wishes to 'include himself out' of the story, yet at the same time he wishes to make it clear that he is a reliable witness because he was a close friend of the Lord" (p. 90).

[96] Lord Charnwood, though he does not think that John the apostle wrote this Gospel, is scathing about those who see in the beloved disciple another than John. He regards this as a "remarkable feat of criticism," and again he speaks of "the plainest fact in the whole problem, namely, the reference in this Gospel to a certain Disciple who, if we attend at all to the Gospels, can be none but the Apostle, John the son of Zebedee." He refers to the evidence in favor of this view as "evidence which, outside the ranks of theology, no reasonable man would dream of setting aside except for very substantial and well-tested reasons (According to St. John, London, n. d., pp. 28, 36).

[97] R. E. Brown carefully marshalls the evidence. He makes full allowance for the objections to seeing John bar Zebedee as the beloved disciple, three of which in particular "offer real difficulty," namely the attention given to Jerusalem whereas John was a Galilean, the description of John as "illiterate and ignorant" (Acts 4: 13), which scarcely fits the author of this Gospel, and the omission of the transfiguration and the agony in the garden. But he sees greater difficulties in the way of any other hypothesis and concludes, "... The combination of external and internal evidence associating the Fourth Gospel with John son of Zebedee makes this the strongest hypothesis, if one is prepared to give credence to the Gospel's claim of an eyewitness source" (op. cit., p. XCVIII).

the house where the last supper was held." He fits better than John the description "known to the high priest." This may be so, but the view suffers from the not inconsiderable drawback that "there is no evidence for it." The man obviously existed. "But nothing whatever is related of him. Not even his name is known. And it is hard to believe that anyone who played the important role assigned to the beloved disciple in the story of our Lord's passion and resurrection would have vanished so conclusively from the pages of both history and legend."[98] Green-Armytage is highly critical of the view that the beloved disciple means "the ideal disciple." A Jew of the first century would not imagine an "ideal" disciple. In any case he says practically nothing, does practically nothing. The only thing is that Jesus loved him and "confided St. Mary to his care."

Other suggestions have been made. Thus Lewis Johnson argues for John Mark as the beloved disciple,[99] but his arguments appear to have been met by Donald Rogers.[100] And so with other suggestions. None has anything like the probability that the Son of Zebedee is meant.

DIRECT EVIDENCE

WHEN HE TURNS HIS ATTENTION TO THE DIRECT EVIDENCE afforded by the Gospel, Westcott finds three passages. The first is John 1:14, "The word became flesh and tabernacled among us, and we beheld his glory." The same verb for "beheld," $\theta\epsilon\acute{a}o\mu\alpha\iota$, is found in 1 John 1:1, "That which was from the beginning, which we have heard, which we have seen with our eyes, which we beheld, and our hands handled, concerning the Word of life. . . ." It refers to a literal seeing with the eyes, the verb never being used anywhere in the New Testament for mental vision (as is $\theta\epsilon\omega\rho\acute{\epsilon}\omega$). While "dwelt among us" might be understood of all Christians or even of all men, it does not exclude apostles. And it does not affect the

---

[98] Green-Armytage, *op. cit.*, p. 88.
[99] ET, 77, 1965-66, pp. 157f.
[100] ET, 77, 1965-66, p. 214.

sense of "beheld" which affirms the activity of an eye-witness. "The words cannot without violence be made to give any other testimony."[101] Barrett, having rejected the possibility of apostolic authorship, says, "It remains possible only that it should mean 'we, the Church,' 'we Christians': we beheld the glory of Christ when he abode with us."[102] I cannot see that exegetically this interpretation has anything to commend it above that of Westcott. Indeed, without the prior assumption that it could not refer to apostles, it would not, I think, be put forward.[103]

The second passage is in the crucifixion narrative: "And forthwith came there out blood and water. And he that hath seen hath borne witness, and his witness is true: and he knoweth that he saith true, that ye also may believe" (John 19:35). Westcott sees no great difficulty in referring the pronoun ἐκεῖνος to the speaker, this being found in the classics and also in this Gospel (9:37). Considering the way this Gospel is drawn up, the introduction of the first person at this point would have been more strange than the construction we have, especially

---

[101] Westcott, *op. cit.*, p. liii.

[102] *Op. cit.*, p. 119.

[103] Cf. Sir Edwin Hoskyns' view of the "we." "The point is that, in the perspective of the Johannine Writings, the first person plural means primarily the original disciples of Jesus, and that it is precisely this plural that is capable of expansion to a general 'we' and of contraction to a particular 'ego'. This expansion and contraction is, however, possible only within the sphere of those who, though belonging to a later generation, have been so completely created by apostolic witness and formed by apostolic obedience that they are veritably carried across into the company of the original disciples of Jesus and invested with the authority of their mission. In this context the possibility has to be taken seriously into account that a man, not himself one of the original disciples of Jesus, may have been so completely absorbed by their testimony as to have been driven not only to bear witness to the world, but also to the Church, and to have done this with true, though derived, apostolic authority" (*The Fourth Gospel*, London, 1950, p. 92). Here the "inspired" like Hoskyns have the advantage. To reject this as way beyond the evidence and outside the realm of probability (not to say possibility) is to stamp oneself as hum-drum, plebian, unable to enter the soaring thoughts of great minds. Yet despite his eloquence, Hoskyns has not made his case. It is a curious use of "we" that he postulates and one to be accepted only after rigorous demonstration.

since John has been already introduced in this scene (vv. 26, 27). The use of the third person is thus natural. This is supported by the use of the perfect tense rather than the aorist, which would have been the natural tense to use of the witness of someone else. Westcott concludes,

> On the whole, therefore, the statement which we have considered is not only compatible with the identity of the eye-witness and the writer of the Gospel, but it also suggests, even if it does not necessarily involve, the identification of the two. On the other hand, the only other possible interpretation of the passage is wholly pointless. It supposes that an appeal is made with singular emphasis to an unknown witness, who is said to be conscious of the truthfulness of his own testimony. Such a comment could find no place in the connexion in which the words stand.[104]

Modern scholars in general would not be as ready as Westcott to see a reference to John as the author of the Gospel. Most would agree, I think, that appeal is being made to the witness behind the Gospel, and that the witness is the beloved disciple. But they would distinguish between the author and the witness. I agree that this is the more natural way, though not the only way, of understanding the third person. Many also draw attention to the context with its mention of the water and blood coming out from the Saviour's side and think of this as probably unhistorical. Thus they place no very great reliance on the passage. But the author of the Gospel seems to have thought it important. Granted that there are obscurities about it, it remains at least possible that the words should be understood as Westcott takes them. And on any showing they are meant to indicate that behind what is recorded is the testimony of an eyewitness.

The third passage is John 21:24: "This is the disciple who witnesseth concerning these things, and who wrote these things: and we know that his witness is true." Westcott thinks these words unmistakably assign the writing of this Gospel to the beloved disciple. He points out further, that it is contemporaneous with the publication of the Gospel (there is no evidence that the Gospel

---

[104] *Op. cit.*, p. lvii.

ever circulated without the addition). Again, it speaks both of "substantial authorship" and of "the literal authorship."[105] It does not appear to have been written by the beloved disciple himself, but it attests his authorship.

Here modern students see many difficulties. It is widely held that the Gospel originally ended at 20:31, and that chapter 21 is an addition. The note at the end may thus refer to the addition, or to the whole Gospel. Again, ὁ γράψας, which would not unnaturally be held to mean "who wrote," could possibly mean "who caused to write" and thus be compatible with the theory that the beloved disciple was not the actual author but was the witness whose testimony was behind the Gospel. All these possibilities exist, and we may feel that Westcott did not give sufficient attention to other possibilities than the one he espoused. Yet when all is said and done the idea that the words mean that the beloved disciple both bore the witness to those things and also wrote them is much the most straightforward interpretation of the Greek.

With this we should take the fact that the words at the end of chapter 21 are so early. Kenyon sees the first-century date as very important: "Now if the Gospel had been written after the middle of the second century, such a certificate might be explained away as a forger's attempt to authenticate his work ... but if it were written at the end of the first century, when many persons were alive who could confirm or contradict it, such an explanation is impossible."[106] Perhaps Kenyon puts the point a little too strongly, but it is a good point nevertheless. Few critics even try to explain how a *falsarius* could get away with this kind of authentication at as early a date as this. Such suggestions as are offered carry little conviction. It still remains the most probable view that the words represent an authentication of the preceding by people who knew what they were about.

EXTERNAL EVIDENCE

ALL AGREE THAT THE EXTERNAL EVIDENCE FOR THE

[105] *Ibid.*, pp. lviif.
[106] Cited in Green-Armytage, *op. cit.*, pp. 74f.

authorship of this Gospel by John, the son of Zebedee, is strong, though not strikingly early. Westcott points out that Christian theological literature to all intents and purposes begins with Irenaeus, Clement of Alexandria, and Tertullian, all of whom fully accept Johannine authorship. He begins his case "with the undeniable fact that about the last quarter of the second century, when from the nature of the case clear evidence can first be obtained, the Gospel was accepted as authoritative by heretical writers like Ptolemaeus and Heracleon, and used by the opponents of Christ like Celsus, and assigned to St. John by Fathers in Gaul, Alexandria, and North Africa, who claimed to reproduce the ancient tradition of their churches."[107] He notes that Marcion rejected this Gospel, but on subjective grounds. Also unimportant is its ascription to Cerinthus by the *Alogi*, which "seems to have arisen from the mistaken extension to the authorship of the Gospel, by way of explaining its rejection, of a late conjecture as to the authorship of the Apocalypse."[108]

The first to quote it by name is Theophilus of Antioch (*ca.* AD 181).[109] From him Westcott works back through Athenagoras, Claudius Apollinaris, and Tatian, thus bringing back the date of acceptance of the Gospel to *ca.* AD 160. He notes coincidences of thought with Clement of Rome, Barnabas, and Ignatius, but he sees "the decisive testimony to the authenticity of St. John's writings" as really beginning with Polycarp and Papias.[110] Polycarp spanned the period between the apostle John and Irenaeus, having known them both personally. "Is it conceivable that in his lifetime such a revolution was accomplished that his disciple Irenaeus was not only deceived as to the authorship of the book, but was absolutely

---

[107] *Op. cit.*, p. lx. Notice that this can be extended a little because the heretics Westcott names were of the Gnostic type. It was also accepted, as the Clementine Homilies show, by heretics of Ebionitic or Jewish type. Since it was accepted by both it can scarcely have been originated by either, but must go back to a source both could recognize.

[108] *Ibid.*

[109] Ptolemaeus, the Valentinian, also apparently assigns the Gospel to "John, the disciple of the Lord" (Irenaeus *Adv. Haer.* I, 8.5).

[110] *Op. cit.*, p. lxii.

unaware that the continuity of the tradition in which he boasted had been completely broken?"[111] Papias is cited both as having used 1 John (which, with Westcott, carries the implication that he knew and accepted the Gospel), and as having given an account of the way the Gospel was written similar to that in the Muratorian fragment. Polycarp and Papias and the "elders" cited by Irenaeus show that a school of St. John existed, and this points to his Gospel as authoritative. Westcott goes on to show that Justin Martyr seems to have known the book, and that his teaching on the Word presupposes that of John. He goes on to refer to the Shepherd of Hermas, the Muratorian fragment, the translations into Syriac and Latin, and the works of heretics like Heracleon, Valentinus and Basilides.

Westcott sums up by agreeing that traces of the use of this Gospel in the first 75 years "are less distinct and numerous than those might have expected who are unacquainted with the character of the literary remains of the period. But it will be observed that all the evidence points in one direction."[112] He thus sees the external evidence as forming strong confirmation of the internal evidence.[113]

Work since Westcott has not altered the picture very much. In some respects it has strengthened Westcott's

---

[111] *Ibid.*, p. lxiii.

[112] *Ibid.*, p. lxvii.

[113] Others state much the same evidence in a somewhat different fashion. M. F. Wiles, for example, cites Theophilus and Ptolemaeus, and then lists "four fuller accounts of the writing of the Gospel." The anti-Marcionite prologue says that John dictated the Gospel to Papias "while still in the body." The Muratorian Canon says that John wrote "at the encouragement of his fellow-disciples and bishops." Clement of Alexandria speaks of John as "being urged by his friends and inspired by the Spirit" as a result of which he composed "a spiritual Gospel." Irenaeus says that the Gospel was written by John, the disciple who leaned on Jesus' breast, while he was in Ephesus (*The Spiritual Gospel*, Cambridge, 1960, pp. 7f.). For later commentators it was unquestioned that John, the son of Zebedee, was the author. "To speak of finding confirmation of this fact from the internal evidence of the Gospel itself would be misleading. One cannot confirm that about which one is not in any doubt" (p. 9).

position. For example, the discovery of a little piece of papyrus containing a few verses of this Gospel and confidently dated to the first half of the second century, has shown conclusively that the Gospel must be early.[114] The papyrus comes from Egypt, and allowing time for the work to travel there from its place of origin, it seems plain that extreme theories which once placed the composition of the Gospel well into the second century must be ruled out. With this we should mention the discovery of parts of a composition which looks like a mosaic from the canonical Gospels, including John.[115] This, too, is early (probably AD 140-160), so that if it did use the Fourth Gospel, John must be placed some time before this. Thus from the point of view of the documents the case is stronger now than when Westcott left it.

On the other hand many scholars are inclined to place more stress on the lateness of the ascription of the Gospel to John. They ask, "If this work were written by the apostle John, why does not someone say so before Irenaeus and Theophilus?" They also find little definite evidence of its acceptance, even without citing the name of its author. Thus it is denied that Ignatius or Justin used the Gospel. It is argued that the delay in its being accepted until the end of the second century is inexplicable if it were really penned by an apostle.

One recent piece of work on Papias should be cited. The ancient worthy has usually been accepted at Eusebius' valuation as a man of limited intelligence, and the value of his evidence has been discounted. But C. S. Petrie has reexamined the evidence,[116] and he decides that Eu-

---

[114] C. H. Roberts (ed.): *An Unpublished Fragment of the Fourth Gospel in the John Rylands Library*, Manchester, 1935.

[115] Egerton Papyrus 2; see H. J. Bell and T. C. Skeat (eds.): *Fragments of the Unknown Gospel*, London, 1935. J. Jeremias favors the view that the writer knew John as well as the Synoptics (E. Hennecke, *New Testament Apocrypha*, I, London, 1963, pp. 94ff.). R. Bultmann thinks that this papyrus and that mentioned in the previous note "indicate that John was known in Egypt about 100 A.D." (*Theology of the New Testament*, II, London, 1955, p. 10).

[116] See his article, "The Authorship of 'The Gospel According to Matthew': A Reconsideration of the External Evidence" (NTS, 14, 1967-68, pp. 15-32).

sebius was perhaps unduly influenced by his determination to discredit the chiliastic ideas of Papias. Petrie's argument produces good reason for accepting the evidence that Papias was a hearer of John the apostle. If this is so, and Petrie's case is strong, Papias' evidence on the origin of this Gospel takes on a new importance.

The evidence of the Chenoboskion manuscripts also alters the picture somewhat. In 1945 or 1946 some peasants near Nag Hammadi in Upper Egypt stumbled across the remains of a library of Gnostic manuscripts. There were eleven codices, containing in all about forty-eight works. After a complicated series of happenings most were secured for the Coptic Museum in Cairo. The find is sometimes referred to with the modern name Nag Hammadi, and sometimes with the name of the ancient town of Chenoboskion (where Pachomius had one of the earliest Christian monasteries). For a variety of reasons publication has been slow, and most of the documents have not yet appeared in print. But some of the more important have been published, and these show that John was known and accepted as authoritative before the middle of the second century. Thus the "Gospel of Truth" (probably written by Valentinus), which is dated in the period AD 140-150,[117] gives evidence of familiarity with our Gospel. Quispel says of it, "The 'Gospel of Truth' has borrowed more than a little from the Gospel of St. John, as from a writing which was already old and held in high repute."[118] That the Gospel was "already old" in 140-150 is an important conclusion.

Probably the writing which attracted most attention in this find was the "Gospel of Thomas." This is a collection of sayings, and it has many more affinities with the Synoptic Gospels than with John. But it does appear to reflect John in some passages, and as it is usually dated ca. AD 140-150[119] it is further indication that

---

[117] K. Grobel dates it "150 if not earlier" (*The Gospel of Truth*, London, 1960, p. 28) ; G. Quispel, "earlier than 150, say about 140" (H. C. Puech, G. Quispel, W. C. van Unnik, *The Jung Codex*, London, 1955, p. 54) ; W. C. van Unnik, "round about 140-145" (*ibid.*, p. 104).
[118] *Op. cit.*, p. 49.
[119] Cf. B. Gärtner, "Hitherto there has been a fair measure of

John is significantly earlier than this. Yet another "Gospel," this time the "Gospel of Philip," shows a fondness for John (and for Matthew). The dating of this "Gospel" is uncertain, but it may well be second century, in which case it supports the previously mentioned works.[120]

Another of the Gnostic writings is the "Apocryphon of John." This document shows a knowledge of many New Testament books, including John. Once more, it appears to be quite early, perhaps as early as the beginning of the second century.[121]

This makes a fairly solid body of literature which treats the Fourth Gospel as authoritative in the first half of the second century. In the light of these new discoveries it is not easy to maintain that the attestation of this Gospel is late. It is true that a connection with the apostle John is not explicitly attested in the Chenoboskion finds so far published. Yet we should not overlook the fact that Irenaeus tells us that Ptolemaeus (a disciple of Valentinus) and his followers held this Gospel to have been written by "John, the disciple of the Lord."[122] There is no reason for thinking him in error about this, and it would certainly accord with the way these Gnostics used the Gospel.

Another early figure of some importance is the heretic Marcion. This man produced an edited version of Luke as the only Gospel to be believed and used, discarding the others. But he does not seem to have done this because he held them inauthentic. He appears to have agreed that Matthew and John were written by apostles,

---

agreement over the date A.D. 140-150" (*The Theology of the Gospel of Thomas*, London, 1961, p. 271).

[120] H.-Ch. Puech puts it "in the 2nd century, or at latest in the beginning or the middle of the 3rd" (E. Hennecke, *New Testament Apocrypha*, I, London, 1963, p. 278). R. McL. Wilson sees "a number of indications which seem to point to the second century" (*The Gospel of Philip*, London, 1962, p. 3).

[121] R. M. Grant thinks of a date at the beginning of the second century (Puech, *op. cit.*, p. 331; Puech's view is that "It is scarcely too much to assume that it was composed in the first half of the second century," *op. cit.*, p. 330).

[122] *Adv. Haer.* I. viii. 5; ANF, I, p. 328. Perhaps it should be added that this is Irenaeus' usual way of referring to John: he does not use the title "apostle."

but to have pointed out that apostles can err and that
Paul on one occasion rebuked even Peter (Gal. 2:13f.).[123]
As Marcion appears to have come to Rome *ca.* 140 this
is early evidence for the view that John the apostle wrote
this Gospel.

A further point that receives more stress nowadays
than it did with Westcott is the fact that a number of
early authorities associate others with John in the writing of the Gospel. For example, the Muratorian Canon
says:

> The fourth gospel is that of John, one of the disci-
> ples.... When his fellow-disciples and bishops exhorted
> him he said, "Fast with me for three days from to-day,
> and then let us relate to each other whatever may be
> revealed to each of us." On the same night it was re-
> vealed to Andrew, one of the Apostles, that John should
> narrate all things in his own name as they remembered
> them....[124]

Here others are associated with the idea of composing
this Gospel, and John is said to have been directed to
write "in his own name" certainly, but also "as they
remembered." Other passages linking his fellows with
John in this Gospel have been noted above.[125] This kind
of evidence, coupled with the absence of express ascription to John in early years, leads many to think of John
as the witness whose testimony guaranteed the Gospel,
but of a friend or pupil of his as the actual author. If this
associate was not himself an original follower of Christ
this may account for such things as the absence of
parables. In fact, to many this theory gains the best of

---

[123] Tertullian says that Marcion labored "very hard to destroy
the character of those Gospels which are published as genuine and
under the name of apostles" (*Adv. Marc.* IV. iii; ANF, III, p. 348).
In this connection he says that Marcion cited the Galatians passage
and "Marcion complains that apostles are suspected (for their
prevarication and dissimulation) of having even depraved the
gospel" (*ibid.*). It is not easy to see why he should have taken
this line unless he held that John was responsible for the Fourth
Gospel.

[124] Cited from H. Bettenson, *Documents of the Christian Church*,
London, 1944, p. 40.

[125] See above, p. 258, n. 113.

both worlds, allowing as it does for the objections to apostolic authorship, while seeing John's testimony as behind the Gospel.

On the whole I think that Westcott's estimate should stand. It is perhaps true that he did not give sufficient consideration to the significance of the delay in the acceptance both of the Gospel itself, and also of the Johannine authorship.[126] But it is just as certain that his critics do not give sufficient attention to the difficulty in seeing how such a Gospel, so very different as it is from the Synoptics, and being in such favor as it was with Gnostic heretics, could have been accepted unless there was strong evidence.[127] It is certain that its credentials were scrutinized closely by determined opponents. That they came up with no alternative candidate for authorship (or none that has left a mark on the tradition) is surely significant. And it is also worth reflecting that the

---

[126] Yet this should not be exaggerated. Long ago J. B. Lightfoot wrote, "If we ask ourselves why we attribute this or that ancient writing to the author whose name it bears, — why, for instance, we accept this tragedy as a play of Sophocles, or that speech as an oration of Demosthenes, — our answer will be that it bears the name of the author, and (so far as we know) has always been ascribed to him. In very many cases we know nothing, or next to nothing, about the history of the writing in question. In a few instances we are fortunate enough to find a reference to it, or a quotation from it, in some author who lived a century or two later. The cases are exceptionally rare when there is an indisputable allusion in a contemporary, or nearly contemporary, writer. ... The external testimony in favor of Saint John's Gospel reaches back much nearer to the writer's own time and is far more extensive than can be produced in the case of most classical writings of the same antiquity" (*op. cit.*, pp. 136f.). A little later he says that if the external testimony "is as great, and more than as great as would satisfy us in any other case, this should suffice us" (p. 137). We should be on our guard against demanding too much. Elsewhere Lightfoot has a much more thorough and detailed survey of the external evidence than Westcott's, and he comes to the same conclusion (*Biblical Essays*, London, 1893, pp. 47-122). This massive work of a profound scholar is not to be rejected lightly.

[127] A. P. Peabody says, "... There is no book of the New Testament as to the authorship of which there is a more absolute unanimity among early Christian writers" (E. Abbot, A. P. Peabody and J. B. Lightfoot, *The Fourth Gospel*, London, 1892, p. 109).

reception of this Gospel into the canon is not easy to explain if we reject the Johannine authorship. It certainly was not due to the fact that the Gospel was so widely popular that it just had to be included. The opponents of apostolic authorship make this point very effectively. They show that quotations from John are few in the early days. Why should the Christians accept as canonical a book which, demonstrably, few were using (and many of them were heretics!), unless there was good evidence for its connection with an apostle?

* * *

FROM ALL THIS IT IS PLAIN THAT THERE IS STILL GOOD reason for thinking of the apostle John as the author of the Fourth Gospel. It is far from being a fashionable view. Even among fairly conservative critics many prefer to hold that the apostle was the witness behind the Gospel rather than its actual author. Neither apostolic nor non-apostolic authorship can be held to have been proved up to the hilt.

When all is said and done it may well be that the conclusion of, say R. V. G. Tasker, that the Gospel was authenticated but not written by John, should be accepted.[128] It agrees with much of the evidence, and it safeguards what is valuable. But for all its current popularity I am not sure that it is to be preferred to that of Westcott.

For the fact is that the massive argument of Westcott has not been decisively refuted. Modifications in detail

---

[128] Tasker notes approvingly the Christian tradition "that the authority of the apostle John, the son of Zebedee, lies behind it, and that it embodies his testimony to the life and teaching of Jesus." He finds that the evidence does not prove conclusively "that John the son of Zebedee was the actual *writer* of the book." He goes on, "But it cannot be too strongly asserted that, even though an objective study of the evidence may lead us to regard it as probable that a friend or disciple of the son of Zebedee was the amanuensis of the Gospel, nothing of primary importance is lost. . . . What we need to be assured about is that the Fourth Gospel contains not the imaginative reflections of some second-century mystic, but the testimony of one of the original apostles to the life and teaching of Jesus" (*The Gospel According to St. John*, TNTC, London and Grand Rapids, 1960, p. 11).

are demanded, but few of the main points have been really overthrown. Westcott these days is not so much controverted as by-passed. Scholars are putting their emphasis on points other than those that mattered to Westcott. But they are not producing new evidence.

A. M. Hunter, for example, sees three main arguments against the apostolic authorship.

1. It is improbable that one of the Twelve would have used Mark and Luke as John evidently did.

2. There is a difference in style. In the Synoptics Jesus speaks in a wealth of parables and short, pithy sentences. John has no parables, but long mystical discourses in a style resembling that of the Evangelist himself.

3. It is psychologically unlikely that the apostle John would style himself "the disciple whom Jesus loved."

Hunter concludes: "For these and other reasons, scarcely a reputable scholar in this country nowadays is prepared to affirm that the Fourth Gospel was written by John the Apostle."[129]

It is not without its interest that the three things that weigh so heavily with Hunter that he counts them decisive were all known to Westcott. He, however, thought them of comparatively little weight. In other words we have here, not something new, but a new evaluation of something old (together, of course, with an almost complete neglect of the strength of the case made out by Westcott).

Hunter's first point seems to have little weight. There is no adequate evidence that John used any of the other Gospels, as I have tried to make clear in Chapter I. Scholars of the caliber of Gardner-Smith and Goodenough, to name no others, have been convinced that John had neither Mark nor Luke before him as he wrote, and the view is winning wide acceptance. No real weight can be put on this point.

The third point, as I have already tried to make clear, tells against the apostolic authorship, though not decisively. It is not what would have been expected, that John should describe himself in this way. It is not easy

---

[129] *Introducing the New Testament*, London, 1945, p. 50.

to see why he should have chosen this designation for himself. But then it is not easy to see why anyone should have chosen it for someone else either. The argument is not decisive.

Hunter's second point is his important one. There is a difference in style and it is difficult to account for. Indeed, F. C. Grant says flatly, "... It is impossible to believe that one person uttered the sayings in the synoptics and those in the Fourth Gospel."[130] But this impossibility has not appeared so obvious to all. I have elsewhere noted the position taken up by H. Riesenfeld and his followers. They see the difference as that between the formal, more or less systematic public teaching of Jesus given in a form intended for committing to memory, and the more informal kind of teaching which arose both from disputes with His enemies and discussions with His friends.[131]

Another possibility is that put so clearly by W. C. van Unnik:

> The evangelist ... has only one theme which he develops in recurring variations: Jesus is the Anointed One, the Son of God. He shows a tremendous concentration on this sole issue: *Solus Christus!* It is important to take this into account, because one has often wondered that so many themes which are mentioned in the Synoptics and Paul are not found here.... He absolutely stuck to his program and made everything subordinate to it."[132]

This must be taken very seriously. This Evangelist was quite capable of sticking to his program without distortion of the facts.[133] And he tells us plainly that he wrote to make men see that Jesus is the Christ (John 20:31). When an able theological writer sets himself to handle the facts in such a way as to bring out a truth that he sees clearly in them, we need not expect

---

[130] F. C. Grant, *The Gospel of John*, New York and London, 1956, p. 6.

[131] See above, pp. 131ff.

[132] SE, I, p. 398.

[133] Cf. his treatment of John the Baptist, whom he sees only in the capacity of witness, yet without falsifying the evidence (see above, pp. 110ff.).

to find him repeating the language of others. But neither must we affirm that he is ignorant of the things that loom so large in their writings. When all is said and done it must remain a possibility that John has of set purpose described one facet of Jesus' ministry to the exclusion of other facets that he knew.

Perhaps as good a summary as any of the reasons against the view that John the son of Zebedee was the author of this Gospel, is that given by W. F. Howard:

> The Evangelist was almost certainly not the Apostle John. He was too dependent upon Synoptic records of incidents where personal memory would have made such reliance upon the words of others, not only unnecessary, but even unthinkable. He is silent regarding those very events where the Son of Zebedee was one of the three disciples chosen by the Master to share with Him some signal manifestation of His glory or His grief. It is most improbable that an intimate disciple, who had followed Jesus from the beginning of His ministry, should have found no place for a single parable or illustrative story, and should give no conception to his readers of the gradual disclosure in the self-revelation which occupied so large a place in the training of the Twelve. There is also the difficulty of accounting for the slow recognition of the Fourth Gospel, and for the absence of any reference to its apostolic authorship before the time of Irenaeus, if it were known to have come from the pen of the last survivor of the glorious company of the Apostles.[134]

Elsewhere he adds to this, by specifying the transfiguration and the agony in the garden as the kind of event at which John was present and which he would have expected to be mentioned in a Gospel from his pen.[135]

---

[134] FGRCI, pp. 228f.

[135] *Ibid.*, p. 8. He thinks that "it is possible to account for some of these variations by supposing that in advanced age the venerable Apostle looked at distant events through a golden haze of devotional reflection. But, if that is so, the value of apostolic authorship diminishes as a historical guarantee" *(ibid.)*. This must be conceded. Unless we can think of the apostle as writing with a clear mind there is no point in thinking of him as the author. But I do not think that the evidence supports the view that he wrote through "a golden haze."

This is a formidable case. But no item in Howard's list is beyond dispute. We have already noticed that there are no good grounds for holding that the Fourth Evangelist was dependent on the Synoptic Gospels, so his first point cannot be sustained. And if there is anything in van Unnik's statement cited in the preceding paragraph, not much can be made of the omission of certain Synoptic incidents. We may say that if we had been the son of Zebedee and had been writing a gospel we should certainly have included such and such incidents. But we cannot say that John *must* have done this. He must be allowed to be the judge of whether or not a given incident fits his purpose; at our distance in space and time we are not competent to say what he would or would not have done.

The same consideration takes care of Howard's next point, the omission of parables. John is entitled to insert what he wishes, and we cannot say that he *must* use parables if he is familiar with the authentic Jesus. Such *a priori* arguments are always suspect. Freedom of selection must be permitted to an author. And we have no reason for thinking that the parables of Jesus appealed to all His hearers in the same way. We are greatly attracted by them. Yet for some purposes we can speak or write at great length without mentioning them. If John had set out to give a complete account of Jesus' teaching we might legitimately have demanded parables. As he did not, we can do no such thing.

In any case it is worth pointing out that there is dispute as to whether the parables are so completely absent from John. They certainly do not occur in the Synoptic fashion, but that is not the same as saying that they are not there. C. H. Dodd devotes some twenty pages to what he calls "Parabolic Forms" in the Fourth Gospel.[136] We may profitably cite his conclusion:

> To sum up: while the usual method of employing imagery in the Fourth Gospel is characteristic of the author, and strikingly different from that of the Synoptic Gospels, we have found six passages which stand out from the rest by their unlikeness to the usual

[136] HTFG, pp. 366-387.

Johannine type, and their similarity to passages in the Synoptics. They are genuinely parabolic, and not allegorical; in form, content, and purport, often even in vocabulary, in spite of such degree of rewriting as we must always expect from our evangelist, they find their natural place in the family to which the Synoptic parables belong. Yet in no case is there the remotest likelihood of derivation from Synoptic sources. It appears therefore in the highest degree probable that at any rate for parts of the teaching of Jesus John drew independently upon the common and primitive tradition, and that he has preserved valuable elements in that tradition which the Synoptic evangelists have neglected.[137]

In the light of all this it is difficult to cite the absence of parables as a conclusive argument against the traditional authorship. Nor is the "gradual disclosure in the self-revelation" as obvious a difference to all as it is to Howard. In the Synoptics the apostles must from the very beginning have had a fairly high view of Jesus' person. For they left home, friends, jobs, and all that life had held for them in order to be with Him, and that at a very early stage in their knowledge of Him. If the form critics have achieved anything they have shown that the order of events is not easy to determine from the Synoptic Gospels, and that, in fact, we know little about the timetable by which the apostles came into a fuller knowledge of Jesus.

And by the same token it is not as easy as is sometimes assumed to conclude that John gives us no evidence of development. Let us notice just two reasons. One is that it is not always clear what content is to be put into the expressions used. Thus Andrew is recorded as having told his brother that he and his friend had found "the Messiah" (John 1:41). But what does this mean? There were many ideas of messiahship current in the first century, and it is not easy to be certain which of them Andrew is espousing. We must beware

---

[137] *Ibid.*, pp. 386f. J. A. T. Robinson also argues that the parable is not absent from John. He cites John 10:1-5 as a genuine parable. See his article, "The Parable of the Shepherd," reprinted in *Twelve New Testament Studies*, London, 1962, pp. 67-75.

of reading into the term the full idea of messiahship that the Christians later came to hold. It is a Johannine habit to use words capable of more than one meaning, and it would be quite in keeping with the author's style for him to use a term that had a very limited meaning for the man who originally uttered it and a much fuller one for John who records it. The second reason is that John is not indiscriminate in his use of terms. Take, for example, his use of *kurios*. This was common in polite conversation in a sense much like our "Sir," and John uses it in this way early in his Gospel (4:11, 15, etc.). But in the sense "Lord," which it came to have in Christian theology, it is not used of Jesus by any of the disciples at all until after Peter's confession (John 6:68). And even after that it is used but rarely until the resurrection narratives, where its appropriateness is obvious.

Howard's last argument cuts both ways. It is difficult to explain the absence of any reference to the apostle John as the author of the Gospel until the time of Irenaeus. But this can be accounted for in part at any rate by this Gospel's popularity with heretics of a Gnostic type. Ordinary Christians may well have hesitated to use the Gospel at first. And if they hesitated to use it, much more would they hesitate to speak about John as its author even if they had heard that this was the case. They would not have wished to associate heresy with one of our Lord's intimates. That this Gospel was used by heretics is beyond doubt. It therefore becomes difficult to explain why as early as the time of Irenaeus it should have been ascribed to John the apostle if this was not, in fact, the case. We have already made the point that, in view of the opposition to its acceptance in the church, we cannot doubt but that its credentials were subjected to close scrutiny,[138] and it is significant

---

[138] Howard, in summarizing the position of V. H. Stanton, points out that "this belief in the Asiatic residence of John the Apostle was unchallenged in the latter part of the century, even when in three different controversies, those with the Gnostics, with the Quartodecimans, and with the Alogi, it was in the interest of one of the parties to support its case by disputing the apostolic authority of the Fourth Gospel" (*op. cit.*, p. 21).

that in the early church no one else appears to have been suggested as the author. It may be true, as Howard says, that it is difficult to account for the omission of its ascription to John the apostle until the days of Irenaeus. But in view of its heretical associations it is just as difficult to account for its universal acceptance as from that author from that time on unless there was some good reason.

The difficulties in the way of the traditional view must not be minimized. They are real, and they convince men like Hunter and Howard. But they are far from conclusive, and it is not mere obscurantism that causes many conservatives to remain unconvinced. There are real difficulties whichever view we adopt. Conservatives contend, not that there are no objections to their view, but only that there are more serious problems which confront those who take the other view.

Of other objections urged, one is that the son of Zebedee was a simple fisherman, and that it is impossible to see in him one "known to the chief priest." On this point Green-Armytage has some interesting observations. He points out that Zebedee's fishing business "does not suggest anything very abject." Indeed its prosperity leads him to conjecture that Salome, Zebedee's wife, may have helped finance Jesus' activities. Her request for places of honor for her sons (Matt. 20:20f.) "may have been due to a quite human snobbishness and a feeling that the Zebedees were a cut above the rest of the disciples."[139] The point is well taken that all that we know of the Zebedees points to a well-to-do family. If it be objected that even so Galilee was a long way from Jerusalem, and we cannot think of any close connection, it is fair to retort that we do not know what opportunities existed for people from Galilee to get to know the priestly families. We do know that it was common for large numbers of people to go up to Jerusalem for the feasts, so that the distance was not an insuperable problem.

Green-Armytage deals also with the objection that the son of Zebedee would not have the knowledge which this

---

[139] *Op. cit.*, p. 95.

Gospel shows of Jerusalem in general and of the events in priestly circles there in particular. "They ask, how did the provincial fisherman come to be so well informed about events in priestly circles at Jerusalem? We may ask, in return, how did your young Sadducee come to be so well informed about events in Galilee and Samaria?"[140] It is important to be clear that this Gospel shows a knowledge of things in Galilee and Samaria as well as in Judea. It is easier to think of a Galilean who had acquired some knowledge of what went on in Jerusalem than it is to think of a member of the Jerusalem aristocracy who had discovered certain things that had happened elsewhere. It is easier, because Jerusalem was the capital, and people went up to it regularly, especially at the feasts. This would give Galileans opportunities of getting acquainted with many people and of acquiring information about local happenings. But what would bring a Jerusalem aristocrat to Samaria and Galilee?

It is also worth asking ourselves what we are offered if the traditional arguments be rejected. We are faced with the facts of the existence of the Gospel and of the tradition that it was written by the apostle John. What explanation is there? Many find their confidence in the work of radical scholars shaken when they turn to the bizarre and often contradictory solutions that emerge.[141] With no desire to appear hypercritical, one wonders whether some of them, when they come from criticizing the views of the orthodox to setting out their own account of what happened, do not forget the real world

---

[140] *Ibid.*, pp. 91f.

[141] G. A. Broomfield cites these two passages from consecutive pages of a work by E. F. Scott: "An eyewitness of the events could hardly have allowed himself those many departures from what, to all appearance, is the correct historical tradition"; "Almost all the incidents he (the Fourth Evangelist) records are derived, more or less obviously, from the Synoptic narrative.... An Apostle, who had his own store of personal reminiscence from which to draw, would not have leaned in this way on written documents" (*John, Peter, and the Fourth Gospel*, London, 1934, pp. 83f.). Thus the writer cannot be an apostle in the first quotation if he disagrees with Mark, and in the second if he agrees!

and retreat into a kind of Alice's Wonderland where everything is possible. R. A. Edwards tells us that this is one of the factors which leads him to think of John the son of Zebedee as the author of this Gospel. He holds this position in part "because the alternative solutions seemed far too complicated for them to be possible in a real world where living men met and talked. Indeed, some of the suggestions made about the Gospel seemed to pass so far beyond the reasonable that it was sometimes difficult to believe that they were offered seriously."[142] If the apostolic authorship is to be rejected some really credible alternative must be suggested. J. B. Lightfoot points out that there is usually a contradiction in the attitude of modern critics at this point.

---

[142] *Op. cit.*, p. ix. Green-Armytage has some strong words on the subject: "There is a world — I do not say a world in which all scholars live but one at any rate into which all of them sometimes stray, and which some of them seem permanently to inhabit — which is not the world in which I live. In my world, if *The Times* and the *Telegraph* both tell one story in somewhat different terms, nobody concludes that one of them must have copied the other, nor that the variations in the story have some esoteric significance. But in that world of which I am speaking this would be taken for granted. There, no story is ever derived from facts but always from somebody else's version of the same story.... In my world, almost every book, except some of those produced by Government departments, is written by one author. In that world almost every book is produced by a committee, and some of them by a whole series of committees. In my world, if I read that Mr. Churchill, in 1935, said that Europe was heading for a disastrous war, I applaud his foresight. In that world no prophecy, however vaguely worded, is ever made except after the event. In my world we say, 'The first world war took place in 1914-1918'. In that world they say, 'The world-war narrative took shape in the third decade of the twentieth century'. In my world men and women live for a considerable time — seventy, eighty, even a hundred years — and they are equipped with a thing called memory. In that world (it would appear) they come into being, write a book, and forthwith perish, all in a flash, and it is noted of them with astonishment that they 'preserve traces of a primitive tradition' about things which happened well within their own adult lifetime" (*op. cit.*, pp. 12f.). W. F. Howard says of some critics, "Originality rather than probability has been the guide of life, and in the desire to sustain a novel hypothesis important factors are often sacrificed, not because they are disproved, but because they are old-established" (FGRCI, pp. 89f.).

They suggest that the early church was too critical to detect a forgery when a nonapostolic work was passed off as a writing of the apostle John. But they regard it as sophisticated enough to produce at any rate one man who could write about the time of Jesus with such delicate artistry, and such accuracy. He puts his objection to this procedure in a sentence: "The age which could not expose a coarse forgery was incapable of constructing a subtle historical romance."[143]

Those who reject the Johannine authorship offer us a miscellany of extraordinary hypotheses. The tradition is respected to the extent that some connection with John the son of Zebedee is often postulated (though the link may be rather tenuous). William Temple is often cited: "I regard as self-condemned any theory which fails to find a very close connexion between the Gospel and the son of Zebedee."[144] But the "connection" may be understood in very varied ways. The reconstructions that follow differ bewilderingly. Let us consider but two.

This is the way Barrett sees events:

> John the Apostle migrated from Palestine and lived in Ephesus, where, true to character as a Son of Thunder, he composed apocalyptic works. These, together with his advancing years, the death of other apostles, and predictions much as Mark 9.1, not unnaturally gave rise to the common belief that he would survive to the *parousia*. A man of commanding influence, he gathered about him a number of pupils. In course of time he died; his death fanned the apocalyptic hopes of some, scandalized others, and induced a few to ponder deeply over the meaning of Christian eschatology. One pupil of the apostle incorporated his

---

[143] *Op. cit.*, pp. 142f. He goes on to point out that the *Protevangelium* and the *Clementine Homilies* show us the kind of thing the early church produced when it composed romances: "the former, a vulgar daub dashed in by a coarse hand in bright and startling colors; the other, a subtle philosophical romance, elaborately drawn by an able and skilful artist. But both the one and the other are obviously artificial in all their traits, and utterly alien to the tone of genuine history" (p. 143). No one would place the Fourth Gospel in the same category.

[144] William Temple, *Readings in St. John's Gospel*, London, 1947, p. x.

written works in the canonical Apocalypse; this was
at a date about the close of the life of Domitian —
c. A.D. 96. Another pupil was responsible for the
epistles (possibly 1 John came from one writer, 2 and
3 John from another). Yet another, a bolder thinker,
and one more widely read both in Judaism and Hellenism, produced John 1-20. Comparison with 1, 2, and 3
John shows at once that the evangelist stood apart
from the busy and quarrelsome ecclesiastical life of
the age. Probably he was not popular; probably he
died with his gospel still unpublished. It was too original and daring a work for official backing. It was first
seized upon by gnostic speculators, who saw the superficial contact which existed between it and their own
work; they at least could recognize the language John
spoke. Only gradually did the main body of the Church
come to perceive that, while John used (at times) the
language of gnosticism, his work was in fact the strongest possible reply to the gnostic challenge; that he had
beaten the gnostics with their own weapons, and vindicated the permanent validity of the primitive Gospel.
The gospel was now edited together with ch. 21; the
narratives of the final chapter were probably based on
traditional material; perhaps material which the evangelist had left but had not worked into the main body
of his work. The evangelist, perhaps the greatest theologian in all the history of the Church, was now
forgotten. His name was unknown. But he had put
in his gospel references to the beloved disciple — the
highly honoured apostle who years before had died in
Ephesus. These were now partly understood, and partly
misunderstood. It was perceived that they referred to
John the son of Zebedee, but wrongly thought that
they meant that this apostle was the author of the
gospel. 21.24 was now composed on the model of
19.35, and the book was sent out on its long career
as the work of John, foe of heretics and beloved of
his Lord.[145]

Contrast the reconstruction of J. Ernest Davey:

I would suggest that, after the deaths of Peter and
Paul in Rome, Mark left for the East, surrendering
in disgust the use of his Roman name Marcus and
henceforth using the name of John, and that he ar-

---

[145] *Op. cit.,* pp. 113f.

rived finally at Ephesus, where his friend Timothy was head of the Church; though it is quite possible that he spent some time on the way at Alexandria, for the Church at Alexandria made later very definite claims for a residence of John Mark there. In Ephesus, after the death of Timothy, he was probably recognized as the head of the Church there and in "Asia" generally, and so may have become the John of Ephesus, an apostolic figure, a disciple of Jesus — not the son of Zebedee, who had died in the sixties in Jerusalem, according to my suggested reconstruction.[146]

Clearly this position is far from that of Barrett. So is Davey's view of the way the Gospel came to be written. He thinks that "the tradition in *John*, the tradition of Asia Minor, rests upon the evidence or authority of a John who is John Mark."[147] He says further:

My own theory of the Gospel is that behind it lie the memoirs of a witness, on the basis of which has been written a Gospel on topical lines, i.e. grouped round great ideas like the Old and the New, Water, Bread, Light, Life and so forth, the order of the material being thus determined, not by chronology normally, but by kinship of ideas (e.g. the cleansing of the Temple belongs to the topic of the New and the Old (Chapters 1-4) and so is chronologically out of place), while finally a redactor (or redactors) has added a chronological scheme which does not really fit the book well.[148]

It is, I suppose, just possible that one or the other of these reconstructions is true. Both cannot be. It is worth noticing that both are complicated, especially

---

[146] J. E. Davey, *The Jesus of St. John*, London, 1958, p. 25. Johannes Weiss had, of course, earlier linked the Fourth Gospel with John Mark, though he denied that he had written the Second Gospel (see W. F. Howard, FGRCI, pp. 66f.). Davey sees "the possibility that some memoranda of John Mark are used in both Gospels, and that they both go back, for part of their sources at least, to one authority, who may possibly have *written* the Second Gospel but who, in the case of *John* (published some thirty or forty years later) is at most only a basis, representing teaching or memoranda which have been employed by others" (p. 26).

[147] *Ibid.*, p. 26.

[148] *Ibid.*, p. 29.

that of Barrett. Neither hypothesis is nearly as convincing as the simpler view that John the son of Zebedee, the beloved disciple, wrote the Gospel. The traditional view may not account for all the facts. But then, neither do these new views. At least the traditional view has the merit of simplicity.

One defect common to the reconstruction of both Barrett and Davey, and for that matter to most of the suggested reconstructions, is the problem of the disappearance of the hero. In fact there are two heroes who disappear, the author and the apostle John. Barrett speaks of the Evangelist as "perhaps the greatest theologian in all the history of the Church." Yet he is completely forgotten! Even his name is unknown. Barrett pays no attention to the problem of why this greatest of all theologians, this man who could interpret the thought of Jesus with such penetrating insight, has left no trace in Christian history. Why should such a man have made such a negligible impact?

Moreover Barrett invites us to believe that this man was a disciple of John the son of Zebedee, *yet never mentions John throughout his entire Gospel!*[149] That John should write a gospel and never mention himself or his brother is credible. It is perhaps not what we would have anticipated, but we can understand it. That a follower of John, one who by definition esteemed him highly and had derived from him his basic understanding of the Christian faith, should have done this is much more difficult. In fact I for one find it incredible. I am surprised that those who reject the Johannine authorship take it so calmly. For what conceivable reason could a man follow such a curious procedure?

Sometimes it is suggested that there was simply a

---

[149] Green-Armytage is scornful: ". . . What to my mind is not credible is the figure of John the Presbyter which then emerges. A disciple of the Apostle John who resolutely ignored his very existence and omits all reference both to St. John and his brother James? A disciple of St. John who never hints that there was or ever had been anyone of that name (bar the Baptist) besides himself? A man, moreover, who gives pretty clear hints in his Gospel that he himself is the Apostle? Such a man, surely, is a psychological monstrosity" (*op. cit.*, p. 132).

confusion between two Johns, John the apostle and
John the presbyter. Now even if this could be established,
and if it could be shown that John the presbyter wrote
the Gospel, the difficulty remains. Why does he never
mention his mentor? It is putting a very great strain
on our credulity to ask us to believe that a disciple should
write a book about scenes and events in which his teacher
figured prominently and should pass him by so completely
that he does not so much as once mention his name!

But the view that there are two Johns is far from
having been established. It rests on Eusebius' interpretation of a single sentence in Papias, plus a traveller's
tale of a much later date that there were two tombs in
Ephesus, each said to be John's. Papias' words are these:
"I would inquire as to the discourses of the elders, what
Andrew or what Peter said, or what Philip, or what
Thomas, or James, or what John or Matthew or any
other of the Lord's disciples; and the things which Aristion and John the elder, disciples of the Lord, say."[150]
It is pointed out that John is mentioned twice and the
second time called "the elder." Not much stress can be
put on this designation, however, for Papias introduces
his list by apparently calling all the apostles he mentions elders. The double mention of John is inevitable
in accordance with Papias' method. He figures in the
first list because he ranks with the apostles. He is mentioned again[151] because he is one whom Papias claims
to have heard personally[152] (as Eusebius says a para-

---

[150] Cited from J. Stevenson, *A New Eusebius*, London, 1963, p. 50.

[151] Petrie makes a most important grammatical point when he
draws attention to the article at the second mention of John. He
points out that ὁ πρεσβύτερος Ἰωάννης "is naturally rendered, 'the
(aforementioned) ancient worthy John' " and that "John the Elder"
would be Ἰωάννης ὁ πρεσβύτερος. He further says, "It is the practice
in Greek at first mention of a person to use his name without the
article, and then, if he is mentioned again, to use the article with
reference to the former mention, the article indicating 'the aforementioned'. Hence, the names here are all anarthrous until John's
name is repeated, when the article appears: 'the John already
mentioned' " (*op. cit.*, p. 21). Very little attention appears to have
been paid to this one article in a considerable list of anarthrous
names.

[152] T. Zahn sees this in the very form Papias uses in the questions: "The inquiries, τί εἶπεν, he asked of such as had lived

graph or two earlier). Admittedly the passage could be understood to mean that there were two Johns, but we must bear in mind that Eusebius was rather anxious to find a John other than the apostle on whom he could father the Apocalypse, a book which he disliked. And there is nobody else in early days who has any notion of this second John. W. Bousset puts this objection strongly: ". . . It is at least certain that Papias speaks not of two Johns in Asia Minor — the apostle and the presbyter — but of one John. . . . Of a second John the second century and the first half of the third know nothing; he is unknown to Irenaeus and to those who disputed the claims of the Fourth Gospel, to the Alogi and to Caius, to Tertullian, to Clement, and to Origen."[153] This one sentence of Papias (in which he does not even say there are two Johns) known to us only in Eusebius, a man who was keen on finding another John than the apostle, cannot be said to be strong evidence on which to build a theory.[154]

---

in Palestine for a long time and had had there opportunity to hear many apostles and other disciples of Jesus: the inquiries, ἅ τε λέγουσιν, he made of such, like Papias himself, as had had for a time intercourse with the disciples of Jesus, then living in the province of Asia, or also still had intercourse with them, while it was denied him. The apostle John belonged to both groups of the disciples of Jesus, whose words Papias wished to ascertain from their own disciples. This accounts for the double mention of the name. There remains only a certain clumsiness, rhetorically considered, on Papias' part" (*Introduction to the New Testament*, II, Edinburgh, 1909, p. 453).

[153] *Encyclopedia Biblica*, London, 1914, col. 198. He goes on to speak of the view that there were two Johns as "a baseless hypothesis." He is not arguing for the conservative opinion, but his firm rejection of two Johns is significant.

[154] C. F. Nolloth maintains that if Papias' meaning is that there were two Johns, "he has done all that language can do to hide it" (*op. cit.*, p. 61). Donald Guthrie ingeniously asks whether if the later church "mixed up apostles and elders might not Papias have done the same, which might well destroy the *raison d'être* for John the Elder's existence?" (*New Testament Introduction, The Gospels and Acts*, London, 1965, p. 243). He also says, "It is not without strong reason that B. W. Bacon concluded that the Elder at Ephesus theory was 'a higher critical mare's nest'" (*ibid.*, n. 2). Broomfield says of the hypothesis, ". . . In my view the evidence of

The legitimate difficulties in the way of their views then and the diversity afforded by the reconstructions of the radical critics tell against the likelihood of their guesses being correct. Once we get away from the conservative position there is not much unity. The contentions of one critic often represent the demolition of those of another. We cannot have confidence in a method that leads to such results. On all counts it seems better to accept the simpler solution, that John the apostle is responsible for the Gospel.[155]

Additional Note A — The Tradition That John the Apostle Was Martyred Early

SOME SCHOLARS ACCEPT THE VIEW THAT JOHN THE SON of Zebedee suffered martyrdom very early and that he could not therefore be the author of the Fourth Gospel. The evidence cannot be said to be very impressive. The points adduced appear to be the following:

(1) A seventh-century epitome of the history of Philip of Side (fl. *ca.* 450) contains this passage: "Papias in

---

Papias makes this impossible. Apart from the fact that Papias would certainly have known, and commented on, the production of anything in the nature of a Gospel by John the Elder, there is reason to think that the latter's theological outlook was entirely different from that of the Fourth Gospel. John the Elder will not do" (*op. cit.*, p. 180).

[155] A. C. Headlam sees two alternatives to the apostolic authorship, namely that there was another disciple, probably resident in Jerusalem and later in Asia Minor, and that there was no such person as the beloved disciple — he was simply an ideal figure to give authority to the Gospel. He dismisses both, affirming (when dealing with the former) that "what the Gospel (as I believe) demands for its author is some one who had a very close intimacy with Jesus and could interpret his thoughts as no one else could, and I cannot believe that there was a disciple who could be styled the 'disciple whom Jesus loved' who is not mentioned in the other Gospels" (*The Fourth Gospel as History*, Oxford, 1948, p. 44). This leaves him with the apostolic authorship. Green-Armytage also sees three possibilities: that the author was John the apostle, that he was someone pretending to be John the apostle, and that he was neither John nor pretending to be John. He eliminates the last two, and is left with the first (*op. cit.*, pp. 96f.).

his second book says that John the Divine and James his brother were killed by the Jews."[1]

(2) The ninth-century George the Sinner says of John that he "after writing his Gospel received the honour of martyrdom. For Papias, bishop of Hierapolis, who was an eye-witness of him, in the second book of the Oracles of the Lord says that he was killed by the Jews."[2] But we should bear in mind that the passage appears to be in one manuscript only of George's text, and may be an insertion from an unknown source.

(3) In a Syriac martyrology (before 411) James and John, apostles, are commemorated on December 27th. The suggestion is that the commemoration together probably means martyrdom together or at least somewhere near each other. But this overlooks the fact that inclusion in such a list does not depend on having suffered death by martyrdom. And even if it did, brothers might well be commemorated together though having suffered at widely differing times.

(4) The Calendar of Carthage (AD 505) lists for commemoration on December 27, "S. Iohannis Baptistae et Jacobi apostoli quem Herodes occidit."[3] Since John the Baptist is commemorated elsewhere in this Calendar it is concluded that the entry is a slip and that John the apostle is meant. The same weakness is apparent in this as in the previous argument.

(5) Mark 10:39f. is said to be a *vaticinium ex eventu*, a prophecy after the event, or at least it is urged that the prophecy could not have been recorded if it was

---

[1] Cited from J. B. Lightfoot, *The Apostolic Fathers*, London, 1926, pp. 530f. Of this epitome Bernard says scathingly, ". . . No historical inference can be drawn from a corrupt sentence in a late epitome of the work of a careless and blundering historian"; and he cites Harnack's characterization of any argument based on it for the martyrdom of John as "an uncritical caprice" (St. John, ICC, I, p. xlii).

[2] Cited from J. B. Lightfoot, *op. cit.*, p. 531. There is no evidence that George had any authority for his statement other than Philip or the epitomizer. See Nolloth, *op. cit.*, p. 74, n. 4 on this. See also H. P. V. Nunn, *The Son of Zebedee*, London, 1927, pp. 56f.

[3] Cited from Bernard, *op. cit.*, p. xliii.

known not to have been fulfilled. This is a libel on the Evangelist, and the subjective nature of the argument is apparent. There is no reason for thinking that when the words were originally spoken anyone applied them to death, whether of Christ or of His followers. An argument for martyrdom from this is worthless.

(6) Heracleon, commenting on Luke 12:8f., lists Matthew, Philip, Thomas, and Levi as not having suffered martyrdom.[4] John is not mentioned and some infer that he was held by Heracleon to have died as a martyr. But Heracleon is contrasting those who "confessed" only by their manner of life with those who did so before the authorities. Since the general Christian tradition was that John had so confessed before the authorities and had been exiled to Patmos as a result, he could not be included.

(7) Occasionally an argument is drawn from Revelation 11:3-13. This speaks of two witnesses as dead in Jerusalem at a time later than Jesus' death. The inference drawn is that the two are leaders of the church, and, in fact, are James and John. J. E. Davey thinks of James the Lord's brother and John:

> It seems to me, then, a very reasonable assumption that it was on this same occasion (about A.D. 62) that John, the son of Zebedee, died at the hands of the Jews, i.e. along with James the Just, and that the Papias reference (in the vague form in which it has come to us) represents an easy and very natural confusion between the Jameses. . . . The passage in *Revelation* rather suggests that the deaths are recent and the 3½ days not yet over, i.e. their resurrection was still expected at the time the fragment was composed.[5]

It scarcely seems necessary to deal with this. There is no evidence for it. And believing the traditional view is easy by comparison with this elaboration.

(8) C. H. Dodd cites a Syriac manuscript (Mingana Syriac 540) which heads the Fourth Gospel, "The holy Gospel of our Lord Jesus Christ (according to) the

---

[4] Quoted by Clement of Alexandria, *Stromata* IV. 9.
[5] *Op. cit.*, p. 22.

preaching of John the younger." The manuscript is dated 1749, but, Dodd says, "is believed to be a copy of an eighth-century archetype."[6] Even if it is a copy of such a manuscript it is a long distance from the event of which it speaks. And in any case "John the younger" is a curious description of "John the elder."

Thus, while appeal is made to a variety of considerations, not one of them can be said to have real weight. Against this view we may set the succinct summary of Vincent Taylor:

> (1) The unreliability of Philip of Side as a historian and the doubt whether he or the epitomizer has correctly reported the Papias statement; (2) The probability that Georgius Hamartolus is dependent on Philip or the epitomizer; (3) The doubtful value of the evidence based on the calendars; (4) The precarious character of the view that Mk. x.39 predicts 'red' martyrdom; (5) The silence of Asian tradition regarding the martyrdom of John; (6) The silence of Irenaeus and, in particular, of Eusebius who had read Papias; (7) The strength of the tradition that John lived to a peaceful old age in Ephesus.

He concludes, "On these grounds the alleged tradition ought to be dismissed."[7] This is surely the only reasonable conclusion to which we can come on the basis of the evidence.[8]

Additional Note B — The Date of the Fourth Gospel

IN MODERN WRITING IT IS USUALLY HELD, BY CONSERVATIVES and radicals alike, that the Fourth Gospel must be late. If it is late enough, say in the second century,

---

[6] HTFG, p. 11, n. 2.

[7] Vincent Taylor, *The Gospel according to St. Mark*, London, 1959, p. 442.

[8] R. A. Edwards speaks of the view that John was martyred with James as "one of the absurdities with which modern Johannine scholarship has been bedevilled" (*op. cit.*, p. 3). Lord Charnwood comments, "There could be no better example of a vice which microscopic research seems often to induce, that of abnormal suspiciousness towards the evidence which suffices ordinary people,

plainly John cannot have been its author. For this reason we must look, if only briefly, at the considerations
that are adduced. Sometimes the late date is argued in
a reasoned fashion, and sometimes argument is regarded
as superfluous. As an example of the latter one might
point to the words of Morton Enslin: "Enough has been
said to make argument unnecessary that the date of the
gospel cannot be set before 100 A.D. Its use of the Synoptic gospels, its obvious antipathy to the Docetic heresy,
its utter recasting and evaluation of the early traditions
are definitive."[1] More systematically we may give the
general viewpoint on the date in this way:

(1) Patristic writers normally date this Gospel after
the other three. For example, Irenaeus speaks of the first
three Evangelists and proceeds, "Afterwards, John, the
disciple of the Lord, who also had leaned upon His
breast, did himself publish a Gospel during his residence
at Ephesus in Asia."[2]

Or we might cite Clement of Alexandria. Eusebius
records that he wrote: "But that John, last of all, conscious that the outward facts had been set forth in the
Gospels, was urged on by his disciples, and, divinely
moved by the Spirit, composed a spiritual Gospel. This
is Clement's account."[3]

(2) The manner of referring to "the Jews" points
to a time when they had become confirmed enemies of
the church.

(3) It is commonly said that John made use of some
of the Synoptics. Usually it is held that he used Mark,
sometimes that he used Luke, more rarely that he used
Matthew. But if he used any of them obviously he must

---

coupled with abnormal credulity towards evidence which is trifling
or null" (*op. cit.*, p. 35). W. F. Howard quotes A. S. Peake that
this view "has gained a credence which seems to me amazing in
view of the slenderness of the evidence on which it is built, which
would have provoked derision if it had been adduced in favour of a
conservative conclusion" (*op. cit.*, p. 232).

[1] Morton S. Enslin, *Christian Beginnings*, New York and London,
1938, p. 451.

[2] *Adv. Haer.* III. i. 1 (cited from Eerdmans edn., n.d., p. 414).

[3] Eusebius H.E. VI. xiv. 7 (Loeb edn., II, p. 49).

be later than his source. The conviction that he is later than Mark is usually held in the form that he is considerably later.

(4) The absence of any reference to the destruction of Jerusalem points either to a time before that event or to a time long enough after it for interest to have subsided. As it is felt unlikely that it would have been written before the destruction of Jerusalem, this evidence is held to point to a date considerably later.

(5) The theology of John is held to be highly developed. Most scholars feel that this fully developed appreciation of Christianity must have taken time to form. They think accordingly of a date toward the end of the first century.

(6) A number of arguments depend on affinities with 1 John. Some argue that 1 John is clearly the work of an old man and that the Fourth Gospel must have been written about the same time as this Epistle. Another argument of a similar kind is that this Epistle shows evidences of the Docetic heresy. If this heresy was in existence at the time that the Fourth Gospel was written then clearly it must have been written late in the first century at the earliest.

(7) Johannine ecclesiasticism is said to be too advanced for an early period in the life of the church. Particularly is this held to be so with respect to the sacramental system underlying this Gospel. Thus John 3 is said to indicate a developed view of Baptism and John 6 is the result of much reflection on the Holy Communion.

(8) There are references to excommunication in John (9:22; 12:42; 16:2). It is urged that it was not until the 80's that the Jews made systematic attempts to remove Christians from their synagogues. Since John reflects the practice it must be later than this.[4]

Arguments of this kind have convinced the majority of scholars that this Gospel must be put late in the first

---

[4] See, for example, R. E. Brown, *The Gospel according to John (i-xii)*, New York, 1966, pp. LXXIIIff.

century. But it is usually held that it cannot be put
very far if at all into the second century. Many believe
that Ignatius shows some knowledge of this Gospel.
Sometimes this is indicated by express allusion and sometimes by the general theology of Ignatius. It is beyond
doubt that the Gospel was in existence in the first half
of the second century, for a fragment of it has been
found in Egypt.[5] This is the oldest extant part of any
of the New Testament writings, and it is confidently
dated to the first half of the second century. There is
also in Egerton Papyrus 2 a writing that gives every
indication of knowledge of the Fourth Gospel.[6] Few these
days would dispute the contention that the evidence of
these two papyri indicates that John was already in
existence in the early second century. Thus a date between AD 90 and 100 seems to most scholars to be the
most satisfactory.

However in recent years some scholars have suggested
that the date may perhaps be considerably earlier. It
is pointed out that most of the arguments for a late
date are vulnerable. The two most considerable are the
developed theology of this Gospel and its dependence
on the Synoptics.

The argument from developed theology proves very
little. It seems to rest on a view of the way in which
Christian doctrine must have evolved. It is rarely put
into words, but the reasoning appears to be that we
see Jesus most clearly in the Synoptic Gospels. There
is an evolution from Mark to the other Synoptists, and
then to John and then to the second-century Fathers.
This sounds quite impressive. However, it conflicts with
the fact that the oldest documents of Christianity are
the Pauline Epistles. But the figure of Christ that

---

[5] Rylands Papyrus 457. See C. H. Roberts, *An Unpublished Fragment of the Fourth Gospel*, Manchester, 1935. The official designation of the papyrus is P[52]. K. Aland dates it at the "beginning of
the 2nd cent." (NTS, 9, 1962-63, p. 307; see Brown, *op. cit.*, p.
LXXXIII).

[6] It is also possible that the Fourth Gospel is dependent on this
writing, or that both are drawing on traditional material. But the
weight of scholarly opinion is that the papyrus depends on St.
John's Gospel.

emerges from the Pauline references to Him is closer to that of John than to that of the Synoptists. We could put this argument another way. If Romans and Colossians could have been written by the mid-fifties there seems no reason why John could not have been written just as early. This, of course, does not prove an early date. But it indicates that one argument commonly used for a late date is untenable. The existence of the Pauline corpus before AD 60 shows us that there is no necessity on the grounds of a late development of theology for putting John late.

A very similar argument can be used with regard to the so-called sacramentalism of the Fourth Gospel. It is in my judgment more than dubious whether John 3 refers to Baptism and John 6 to the Eucharist. But if there is a sacramental reference in these two chapters it can fairly be said that there is nothing in John 3 that requires a later date than Romans 6, and that there is nothing in John 6 that gives us a more developed view of the Holy Communion than 1 Corinthians 10:2-4, 16ff.

Any argument that depends on development is subject to the heavy discount that we have no means of knowing at what rate development took place. It is unlikely that it took place at a uniform pace throughout the church. We must bear in mind P. Gardner-Smith's warning: "... If once it is admitted that the Evangelist shows no positive signs of acquaintance with the synoptic writers it can no longer be assumed that his is literally the *Fourth* Gospel. It is just conceivable that its later and more developed tone is due to the fact that it was produced in some locality in which development had been more rapid than in other parts of the Church."[7] The whole argument from development is weak and proves nothing. On this score, John might as easily be the first as the fourth of the Gospels.

Arguments that depend on a linking of authorship with that of the First Epistle of John are also vulnerable. There are some first-rate scholars who argue solidly for a different authorship. It cannot simply be as-

---

[7] P. Gardner-Smith, *Saint John and the Synoptic Gospels*, Cambridge, 1938, p. 93.

sumed that the same man wrote both. But if it be held
that one man did write both books (as I think it should
be) it is a further assumption that that author was
an old man. Nothing in 1 John compels this view. Nor
have we such a detailed knowledge of first-century Christianity that we can say that the heretics being opposed
in 1 John must have flourished at the end of the century.
When we consider the erroneous views of Christianity
implied in some of the Pauline Epistles it is difficult
to affirm dogmatically that the error denounced in 1
John cannot be early.

There are some other arguments for an early date
that should be noted.

(1) The ignorance of the Synoptic tradition. One of
the arguments put forward for a late date is that John
knew at least Mark, possibly also Luke or even Matthew. This is now strenuously contested. It is very difficult to cite any passage that gives much of a case for
dependence. In another chapter of this book I have indicated strong reasons for believing that the Synoptic
and Johannine traditions are independent. This has been
argued most convincingly by C. H. Dodd in his monu-
mental work, *Historical Tradition in the Fourth Gospel*.
Ever since the work of Percy Gardner-Smith it has been
difficult to hold that John depended on the Synoptics.
Any argument resting on such dependence must now
be held to be dubious.

The fact is that John writes as though he had not
seen the Synoptics. And if he had not seen them his
Gospel must be very early indeed. The evidence is that
the Synoptic Gospels won acceptance fairly quickly. The
later we date John the more difficult it is to hold that
either the author would not have known these Gospels
or that if he knew them he could have neglected them.

It is also noteworthy that John omits much that is
in the Synoptic Gospels that would have been valuable
for his purpose. He was apparently uninterested in gathering such material. And he concentrates on what E. R.
Goodenough calls "his allegory and creative writing of
sermons for Jesus, because like Paul he felt that Jesus'

nature, incarnation, death, and resurrection were the essence of the Christian message."[8] In Paul this is early, and the implication is that it is early in John also.

(2) The virgin birth. It is often said that Mark and Paul omit the virgin birth because they did not know it. I do not think that this reasoning is valid. It is possible for a man to omit something that he knows because it is not relevant to his purpose. But it is quite possible that in the earliest time Christian preachers and writers did not refer to this concept. John omits all reference to the virgin birth and this may be a sign of earliness.

(3) The way John refers to the immediate followers of Jesus is worth noting. He does not speak of them as "apostles" but as "disciples." This seems a mark of early tradition. Moreover he usually uses the expression "His disciples" rather than "The disciples." The former term would be used in the earliest days when it would be needed to distinguish Jesus' disciples from those of other Rabbis. But in later times, for Christians at any rate, Jesus' disciples were THE disciples.

(4) It is worth noting also that in John 5 we read "there is," not "there was" a pool. It is often pointed out that John can and does use the present tense when referring to what is past. This is true, and therefore the point is not absolute proof. Nevertheless it is more usual to use "is" for what is at present in existence than for what has ceased to be.

(5) The discoveries at Qumran prove to have many affinities with the Fourth Gospel. Yet the monastery at Qumran appears to have been finally destroyed before AD 70. It seems accordingly that the Fourth Gospel may well be early, as there is no question of documentary dependence (which could well take place later). E. K. Lee thinks that the scrolls have shown that "The date of the Gospel may be placed much earlier than used to be thought possible." He sees this as reinforced by the view that it is not dependent on Mark. Thus, "It is not

---

[8] JBL, 64 (1945), p. 170.

necessary to postulate a date some years after the publication of the Synoptic Gospels."[9]

It is perhaps worth drawing attention to the view of
A. T. Olmstead that this Gospel, or at least part of it,
was written very early indeed. He can say, "When shortly after the crucifixion, John had published his Memoirs,
he had mentioned without comment the belief of some
that Jesus was the Messiah and the objection of others:
'Does the Messiah come from Galilee?'. . ."[10] This last
point appears to mean a great deal to him. Thus with
respect to the argument, "Hath not the scripture said
that the Christ cometh of the seed of David, and from
Bethlehem, the village where David was?" (John 7:42),
he says, "John has no answer to the objection; when he
wrote, it had not yet been 'discovered' that Jesus was
in truth of David's seed, that Jesus was actually born
in David's town."[11] In a footnote he adds, "This is incontrovertible evidence that John's narrative was written before the 'discovery' of the Davidic birth and birth-
place as a consequence of the expected second return in
A.D. 40." Part of this argument is subject to a heavy
discount. I see no real evidence that the Davidic line
and the birth of Jesus in Bethlehem was a comparatively
late "discovery" so that any reference to it must be
late. But in early days it may well be that it was not
as widely known as some other parts of the Gospel,
and John may not have felt free to appeal to it if this
was the case. But it still remains that a writer who
is far from being conservative can yet confidently speak
of John's narrative as having been written before AD 40.

W. F. Albright is another who thinks an early date
probable, though not as early as that suggested by Olmstead. Albright maintains that "All the concrete arguments for a late date for the Johannine literature have

[9] CQR, 167, 1966, pp. 299f.

[10] A. T. Olmstead, *Jesus in the Light of History*, New York, 1942,
pp. 255f.

[11] *Ibid.*, p. 159. He does not think of the whole Gospel as early.
His viewpoint may be seen from the following extract: "The
author's discovery that the narratives proper are fully trustworthy
while the interpolations agree with the long sermons in style and
thought is the basis of this present life of Jesus" (p. 291).

now been dissipated." He proceeds to suggest "the late 70's or early 80's" as his preferred date for this literature.[12] Vacher Burch does not give a precise date. But he argues that the Gospel must be before AD 70 and he thinks that its date should "be put near to the time of the Crucifixion of Jesus Christ."[13]

We should also notice C. C. Tarelli's point that the references to the Jews look early. He reminds us that this Gospel is not preoccupied with heresies of the type that are the target of the First Epistle of John. Rather its concern is with Jesus' rejection by the Jews. Tarelli goes on,

> The prominence of this theme would be rather strange in a work written as late as the last decade of the first century, unless it aimed, like Justin's dialogue, at the conversion of Jews. It is also strange that a work so much filled with this theme should make no allusion to the destruction of Jerusalem, if it was written after that event. To suggest a date before A.D. 70 is perhaps too daring, and yet the Palestinian atmosphere which many scholars find in the Gospel is certainly the atmosphere of Palestine before that date, however little weight is to be attached to v.2: 'There is in Jerusalem'.[14]

This argument is no more final than the others we have adduced, but it is worth weighing none the less. Too little consideration has usually been given to the fact that John has so much to say about the rejection of Jesus by the Jews and so little about the kind of heresy that was found later.

From all this it is plain that the dating of the Fourth Gospel is not easy. In view of the many uncertainties it may not be wise to attempt to date it with too great precision. It seems to me that there is nothing that demands a date later than AD 70, though I doubt whether we can go much beyond that. But for our present pur-

---

[12] W. F. Albright, *New Horizons in Biblical Research*, London, 1966, p. 46.

[13] V. Burch, *The Structure and Message of St. John's Gospel*, London, 1928, p. 228.

[14] JTS, 48, 1947, p. 209.

pose it is sufficient to notice that the evidence is not such as to compel us to assign to the writing a date incompatible with authorship by John, the son of Zebedee.

Chapter Five

Variation — A Feature of the Johannine Style

IT IS WELL KNOWN THAT IN THE FINAL CHAPTER OF THE Fourth Gospel two different words for love are used in the conversation between our Lord and the apostle Peter. Different words are used also for "know," and there are other differences. Sometimes these are regarded as highly significant, and the exegesis of the passage is made to turn on them. Is this justified? Before concluding that it is, we must reckon with the fact that John has quite a habit of introducing slight variations. In fact this happens almost every time he repeats a statement, and this whether in narrative or in the words of Jesus or someone else. This is often obscured by English translations which are identical, but the Greek almost always has some variation. It is, I fear, rather tedious to go through the evidence. But it is necessary if we are to grasp this feature of Johannine style.

TWOFOLD VARIATION

LET US CONSIDER FIRST OF ALL PASSAGES WHEREIN A word or expression is used and then repeated once only. This twofold variation is found quite widely.

1:11, 12. John refers to those who "received" not the Word and those who "received him." In v. 11 "received" translates παρέλαβον, and in v. 12 ἔλαβον. The difference is not very important and there is no reason for looking for a difference in meaning. But it illustrates John's method.

1:15, 30. "He of whom I said" is identical in the English in both places. But in v. 15 the Greek for "he of whom" is ὅν, and in v. 30 ὑπὲρ οὖ. When we go on to the content of what was said there is an emphatic ἐγώ in the latter verse but not in the former; and again the expression, "He that cometh after me is become before me" becomes, "After me cometh a man who is become before me."

1:18; 13:23. Twice John uses the expression "in the bosom." On the first occasion it is εἰς τὸν κόλπον, and on the second, ἐν τῷ κόλπῳ.

1:28; 10:40. The words "where John was baptizing" occur in both places, but on the second occasion the article is omitted before Ἰωάννης and "at the first" (τὸ πρῶτον) is inserted between Ἰωάννης and βαπτίζων.

1:29, 36. Both these verses refer to Jesus as "the Lamb of God." But the first describes the Lamb in the words, "that taketh away the sin of the world!" The addition is lacking in the second passage.

1:49. Nathanael says, "Thou art the Son of God; Thou art King of Israel." Here we have a slight difference in word order. εἰ precedes ὁ Υἱὸς τοῦ Θεοῦ, but follows Βασιλεύς. There is an article with Υἱός, but not with Βασιλεύς, but this is probably a consequence of the different order.

2:12; 4:40. The adverb ἐκεῖ, "there," precedes the verb in the former passage and follows it in the latter.

2:13; 5:1. In both passages Jesus is said to have gone up to Jerusalem, but the word order is different and the second passage lacks the article with Ἰησοῦς. 2:13 reads ἀνέβη εἰς Ἱεροσόλυμα ὁ Ἰησοῦς and 5:1 ἀνέβη Ἰησοῦς εἰς Ἱεροσόλυμα.

2:14, 16. There are two references to them "that sold" with a difference of word order. The object of the participle πωλοῦντας in v. 14 follows it, but that of πωλοῦσιν in v. 16 precedes.

2:18; 6:30. "What sign showest thou unto us ..." in 2:18 becomes "What then doest thou for a sign..." in 6:30. In the Greek σημεῖον precedes the verb in the former passage but follows it in the latter, where also the emphatic σύ strengthens the subject. These two passages, of course, refer to quite different occasions. There is no reason why the words should be identical. But I cite them because they illustrate John's habit of varying statements. Even such a simple question as "What sign do you show us?" is worded differently on different occasions.

3:3, 5. There is a slight difference with regard to the kingdom. In v. 3 Jesus says that the new birth is necessary if one would "see" it, and in v. 5 if one would "enter" it.

3:12. In the clauses, "If I told you earthly things ... if I tell you heavenly things," the order of the objects of the verbs varies: "earthly things" precedes its verb, while "heavenly things" follows.

3:15, 16. Both these verses speak of believing, of Christ, and of eternal life as the possession of the believer. In the latter verse we have the regular construction "believeth on him" (ὁ πιστεύων εἰς αὐτόν). But in the former "in him" (ἐν αὐτῷ) is probably not to be connected with "believeth." Cf. the ARV, "whosoever believeth may in him have eternal life." If with the RSV we regard the two expressions as of identical meaning, "whoever believes in him," it still remains that John uses two different Greek expressions. He also inserts "should not perish" in v. 16 but not in v. 15.

3:17; 12:47. We are twice told that the purpose of the Incarnation was to save the world, not to judge it. The former is in the third person, the latter in the first person. Again, the former tells us that God sent the Son into the world; in the latter Christ simply says "I came." The words about salvation are also different. In 3:17 they are passive: "that the world should be saved through him." But in 12:47 they are active, "that I might save the world."

3:19; 12:43. In both verses there is a comparison, and in both, men loved the wrong thing. In 3:19 "than" is ἤ, and in 12:43 ἤπερ.

3:20, 21. The participial construction changes from "every one that" (πᾶς ὁ πράσσων) to "he that" (ὁ ποιῶν). In the former the object comes between the article and the participle; in the latter it follows the participle. There is a somewhat similar variation in 4:13, 14, but here the participle in the former verse (πᾶς ὁ πίνων) gives way to the subjunctive (ὃς δ' ἂν πίῃ).

3:31. The celestial being is first called "He that cometh from above," and when referred to again, "he that cometh from heaven." Another small variant is that both ἄνωθεν and ἐκ τοῦ οὐρανοῦ are placed between the article and participle, whereas ἐκ τῆς γῆς follows its participle.

3:35; 13:3. In one place "The Father ... hath given all things into his hand," and in the other "the Father had given all things into his hands." It is difficult to see why there is the singular "hand" in the one case and the plural "hands" in the other. Other small changes are in tense (δέδωκεν and ἔδωκεν), in the prepositional construction (ἐν τῇ χειρί and εἰς τὰς χεῖρας), and in the use of possessive αὐτοῦ in the former but not the latter, which instead has αὐτῷ after ἔδωκεν.

3:36. To balance ὁ πιστεύων we should have anticipated ὁ ἀπιστῶν or the like. But we get ὁ ἀπειθῶν.

4:10. In the first of the two clauses in which it occurs ἄν follows the subject, in the second the verb, viz. σὺ ἂν ᾔτησας ... ἔδωκεν ἄν.

4:14. There are two references to "the water that I shall give him," but in the first there is an emphatic ἐγώ which is lacking in the second.

4:23, 24. Twice we read of worship "in spirit and truth." In the first "the true worshippers shall" worship in this way, in the second worshippers "must" worship in this way.

4:37; 9:30. These two verses contain an almost identical expression rendered "For herein" and "Why, herein." But the word order is different, ἐν γὰρ τούτῳ and ἐν τούτῳ γάρ.

5:19, 30. Twice Jesus stresses His dependence on the Father, "The Son can do nothing of himself," and, "I can of myself do nothing."

5:25, 28. Here we have two ways of describing the general resurrection, "the dead shall hear the voice of the Son of God," and, "all that are in the tombs shall hear his voice."

5:26. In the two expressions about having life the word order is reversed, ἔχει ζωήν and ζωὴν ἔχει.

5:30; 6:38. There is a readiness on Christ's part to do the will of the Father, but this can be variously put. In 5:30 it is, "I seek not mine own will, but the will of him that sent me," and in the other passage, "For I am come down from heaven, not to do mine own will, but the will of him that sent me."

5:31, 32. There is a change of word order in the two references to the witness being true or not. We could bring this out in English with, "my witness is not true ... true is his witness" (ἡ μαρτυρία μου οὐκ ἔστιν ἀληθής ... ἀληθής ἐστιν ἡ μαρτυρία).

5:34, 41. Both verses speak of Christ as not receiving from men. In the first case it is witness and in the second glory.

5:36; 10:25. Both times the works of Jesus are said to bear witness to Him, but there are slight differences. "The works which the Father hath given me to accomplish, the very works that I do, bear witness of me"; "the works that I do in my Father's name, these bear witness of me."

5:43. There is a difference of word order in the placing of the object before the verb in one case and after it in the other. This is brought out in the ARV, "ye receive me not ... him ye will receive."

6:14; 11:27. Both refer to Christ as coming into the world, but the word order differs, ὁ ἐρχόμενος εἰς τὸν κόσμον and ὁ εἰς τὸν κόσμον ἐρχόμενος.

6:38, 42. Here are two references to Christ as having come down from heaven, but the word order differs and so does the preposition rendered "from": καταβέβηκα ἀπὸ τοῦ οὐρανοῦ and ἐκ τοῦ οὐρανοῦ καταβέβηκα.

6:46. Another change of word order with the subject and object changing places in the otherwise similar clauses, "Not that any man hath seen the Father ... he hath seen the Father": οὐχ ὅτι τὸν Πατέρα ἑώρακεν τις ... οὗτος ἑώρακεν τὸν Πατέρα.

7:6, 8. It is not yet time for Jesus to go up to Jerusalem, but this is put in slightly different ways, "My time is not yet come," and, "my time is not yet fulfilled."

7:16; 14:24. Jesus' teaching is not His own, but comes from the Father: "My teaching is not mine, but his that sent me"; "the word which ye hear is not mine, but the Father's who sent me."

7:18. Another example of the reversal of the places of verb and object: τὴν δόξαν τὴν ἰδίαν ζητεῖ . . . ζητῶν τὴν δόξαν. . . .

7:22, 23. Here is a change of order with "on the sabbath" in the first place in one clause and in the last place in the next. There is also a difference in the manner of expressing circumcision, "ye circumcise a man . . . a man receiveth circumcision."

7:30, 44. On the two occasions here referred to, Jesus was not arrested. In the first of them no man laid his "hand" on Jesus, but in the second it is "hands."

7:34; 8:21. Twice Jesus tells the Jews that they will look for Him and not find Him. "Ye shall seek me, and shall not find me: and where I am, ye cannot come"; "ye shall seek me, and shall die in your sin: whither I go, ye cannot come."

7:41, 42. A reversal of order in the words referring to the coming of the Christ: ὁ Χριστὸς ἔρχεται . . . ἔρχεται ὁ Χριστός.

8:13, 14. This is similar to 5:31, 32. The word order in the references to the truth of the witness is reversed: "thy witness is not true . . . true is my witness."

8:23. There is a reversal of order in the words referring to this world: "you, of this world you are; I, I am not of this world." This is the more striking in this case in that the emphatic pronouns stand at the heads of the two clauses as indicated, and also in that in the first part of the verse the corresponding clauses have the same word order.

9:10, 26. The neighbors of the man born blind asked, "How then were thine eyes opened?" The same inquiry was made by the Pharisees in these terms, "How opened he thine eyes?"

9:28. Another change in word order, "disciple of him . . . of Moses disciples."

10:18. Christ says that no one "taketh" (or "took" — the MSS are divided) His life from Him. Then He says

that He has power to "take" it again. But in the first
instance "taketh" is αἴρει (ἦρεν), and in the second "take"
is λαβεῖν.

10:25, 26. Twice Jesus says to the Jews, "ye believe not."
The first time there is no pronoun, the second time ὑμεῖς
emphasizes the subject.

10:32, 33. When the Jews threatened to stone Jesus He
asked, "For (διά) which of those works do ye stone me?"
They reply, "For (περί) a good work we stone thee not."

11:3, 5. In both these verses Jesus is said to love Lazarus
(in the second Martha and her sister as well). The verb
on the first occasion is φιλεῖς and on the second ἠγάπα.

11:21, 32. In the English Martha and Mary greet the
Lord in identical fashion, "Lord, if thou hadst been here,
my brother had not died." But in the Greek μου is differently placed. In some MSS the verb for "died" is different also (ἀπέθανεν is accepted as the correct reading
in v. 32, but we should probably read ἐτεθνήκει in v. 21).

11:29, 31. V. 29 tells us that Mary rose quickly and went
out, while v. 31 adds the information that the Jews saw
her do this. But in the repetition the word for "quickly"
is different (ταχύ in v. 29, ταχέως in v. 31), as is that for
"arose" (ἐγείρεται in v. 29, ἀνέστη in v. 31). The first statement tells us that Mary "was going to him" (ἤχετο πρὸς
αὐτόν) and the second simply that she "went out" (ἐξῆλθεν).

11:39, 44. The words for "him that was dead" differ,
τοῦ τετελευτηκότος in v. 39 and ὁ τεθνηκώς in v. 44.

11:41f. Twice Jesus refers to the Father as hearing
Him, "I thank thee that thou heardest me. And I knew
that thou hearest me always." There is the change of
tense, from past to present, and also a change of word
order, with μου following ἤκουσας but preceding ἀκούεις.
The adverb "always" is inserted in the second clause but
not the first, but not too much can be made of this, for
it is the reason for the repetition.

12:26. The expression, "If any man serve me" occurs
twice in this verse, but the word order is different, ἐὰν
ἐμοί τις διακονῇ . . . ἐάν τις ἐμοὶ διακονῇ.

12:35, 36. There are two references to "while ye have
the light," but the word order is different in that the first

is preceded by "walk" and the second followed by "believe."

12:46, 47. Twice Jesus speaks of His coming into the world, the first time with the pronoun ἐγώ, the second time without it. The first time the verb is in the perfect, "I am come" (ἐλήλυθα), and the second time it is in the aorist, " I came" (ἦλθον).

13:19; 14:29. Twice Jesus speaks of His foretelling coming events so that His disciples may believe. He says, "From henceforth I tell you before it come to pass, that, when it is come to pass, ye may believe that I am he." But again He says, "And now I have told you before it come to pass, that, when it is come to pass, ye may believe." There are obvious slight differences in the English, and there are more in the Greek. For example, "before it come to pass" is the translation of πρὸ τοῦ γενέσθαι in 13:19, and of πρὶν γενέσθαι in 14:29. The word order also varies with ἵνα πιστεύητε ὅταν γένηται in the former passage and ἵνα ὅταν γένηται πιστεύσητε in the latter. The tense of "believe" also varies, being present in 13:19 and aorist in 14:29.

13:33, 36. Jesus twice introduces sayings with "Whither I go," but in v. 33 He adds, "ye cannot come" and in v. 36, "thou canst not follow me now." There is also a difference in the "Whither I go." On the first occasion the subject is strengthened with the pronoun ἐγώ but this is absent the second time.

14:1, 27. The words "Let not your heart be troubled" occur in both these verses, but the reason is given in the first of them in terms of faith ("Believe in God, believe also in me") and in the other in terms of peace ("Peace I leave with you; my peace give I unto you").

14:10, 11. The two sayings about Jesus' being in the Father and the Father in Him are differently introduced. The first time it is with "Believest thou not" and the second with "Believe me." Again, the first time the verb ἐστιν occurs after ἐν ἐμοί, but this is lacking the second time.

14:15, 23. In the former verse Jesus says, "If ye love me, ye will keep my commandments." In the latter, which is making essentially the same point, He uses the third person, "If a man love me"; and instead of a reference to keeping Jesus' "commandments" we have one to keeping His "word."

14:19. There is a difference of word order in the two references to beholding Jesus. The first time we read με ... θεωρεῖ, and the second time θεωρεῖτέ με.

14:23, 24. These two verses confront us with the positive and the negative forms of the same saying, "If a man love me, he will keep my word ... He that loveth me not keepeth not my words." But in the negative the conditional clause of the positive is replaced by a participle with an article, and the singular, "word," is replaced with the plural, "words."

14:26, 28. Here we have an unimportant alteration of word order. In both verses Jesus says, "I said unto you"; but this is εἶπον ὑμῖν ἐγώ in v. 26, and ἐγὼ εἶπον ὑμῖν in v. 28.

14:27. In the two references to peace it is first "Peace" and then "my peace"; first Jesus says "I leave" and then, "I give."

15:9-11. There are several slight variations here. Thus when Jesus says "abide ye in my love" it is ἐν τῇ ἀγάπῃ τῇ ἐμῇ, whereas "ye shall abide in my love" yields ἐν τῇ ἀγάπῃ μου. "Abide in his love" gives another order, namely, αὐτοῦ ἐν τῇ ἀγάπῃ. When we move on to joy, "my joy" is ἡ χαρὰ ἡ ἐμή, but "your joy" is ἡ χαρὰ ὑμῶν.

15:12, 17. Here are two references to Christ's command that His followers love one another: "This is my commandment, that ye love one another, even as I have loved you," and "These things I command you, that ye may love one another." There is similarity, but there is also variation.

15:15. This verse yields changes of order and of verb: "do I call you servants" is λέγω ὑμᾶς δούλους, but "I have called you friends" changes the verb from λέγω to εἴρηκα, and gives us the order ὑμᾶς ... εἴρηκα φίλους.

15:16; 16:23. Jesus is speaking of the efficacy of prayer in His name. He tells His apostles that He chose and appointed them "that whatsoever ye shall ask of the Father in my name, he may give it you." Later He says, "If ye shall ask anything of the Father, he will give it you in my name." Obviously the two are closely related, but "in my name" is connected first with the asking and then with the giving.

15:18, 19. Twice Jesus says, "The world hateth you." The first time it is preceded by "if" and the second by "therefore," and there is a change in word order: ὁ κόσμος ὑμᾶς μισεῖ . . . μισεῖ ὑμᾶς ὁ κόσμος.

15:19. There are changes in order and the like here. Thus "the world would love its own . . . the world hateth you" gives this variety in order: ὁ κόσμος . . . τὸ ἴδιον ἐφίλει . . . μισεῖ ὑμᾶς ὁ κόσμος. Again, ἐκ τοῦ κόσμου precedes its verb on its first two occurrences and follows it the third time. There is nothing in the first half of the verse to balance the clause, "but I chose you out of the world" in the second half.

15:21; 16:3. Jesus' followers will be ill-treated because of the ignorance of their enemies. This is put first in this way, "But all these things will they do unto you for my name's sake, because they know not him that sent me." The second time it is, "And these things they will do, because they have not known the Father, nor me." The repetition lacks "all," and "for my name's sake," probably also "unto you" (there are textual variants). It reads "the Father" instead of "him that sent me," and adds "me" (i.e. Christ) as an additional person not known. There is also change of verb from οἶδα to γινώσκω and of tense from the present to the aorist.

16:10, 11. Here is another small change of world order. The Spirit will convict men in respect of righteousness (περὶ δικαιοσύνης δέ) and in respect of judgment (περὶ δὲ κρίσεως).

17:1, 5. Twice Christ prays that the Father will glorify Him, "glorify thy Son . . . glorify thou me."

17:12. There is a curious change of tense here as Christ refers to safeguarding the disciples. "I kept" is in the imperfect, and "I guarded" in the aorist.

17:14, 16. In the English we have identical translations, "they are not of the world, even as I am not of the world." But the word order is different: οὐκ εἰσὶν ἐκ τοῦ κόσμου . . . ἐκ τοῦ κόσμου οὐκ εἰσίν.

17:18; 20:21. The first of these passages is in Jesus' great prayer. He says, "As thou didst send me into the world, even so sent I them into the world." Then, after the resurrection, He says to the disciples, "As the Father hath sent me, even so send I you." In the former passage both the verbs of sending are in the aorist, both are from the verb ἀποστέλλω, and the sending is qualified as "into the world." In the latter we have a perfect and a present tense, the verb is first ἀποστέλλω and then πέμπω, and the sending is left quite general.

17:21-23. We have here two typical variations of order. "That the world may believe" is ἵνα ὁ κόσμος πιστεύῃ, but "that the world may know" is ἵνα γινώσκῃ ὁ κόσμος. Similarly "lovedst them" is ἠγάπησας αὐτούς whereas "lovedst me" is ἐμὲ ἠγάπησας.

18:1, 2. The phrase "with his disciples" occurs in both these verses. But in v. 1 the preposition is σύν and in v. 2 μετά.

18:5, 7. Twice it is recorded that Jesus asked, "Whom seek ye?" The first time "They answered," and the second, "they said."

18:33; 19:9. In both these verses Pilate is said to have entered the Praetorium again and spoken to Jesus. The word order is different, πάλιν εἰς τὸ πραιτώριον . . . εἰς τὸ πραιτώριον πάλιν. The verb also changes from εἶπεν to λέγει.

19:8, 13. Pilate is twice said to have heard certain things. On the first occasion this is expressed by a subordinate clause and the use of the singular, ὅτε οὖν ἤκουσεν ὁ Πειλᾶτος τοῦτον τὸν λόγον, whereas on the second we have a participle and the plural, ὁ οὖν Πειλᾶτος ἀκούσας τῶν λόγων τούτων.

19:35. John tells us that "he that hath seen hath borne witness, and his witness is true: and he knoweth that he saith true. . . ." Here he uses two different words for "witness" (μεμαρτύρηκεν and μαρτυρία), and two different words for "true" (ἀληθινή and ἀληθῆ).

20:19, 26. Twice it is said that Jesus came to the disciples when the doors were shut and spoke to them. There is a change of word order and a change in the word for speaking: τῶν θυρῶν κεκλεισμένων . . . ἦλθεν ὁ Ἰησοῦς, and ἔρχεται ὁ Ἰησοῦς τῶν θυρῶν κεκλεισμένων. So we have λέγει in the former passage and εἶπεν in the latter. There is

also a change in the tense of the verb coming, from
ἦλθεν to ἔρχεται.
21:19, 22. Twice Jesus tells Peter to follow Him, there
being a slight difference in the English, "Follow me" and
"follow thou me." This corresponds to a different word
order in the Greek, together with the use of the personal
pronoun in the latter passage, ἀκολούθει μοι and σύ μοι
ἀκολούθει.

VARIATIONS WHEN CHRIST'S WORDS ARE QUOTED

THE PASSAGES SO FAR LISTED INDICATE THAT THIS WRITER
was not averse to introducing slight variations when
similar statements are made. Even more significant for
an understanding of his method is the fact that when
he gives us a saying of Jesus twice over, the second being
introduced by some such formula as "I said unto thee,"
there is usually some slight variation. It is only on rare
occasions that he reproduces the words of Jesus exactly.
This is true whether Jesus is recalling His words,[1] or
whether it is someone else. The following may be noted.
1:48, 50. In Jesus' address to Nathanael the words occur,
"when thou wast under the fig tree." Later Jesus says,
"Because I said unto thee, I saw thee underneath the
fig tree...." On the second occasion, though the words
are introduced by "I said unto thee" the word order is
different, the preposition ὑπό is replaced by ὑποκάτω, and
the participle ὄντα is lacking. The word order is ὄντα ὑπὸ
τὴν συκῆν εἶδόν σε and εἶδόν σε ὑποκάτω τῆς συκῆς. The changes
do not affect the sense of the saying, and it would be fair
comment that the repetition faithfully reproduces the
thought of the original. But it does not reproduce the
exact words, despite the introduction, "I said unto thee."
This is the point I am making.
5:8, 11, 12. For this triple repetition see below, p. 308.
6:38, 42. In His address in the synagogue at Capernaum

---

[1] This is not always realized. Thus R. E. Brown speaks of "the
instances in John where Jesus cites his own words quite exactly
(viii 24 citing 21; xiii 33 citing viii 21; xv 20 citing xiii 16;
xvi 15 citing 14)" (*The Gospel according to John (i-xii)*, New
York, 1966, p. 297). But he has not subjected his first and fourth
examples to a sufficiently close scrutiny.

Jesus says, "I am come down from heaven." The Jews presently ask, "How doth he now say, I am come down out of heaven?" Their word order is different, for they put "out of heaven" before "I am come down" where Jesus has it the other way around. And they change the preposition from ἀπό to ἐκ.

6:44, 65. Jesus said, "No man can come to me, except the Father that sent me draw him." Later He refers back to this with the words, "For this cause have I said unto you, that no man can come unto me, except it be given unto him of the Father." Obviously these two mean the same thing. But equally obviously "I said unto you" does not introduce a verbatim quotation.

8:21, 24. For this triple repetition see below, p. 308.

8:51, 52. Jesus told the Jews, "If a man keep my word, he shall never see death." As they argue they proceed to quote Him, "Thou sayest, If a man keep my word, he shall never taste of death." The English preserves one of their changes, namely the use of "taste of" for "see." But they also change τὸν ἐμὸν λόγον to τὸν λόγον μου, and put θανάτου after the verb whereas Jesus had put θάνατον before it.

9:7, 11. In the healing of the man born blind Jesus told him, "Go, wash in the pool of Siloam." Later he told his neighbors, "Jesus . . . said unto me, Go to Siloam, and wash."

12:32, 34. Jesus said, "I, if I be lifted up from the earth. . . ." But when the crowd refer to His words they quote them in the form "how sayest thou, The Son of man must be lifted up?" The quotation is so different from Jesus' words that some have wondered whether the crowd has another saying in mind.

13:10, 11. In the upper room Jesus said to Peter, "Ye are clean, but not all." John goes on to explain, "For he knew him that should betray him; therefore said he, Ye are not all clean."

14:3, 28. During the discourse in the upper room Jesus spoke of leaving the disciples and of returning to them, "If I go and prepare a place for you, I come again." It is apparently these words which are in mind when He says, "Ye heard how I said to you, I go away, and I come unto you." The reference to preparing a place is omitted and the thought confined to going and returning. The words for "go" are different, being πορεύθω in v. 3 and ὑπάγω in v. 28.

16:14, 15. Later in the farewell discourses Jesus speaks of the Holy Spirit: "He shall take of mine, and shall declare it unto you." Then he goes on, "All things whatsoever the Father hath are mine: therefore said I, that he taketh of mine, and shall declare it unto you." In quoting His words Jesus changes the future tense to the present.

16:16, 17, 19. For this triple repetition see below, p. 308.

17:12; 18:9. In His prayer Jesus prays, "I guarded them, and not one of them perished. . . ." When later He intercedes with those arresting Him to let His followers go, John quotes Him in this way: "that the word might be fulfilled which he spake, Of those whom thou hast given me I lost not one." There are several slight changes here, both by way of alteration and of omission.

From all this it is clear that the Evangelist attaches no great importance to verbatim quotation of Jesus' words. Sometimes Jesus quotes Himself, sometimes He is quoted by His friends, sometimes by His enemies, and sometimes the Evangelist recalls His words. But in each case there is slight alteration. It is never enough to distort the sense, and we can truthfully say that the Master's thought is faithfully reproduced. But our point is that small changes in the wording are habitual, even though no change in the sense is signified.

VARIATIONS WHEN OTHER PEOPLE ARE QUOTED

AS WE MIGHT EXPECT, THE SAME PHENOMENON RECURS when John reports the quotation of words of others than Jesus.

1:20; 3:28. The Baptist said plainly, "I am not the Christ" (ἐγὼ οὐκ εἰμὶ ὁ Χριστός). Later he reminded his followers of this, "Ye yourselves bear me witness, that I said, I am not the Christ, but, that I am sent before him." His words about not being the Christ this time are οὐκ εἰμὶ ἐγὼ ὁ Χριστός, a different word order. And his addition is not given in exactly this form previously

though the substance of it is perhaps to be found in
1:15, 30.

4:17. The woman of Samaria said, "I have no husband"
(οὐκ ἔχω ἄνδρα). But when Jesus quoted her words He
altered the order a little. The English is the same, but
the Greek is ἄνδρα οὐκ ἔχω.

9:21, 23. The parents of the man born blind thought
that he, not they, should be questioned. "Ask him (αὐτὸν
ἐρωτήσατε); he is of age; he shall speak for himself."
But John quotes them in this way, "Therefore said his
parents, He is of age; ask him (αὐτὸν ἐπερωτήσατε)." In
the repetition the clause "he is of age" is placed differently, there is a change of verb, and the final clause is
omitted.

11:50, 51. John records Caiaphas' prophecy that Jesus
should die "for the people" (ὑπὲρ τοῦ λαοῦ). Then he
explains that it was because he was high priest that he
so prophesied that Jesus would die "for the nation" (ὑπὲρ
τοῦ ἔθνους).

13:25; 21:20. In the last chapter the beloved disciple is
identified as the one who said at the Supper, "Lord, who
is he that betrayeth thee?" But the actual words used
at the Supper were, "Lord, who is it?" The reference to
betrayal is easily understood from 13:21, where Jesus
said, "One of you shall betray me," with reference to
which the question is asked. This is another example of
the slight change in wording which in no way distorts
the sense but which is not an exact quotation.

THREEFOLD REPETITION WITH TWO THE SAME

THERE ARE SEVERAL EXAMPLES OF THREEFOLD REPETITION
in this Gospel. Sometimes two of the three are identical
and the variation is introduced into the third occurrence,
and sometimes all three are different. We begin with those
passages where two of the three passages are the same.

6:35, 48, 51. In the first two passages Jesus says, "I am
the bread of life," but in the third His words are, "I am
the living bread."

6:54, 56, 57. Twice Jesus says, "He that eateth my flesh
and drinketh my blood," but the third time, "He that
eateth me."

8:21, 24. Here the variation is the reverse of what we have seen in the two previous examples, for it is the last two that are identical. This time Jesus says, "Ye ... shall die in your sin." Then He twice repeats His saying with a slightly different word order and with the plural "sins" instead of "sin," the two repetitions being identical (the original saying is ἐν τῇ ἁμαρτίᾳ ὑμῶν ἀποθανεῖσθε; the repetitions read ἀποθανεῖσθε ἐν ταῖς ἁμαρτίαις ὑμῶν).

16:16, 17, 19. Here again the single form is the first. Jesus says, "A little while, and ye behold me no more"; but the disciples take this up as "A little while, and ye behold me not." Then Jesus repeats His saying in the form in which the disciples have quoted it.

TRIPLE VARIATION, ALL DIFFERENT

WHEN JOHN REPEATS AN EXPRESSION THREE TIMES IT IS more usual for him to vary it on all three occasions. The places where two of the three are identical are interesting, and it may be that some special significance attaches to the exact repetition. But they are not typical. There are many passages where we find three different ways of saying essentially the same thing.

1:26, 31, 33. There are three references to John's baptizing in water: "I baptize in water," "for this cause came I baptizing in water," and "he that sent me to baptize in water."

1:32, 33, 34. John speaks three times of seeing the Spirit descend on Jesus and the Greek verb is different in each case, τεθέαμαι, ἴδῃς, and ἑώρακα.

5:8, 11, 12. Here some words of Jesus are twice reported, each time a little differently. Jesus said, "Arise, take up thy bed, and walk." When the lame man repeated this it was without the preliminary "Arise." The Jews further shortened the saying by omitting "thy bed."

6:5; 11:41; 17:1. Three times Jesus is said to have lifted up His eyes. "Jesus therefore lifting up his eyes"; "And Jesus lifted up his eyes"; "and lifting up his eyes to heaven." There seems no particular reason for varying such a phrase, but there are three different ways of putting it. The verb in the second is ἦρεν, whereas the first and third have the participle ἐπάρας. It is perhaps also worth noticing that "and said" or the like occurs each time, and that the verb on the first occasion is λέγει and on the others εἶπεν. The possessive pronoun αὐτοῦ is used on the third occasion, but the article suffices on the others. 6:31, 49, 58. Three times John refers to the ancients as eating the manna. The first time the Jews are the speakers and say, "Our fathers ate the manna in the wilderness"; next Jesus says, "Your fathers ate the manna in the wilderness" (He puts τὸ μαννα after ἐν τῇ ἐρήμῳ, whereas the Jews put it before the verb); finally Jesus says, "not as the fathers ate." As sometimes elsewhere the last of the three is considerably abbreviated. 8:12; 9:5; 12:46. These are three references to Christ as the world's light. The first two both read in the English, "I am the light of the world," but there are differences in the Greek. 8:12 is one of the great "I am" sayings, beginning ἐγώ εἰμι. In 9:5 φῶς lacks the article and comes first, and there is no ἐγώ. In the third saying Jesus says, "I am come a light into the world." 8:16, 29; 16:32. Three times Jesus says that the Father's presence means that He is not alone. "I am not alone, but I and the Father that sent me"; "he that sent me is with me; he hath not left me alone"; "and yet I am not alone, because the Father is with me." 9:13, 17, 18. Notice these three ways of referring to the man on whom Jesus performed the miracle: "him that aforetime was blind"; "the blind man"; "him that had received his sight." (We should perhaps add a fourth way, "he that sat and begged," v. 8, but this does not include a reference to blindness or the giving of sight). 10:2, 7, 9. Here we have three descriptions of Jesus with reference to the door. First, "He that entereth in by the door is the shepherd of the sheep," then, "I am the door of the sheep," and finally, "I am the door." 10:11, 14. I am not certain whether this should be taken as a threefold reference to the good shepherd, or a twofold repetition of "I am the good shepherd." Verse 11 reads, "I am the good shepherd: the good shepherd layeth down his life for the sheep," and verse 14, "I am the good shepherd; and I know mine own, and mine own know me." Either way, there is the typical Johannine variation.

10:15, 17, 18. The three references to Christ's laying down of His life are all different, τὴν ψυχήν μου τίθημι ὑπὲρ τῶν προβάτων, then ἐγὼ τίθημι τὴν ψυχήν μου, and finally, ἐγὼ τίθημι αὐτὴν ἀπ᾽ ἐμαυτοῦ. The latter two have additions about taking the life again, but these differ.

11:33; 12:27; 13:21. Three times the verb ταράσσω is used of Jesus: "He groaned in the spirit, and was troubled"; "Now is my soul troubled"; "He was troubled in the spirit."

12:31; 14:30; 16:11. The defeat of Satan is described in three ways and Satan himself in two. In 12:31 and 16:11 he is ὁ ἄρχων τοῦ κόσμου τούτου and in 14:30, ὁ τοῦ κόσμου ἄρχων. In the first passage, "now he will be cast out," in 14:30, "he has nothing in" Christ, while in 16:11, "he has been judged."

12:45; 13:20; 14:9. I am not sure whether this is a double or triple variation. The first reads, "he that beholdeth me (ὁ θεωρῶν ἐμέ) beholdeth him that sent me," and the third, "he that hath seen me (ὁ ἑωρακὼς ἐμέ) hath seen the Father." The second speaks of "receiving" rather than "seeing": "He that receiveth me receiveth him that sent me."

12:46; 16:28; 18:37. Here are three sayings about Christ's coming into the world: "I am come a light into the world"; "I . . . am come into the world"; "to this end am I come into the world."

13:3; 16:27, 30. Now we have three sayings about His coming from God: "he came forth from God, and goeth unto God"; "I came forth from the Father"; "thou camest forth from God." In addition to the interesting variation from third person to first person to second person, the preposition for "from" in the second passage is παρά, whereas in the others it is ἀπό.

13:6, 8, 9. Three times Peter speaks of "my feet" and puts the pronoun μου in a different place each time. First it is σύ μου νίπτεις τοὺς πόδας; then, μου τοὺς πόδας; and finally, τοὺς πόδας μου.

15:1, 4, 5. Jesus speaks of Himself as the vine three times: "I am the true vine, and my Father is the husbandman"; "The branch cannot bear fruit of itself, except it

abide in the vine"; "I am the vine, ye are the branches."
If the second be excluded we have an example of twofold
variation.

14:26; 15:26; 16:7. The Holy Spirit is said three times
to be "sent." Jesus says first, "the Holy Spirit, whom the
Father will send in my name"; then, "the Comforter...
whom I will send unto you from the Father," and thirdly,
"I will send him unto you." Here we have another example of the third member of the trio being the shortest.

16:13, 14, 15. Three times Christ says that the Spirit
will "declare" certain things: "he shall declare unto you
the things that are to come"; "he shall take of mine, and
shall declare it unto you"; "therefore said I, that he taketh
of mine, and shall declare it unto you." Clearly these three
are closely connected, but the way of putting it varies
each time. Notice further that in the last passage Jesus
is expressly quoting Himself. Yet the wording is a little
different.

16:27, 28, 30. Three times Jesus says that He came from
God. The preposition "from" is probably different each
time, παρά, ἐκ (though some MSS read παρά), and ἀπό.
On the first occasion the MSS are divided between "God"
and "the Father"; the second reads "the Father" and the
third "God."

18:29, 38; 19:4. In such a small matter as conveying the
fact that Pilate went out to the Jews we have a triple
variation. First we read, ἐξῆλθεν οὖν ὁ Πειλᾶτος ἔξω   πρὸς
αὐτούς, then,   πάλιν ἐξῆλθεν πρὸς τοὺς Ἰουδαίους, and finally,
καὶ ἐξῆλθεν πάλιν ἔξω ὁ Πειλᾶτος.

18:36. Jesus three times refers to His kingdom. On the
first two occasions there is a change of order, "My kingdom is not of this world; if of this world were my kingdom." On the third occasion "from hence" replaces "of
this world."

18:38; 19:4, 6. John records that three times Pilate said
he found no crime in Jesus. The English varies little from
"I find no crime in him." But in the Greek on the first
occasion the pronoun ἐγώ is employed, and the words
εὑρίσκω ἐν αὐτῷ' are inserted between οὐδεμίαν and αἰτίαν.
On the second occasion the pronoun is lacking and οὐδεμίαν
αἰτίαν occurs without interruption. On the third occasion

the ἐγώ reappears, but οὐδεμίαν is replaced by οὐχ.

20:2, 13, 15. There are three references to taking Jesus' body from the tomb. On the first two occasions the verb is ἦραν, but on the third ἐβάστασας. The first two speak of ignorance of the present location of the body, but the first time it is the plural, "we know not" and the second time the singular, "I know not." The first time it is "the Lord" and the second "my Lord." The first time "out of the tomb" is found, but not the second time. On the final occasion there is no reference to not knowing where they have put the body, though this is implied in "tell me where thou hast laid him."

21:1, 14. Jesus is three times said to have manifested Himself. The first time this is given in full, ἐφανέρωσεν ἑαυτὸν . . . τοῖς μαθηταῖς; the second time is a reference back to the first, ἐφανέρωσεν δὲ οὕτως. On the third occasion we have τοῦτο ἤδη τρίτον ἐφανερώθη . . . τοῖς μαθηταῖς.

21:15ff. There is quite a complicated series of variations in the series of questions and answers between the risen Lord and His servant Peter. When Jesus asked, "Lovest thou me?" his verb on the first two occasions is ἀγαπᾷς, but in his reply Peter uses φιλῶ. On the third occasion Jesus uses Peter's verb (as does John when he tells us that "Peter was grieved because he said unto him the third time, Lovest thou me?"), and Peter retains it in his reply. As Jesus includes "more than these" in His first question but not the others this means that on each occasion His question is phrased a little differently. Peter's reply is identical on the first two occasions, but the third time he prefaces it with, "Lord, thou knowest all things" and changes his verb "knowest" from οἶδας (which, incidentally, he uses in Κύριε, πάντα σὺ οἶδας) to γινώσκεις. There is further variation in Jesus' commission rendered in the ARV, "Feed my lambs," "Tend my sheep," and "Feed my sheep." The initial verb is βόσκε on the first and third occasions and ποίμαινε on the second. There is textual doubt about "lambs" and "sheep" throughout. On the first occasion it seems tolerably clear that we should read αρνια (though some MSS have προβατα). There is more difficulty about the second occurrence, but it seems that προβατια is to be preferred to προβατα. The third time there is more support for πρόβατα, but again it seems to me that the balance of probability lies with πρόβατια. This would give a twofold variation in the verb and a twofold variation in the noun, but so arranged that no two changes are the same.

MULTIPLE VARIATION

NEXT WE SHOULD NOTICE A NUMBER OF PASSAGES IN which the variation is more than triple. Sometimes there are four or even more occurrences, and we find the same tendency that we have already noticed to make small changes.

3:3, 5, 6, 7. In chapter 3 Jesus is discussing the rebirth that is required of Nicodemus, and He refers to it in four different ways. First it is, "Except one be born anew (or 'from above', ἄνωθεν)," then, "Except one be born of water and the Spirit," next, "that which is born of the Spirit is spirit," and finally, "Ye must be born anew (or 'from above')."

6:33, 41, 50, 51, 58. In these five verses Jesus refers to the bread that comes down from heaven, and there is quite a variety of ways of putting it. First we read, "The bread of God is that which cometh down out of heaven, and giveth life unto the world." Then the Jews murmured because Jesus said, "I am the bread which came down out of heaven" (v. 41). On the third occasion Jesus says, "This is the bread which cometh down out of heaven, that a man may eat thereof, and not die" (v. 50). Then He says, "I am the living bread which came down out of heaven: if any man eat of this bread, he shall live for ever" (v. 51). Finally He says, "This is the bread which came down out of heaven: not as the fathers ate, and died; he that eateth this bread shall live for ever" (v. 58). It will be seen that, while the theme in all these sayings is the same, there is considerable variation in detail.

6:39, 40, 44, 54. In the English translation there appears to be almost a refrain, "I will raise him up at the last day." But each of these statements differs slightly from the others in the Greek. In v. 39 the pronoun is neuter, αὐτό, whereas in all the others it is masculine. And this verse lacks the ἐγώ in the subject. In v. 40 we have the word order καὶ ἀναστήσω αὐτὸν ἐγώ, but in v. 44 it is κἀγὼ ἀναστήσω αὐτόν. In the last occurrence of the phrase the word order is as in v. 44, but v. 54 lacks ἐν before τῇ ἐσχάτῃ ἡμέρᾳ, though it is found in all three previous occurrences. This variation is instructive for Johannine method. None of the variations is important from the point of view of the sense. All say the same thing. But no two are the same, and this cannot be put down wholly to a dislike for repeating the same expression too quickly, for there are ten verses between the third and fourth occurrences.

6:71; 12:4; 13:2, 26, 29. These are all references to Judas Iscariot and they manifest an interesting variety. The first time he is τὸν Ἰούδαν Σίμωνος Ἰσκαριώτου, and a reference to the betrayal follows. In 12:4 we have Ἰούδας ὁ Ἰσκαριώτης εἷς τῶν μαθητῶν αὐτοῦ, followed by a reference to the betrayal in a slightly different form (participle instead of indicative and different word order). Next come Ἰούδας Σίμωνος Ἰσκαριώτης and Ἰούδᾳ Σίμωνος Ἰσκαριώτου. Finally we have the simple Ἰούδας. One would have thought that there is nothing profound about the way this man is named. Yet no two of these five references to him are exactly the same.

7:28, 37; 11:43; 12:44. Four times Jesus is said to have cried out (κράζω). First we read, "Jesus therefore cried in the temple, teaching and saying"; next comes, "Jesus stood and cried, saying"; third is, "He cried with a loud voice"; and finally, "And Jesus cried and said."

7:29; 8:55. Here we have several references to knowing God. In 7:29 Jesus says, ἐγὼ οἶδα αὐτόν. The other verse has several occurrences. Of the Jews Jesus says, οὐκ ἐγνώκατε αὐτόν, then of Himself, ἐγὼ δὲ οἶδα αὐτόν (which differs from 7:29 by the insertion of δέ). He proceeds to put the negative supposition οὐκ οἶδα αὐτόν, and finally says οἶδα αὐτόν (differing from both His previous affirmations concerning Himself by the lack of ἐγώ).

12:23; 13:1; 16:32; 17:1. These are all references to Jesus' hour as having come. In the first of them Jesus says, "The hour is come (perfect) that the Son of man should be glorified"; then, "knowing that his hour was come (aorist) that he should depart out of this world unto the Father"; thirdly, "The hour cometh, yea, is come (perfect), that ye shall be scattered"; and finally, "Father, the hour is come (perfect); glorify thy Son. . . ." 13:34, 35; 15:12. All these references are to Christ's new commandment that His disciples love one another. First comes ἵνα ἀγαπᾶτε ἀλλήλους, then ἵνα καὶ ὑμεῖς ἀγαπᾶτε ἀλλήλους. The third time it is ἐὰν ἀγάπην ἔχητε ἐν ἀλλήλοις, but on the fourth occasion Jesus returns to the first form, ἵνα ἀγαπᾶτε ἀλλήλους.

14:13, 14; 15:16; 16:23, 24. Jesus has a good deal to say about asking "in my name." "Whatsoever ye shall ask in my name," He says, "that will I do"; and again, "If ye shall ask anything in my name, that will I do." Now comes this: "that whatsoever ye shall ask of the Father in my name, he may give it you," where He specifically mentions the Father and further says that He, the Father, will give the gift. In 16:23 Jesus says, "If ye shall ask anything of the Father, he will give it you in my name," connecting the "name" with the giving, not the asking. We should probably also include the next verse, "Hitherto have ye asked nothing in my name: ask, and ye shall receive. . . ."

We may well conclude this section by indicating the curious way in which the changes are rung on the verb μένω in the opening section of chapter 15. One would not have thought it possible to get so many statements so close in meaning but with such constant variation.

15:4, μείνατε ἐν ἐμοί
15:4, ἐὰν μὴ μένῃ ἐν τῇ ἀμπέλῳ
15:4, ἐὰν μὴ ἐν ἐμοὶ μένητε
15:5, ὁ μένων ἐν ἐμοί
15:6, ἐὰν μή τις μένῃ ἐν ἐμοί
15:7, ἐὰν μείνητε ἐν ἐμοί
15:7, καὶ τὰ ῥήματά μου ἐν ὑμῖν μείνῃ
15:9, μείνατε ἐν τῇ ἀγάπῃ τῇ ἐμῇ
15:10, μενεῖτε ἐν τῇ ἀγάπῃ μου
15:10, καὶ μένω αὐτοῦ ἐν τῇ ἀγάπῃ
15:16, καὶ ὁ καρπὸς ὑμῶν μένῃ

EXACT REPETITION

OCCASIONALLY JOHN GIVES US EXACT REPETITION. SINCE his habit is to introduce slight variation even when there is no real difference of meaning perceptible we must hold that in some, at any rate, of these cases it seemed important to him to make the point exactly. The cases I have noted are as follows:

1:7, 8. John the Baptist came for witness, "that he might bear witness of the light." It is our Evangelist's constant concern to depict the Baptist as a witness to Jesus. This statement is thus very important to him, and we can understand its being repeated carefully.

7:34, 36. Here Jesus is speaking of His departure. "Ye shall seek me, and shall not find me: and where I am, ye cannot come." The Jews repeat His words exactly.

8:21, 22; 13:33. This is of interest as being the only threefold repetition in exact terms that I have been able to find. After telling the Jews that He will go from them and that they will seek Him and die in their sins, Jesus says, "Whither I go, ye cannot come." The Jews immediately ask, "Will he kill himself, that he saith ... ?" and they repeat His words exactly. Later in the upper room Jesus recalls the occasion and reiterates His words with the introduction, "as I said unto the Jews."[2] It is not without its interest that this triple repetition is akin to the twofold repetition noted in the preceding paragraph. Clearly the sayings about Jesus' going away where the Jews could not reach Him greatly impressed John, so that he recorded them with exactness.

9:34, 35. After Jesus had healed the man born blind and after there had been some vigorous discussion, it is recorded that "they cast him out." This expression is taken up in the next verse, where we read that "Jesus heard that they had cast him out." However this is so short (three words in the Greek) and so natural a way

---

[2] In 13:36 Jesus says to Peter, "Whither I go, thou canst not follow me now; but thou shalt follow afterwards." This is similar to the repetition just noted, but not exactly the same. However, it cannot be held to introduce a serious qualification into what was said above, for the saying to Peter stands apart from the saying to the Jews.

of putting it that probably not much should be built on this.

12:33; 18:32. Jesus spoke of being "lifted up" from the earth, and John explains that He said this, "signifying by what manner of death he should die." When later he speaks of the Jews as demanding Roman intervention he says this was so that Jesus' word might be fulfilled, "signifying by what manner of death he should die." It is of interest that this expression should be repeated so many chapters later.

13:16; 15:20. "A servant is not greater than his Lord," said Jesus in connection with the foot-washing. When later He called on His disciples to remember His words He cited them exactly. Clearly the saying is important. In slightly variant form it is found in two other Gospels (Matt. 10:24; Luke 6:40), so evidently Jesus loved to revert to it.

21:22, 23. When Peter inquired as to what John would do Jesus said, "If I will that he tarry till I come, what is that to thee?" The saying was misunderstood and some thought that that disciple would not die. So the writer explains that this is not what Jesus said: He said, "If I will that he tarry till I come, what is that to thee?" Obviously this is a place where the exact words are important and John accordingly gives them.[3]

*   *   *

SUCH THEN IS THE EVIDENCE. I DO NOT CLAIM THAT THESE lists are complete. For that a more exhaustive investigation would be necessary. But I do claim that they are representative. John makes it a habit to repeat his sayings usually with a slight variation. When the subject is sufficiently important he can and does make his repetition exact. But his normal habit is not to do this, even where he is quoting a saying of Jesus or of someone else. It is fair to say that he rarely alters the sense materially in such variation, and that the meaning of the original is reproduced faithfully. But the variation is there and it must be taken into account when we

---

[3] The words τι προς σε are omitted by a few MSS, notably ℵ 565 syr^s, but the evidence for their inclusion seems decisive.

are interpreting certain passages. Sometimes the variation is merely stylistic, as when we get a chiastic variation in word order. This is common in many writers
and is not at all remarkable. We have noticed some
examples of this kind of thing because they fall into
the general pattern, and because it is worth noticing
that John is the kind of writer who practices this type
of variation, not the kind who avoids it.

Something similar can be said when the same kind
of thing is repeated in successive (or nearly successive)
verses. It is no more than the sign of a desire to avoid
a monotonous style to introduce variety under such
circumstances. But a glance at our lists will show that
when John is saying something again after an interval
of several verses or even several chapters he usually
varies it. This cannot be put down to a desire to avoid
monotony. It is due to a habit of mind.

This habit must be borne in mind in interpreting
passages like John 3 and 21. In the former there have
been many discussions of the meaning of "Except one
be born of water and the Spirit," but often these do not
allow for the fact that it is John's habit to introduce
slight variations of wording without appreciable difference in meaning. If he is writing in his usual fashion, being born "of water and the Spirit" will mean
much the same as being born "again" and being born
"of the Spirit." Of course this stylistic point is not
sufficient of itself to determine the meaning. But it must
be taken into account as an important consideration.

This applies also to the use of the different words
for love in John 21:15ff. To say that the verbs ἀγαπάω
and φιλέω can be shown to have different meanings in
certain contexts does not mean that John uses them differently here. We must bear in mind that he varies
words very often indeed, so that this is far from being
an exceptional case. And since there is usually no difference in meaning there may well be none here. Again
this is not the only factor to be considered. But any
discussion that overlooks it must be heavily discounted.
John's habit creates a presumption that there will be
no great difference.

Thus the stylistic peculiarity to which we have been drawing attention has its importance in interpreting certain passages. It certainly is a prominent feature, as a careful study of this Gospel amply reveals.

Chapter Six

The Dead Sea Scrolls and St. John's Gospel

THE PHARISEES, BEING SENSIBLE MEN, DID NOT BOTHER themselves with perpetuating ideas they knew to be wrong. Anticipating the excellent practice of our modern scientists they discarded ideas that were shown to be false (or that they held had been shown to be false), and concentrated on those that were true. They held that the distinctive ideas of the Sadducees and the Essenes were erroneous, so they piously eschewed propagating them. This would be of no more than passing interest to us were it not for the fact that in time the Pharisees became the dominant party within Judaism. Jewish writings became to all intents and purposes Pharisaic writings. The rabbinic literature by and large sets forth Pharisaic ideas. We see other Jewish groups not as they saw themselves, but through Pharisaic eyes. None of their writings was copied by the Pharisees, which is both understandable and unfortunate. New Testament scholars have had to be content with a monolithic Judaism.

The great value of the Dead Sea scrolls for New Testament studies is that for the first time we are able to read the views of a Jewish sect other than the Pharisees from within. Whatever be the dates of composition of these documents they let us see something of a sect that

321

was in existence at the time the Christian movement
began, and to see it in the sect's own writings.

Not surprisingly, some of the terms and ideas in the
scrolls are found also in the New Testament. This has
led to the most diverse estimates of the relationship
between the two. Some stress the resemblances. They
think of Christianity as nothing more than a natural
development of the type of religion we see reflected in
the scrolls.[1] Some even think of the scrolls as Christian
documents.[2] Others concentrate their attention on the
differences. They think that there is no significant connection between Christianity and the scrolls.[3] We can-

---

[1] Cf. Edmund Wilson's well-known statement that the Qumran
monastery "is perhaps, more than Bethlehem or Nazareth, the
cradle of Christianity" (*The Scrolls from the Dead Sea*, New York,
1956, p. 98). So also A. Powell Davies, "Surely, what the new
knowledge is revealing to us is the natural historical evolution of
Christianity from a branch of Judaism which preceded it";
"Christianity, we now must see, instead of being a faith 'once for
all delivered to the saints' in the Judea of the first century, is a
development of one branch of Judaism into a religion which
presently, when it mingled with other religions in the Gentile world,
developed by a natural evolution into the religious system, widely
divergent within itself, that we know today" (*The Meaning of the
Dead Sea Scrolls*, New York, 1957, pp. 105, 120). Davies' treatment seizes on anything that looks like a resemblance, and almost
totally ignores the differences. Wilson is not so wild, though he can
make statements like, "... The rites and precepts of the Gospels and
Epistles both are to be found on every other page of the literature
of the sect" (*op. cit.*, p. 94). He, too, glosses over the differences.

[2] J. L. Teicher takes up this position. See the discussion of his
views in ML, pp. 269ff.

[3] R. P. C. Hanson maintains that it is "highly precarious to
recognize in the form and structure of the Christian Church any
significant borrowings from the Qumran community. On this particular point it seems to me that too many writers have been
afflicted by a dewy-eyed susceptibility to dubious points of resemblance" (*Guide*, p. 69, and cf. his list of differences on p. 68). Cf.
also Geoffrey Graystone: "... Many of the most fundamental doctrines of the New Testament find no parallel in the Qumran
scrolls; e.g. Redemption by vicarious expiation, the Blessed Trinity,
the sacraments. Canon Coppens goes further and considers the
'essence of Christianity' according to Christ's teaching, not indeed
as we understand it, but as it is understood by leading liberal
scholars. As the essence of Christianity, some have reckoned
God's tender love for the individual human soul, as preached by
Jesus; others, a combination of Divine Fatherhood, universal

not complain of lack of variety in the views put forward.

By common consent there is no part of the New Testament with more points of contact with the scrolls than the Gospel according to St. John,[4] and it is with these contacts that we shall concern ourselves. We shall examine some of the common terminology and ideas, and try to estimate the significance of the scrolls for the understanding of the Fourth Gospel. As we do so it is well for us to bear in mind F. F. Bruce's warning: "It would be wise to remember that practically every new discovery in the field of Near Eastern religion of the closing years B.C. and early years A.D. has been hailed in its time as the solution to 'the problem of the Fourth Gospel'."[5] It is easy to be led away by enthusiasm for the latest discovery. This, however, should not make us go to the opposite extreme. There are similarities between John and the scrolls and they must be weighed with all seriousness.

---

fraternity and the coming and presence of the Kingdom; others, the presence of the Kingdom and hence the need for man to obey God's will absolutely. Where, indeed, do we find parallels to these things in the Qumran writings? Is there anything to match the picture of God's universal tenderness as painted in the parables of the Good Samaritan and the Prodigal Son? Where do we find that spirit of 'universalism' that pervades the New Testament, that sense of universal redemption issuing in the urge to preach the good tidings to all nations? The Kingdom of God, a fundamental notion in the synoptic gospels, is not even mentioned in the Qumran scrolls. There is only that vague idea of 'domination', not of God, but of the angels who preside over the destiny of the 'two ways'" (*The Dead Sea Scrolls and the Originality of Christ*, New York, 1956, pp. 76f.).

[4] Cf. K. G. Kuhn, "We succeed in reaching in these new texts the native soil *(Mutterboden)* of the Gospel of St. John" (cited in A. Dupont-Sommer, *The Jewish Sect of Qumran and the Essenes*, London, 1954, p. 151). Cf. also O. Cullmann, "If we wish to compare the thought of the two groups, we must turn particularly to the *Gospel of John*. From the start it has been observed that more than the other New Testament writings, this Gospel belongs to an ideological atmosphere most closely related to that of the new texts" (SNT, p. 22).

[5] *Bulletin of the John Rylands Library*, 49, Autumn 1966, p. 81. Bruce proceeds, "Even so, the affinities with Qumran certainly provide additional evidence for the Hebraic foundation of the Fourth Gospel."

There are some resemblances of style and general approach. The style of John is notoriously different from that of the Synoptic Gospels. It is more like that of part, at any rate, of the scrolls than is the style of the Synoptic Gospels. Cross finds this resemblance so striking that he thinks of the origins of John's style as being found among the sectarians.[6] The estimate of style is a subjective thing, but I think that Cross goes too far here. The sectarians wrote in Hebrew or Aramaic and John in Greek, albeit a Greek that shows Aramaic influence. Indeed Dr. H. S. Gehman suggests to me that this may explain such resemblances as there are. But the difference in language makes it more than difficult to establish a dependence stylistically. In any case it must be borne in mind that the style of the scrolls is not uniform. John's style is his own. There are some passages in the scrolls that are not markedly dissimilar, but there is certainly nothing to show that John derived his essential method of writing from the sectarians.

A feature of the scrolls is a dualism which comes to expression in various ways: the good spirit and the evil spirit, the sons of light and the sons of darkness, truth and perversity. Raymond E. Brown can say, "The outstanding resemblance between the Scrolls and the New Testament seems to be the modified dualism that is present in both."[7] Nowhere is John closer to the sectarians than here.

The view of the men of Qumran is outlined in the *Manual of Discipline:*

> He created man to have dominion over the world and made for him two spirits, that he might walk by them until the appointed time of his visitation; they are the spirits of truth and of error. In the abode of light are the origins of truth, and from the source of dark-

---

[6] He cites Preiss on the Johannine literature, "In a style of grandiose monotony, it develops a few unchanging themes," and adds, "No better description could be given of the theological sections of the sectarian document. There can be little doubt that the origins of the Johannine style must be sought after in Essene circles" (ALQ, p. 155, n. 19; he accepts the identification of the sect with the Essenes).

[7] SNT, p. 184.

ness are the origins of error. In the hand of the
prince of lights is dominion over all sons of righteousness; in the ways of light they walk. And in the
hand of the angel of darkness is all dominion over
the sons of error; and in the ways of darkness they
walk. And by the angel of darkness is the straying
of all the sons of righteousness, and all their sin and
their iniquities and their guilt, and the transgressions
of their works in his dominion, according to the mysteries of God, until his time, and all their afflictions
and the appointed times of their distress in the dominion of his enmity. And all the spirits of his lot
try to make the sons of light stumble; but the God
of Israel and his angel of truth have helped all the
sons of light.[8]

Here we have a clear expression of the thought of
two spirits, one good and one evil. Both are made by
God. One rules over "the sons of light" and the other
over "the sons of darkness." To the angel of darkness
is ascribed the responsibility for all evil, including that
in the sons of light as well as that in his own sons of
darkness. The two spirits struggle for men and in men.
Though some men belong to the good spirit, that does
not mean that they are sinless. It means that they are
on his side. But the evil spirit is always eager to lead
them astray and thus he and his henchmen "try to make
the sons of light stumble." The result is a grim struggle
between evenly balanced opponents. "For God has established the two spirits in equal measure until the last
period, and has put eternal enmity between their divisions."[9] "For in equal measure God has established the
two spirits until the period which has been decreed
and the making new."[10] These sayings preserve the great
truth of God's sovereignty over all, and of the final victory of good. But until that final victory the good and
the evil are evenly matched.

In time of war there are usually no tender feelings
toward the enemy, and the scrolls make no bones about

[8] DSS, p. 374. Here and throughout this chapter, unless otherwise noted, I use Millar Burrows' translation.
[9] DSS, p. 375.
[10] DSS, p. 376.

the harsh attitude to be adopted toward the other side. The writers think of God as having put "eternal enmity between their divisions." He Himself loves one of the spirits, but "as for the other, he abhors its company, and all its ways he hates forever."[11] A like attitude is required from those who serve Him. The final section of the regulations in the *Manual of Discipline* sums up with, "These are the regulations of the way for the wise man in these times, for his love together with his hate, eternal hate for the men of the pit. . . ."[12]

A variety of names is given to the spirits. There are references to "his holy spirit," "the prince of lights," "the spirit of truth," "his angel of truth." Other references may have this spirit in mind, though possibly the spirit of the man is meant, as in the psalm that says, "I know thee, my God; by the spirit thou didst put in me, which is trustworthy,"[13] or in the *Blessing of the Prince of the Congregation*, ". . . With the breath of your lips you shall slay the wicked, with a spirit of counsel and everlasting power, a spirit of knowledge and the fear of God."[14] The most common name for the other spirit is "the spirit of Belial"; but other designations also appear, "a spirit of error," "a spirit of confusion," "the angel of darkness." His helpers are "the spirits of his lot," or "destroying angels."

The discussion of the spirits is complicated by the fact that the scrolls sometimes speak of the spirit of man. It is not always easy to determine whether the spirit in a given passage refers to the man's human spirit or to the spirit in whose lot he is. When a candidate for membership in the sect appears, "they shall investigate his spirit in the community, between a man and his neighbour, according to his understanding and his works in the law."[15] This might refer to the man's own spirit, his inner disposition, his nature, what he is. More likely it means that examination is made to

---

[11] DSS, pp. 375, 374.
[12] DSS, p. 384.
[13] DSS, p. 415.
[14] ML, p. 398.
[15] *Manual*, DSS, p. 378.

determine whether he really belongs to the good spirit, for only if this were so might he belong to the community. The community is especially the province of the good spirit, and "holy angels are in their congregation."[16] By contrast those outside may be termed "a congregation of Belial."[17]

This goes a long way beyond the Old Testament. There we see references to an evil spirit, but we do not get the picture of two spirits with their followers engaging in incessant struggle. The view of the sectarians is also very different from the usual teaching of contemporary Judaism as far as it is known to us. There does not seem to be much emphasis there on present activities of the Spirit at all. The Spirit of the Lord is understood to have worked in the days of old as recorded in the Scripture. And in the messianic age He may be expected to work again. But there was little thought of a present activity, whereas Qumran and John both stress the work of the Spirit in this age. This is not completely lacking in Judaism, and it is to be found, for example, in the *Testaments of the Twelve Patriarchs*.[18] But it is far from common, and it is this fact, that John shares with the scrolls a series of ideas not found in the Old Testament or widely in contemporary Judaism, which shows that there is some connection between the two.

K. G. Kuhn seems to have shown that the Qumran view is indebted to Iranian Zoroastrianism.[19] Whatever

[16] *Rule*, ML, p. 395.

[17] *Psalms*, DSS, p. 402.

[18] See, for example, Test. Jud. 20:1-5; perhaps also Test, Ash. 1:1ff.; Test. Ben. 6:1. E. M. Sidebottom is of opinion that "The doctrine of the two spirits ... is closer to that of the Testaments of the Twelve Patriarchs than to John. The same is true of the dualism generally" (*The Christ of the Fourth Gospel*, London, 1961, p. 20).

[19] SNT, pp. 98, 185. S. Neill admits that Kuhn may be right. But he points out that Qumran differs from Iranian religion in that it "holds fast to the tradition of an uncompromising monotheism — it is God who has *created* both spirits, the spirit of truth and the spirit of error." Further, in Qumran "the victory of the good is not attained by the deliverance of the fragments of the light-world out of the world of darkness, but by God's intervention at the appointed time" (*The Interpretation of the New Testament*

be the truth of this it is important to notice that John
shares to some extent with the men of Qumran a particular view of the ethical struggle that we do not find
elsewhere.[20] The qualification "to some extent" is not
without point. John does speak of a continuing conflict
between light and darkness.[21] He does refer to "the Holy
Spirit" and "the Spirit of truth." But John does not
endorse the sect's view on spirits as a whole. Indeed,
the Qumran view of "spirit" is inexact and bewildering.
Sometimes it refers to the two spirits, sometimes to the
spirit of a man, sometimes to angelic or demonic beings,
sometimes to influences exerted by such beings. John does
not share the sect's view that the two spirits are evenly
matched. He does not see the Holy Spirit as a created
being on a level with Satan. Rather He partakes of the
nature of deity, and proceeds from the Father and the
Son. It is also worth noticing that John speaks of Jesus
as "the light of the world" (John 8:12), which contrasts
with the Qumran view of a created "prince of lights."
Again, the Johannine writings tend to link light with
Christ, while "the Spirit of truth" is the Third Person
of the Trinity. The scrolls make no such distinction.
Their "prince of lights" is identical with their "spirit
of truth." Moreover, while John speaks of a struggle
it is not an even contest. Christ has won the victory
(John 16:33). Satan has already been defeated, and
believers even now pass from death to life. The resemblances to Qumran thought should not be overlooked.
But the differences are striking.

1861-1961, London, 1964, p. 312). In both points John and Qumran
are in agreement.

[20] Lucetta Mowry maintains that a dualistic system of thought
like that of John "was unintelligible to one trained in the Jewish
outlook derived from a study of the Law and the prophets." She
sees in this the difficulty of a man like Nicodemus (*The Biblical
Archaeologist*, 17, Dec. 1954, p. 79).

[21] J. Danielou stresses this. He says, "As is known, the Gospel
of John is entirely constructed on the theme of the conflict between
light and darkness.... Now this is nothing else but the *leitmotif*
of Qumran" (*The Dead Sea Scrolls and Primitive Christianity*,
New York, 1962, p. 107).

THE SONS OF LIGHT AND THE SONS OF DARKNESS

THE DIVISION OF MANKIND INTO TWO GROUPS IS FUNDA-mental for the men of Qumran. They refer to both in a variety of ways. The sect, of course, takes up an exclusive position. Only its members are in right relation to God. They are spoken of in the *Damascus Document* as "those in the covenant," "the many," "the sons of the camp." The *Habakkuk Commentary* sees them as "the simple ones of Judah, the doers of the law," as "the teacher of righteousness and the men of his party," as "(God's) people and his congregation," as "the poor." The *Manual of Discipline* refers to "sons of righteousness," "the sons of the truth," "the wise man," "the men of the community," "the men of perfect holiness," "a holy man," "all who have offered themselves," those "who have offered themselves together to his truth," "those who choose the way," "all the men of God's lot." In the *War Scroll* we read of "sons of light," "all the men of (God's) lot," "the congregation of the sons of heaven," "thy people," "the sons of thy truth." The *Rule of the Congregation* refers to "the whole congregation of Israel," "the sons of Zadok the priests and the men of their covenant, who turned back from walking in the way of the people," "the men of his counsel." The *Commentary on Psalm 37* mentions "the congregation of his elect, those who do his will," "the congregation of his elect, who will be chiefs and princes," "sheep in the midst of their pastures," "the congregation of the poor," "his holy people."

Those outside may be described as "all who despise" God, "a congregation of treacherous men, those who turned aside out of the way," "the sons of the pit," "the men of the pit," "the wicked," "the house of Absalom and the men of their party," "the house of judgment," "men of violence who rebelled against God," "a congregation in falsehood," "the sons of error," "the sons of darkness," "the seekers of smooth things," "men of deceit," "seers of error," "the men of Belial's lot."

The very wealth of nomenclature (and this is not an exhaustive list) indicates the manysidedness of light and darkness. For the men of Qumran the subject was of absorbing interest, and they evolved a rich terminology in which to describe it. John likewise has many ways of referring to those in the right way and those in the wrong one. The former are "disciples," "his disciples," "true worshippers," "my sheep." We are told that "the sons of God" are "as many as received" Christ, or again "them that believe on his name." Other expressions are "he that doeth the truth" (cf. "I am the truth"), "he that believeth on him," "whosoever liveth and believeth on me," "he that heareth my word, and believeth him that sent me," "he that eateth my flesh and drinketh my blood," "he that abideth in me, and I in him," "my friends," "every one that is born of the Spirit." John refers to those who continue in Christ's work, and to those who are drawn to Him. He can speak of those in the wrong way as "the world," or "the Jews," or refer to them as loving darkness or doing evil. But he also refers to men who do not "come to" Christ or "receive" Him, and to those who "went back, and walked no more with him." Cf. also he that "hath not believed on the name of the only begotten Son of God," "he that rejecteth me, and receiveth not my sayings," "he that honoreth not the Son," them "that believed not," "not of my sheep."

The interesting thing about John's usage is that his terms tend to center on Jesus. People are characteristically described according to their relation to Him. Especially important is the stress on faith. Though he never uses the noun "faith" John employs the verb "to believe" over ninety times, and this is the measure of the importance he attaches to believing. Indeed, he tells us that he wrote his Gospel "that ye may believe that Jesus is the Christ, the Son of God; and that believing ye may have life in his name" (John 20:31). While there is occasional mention of faith in the scrolls there is no counterpart to this emphasis. The *Habakkuk Commentary* once speaks of "faith in the teacher of righteousness,"[22] but this signifies no more than wholehearted acceptance of his teaching. It is not trust in the New

---

[22] DSS, p. 368.

Testament sense.[23] Indeed, since it means acceptance of the Teacher's doctrine of salvation by keeping the Law it cuts clean across one of the more important New Testament ideas, namely that works of law-righteousness will never save.[24] John puts relationship to Jesus, and specifically the relationship of faith in Jesus, in the very center of the picture. That is the one thing that matters. The Teacher of Righteousness is for the men of Qumran an honored figure, but at the center of their religion is not a person but the Law. For John the great truth was that the Messiah has come. Men must put their faith in Him, not in any ability to keep the Law.

The sectarians give unambiguous expression to the doctrine of salvation by works. Thus the *Manual of Discipline* opens with the words, "the order of the community; to seek God ... to do what is good and upright before him ... to do truth and righteousness and justice in the land...."[25] Shortly it refers to "all the men of God's lot, who walk perfectly in all his ways."[26] Here and there statements will be found that are more humble, but for the most part the covenanters have no mock modesty about their ethical achievements.

It is true that there are some passages, especially in the *Thanksgiving Psalms*, that regard the members of the community as men who have been forgiven. Thus we may read,

Who will be justified before thee when he is judged?
There is no spirit that can reply to thy accusation,

---

[23] Cf. F. F. Bruce: "... Faith in the Teacher of Righteousness implied mainly faith in his teaching, whereas saving faith in Jesus, according to the New Testament, includes in addition personal commitment to Him as Lord and Redeemer. To His first followers Jesus was the promised Messiah; there is no evidence, on the other hand, that the Teacher of Righteousness ever claimed that dignity for himself or received it from His followers" (*Second Thoughts on the Dead Sea Scrolls*, Grand Rapids, 1956, p. 96).

[24] Cf. C. G. Howie: "... The salvation by personal faith in this figure actually amounted to salvation by works of law which Paul so desperately denied and detested" (*The Dead Sea Scrolls and the Living Church*, Richmond, Va., 1958, p. 93). We might add that this doctrine is just as abhorrent to John as to Paul.

[25] DSS, p. 371.

[26] DSS, p. 372.

and none is able to stand before thy wrath.
But all the sons of thy truth thou wilt bring in
pardon before thee,
cleansing them from their transgressions.[27]

Other passages might be cited to similar effect, but the sectarians are not thinking of all men as sharing in a corrupt nature. As T. H. Gaster puts it,

> There is ... no vestige of the idea of Original Sin. On the contrary, the idea is affirmed constantly in the *Book of Hymns* that every man is endowed at birth with the charisma of knowledge and discernment and that any sinfulness which he incurs is due only to his individual neglect of these gifts. ... Because sin is individual and not the inherited lot of man, and because it is incurred by his own personal disposition, it can be removed also by his own individual experience. ... Since there is no concept of original, universal sin, there is obviously no place for universal vicarious atonement. Men suffer their individual crucifixions and resurrections; there is no Calvary.[28]

Men outside the community are regarded as sinners exceedingly. Anyone who seeks admission must therefore first confess his sins and seek forgiveness. But thereafter the emphasis is overwhelmingly on works.

The Fourth Gospel sees salvation as the gift of God in Christ. It is received by believing on Christ, and not by any works of righteousness whatever. While John does not neglect the importance of good works he does not regard them as meriting salvation, and he does not think of any man as having reason for self-satisfaction before God. The conviction that salvation is God's free gift, and that it cost Christ His life, cannot but make for humility in the recipients.

TRUTH AND ERROR

THE PASSAGE TELLING OF THE CREATION OF THE TWO spirits refers to them as "the spirits of truth and of error."[29] Truth is often connected with God, as when

---

[27] DSS, p. 410.
[28] *The Dead Sea Scriptures*, New York, 1956, p. 19.
[29] DSS, p. 374.

the sectarians write on their banner as they go to war, "The Truth of God,"[30] or when their psalmist speaks of "all the works of thy truth."[31] The psalms in fact have quite a number of passages of this kind. Somewhat in the Johannine manner truth is thought of now and then as a means of purification. "God will refine in his truth all the deeds of a man ... cleansing him with a holy spirit from all wicked deeds. And he will sprinkle upon him a spirit of truth, like water for impurity...."[32] With this we might compare, "Sanctify them in the truth ... I sanctify myself, that they themselves also may be sanctified in truth" (John 17:17-19).

John speaks of "doing" the truth (John 3:21), an expression found also in the opening section of the *Manual of Discipline*. The community is "to seek God ... to do truth and righteousness and justice in the land."[33] But before we conclude that the men of Qumran had the same idea as did John it is important to notice the way they connect truth and the Law. For example, they explain Habakkuk 2:3 in this way: "This means the men of truth, the doers of the law, whose hands do not grow slack from the service of the truth."[34] A close examination of their writings shows that the sectarians connected truth closely with the Law, whereas the distinctive Johannine teaching is that which associates truth with Jesus, who said, "I am the way, and the truth, and the life" (John 14:6). The terminology is arrestingly similar, but the basic ideas are fundamentally diverse.

PREDESTINATION

A MARKED FEATURE OF THE SCROLLS IS THEIR INSISTENCE that all takes place according to the will of God.[35] Thus

---

[30] DSS, p. 393.

[31] DSS, p. 401.

[32] *Manual*, DSS, p. 376.

[33] DSS, p. 371. Cf. also the expression "to practice truth," pp. 376, 381.

[34] DSS, p. 368. Cf. also the *Manual*, "every case regarding law, wealth, or justice, to practice truth..." (DSS, p. 376).

[35] Cf. Millar Burrows: "In recent discussions of the Dead Sea Scrolls the conviction of the absolute sovereignty of God is seen more and more to be basic for the sect" (ML, p. 278).

the concluding psalm in the *Manual of Discipline* says: "By his knowledge everything comes to pass; and everything that is he establishes by his purpose; and without him it is not done ... apart from thy will nothing will be done ... there is no other besides thee to oppose thy counsel."[36] So in the *Thanksgiving Psalms* we find, "What can I plan unless thou hast desired it, and what can I think apart from thy will? ... Apart from thee nothing is done,"[37] and again, "It is thy counsel that will stand, and the purpose of thy heart that is established forever."[38] There are many references throughout the scrolls to God's "elect," which, of course, points to the same basic idea. It means that God chooses men and not men God. Sometimes the sectarians seem to think of evil as well as of good as being determined: "... According to each man's inheritance in truth he does right, and so he hates error; but according to his possession in the lot of error he does wickedly in it, and so he abhors truth."[39] It is this sort of thing that leads Kuhn to say, "For each individual, God has determined beforehand to which side he shall belong, and once he is in existence his acts and destiny are unchangeable."[40]

This is not the whole teaching of the scrolls. There are many passages that regard men as responsible beings, particularly in the matter of their guilt. Those who perished in the flood, for example, are blamed in the *Damascus Document* "because they did their own will and did not keep the commandment of their Maker."[41] By contrast, Abraham "kept the commandments of God and did not choose the will of his own spirit."[42] There are frequent appeals for repentance, which presupposes that men may respond.

There are thus two different ideas taught in the scrolls. One conception is that wickedness is reprehensible and

---

[36] DSS, pp. 388f.

[37] DSS, p. 413. The next psalm also speaks of "the sons of thy good pleasure" (p. 414).

[38] DSS, p. 406.

[39] *Manual*, DSS, p. 376.

[40] SNT, p. 285, n. 40.

[41] DSS, p. 351.

[42] *Ibid.*

goodness to be praised. Men have chosen the evil or the good, and are adjudged accordingly. Side by side with this is the thought that the will of God is done. Men act according to the lot in which they have been placed. No attempt is made to reconcile the two. Indeed, it may be doubted whether the sectarians realized any need to reconcile them. They simply passed from the one to the other with no sense of incongruity.

John also has a strongly predestinarian strain. Men cannot come to God (more exactly, to Christ) of themselves; there must first be a divine work in them. "No man can come to me, except the Father that sent me draw him" (John 6:44, 65). Characteristically John has Jesus in the central place. Again, as in the scrolls, there is the thought that those who perish do so of their own fault: "This is the judgment, that the light is come into the world, and men loved the darkness rather than the light; for their works were evil" (John 3:19). But there is no trace of the idea that evil is predetermined. Sinners are always viewed as responsible men; they are to be blamed for their sin.[43]

Perhaps this is the place to notice the point made several times in the scrolls that knowledge in things religious comes by revelation from God, i.e. it comes as and when God wills. Thus we read in the *Psalms*, "Thou hast given me knowledge of thy wondrous mysteries";[44] "Of thy true counsel thou wilt give him knowledge."[45] Throughout the Fourth Gospel there runs the thought that the only true knowledge comes from God. But characteristically John thinks of it as mediated by Jesus. It is through Him that the knowledge comes to us.

---

[43] Cf. Menahem Mansoor, "On predestination John differed from the sect.
   a. John emphasized faith as a decision by which men determine their own judgment.
   b. Determinism was stronger in Qumran thought. Human will was negated and the omnipotence of God was asserted: that man can look only to God's grace and will for predestination" (*The Dead Sea Scrolls*, Leiden, 1964, p. 156).

[44] DSS, p. 407. The expression is repeated almost exactly in a later psalm (see DSS, p. 410).

[45] DSS, p. 413.

THE ESCHATOLOGICAL STRUGGLE

THE SCROLLS ARE CLEAR THAT THE STRUGGLE BETWEEN good and evil, and specifically between the spirit of truth and the spirit of error, will continue throughout this life and come to an end only at the last time. Then there will be a terrific battle. The two armies of good and evil will engage in a cataclysmic engagement the result of which will be the total destruction of the hosts of darkness and the final victory of God.

The present situation is that "God has established the two spirits in equal measure," but this is specifically "until the last period."[46] The end time will see a very different pattern. "God in the mysteries of his understanding and in his glorious wisdom has ordained a period for the ruin of error, and in the appointed time of punishment he will destroy it forever."[47] For the wicked there will be "eternal perdition in the fury of the God of vengeance, to eternal trembling and everlasting dishonor, with destroying disgrace in the fire of dark places. And all their periods to their generations will be in sorrowful mourning and bitter calamity, in dark disasters until they are destroyed, having no remnant or any that escape."[48]

With a wealth of vivid detail the *War Scroll* portrays the final battle, telling us of the organization and battle tactics that will be employed. It looks for the total destruction of the wicked and the eternal joy of the sons of light. The final bliss is in mind in many places in the scrolls, and, for example, there are several references to it in the *Benedictions*.[49]

There are some points of resemblance between all this

---

[46] *Manual,* DSS, p. 375.

[47] DSS, pp. 375f.

[48] DSS, p. 375.

[49] Thus the *Blessing of the Congregation* speaks of a "covenant eternal which shall stand forever"; that *of the Chief Priest* says, ". . . May he graciously grant you an eternal covenant," that *of the Priests,* "A covenant of eternal priesthood may he renew for you . . . who has consecrated you for an everlasting time and for all the periods of eternity," that *of the Prince of the Congregation,* ". . . May he renew for him the covenant of community, to establish the kingdom of his people forever" (ML, pp. 396f.).

and John's view of the triumph of God, but the differences are more striking. John does not think of eternal life as coming to man only at the last. It comes to believers now. He emphasizes God's present activity, and there are many references to present condemnation or to present judgment, or to the present gift of everlasting life. The eschatological triumph is real to John, as we see, for example, from John 5:28f. But it is not a prominent feature of his Gospel. Certainly it receives nothing like the stress it gets in some of the scrolls. There is no parallel in John to the lurid imagery of the *War Scroll* with its bitterly contested battle. Moreover, John writes as one for whom the victory is already won. The end time means but the unfolding of the implications of the victory that Christ has already obtained by His death. As H. H. Rowley well says, "The Qumran sectaries hoped to establish the kingdom by killing; Christ by dying."[50]

BROTHERLY LOVE

THE SCROLLS HAVE SOME BEAUTIFUL PASSAGES ON THE importance of love among the brethren. The covenanters according to the *Manual of Discipline* are "to love all the sons of light";[51] they "shall all be in true community and good humility and loyal love and righteous thought, each for his fellow in the holy council."[52] The final psalm in this document speaks of "loyal love for the humble."[53] In the *Damascus Document* we find the requirement "to love each his brother as himself."[54] Of course brethren will not always see eye to eye, but when a brother is to be rebuked it must be "according to the commandment."[55] The *Manual* decrees that "One shall not speak to his brother in anger or in resentment, or with a stiff neck or a hard heart or a wicked spirit; one shall not hate him in the folly of his heart. In his days he shall reprove

---

[50] *The Dead Sea Scrolls and the New Testament*, London, 1957, p. 22.
[51] DSS, p. 371.
[52] DSS, p. 373.
[53] DSS, p. 387.
[54] DSS, p. 354.
[55] *Ibid.*

him and shall not bring upon him iniquity; and also a man shall not bring against his neighbour a word before the masters without having rebuked him before witnesses."[56]

These are outstanding passages. We are reminded that John records our Lord's words, "A new commandment I give unto you, that ye love one another; even as I have loved you, that ye also love one another. By this shall all men know that ye are my disciples, if ye have love one to another" (John 13:34f.). Nowhere in the New Testament is there a greater emphasis on the importance of Christian love than in the Johannine writings.

But we should not without further ado assume that the attitudes of Qumran and of John are the same, or even basically similar. If it is true that the men of Qumran inculcate love to the brethren it is also true that they demand hate for those outside the community. The first passage quoted in the preceding paragraph goes on, "and to hate all the sons of darkness," which is very different from anything in John.[57] Again, the *Manual* bids the Levites curse "all the men of Belial's lot" in these forthright terms,

> Accursed may you be in all your wicked, guilty works; may God make you a horror through all those that wreak vengeance and send after you destruction through all those that pay recompense; accursed may you be without mercy according to the darkness of your works, and may you suffer wrath in the deep darkness of eternal fire. May God not be gracious to you when you call, and may he not pardon, forgiving your iniquities; may he lift up his angry countenance for vengeance upon you, and may there be no peace for you....[58]

---

[56] DSS, p. 378. The last mentioned provision is found also in the *Damascus Document* (DSS, p. 358).

[57] Somewhat curiously Lucetta Mowry says of John, "To be sure, the evangelist hesitates to press his exclusivism to an attitude of hatred for outsiders, but by implication he approaches this Qumran point of view" (*The Dead Sea Scrolls and the Early Church*, Chicago, 1962, p. 30). This is a passing strange inference to draw from John's exhortations to love!

[58] DSS, p. 372.

Sometimes a better note is struck, as in the closing psalm in the same document, "I will not render to a man the recompense of evil; with good I will pursue a man."[59] But this attitude is not sustained, for this very stanza goes on, "... My anger I will not turn back from men of error.... I will not have mercy on any who turn aside from the way."

For all the heights to which the men of Qumran might at times attain we cannot say that they are enunciating the doctrine of love that means so much to John. At best they have no more than a feeling out after the type of love that John depicts so movingly. John had the cross before him and they did not. Nevertheless it is of interest that the Qumran exhortations to brotherly love should be more nearly paralleled in John than in other parts of the New Testament.

LIVING WATERS

JESUS SPOKE TO THE WOMAN OF SAMARIA ABOUT "LIVING water," water that becomes in the recipient "a well of water springing up unto eternal life" (John 4:10, 14). Again, He spoke of living water as flowing out of the believer, which John explains in the words, "this spake he of the Spirit" (John 7:39). The scrolls sometimes use this kind of imagery and even speak of "living water." The *Damascus Document* makes the statement, "they dug the well," and goes on to explain, "The well is the law, and those who dug it are the captivity of Israel, who went out from the land of Judah and sojourned in the land of Damascus."[60] Those who apostatized are those who "turned back and acted treacherously and departed from the well of living water."[61] One of the *Thanksgiving Psalms* begins, "I thank thee, O Lord, because thou hast put me at a source of flowing streams in dry ground ... trees of life in a fount of mystery...."

---

[59] DSS, p. 386.

[60] DSS, p. 353. Cf. also "they dug a well for many waters" (p. 351).

[61] DSS, p. 356 (MS B).

They shall send out their roots to the stream; its stump shall be exposed to the living water."[62]

Here again there are coincidences of language and thought. But they are not sufficient to compel us to think of dependence, all the more so in view of Old Testament passages like Jeremiah 2:13, "They have forsaken me, the fountain of living waters," which might well be the common source. The differences are as important as the agreements. For the sectarians "living waters" evoked memories of the Law. Their basic idea that the keeping of the Law is central shines through here. For John the expression signified the gift that Christ would give, the Holy Spirit. He saw in it the very antithesis of law-keeping.

FESTIVALS

THROUGHOUT THE SCROLLS THERE IS A DEEP INTEREST IN the correct observance of the liturgical year. It is generally agreed that the men of Qumran observed a different calendar from that in use in the temple at Jerusalem, and that theirs was the calendar used also in Jubilees and 1 Enoch. This is a solar calendar, consisting of twelve months each of thirty days, with four days intercalated, one in each period of three months. This makes exactly thirteen weeks in each period of three months, and it has the advantage that any given date will always fall on the same day of the week. New Year's Day, for example, is always a Wednesday, and similarly all the other feasts have their set day year by year.[63]

The sectarians put great emphasis on the festivals and they clung to their calendar with fierce tenacity. It was not only a matter of custom or convenience but a point of honor and even faith to respect the difference between their calendar and that in the temple. The *Manual* tells us that those admitted to the community had to pledge themselves "not to advance their times or postpone any of their appointed festivals."[64] The exag-

---

[62] DSS, p. 411.

[63] See further J. T. Milik, *Ten Years of Discovery in the Wilderness of Judaea*, London, 1959, pp. 107-113.

[64] DSS, p. 371.

gerated emphasis on the calendar may be illustrated in the *Damascus Document,* which, in speaking of the obligations laid on the covenanters, puts "His holy Sabbaths and his glorious festivals" before "his righteous testimonies and his true ways, and the desires of his will."[65] The thirteenth section of this document contains detailed regulations for sabbath observance (including, interestingly, a prohibition of raising an animal from a pit into which it had fallen). Right through the scrolls runs a tremendous stress on the due observance of the liturgical year.

There is no such thing, of course, in the Fourth Gospel. Yet it is not to be overlooked that there are more frequent references to the Jewish festivals in this Gospel than in the others. It cannot be maintained that John has as a primary interest the due observance of the liturgical year, but it is not without its interest that he so faithfully notices that such and such happenings took place when such and such a feast was near. "For him the festivals became an occasion for Jesus' pronouncement of a new and higher expression of the meaning of each feast. The basic idea seems to be that Christ in his signs, discourses, and religious ideas associated with each of the Jewish feasts finds a higher and absolute meaning in them."[66]

MESSIANISM

THE MEN OF QUMRAN LOOKED FOR THE COMING OF THE Messiah, indeed of two Messiahs,[67] and they have quite

---

[65] DSS, p. 351.

[66] L. Mowry, *The Biblical Archaeologist,* 17, December, 1954, p. 88. Again she says, ". . . It would seem that the writer of the Fourth Gospel, prodded by the calendar quarrel, used with remarkable creativity the cycle of festivals as a literary device to interpret the meaning of Christ for a Christian group living in the midst of an Essene group in Syria" (*op. cit.,* p. 89).

[67] Some scholars deny outright the propriety of referring to "the Messiah" in the scrolls. Thus W. LaSor maintains that the evidence as so far known has been too confidently interpreted. He says, ". . . It is my opinion, on the basis of materials now available, that the word *messiah* in the Qumran writings partakes more of the nature of a common noun ('anointed one'). There is no clear evi-

a bit to say about them. There is an interesting trio of
messianic personages in the *Manual,* which looks for the
coming of "a prophet and the Messiahs of Aaron and
Israel."[68] We are reminded of the triple question about
the Christ, Elijah, and the prophet (cf. Deut. 18:15)
in John 1:19-21, though the personages are different.
In the *Damascus Document* we read of "the Messiah of
Aaron and Israel"[69] where the two Messiahs have apparently become fused into one. The *Commentary on
Genesis 49* looks for "the coming of the Messiah of righteousness, the branch of David";[70] and there are other
passages referring to one Messiah only. The Davidic
Messiah is not regarded as preeminent, but is subordinate to the priestly Messiah, and perhaps to the priests.
The *Rule of the Congregation* looks for a time "when
God begets the Messiah:[71] with them shall come the
priest at the head of the whole congregation of Israel,
and all the fathers of the sons of Aaron, the priests,
summoned to the meeting, men of renown; and they shall

---

dence that any specific personage was known as 'the Messiah'"
(*Amazing Dead Sea Scrolls,* Chicago, 1956, p. 163). Again, T. H.
Gaster says, "The 'Messiah' in question is no divine eschatological
figure. He is simply the duly anointed king of Israel *at any future
epoch*" (*op. cit.,* pp. 19f.). There is need for caution, but it is
worth noticing that even LaSor admits that the scrolls have a
messianic doctrine. "To say that there is no messianic doctrine in
the Qumran writings would be too extreme" *(loc. cit.).* But if there
is a messianic doctrine where shall we find it other than in the
references to the "Messiahs"? On the whole it seems to me that the
scrolls do refer to two Messiahs. Cf. J. van der Ploeg: "[while
earlier] the doctrine of the sect about the two Messiahs was not
yet quite clear; at present it is incontrovertible, because not
merely one but several texts have been found which contain it
unmistakably" (*The Excavations at Qumran,* London, 1958, p. 200).
Matthew Black has a very useful discussion of the point (*The
Scrolls and Christian Origins,* London, 1961, ch. VII). He concludes that the scrolls probably indicate one Messiah, though he
agrees that most scholars see two (*op. cit.,* p. 171).

[68] DSS, p. 383.

[69] DSS, p. 355 (MS B). So also later in the same section (p. 356),
and in a subsequent section (p. 361).

[70] ML, p. 401.

[71] The reading here is not certain and nothing should be built
upon it. See the discussions by A. R. Leaney, *Guide,* p. 82, and
Millar Burrows, ML, pp. 300-304.

sit before him, each according to his rank. Next shall come the Messiah of Israel. . . ."[72] It is provided that in the meal the priest "shall put forth his hand on the bread first; and next the Messiah of Israel shall put forth his hand on the bread."[73]

There are many references in the scrolls to a figure called "the Teacher of Righteousness," and some think of him as the Messiah. He was a priest, plainly of the legitimate line. Some scholars have made extraordinary claims for him, even going so far as to say that he was crucified and that his followers looked for his resurrection and return. He is thus held to have been the pattern for the Christian view of Jesus' death and resurrection.[74] This, however, seems the result of a lively imagination rather than close attention to what the scrolls say. One cannot but feel that some scholars have read back into the scrolls things that the Gospels tell us about Jesus. Not surprisingly they have then been able to detect "resemblances." The truth is, in the words of C. G. Howie, that "never have a few writers drawn so many conclusions from so little evidence as has been done in the comparisons of Jesus and the Teacher of Righteousness. In no sense at all was Jesus a late copy or reincarnation of the earlier model."[75]

The passage cited to show the martyrdom of the Teacher is in the *Habakkuk Commentary:* "This means the wicked priest, who persecuted the teacher of righteousness in order to confound him in the indignation

---

[72] ML, p. 395.

[73] *Ibid.*

[74] A. Dupont-Sommer says, "It is now certain — and this is one of the most important revelations of the Dead Sea discoveries — that Judaism in the first century B.C. saw a whole theology of the suffering Messiah, of a Messiah who should be the redeemer of the world, developing around the person of the Master of Justice" (*The Dead Sea Scrolls,* Oxford, 1952, pp. 95f.). Jesus "appears in many respects as an astonishing reincarnation of the Master of Justice" (p. 99). In a later work he italicizes the words "appears in many respects" to emphasize that the resemblance is not complete (*The Jewish Sect of Qumran and the Essenes,* London, 1954, p. 160).

[75] *Op. cit.,* p. 107.

of his wrath, wishing to banish him. ..."[76] The concluding words make it doubtful whether death is in
view at all, and it is certainly more than difficult to see
a reference to crucifixion. Crucifixion is more likely
to be in mind in the *Nahum Commentary*, where we
read of "the lion of wrath ... who hangs men alive."[77]
But the Teacher is not mentioned at all in this text, so
that if anyone is being crucified it is not he.[78] There are
references to "the gathering in of the unique teacher"
in the *Damascus Document*,[79] but this does not necessarily denote violent death at all, let alone death by crucifixion.[80] The same document looks for "the arising of
him who will teach righteousness at the end of the
days,"[81] but this is a slender basis indeed on which to
erect a doctrine of resurrection. While the expression
"him who will teach righteousness" is very similar to
"teacher of righteousness" it is not identical with it,
and it is far from certain that the future teacher is the
same as the past one. Indeed, Cross can say bluntly,
"There are no references to a resurrection of the Righteous Teacher in the Qumran literature."[82]

The scrolls look back to the Teacher with affection
and admiration. It is not too much to say that he is
esteemed as practically the founder of the sect. While
"the consummation of the period (God) did not make
known" to Habakkuk. He did reveal to the Teacher "all
the mysteries of the words of his servants the prophets."[83]
The work of the Teacher was thus to initiate a sect
with special significance for the events of the end time.
But this does not constitute him the Messiah,[84] and, as

---

[76] DSS, p. 370. For difficulties in the interpretation of this
passage, see *Guide*, p. 118.

[77] ML, p. 404.

[78] See H. H. Rowley's discussion of this passage, JBL, 75, 1956,
pp. 188-193.

[79] DSS, pp. 356, 357.

[80] Leaney sees in the expression evidence of a peaceful death
(*Guide*, p. 119).

[81] DSS, p. 354.

[82] ALQ, p. 167, n. 54.

[83] *Habakkuk Commentary*, DSS, pp. 367f.

[84] "If the teacher of righteousness was believed to have any
eschatological role at all, it was certainly not that of the Messiah

we have seen, the coming of the Messiah(s) is looked for in the future. There is a passage in the *Psalms* which speaks of a woman who "gives birth to a man-child; with pains of Sheol he bursts forth from the crucible of the pregnant one, a wonderful counselor with his power...."[85] There seems no reasonable doubt but that this pictures the Messiah as issuing from the womb of the community.[86] But it looks forward to a future coming, not back to the Teacher and the foundation of the sect. In any case it must be borne in mind that the attitude of the community to the Teacher was not that which would be taken up toward the Messiah. "His name is unknown, his person, as the instrument of God, disappears wholly and entirely behind the divine majesty. No one invokes him, no one worships him after his death, his name and work are not made part of a profession of faith."[87] It is, moreover, far from certain that all the references to the Teacher point to the same person. T. H. Gaster and others have no doubt that the expression is the title of an office, held at different times by different persons, rather 'than the designation of an individual. When the sect's teaching on the Messiah is being considered, then the references to the Teacher must be firmly rejected.

In fact the sect does not appear to be tremendously interested in the Messiah or Messiahs as such. It is easy to read what the scrolls say with Christian eyes and unconsciously to infer that, as the Messiah is central to Christianity so must it be with the sectarians. This, however, appears not to be the case. From the information at our command it would appear as though it was

---

of Israel and probably not that of the priestly Messiah. If he was expected to come again in any capacity, he would come as the promised prophet" (ML, p. 334).

[85] DSS, p. 403.

[86] Though some disagree; ML, pp. 317f.

[87] J. van der Ploeg, *op. cit.*, p. 200. He further says, "... The description of the Teacher offered by Dupont-Sommer is taken not from the Qumran scrolls but from the Gospel of Jesus of Nazareth"; "There is not much left of the parallelism between the Teacher and Jesus of Nazareth, since the most important elements appear conspicuous by their absence" (pp. 202, 206).

the eschatological drama that gripped them, not the person of the Messiah. As Lucetta Mowry says, "Unless some of the unpublished material from the Qumran caves gives evidence to the contrary, it would seem that the Sectaries were not as concerned with this third theme as was the Church. The Sectaries, therefore, apparently regarded their messianic hopes as a detail of the eschatological drama which did not demand the attention given to the theme by the Church."[88] For the Christians generally and John in particular the Messiah was central. For Qumran he was not.

It is obvious that the sect's messianism has affinities with John. He begins the narrative section of his Gospel with an incident featuring the coming of the Messiah. There are references to Messiah throughout the Gospel. Indeed, John tells us that he wrote his book expressly "that ye may believe that Jesus is the Christ" (John 20:31). But there is this great and fundamental difference between the two. For the men of Qumran the coming of the Messiah(s) was yet future. It was a consummation devoutly to be wished, but in the meantime men must live without all that that coming would bring. There was a messianic community awaiting the Messiah, but that was all.[89] And their ideas about the Messiah are far from clear. Different conceptions are found in different places, and it is impossible to be sure of what the community really expected, as Millar Burrows' discussion plainly shows.[90] John's ideas, by contrast, are clearly formulated. For John the Messiah has come. All of life has been transformed by that fact. In this, as in many other points, the difference between the scrolls and John is — Jesus.[91]

---

[88] *The Dead Sea Scrolls and the Early Church*, Chicago, 1962, p. 118.

[89] It seems to me that Stendahl (SNT, pp. 12f.) exaggerates the messianic significance of the Teacher. It is possible to read practically all the scrolls without coming across even a hint that he was expected to return as Messiah. This idea is, in fact, confined to a particular interpretation of a very small number of passages. The attitude of John, and of all the New Testament writers, to Jesus, is in marked contrast.

[90] ML, chs. XXVI, XXVII.

[91] D. Howlett stresses the point that this is not merely opinion

CEREMONIAL ORDINANCES

THE COVENANTERS WERE MORE THAN STRICT ON CEREMO-
nial purity. The *War Scroll* decrees that "No lame or
blind man or halt man, or one with a permanent blemish
on his flesh, or a man afflicted with the uncleanness of his
flesh — none of these shall go with them to battle";[92] "no
man who is not clean from his issue on the day of battle
shall go down with them; for holy angels are together
with their armies."[93] References to uncleanness are common throughout the scrolls. The remedy is baptism. This
is not a single, unrepeatable act, as in Christianity, but a
regular ritual cleansing.[94] There are pools and cisterns on
the site of the monastery, though it is not certain that
baptism took place there. The waters of Ain Feshka or
the Jordan may have been preferred. Similar pools are
found in other sites where there is no question of baptism.
Baptism of itself is not regarded as sufficient. There must
also be right dispositions in the worshipper. Of the sinner
who gives "free rein to the stubbornness of his heart"
the *Manual* says, "He will not be purified by atonement
offerings, and he will not be made clean with the water
for impurity."[95] But this does not mean that the ritual

---

but fact. "Jesus Christ towers above his contemporaries because of
what he *was*, not because of what people *thought* he was. The
beliefs *about him* stemmed from the kind of person he *was*" (*The
Essenes and Christianity*, New York, 1957, p. 189). Again, the
scrolls "enable us to see more clearly than we have ever been
able to see before, that our faith is grounded in fact rather than
fancy — that Christianity comes to us through him and because of
him" (p. 190).

[92] DSS, p. 395.

[93] *Ibid.*

[94] Matthew Black reminds us that there were many Jewish sects
that practiced baptismal rites. "What is unique about Qumran is
that such rites were practised in relation to a movement of repentance, of entry into a New Covenant (that of Jeremiah and Ezekiel)
and of a new Covenanted Israel — the sect itself — in preparation
for an impending divine Judgment." While such views have obvious
affinities with the New Testament there are significant differences.
Thus "The Qumran New Covenant was largely a renewal of the
Old Covenant." But Black goes on to cite as the main differences
between Qumran and early Christianity "the persons of John and
Jesus, both towering figures" (*op. cit.*, p. 168).

[95] DSS, p. 373.

requirements are unimportant. The state and quantity of water to be used are rigidly prescribed.[96] K. G. Kuhn goes so far as to say that baptism had acquired "the sacramental function of mediating in the divine forgiveness of sins (I QS iii, 3ff.). In place of the sacrificial cultus of the Temple, which was no longer possible for them by reason of their distance from it, the baths, and apparently also the communal meal, took on a new meaning, mediating salvation from God."[97]

There are also strict food laws.[98] And many regulations stress the importance of a man's keeping his proper place. "Every man of Israel may know his appointed position in the community of God for the eternal council. And none shall be abased below his appointed position or exalted above his allotted place."[99]

This interest is not found in John. He speaks of John the Baptist, but says little about his baptism. He tells us that Jesus' followers baptized some people, but again says little about it. It may not be without significance that he makes much of the symbolism of water, and that incidents in which water figures are common in this Gospel. But he does not relate this to ritual observances. Oscar Cullmann sees in most such passages references to Christian baptism, but it is more than difficult to follow him here. The plain fact is that John makes no specific reference to either of the two Christian sacraments. He has no interest in ceremonial cleanness and little in ritual ordinances. He is concerned with believing in Christ, with responding in the right manner to God's sending of His Son. In this he contrasts sharply with the sectarians.

Perhaps this is the place to notice the prominent place assigned to the priesthood throughout the scrolls. There can be not the slightest doubt but that, for the men of Qumran, a regularly established priesthood was of the first importance. No one takes precedence to their priestly caste, not even the Messiah. The atmosphere of the Fourth Gospel is altogether different. Priesthood is never

---

[96] E.g. *Damascus Document*, DSS, p. 359.
[97] SNT, p. 68.
[98] *Damascus Document*, DSS, pp. 360f.
[99] *Manual*, DSS, p. 373.

mentioned there in connection with the followers of Christ.

ETERNAL LIFE

ONE OF JOHN'S LEADING IDEAS IS ETERNAL LIFE, WHICH, he stresses, comes through believing on Jesus Christ. There are occasional references to eternal life in the scrolls, as when the *Damascus Document* speaks of "His holy Sabbaths and his glorious festivals, his righteous testimonies and his true ways, and the desires of his will, by which, if a man does them, he shall live,"[100] or again, "Those who hold fast to (the sure house in Israel) are for eternal life."[101] Similarly the *Manual* speaks of "the counsels of the Spirit for the sons of the truth of the world and the visitation of all who walk by it, for healing and abundance of peace in length of days, and bringing forth seed, with all eternal blessings and everlasting joy in the life of eternity, and a crown of glory with raiment of majesty in everlasting light."[102] But while such passages are found they are not typical.[103] The covenanters certainly regarded themselves as the community which would be vindicated in the end of time, and whose members would live eternally. But the thought is not prominent. There were too many things to occupy their attention until the blessed state came to pass. And there is no trace of John's characteristic idea that the believer already experiences the life of the age to come.

Much more characteristic is their interest in the Law. The *Damascus Document* says, "They shall walk according to the law,"[104] and it regards accepting the obligation "to return to the law of Moses" as identical with joining

---

[100] DSS, p. 351.

[101] DSS, p. 352.

[102] DSS, p. 375.

[103] Robert B. Laurin argues that there is no idea of immortality in the scrolls, "Immortality in the Qumran 'Hodayot'," *Journal of Semitic Studies*, 3, pp. 344-355. His conclusion is, "To the men of Qumran there was no hope after death. The grave would be man's final resting-place." I am not fully persuaded by his argument, but the fact that he can take up such a position shows that the idea of eternal life is not prominent.

[104] DSS, p. 354.

the community.[105] The *Manual* dictates that "every one who comes into the council of the community shall enter into the covenant of God ... he shall take it upon himself by a binding oath to turn to the law of Moses."[106] The writer of a psalm rejoices that "Thy law is hidden in my heart, until the time when thy salvation will be revealed to me."[107] Typical of the whole attitude to the Law is the provision that "from the place where the ten are there shall never be absent a man who searches the law day and night, by turns, one after another. And the masters shall keep watch together a third of all the nights of the year, reading the book and searching for justice, and worshipping together."[108] One of the documents, *The Oration of Moses*, is nothing more than a paraphrase of Moses' farewell address,[109] and illustrates vividly the keen interest in the Law and the lawgiver so characteristic of the sect.

John treats the Law with respect, but assigns it a different function. For him it points to Christ. He records Philip as saying, "We have found him, of whom Moses in the law, and the prophets, wrote, Jesus of Nazareth" (John 1:45). He tells us that Jesus said, "If ye believed Moses, ye would believe me; for he wrote of me" (John 5:46). He says nothing that is disrespectful of the Law, but he does not accord it the central place that the sectarians did. Cullmann can say, "... The new texts are in fact the strongest expression of Judaism's legalistic piety. Legalism is driven to the utter limit."[110] But John is no legalist.

---

105 DSS, p. 363.
106 DSS, p. 377.
107 DSS, p. 408.
108 *Manual*, DSS, p. 378.
109 See T. H. Gaster, *op. cit.*, pp. 233ff.
110 SNT, p. 22. Similarly Raymond E. Brown says, "... While Qumran and St. John characterize good men in much the same way, they differ greatly in their notion of what brings one into the domain of light. For Qumran it is acceptance of the community's interpretation of the Law; for John it is faith in Jesus Christ" (SNT, p. 194). So also Geoffrey Graystone: "... The Qumran sect was based essentially on the Mosaic Law, it was contained within the framework of the Sinaitic Covenant, even though it claimed fuller lights for understanding its extent and obligations. The

One of John's great concepts is that of judgment. Sometimes he thinks of this as taking place at the last great day (John 5:26ff.), and sometimes as a present activity: "This is the judgment, that the light is come into the world, and men loved the darkness rather than the light; for their works were evil" (John 3:19). The men of Qumran likewise think of judgment under more than one aspect. There is the final judgment, as in the "judgments of fire" of the *Habakkuk Commentary*,[111] or the saying in the concluding psalm in the *Manual*, "With God is the judgment of every living man; and he will repay to a man his recompense."[112]

Present judgment is also found, but it is not John's profound conception of a man passing judgment on himself by his attitude to the light that is come into the world. Rather it is the activity of the covenanters themselves as they pass judgment on their fellows. The eleventh section of the *Damascus Document* sets forth "the order for the judges of the congregation," and the many references throughout the scrolls indicate that this role was taken seriously. Before he can take part in this judgment a man must be at least thirty years of age and "no simpleton."[113]

Again we see that, though the interest is in the same subject, the differences are more striking than the resemblances. For the men of Qumran the important thing about the present judgment was that it was passed by qualified members of the sect upon others, and about the future judgment that it marked the destruction of their enemies. For John the present judgment is passed by men on themselves according to their reaction to Christ, and the future judgment is to be dispensed by Christ. Again it is Christ who is the difference.

The story might be continued. A study of the term

Christian faith was based on the belief that the Death of Christ had abrogated the Sinaitic Covenant and terminated the regime of the Mosaic Law" (*op. cit.*, p. 26).

[111] DSS, p. 369. Cf. also, "In the day of judgment God will destroy all the worshippers of idols and the wicked from the earth" (DSS, p. 370).

[112] DSS, p. 386.

[113] *Rule of the Congregation*, ML, p. 394.

"glory," which figures in both literatures, would yield much the same result. For the covenanters it means the triumph of their sect. For John the idea is transformed by Christ, and the true glory is seen in lowly service and especially in the cross. And so with other terms. The men of Qumran see themselves as the sons of light, and they glory in their sect, both in its present manifestation and in its future triumph. John is concerned primarily with the action of God in Christ. The coming of Christ has transformed everything for him. And therefore even in those matters where he comes closest to Qumran there is a basic difference.

CONCLUSION

WHAT SHALL WE SAY THEN OF THE RELATION BETWEEN the Fourth Gospel and the scrolls? In the first place, that there is a tremendous gap[114] between them. In this study we have been concerned to consider only those points where there is some relation, and this may easily give the impression that the two are closer than in point of fact they are. But to read the whole of the Qumran documents, including the detailed regulations in the *Manual of Discipline* and the *Rule of the Congregation*, the curious exegesis of the commentaries, the martial regulations of the *War Scroll*, and all the rest, is to be transported into a different world. It is true that in some of the *Thanksgiving Psalms* we come in contact with a spirit not out of harmony with that of the men of the New Testament, but this fleeting glimpse of better things serves only to underline the fact that basically the sect is concerned with different purposes from those that underlie Christian service. This great gap should not be overlooked.

Yet when full allowance has been made for it the coincidences of language and thought are striking. There are far too many of them for us to assume that they are

---

[114] Cf. Raymond E. Brown, ". . . There remains a tremendous chasm between Qumran thought and Christianity" (SNT, p. 205). So also Mowry, ". . . The evangelist borrows, not, however, without radical modification of the ideas accepted by him" (*The Biblical Archaeologist*, 17, Dec. 1954, p. 97).

accidental, the result of mere chance. It is asking too much to assume that at roughly the same time, and in roughly the same part of the world, two different groups of men independently evolved the same terminology and thought of the same ideas. It is much more likely that there was some point of contact.

Yet the relationship can hardly be one of direct dependence. We have seen how at point after point, even where John and the covenanters are using similar language and dealing with similar concepts, there are vast differences. Again it is too much to assume that John had the Qumran writings before him, and that as he borrowed their language and concepts he systematically distorted their sense.

What the relationship was we cannot be sure at this distance in time. But it was surely indirect. We may conjecture (though I stress that it is no more than conjecture) that the connection came through John the Baptist. W. H. Brownlee has pointed out that "Almost every detail of the Baptist's teaching in both the Synoptic and the Fourth Gospels has points of contact with Essene belief"[115] (he identifies the Qumran sect with the Essenes). Now the Gospels tell us that John the Baptist's parents were old when he was born (Luke 1:18), and that "the child ... was in the deserts till the day of his showing unto Israel" (Luke 1:80). What being "in the deserts" means is difficult to establish. If it means that John was brought up there then the conclusion seems inescapable that he was brought up by some such sect as the men of Qumran (Josephus tells us that the Essenes adopted other people's children and brought them up). While we have no evidence for this there is nothing at all improbable in it. John's parents were old and may well have died while the child was young, leaving no one to look after him. Alternatively, realizing their age and incapacity, they may have handed him over to the sectarians. The connecting link in either case would be the very high regard the Qumran men had for those of priestly stock

---

[115] SNT, p. 52. So also Raymond E. Brown: "...Almost every detail of his life and preaching has a *possible* Qumran affinity" (SNT, p. 207).

(though we should not overlook the fact that they rejected the Jerusalem priesthood to which John's father belonged). If this is not what happened, being "in the deserts" means at least that John was in those parts where the sectarians lived, and he would have some knowledge of them. Either way he would have some knowledge of the teaching of the sect, in the one case a full and complete knowledge, in the other case a partial knowledge. Whichever be the truth he rebelled against Qumran's distinctive message, for his recorded teaching contradicts some of the essential ideas of the scrolls, even though it shows points of contact. But he did have the terminology of the sect and some of its ideas.

John 1:35ff. makes it clear that some of the first disciples of Jesus came out of the circle that gathered around John the Baptist. This gives us a natural channel whereby some of the sect's terms and ideas may have flowed into Christianity. Especially would this be the case if the unnamed disciple of John 1:35, 40 was the beloved disciple (as has been widely held).[116] Thus the ideas and language of the covenanters would have come to the author of the Gospel, but only at second hand, and that by way of one who was no longer a member of the sect even if he ever had been. He would not reproduce its teaching with anything like fidelity. This would account for the fact that the Evangelist reproduces Qumran language sometimes with minute exactness, while at the same time his basic thought is poles apart from theirs.[117]

---

[116] Cf. F. F. Bruce: "Now the unnamed disciple of John the Baptist who attached himself to Jesus along with Andrew (John i. 35ff.) has been identified, very reasonably, with the disciple whose witness attests the record of the Fourth Gospel (John xxi. 24). If the beloved disciple was indeed at one time a follower of John the Baptist, this may indicate an indirect contact with Qumran. For, among all the theories which have been propounded to establish a connection between the Qumran movement and primitive Christianity, the least improbable are those which find such a connection in John the Baptist, on the ground that he may well have been associated with Qumran before the day when the word of the Lord came to him and sent him forth to preach his baptism of repentance for the remission of sins in view of the approach of the Coming One" (*Faith and Thought*, 90, 1958, pp. 98f.).

[117] Mowry thinks of John as directly combating the sect. "The

It remains for us to consider the importance of the scrolls for an understanding of the Fourth Gospel. I wish to make three points in particular.

1. *The Uniqueness of Christianity.* As we have already pointed out, there is a great chasm between the scrolls and the New Testament.[118] It has been clear for long enough that Christianity is very different from any form of Judaism hitherto known to us. Now its uniqueness is seen against a different background. While there are points of contact in both language and ideas the scrolls add their quota of evidence to show that Christianity is distinctively different from every sect known to us from antiquity. There is no reason to doubt that some of the ideas of the men of Qumran have had their influence on Christian thought. But they have been transformed out of all recognition in the process. John may perhaps be indebted to Qumran for the particular way he gives expression to the thought of conflict between light and darkness. But the specific idea that Christ is the Light of the world is John's own. Both Qumran and John may speak about "the Holy Spirit." But there is no real parallel in the scrolls to the Fourth Gospel's conception of the Paraclete who "abideth with you, and shall be in you" (John 14:17). And so we might go on. While there are undoubted resemblances, the differences are far more striking.[119] Christianity is not an advanced Qumranism. It is basically an independent movement.

---

fact that he found himself in conflict with a group maintaining the value of strict adherence to the proper celebration of feasts, rites, and ceremonies, the Law as a means of salvation, and the teacher as an instrument to proclaim a higher righteousness have strengthened and deepened his own thinking, so that through struggle he gained a perspective and soared to a height that few Christian writers have ever attained" (*op. cit.*, p. 97).

[118] Cf. H. H. Rowley: "With all the links of phrase, both in the Fourth Gospel and elsewhere, we must not ignore the vast gulf that separates the New Testament from the Scrolls in thought. The theology of the Qumran texts and that of the New Testament are poles asunder" (*op. cit.*, p. 28). So also B. Rigaux, "... The Qumran texts, by their content, are destined to underline the originality of John the Baptist, of Jesus, of the first Christian community, of Paul and of John" (*Les Documents de la Mer Morte*, Brussels, 1956, p. 12).

[119] Even Dupont-Sommer says, "... The author in no way wishes to

2. *The Fourth Gospel is Palestinian.* Scholars have sometimes argued that the Gospel according to St. John is essentially Hellenistic. That is to say, it is written in a Greek environment, and is designed to appeal to men saturated in Greek culture by the employment of Greek concepts and imagery. Usually there has also been the thought that it is a late writing, composed possibly well into the second century. Such ideas have been losing ground for some time, and the discovery of the scrolls has hastened their demise. The more firmly it is demonstrated that the ideas and the language are basically Palestinian[120] the more difficult it is to claim that the Gospel is essentially Hellenistic.[121] It makes an appeal to Hellenists, but that is another matter.

W. H. Brownlee reminds us that sometimes in the past John's Gospel "has been regarded as more Hellenistic than Jewish — in fact the most Greek of the entire New Testament." Now, however, there appears a literature with much closer parallels to this Gospel. "To our amazement, this literature is not only Jewish, but Palestinian. Consequently the ultimate sources for the Fourth Gospel must be Palestinian in origin."[122] It is difficult to see how

deny the originality of the Christian religion. He has here noted the resemblances, but differences also clearly exist" (*The Dead Sea Scrolls*, p. 100, n. 1). T. H. Gaster points out that there is in the scrolls "no trace of any of the cardinal theological concepts — the incarnate Godhead, Original Sin, redemption through the Cross, and the like — which make Christianity a distinctive faith" (*op. cit.*, p. 12).

[120] Cf. Cross, "It now turns out ... that John has its strongest affinities, not with the Greek world, or Philonic Judaism, but with Palestinian Judaism" (ALQ, p. 161).

[121] K. Stendahl points out that this means that "many of the odysseys of scholars some decades ago over the deep waters of Hellenistic philosophy and religion were more fascinating than they were rewarding" (SNT, p. 5).

[122] *The Meaning of the Qumran Scrolls for the Bible*, New York, 1964, pp. 122f. He goes on, "If the Gospel as we know it was composed elsewhere, we must account for the migration of this thought and vocabulary." Cf. also Roland E. Murphy, "The striking parallels between the Qumran scrolls and the writings of St. John give strong proof of the Palestinian background and origins of the latter. One who reads the scrolls and St. John together has the feeling that the authors belong to the same world, that St. John

this conclusion can be resisted. It is supported further by Raymond E. Brown's "Second Thoughts" on "The Dead Sea Scrolls and the New Testament."[123] He can say, ". . . In our judgment the Scrolls consistently offer better parallels to John than do any of the non-Christian elements in the Mandean documents emphasized by Bultmann or the examples in Philo and the *Hermetica* offered by Dodd."[124]

Moreover, any contact between Christians and the covenanters must be very early. It is impossible to maintain that after the death of Jesus, when Christian preachers dispersed throughout the world, the movement began to be influenced by such a sect as the men of Qumran. The contact must be early. This does not compel an early date for the Fourth Gospel, but it is consistent with one.[125] It demands that the author must have come in contact with the kind of thinking that is typical of Qumran, and as far as we know there was no opportunity for this in later times.

3. *The Centrality of Christ.* To Christians it has always been obvious that Christ is at the very center of their faith. The scrolls bring this home in a new and striking fashion.[126] Now we see what some of the ideas of the Christian faith look like apart from Christ. We see that the coming of the Messiah altered them out of all recognition. The scrolls might divide men into "sons of light" and "sons of darkness," but John insists that the criterion for the separation is men's attitude to Jesus. The scrolls revere the Old Testament and see it as pointing to a

'speaks the language' of the desert dwellers of Qumran" (*The Dead Sea Scrolls and the Bible*, Westminster, Maryland, 1957, p. 67).

[123] ET, 78, 1966-67, pp. 19-23.

[124] *Ibid.*, p. 21.

[125] J. M. Allegro thinks that "the whole framework of (John's) thought is seen now to spring directly from a Jewish sectarianism rooted in Palestinian soil, and his material recognized as founded in the earliest layers of Gospel traditions" (*The Dead Sea Scrolls*, Penguin edn., 1956, p. 128.

[126] Cf. Raymond E. Brown, "No matter how impressive the terminological and ideological similarities are, the difference that Jesus Christ makes between the two cannot be minimized" (SNT, p. 205).

rigorous system of law-works. John reveres the Old Testament and sees it as pointing men to Christ. The scrolls speak of "living water," John speaks of Christ as giving it. At point after point we are compelled to say, "This idea has been transformed for John, because for him the Christ has come." In their own way the scrolls underline for us the cherished truth that Christianity is Christ.

General Index

Aaron, 342
Abraham, 61, 112, 161, 221, 225, 243, 246, 334
Absalom 329
Aenon, 228, 235
Africa, 257
Agrippa, 88
Ain Feshka, 347
Alexandria, 155, 242, 257, 276
Alogi, 257, 270, 279
Andrew, 28, 37f., 52f., 140, 153f., 174, 234, 241, 246, 262, 269, 278, 354
Annas, 18, 48, 187ff., 195, 234, 241
Apocryphon of John, 261
Appreciative reporting, 93
Aramaic, 120, 135, 222ff., 324
Aristion, 38, 278
Asia, 157, 270, 276, 279, 283
Asia Minor, 168, 188, 242, 279f.
Athenagorus, 257
Authorship of Fourth Gospel,
  Arguments against apostolic, 265ff.
  External evidence, 256ff.
  Internal evidence: direct, 253ff., indirect, 218ff.
Authorship of 1 John, 287ff.

Baptism, 285, 287, 308, 318, 347f.
  in the Holy Spirit, 25
Barnabas, 257
Bartimaeus, 31, 52, 239
Basilides, 258
Bastille, 72f.
Beelzebub, 61
Belial, 326f., 329, 338
Beloved disciple, 179f., 186, 202, 206, 240, 246ff., 255f., 265f., 275, 280, 307, 354
Bethany, 31f., 34, 41, 44, 152, 169, 173f., 228, 235
  beyond Jordan, 228, 235
Bethesda, 28, 52, 152, 228
Bethlehem, 290, 322
Bethsaida, 37, 153
Black Death, 99
Blasphemy, 60, 136, 166
Bread, living, 30, 307, 313
Britain, Battle of, 73

Caesar, 113, 196f., 226
Caesarea Philippi, 30, 141f.
Caiaphas, 41, 48, 73, 172, 187ff., 220, 234, 239, 247, 307
Caius, 279
Calendar, 109, 340f.
Cana, 26, 127, 140, 142f., 220, 227f., 235
Canterbury, Archbishop of, 87, 188
Capernaum, 37, 143, 155, 226, 228, 235, 243, 304
Carthage, 281
Celsus, 257
Centrality of Christ, 357f.
Ceremonial ordinances, 347ff.
Cerinthus, 257
Chenoboskion, 260f.
Christ of faith, 80, 97, 100, 102, 217
Chronicle, 71
Chronology, 109, 276, 228
Chrysostom, 60
Churchill, W., 273
Cicero, 69
Claudius Apollinaris, 257

Index of Authors

Index of Biblical References

STUDIES IN THE FOURTH GOSPEL

Leon Morris

"From within the biblical tradition we must insist and confidently expect that the more profoundly and validly we understand and interpret the Bible, the greater the religious depth with which it will challenge and speak to us. It is precisely here that modern biblical scholarship has proved itself so insipid and unstimulating. We are confronted with the paradox of a way of studying the word of God out of which no word of God ever seems to come, with an imposing modern knowledge of the Bible which seems quite incapable of saying anything biblical or thinking biblically." — *J. V. Langmead Casserley*

These in-depth studies on the Gospel of John, written by a man who describes himself as a 'conservative evangelical,' demonstrate that the application of the critical method to an understanding of scripture need not rule out an acceptance of inspiration. Dr. Morris is here concerned with the authorship of the fourth Gospel, its relation to the Synoptists, the origin and date of writing, and with other similar issues. To his discussion of these issues he brings both his impressive scholarship and a firm committment to the revealatory nature of the Bible. The result is an informed and articulate statement of the conservative position on the many crucial questions raised by John's Gospel.

In his Preface to this volume, Dr. Morris notes that "Critical Protestant scholars and Roman Catholics are reading one another's works and discussing one another's writings with charity and mutual profit. Perhaps it is not too much to hope that both will include the conservative evangelicals within the scope of their reading and charity. In the hope that it will make some small contribution to the continuing dialogue this book goes forth."